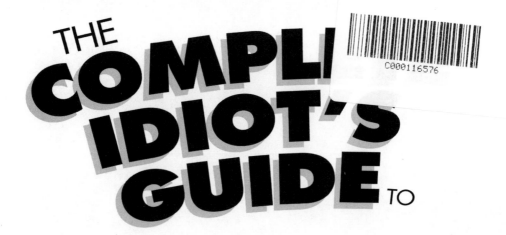

THE

COMPLI
IDIOT'S
GUIDE TO

C000116576

Computer Security

THE COMPLETE IDIOT'S GUIDE TO

Computer Security

by Richard Macdonald

A

Pearson Education

An imp...

...k Mexico City Toronto Sydney Tokyo Singapore
London Boston Indianapolis Madrid Paris Amsterdam Munich Milan Stockholm
Hong Kong Cape Town New...

PEARSON EDUCATION LIMITED

Head Office
Edinburgh Gate
Harlow CM20 2JE
Tel: +44 (0)1279 623623
Fax: +44 (0)1279 431059

London Office:
128 Long Acre
London WC2E 9AN
Tel: +44 (0)20 7447 2000
Fax: +44 (0)20 7447 2170
Website: www.it-minds.com/

First published in Great Britain in 2002

ISBN 0 130 08155 8

British Library Cataloguing in Publication Data
A CIP catalogue record for this book can be obtained from the British Library.

Typeset by Land & Unwin (Data Sciences)
Printed and bound in Great Britain by Biddles, Guildford and King's Lynn.

The Publishers' policy is to use paper manufactured sustainable forests.

Contents At A Glance

Contents

19 Web Crime And Commerce   309

20 Where Do The Children Play?   327

Part 5: Trespassers Will Not Be Forgiven   343

21 Hello Hackers, Everywhere!   345

22 The Trojan Horse   359

23 Building A Wall Around Your Computer   371

Introduction

OK, we lied on the front cover. This is not a book for the complete idiot – it is not even a book for the mildly stupid. The complete idiots are the people who never bother their heads with computer security; the people who are going to find that their computers no longer work, that their precious files have been demolished and that their personal privacy has been invaded by every hacker, cracker and marketing man on the internet. If you have bought this book – and I trust you are not reading it in the store – you are rightly interested in computer security. By definition, you are not a complete idiot!

And I am not going to treat you like one. While many aspects of computer security involve simple procedures, there are areas which are quite technical. I have not tried to avoid such areas since many of them involve tactics which are critical if you are to keep your computer safe from harm. Of course a book of this size cannot explain every procedure in minute detail. I rely on your common sense to fill in some of the gaps. If you stumble on a process that you are not comfortable with, I strongly advise you to take further advice before proceeding. You might ask a computer technician or an experienced systems engineer, or you might track down further information on the web.

I also owe perhaps as many as half of you a profound apology. Throughout the book, where I have needed to refer to a person, I have used 'he' and 'him' and 'his'. I am well aware that computer users come in both flavours. It is simply that I refuse to get tangled up in sentences like: he or she will need to look at his or her hard drive to see whether he or she needs to back up his or her files. Sensitive readers of the more intelligent gender will kindly place a mental 's' in front of every 'he'.

Perhaps I should also apologize to those of you who use the MacOS or one of the many varieties of Linux. This book is distinctly Windows-centric – in fact it's Windows 95/98-centric. If it's any consolation, I am a Mac fan and use it for all my graphics work, but this book is aimed at the overwhelming majority of computer users who, for whatever reason, run Windows. Even as I write this, Windows XP is starting to appear on OEM machines and perhaps the next edition (if there is a next edition) will have to be reworked to cope with Microsoft's new baby. But as it stands, Windows 98 is the dominant OS – which makes this a very democratic book. If you are using a different version, or a different operating system altogether, some of the practical procedures I describe in detail will need to be modified, but in most cases the advice, ideas and commentary will still apply. Try not to feel too hard done by.

This book is an attempt to cover all aspects of computer security. This includes the safety and reliability of your hardware, the security of your programs and data, your personal privacy when accessing a network or the internet, and your right not to be bothered by hackers and unsolicited advertising. I have tried to make the book readable from cover to cover. It might not be as much fun as a novel, but it does have its share of heroes and villains, of high technology weaponry and of strange and mysterious goings-on. No sex, I'm afraid, but there is some pretty sexy software.

For those who can't face the thought of wading through the whole thing, I have done my best to make each chapter a self-contained unit. Sometimes I have failed spectacularly, but where a procedure relies on information from elsewhere in the book, I have inserted a reference to that section – usually something like 'as we noted in Chapter 13'. (A friend once told me that writing like this is 'pedagogically unsound', but since I have absolutely no idea what that means, I have chosen to go my own sweet way.)

If you prefer to treat this book as a reference work – and I am certainly not going to argue with you – you can use the contents at the front and the index at the back to find solutions to particular problems. Remember though that computer troubles seldom appear in isolation and it is always a good idea to read around a problem before jumping into hands-on repair work. At the very least, I urge you to read the whole chapter for background information and general advice.

How Do You Use This Book?

Here are the special icons and boxes used in this book:

Techno Talk

This box contains additional information of interest to the more technical reader. Strictly speaking, you don't need to know this stuff unless you really want to get your hands dirty.

Check This Out

This box has two functions. Mighty though this book is, I cannot hope to cram in all the information on every subject we will be looking at. This box directs you to an address on the web where you will find further details. Where I talk about software you might want to add to your system, this box will also give an internet address from which you can download it. As we go to press, all these web links are valid, but the web is a dynamic medium and addresses change. If I point you to a duff link, accept my apologies and use one of the search engines (www.google.com) to find a valid site.

Tricks of the Trade

Sometimes there are neat little tricks you can use to solve a problem. This box contains often undocumented shortcuts which can save you a heap of time and trouble.

Acknowledgements

We are grateful to the following for permission to reproduce copyright material: Figures 3.9, 3.10, 7.5 and 12.2 Xteq Systems; Figures 5.7 and 5.8 ESET Software; Figure 8.1 Wise Solutions, Inc.; Figure 10.4 PC Dynamics, Inc.; Figure 11.9 Stealthencrypt.com; Figure 11.10 Neil Jones, Codeforge; Figures 11.12, 11.13 and 11.14 SecurStar GmbH; Figure 15.4 Panicware, Inc.; Figure 15.5 webwasher.com AG; Figure 16.3 AtomInterSoft; Figure 16.8 ISL Internet Sicherheitlösungen GmbH; Figure 17.5 Jan ten Hove; Figure 17.6 Trapware Corporation; Figure 17.7 Webroot Software, Inc.; Figure 19.3 Lavasoft; Figure 19.5 PayPal; Figure 20.5 Net Nanny Software, Inc.; Figure 22.3 Lewis Rowan Guest, TrojanShield Development; Figure 22.4 and text extract PestPatrol, Inc.; Figures 23.2 and 23.6 Zone Labs, Inc.; Figure 23.3 Steven M. Gibson, Gibson Research Corporation; Figures 23.4 and 23.5 Time Group Ltd.

Figures 1.3, 3.1, 3.3, 3.5, 3.6, 3.7, 3.8, 4.1, 5.3, 5.4, 5.5, 5.6, 6.4, 6.5, 7.1, 7.2, 7.3, 7.4, 7.6, 7.7, 8.3, 8.5, 9.2, 9.3, 9.4, 9.5, 11.1, 11.2, 11.3, 11.4, 11.5, 11.6, 12.1, 13.3, 13.4, 13.5, 14.4, 14.5, 14.6, 14.7, 14.8, 14.9, 14.10, 14.11, 14.12, 14.13, 15.3, 16.4, 17.1, 17.2, 17.3, 17.4, 18.4, 19.6, 20.2, 20.4, 21.3, 22.2 screenshots reprinted by permission from Microsoft Corporation; Figure 8.4 reprinted by permission from Network Associates Technology, Inc. Copyright 2002 Networks Associates Technology, Inc. All rights reserved. Used with permission. CyberMedia® and Uninstaller® are registered trademarks of Network Associates Technology, Inc.; Figures 11.7 and 11.8 reprinted by permission of Mach 5 Software, Inc., website http://www.kremlinencrypt.com; Figures

12.5, 12.6 and 17.8 reprinted by permission from CyberScrub LLC, a free 30 day fully functional trial is available, this can be downloaded at ftp://cyberscrub.com/cyscrb_E.exe; Figure 14.2 reproduced courtesy of the National Center for Supercomputing Applications (NCSA) and the Board of Trustees of the University of Illinois; Figures 18.2 and 18.3 reproduced courtesy of Mailgate Ltd – http://www.mailgate.com; Figure 20.3 (top) reproduced by permission of InfoSpace, Inc. © 2002 InfoSpace, Inc. All rights reserved. Reprinted by permission of InfoSpace, Inc.; Definitions of 'hack' and 'hacker' from *Que's Computer User's Dictionary*, reprinted by permission from Pearson Technology Group (pub 1994), copyright © by Que Corporation.

In some instances we have been unable to trace the owners of copyright material, and we would appreciate any information that would enable us to do so.

Finally, I should like to thank those people who have helped me to put this book together. I owe a lot to my editor for her reliable dollops of sound advice. I also received a lot of technical help from software manufacturers, technicians and even hackers, too numerous to list. I must thank Colette for putting up with me crawling into bed at 3.00 am most mornings. And lastly I must mention Victoria, Jennifer and Sarah who, in some strange way, provided the inspiration.

Richard Macdonald

Part 1
Know Your Enemy

The first part of this book introduces the concept of computer security and explains why it is important for you to protect your system against accidental and deliberate damage. You'll start by looking at computer hardware and considering why it is inherently unstable. I've provided a checklist for assembling a system that balances your requirements against security issues.

You'll then turn your attention to the operating system to understand how it provides an interface between your hardware and your applications. You'll look at keeping your OS up to date, and configuring it for maximum security. I describe the advantages and disadvantages of building your own computer rather than buying one off the shelf. You will also find some useful advice for undertaking hardware upgrades and repairs.

Finally in Part 1, you'll examine the dangers of computer viruses, worms and bombs. I show you in detail how a virus operates and the damage it can inflict on your system. I suggest some different ways of identifying viruses before they inflict serious harm and help you to evaluate anti-virus measures with a comparison of different anti-virus programs.

By the end of Part 1, assuming you have followed my suggestions, you will have a secure and reliable system, set up to resist most hardware problems. You will also have proofed your computer against virus infection and ensured that your operating system is operating at peak efficiency.

'Don't Buy A Computer, But ...'

In This Chapter

➤ Beware the enemy on your desktop

➤ Are you the master of your own computer?

➤ Meet our cast of characters

➤ Thinking secure thoughts

➤ Operating system alert

➤ Watch out for relatives, friends and colleagues

➤ The balanced approach to computer security

Beware The Enemy On Your Desktop

Are you sitting comfortably? Well, you shouldn't be because you and your computer are under attack! Look over your shoulder and you might spot a horde of shadowy figures lurking behind the couch. Some of them are:

➤ simply criminals anxious to get hold of your credit card number or your bank account details;

➤ cyber-vandals who get their kicks from puréeing your precious computer data;

➤ grasping businessmen who see you as an online wallet and will rummage through your most intimate secrets if it helps them target you as a customer;

➤ even officially sanctioned – government-appointed busybodies who think they have the right to know where you go and what you do.

To all of these potential intruders, your computer is not a safe for storing your secrets. It is an open doorway sprouting a big neon welcome sign. They will gleefully walk in and wallow in your data for their own nefarious purposes. Most people don't realize just how big and welcoming that neon sign really is. They assume that because so many people use computers or because they are just one of billions cruising the internet, they are effectively anonymous. They are wrong. There is no safety in numbers. Everyone is at risk.

Think for a moment about your home. Assuming you don't live in a tent or an igloo, you probably rely on your home to provide a measure of security for yourself and your possessions. When you go out, you close the windows and lock the door; maybe you switch on a burglar alarm or security lighting. What you have done is to secure the obvious access points – the doors and windows – against a human intruder. But there are many other channels into your home. Electricity flows in, water and gas pipes bypass your security, you might have air-bricks, ventilators or chimneys. Imagine an invader who could make use of any of these channels – slipping up your gas main as easily as you walk through the front door. Imagine someone who laughs at your locks and bolts and alarms. Are you feeling paranoid yet? We have hardly started.

If you are still looking over your shoulder, you probably have a crick in your neck by now, so face forward and take a look at that computer sitting on the desk in front of you. It seems innocent enough, doesn't it? It just waits there; your little electronic chum always ready to help you. And these days, how could you survive without it? It lets you stay in touch with the rest of the world. You can use it to visit places and experience sensations you could never hope to aspire to in real life. Without its wondrous data-crunching skills, how could you manage your business? It calculates your accounts, stores your customer records and reminds you of important meetings. Perhaps it has helped you to extend your leisure interests. You might use it to edit your home videos or to touch up digital family photographs. Your computer is your friend. Isn't it?

Your trouble is that you think you have bought a toaster. A toaster is a handy, labour-saving device. You drop in bread, push down the handle and, after a few minutes, up pops your toast. The worst thing a toaster can do is burn the bread. Everywhere in the Western world computers are being sold as toasters. Scarcely computer-literate salesmen line the high street stores to sell you the latest model. They assure you that you need the fastest processor, the largest hard drive and the biggest monitor and that after you have plugged it all together at home, all you will need to do is drop in the bread, push down the handle and up will pop the operating system ready to do your bidding.

But a computer is not a simple household appliance. It is a complex and cantankerous machine designed for no specific purpose. It consists of a mass of compromises and trade-offs, hacked together in a vain attempt to produce a machine which will do a little bit of everything. It is not a fax machine, but it will send and receive faxes. It is not a games console, but it will play games. It is not a filing cabinet, but it will store and retrieve records. Stereo system, video editor, telephone directory, artist's studio – the list goes on and on and keeps getting longer. Would your toaster wash your under-wear or your telephone make the coffee? Naïve people often ask why a computer cannot be as stable and reliable as, say, a television or a video recorder. The simple answer is that a video recorder was designed and built to record videos while the core architecture of a computer was never intended to handle many of the tasks we throw at it. Every so often even the best-behaved computer throws up its hands and collapses. And no wonder. How would your VCR respond if you inserted a cheese sandwich instead of a videotape? Much of the software we cram into our computers is the electronic equivalent of a cheese sandwich. Not only does it fail to work properly, but it also gums up the insides and stops everything else from working properly. Don't blame the machine, blame the sandwich-maker.

We have been deluded by the computer and software manufacturers into believing two great lies. First, we have been persuaded that a computer is a simple, user-friendly home appliance and, second, that anyone who can type a few letters from a keyboard or wiggle a mouse about a bit can become an expert user. All computer advertising emphasizes these two deceits. Of course it does – if the manufacturers admitted the truth, most people would never buy a computer. From the very beginning, you are being misled.

And that's only the start of it. Lug all the boxes and your empty wallet home, and you will find yourself very much on your own. Most operating manuals are totally inadequate – that is if they are not supplied on a CD-ROM, which you can't read because your computer won't start. And just try getting service from that amusingly named 'customer helpline'. It is about now, as you sit alone and unloved among the boxes and wires that paranoia sets in.

Paranoia, according to the dictionary definition in Figure 1.1, is a state of mind 'characterized by delusions of persecution' or 'an abnormal tendency to suspect and mistrust others'. It is also the only sensible approach to all activities that involve using your computer. Unless you cultivate paranoia (and not just ordinary paranoia but a deep and disturbing paranoia), sooner or later, something horrible is going to happen to you. I cannot tell you what it will be. I cannot tell you when it will occur. Maybe you will just lose all your precious data to a hard disk crash or a virus, maybe your computer will be taken over and used by an anonymous hacker for some criminal activity or maybe your private passions will be made glaringly public. But believe me, suffer you will in some, as yet unspecified, way.

Of course you can ignore these warnings and all the other warnings scattered about on the web, in magazines and on the television. You can continue to flutter about in

*Figure 1.1 Paranoia – a
dictionary definition*

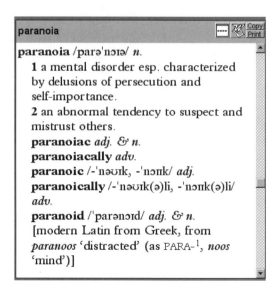

paranoia /parə'nɔɪə/ *n.*
  1 a mental disorder esp. characterized
  by delusions of persecution and
  self-importance.
  2 an abnormal tendency to suspect and
  mistrust others.
paranoiac *adj. & n.*
paranoiacally *adv.*
paranoic /-'nəʊɪk, -'nɒɪk/ *adj.*
paranoically /-'nəʊɪk(ə)li, -'nɒɪk(ə)li/
adv.
paranoid /'parənɔɪd/ *adj. & n.*
[modern Latin from Greek, from
paranoos 'distracted' (as PARA-[1], *noos*
'mind')]

innocence or ignorance. You can even persuade yourself that I am exaggerating the danger. Remember the Y2K bug, you might say, all the hysteria, all those millions spent on millennium proofing and at the end of it all…nothing. A big, damp squib. So go ahead; play the percentages and hope that nothing will ever happen to you. You are wrong. It will!

Are You The Master Of Your Own Computer?

One thing you must decide from the outset is who is in charge. Are you the master of your own computer, or are you going to let it control you. Deep down inside, most of us are a little frightened of our computers. When they do strange and unpleasant things, we look the other way and refuse to acknowledge that there is a problem. By ignoring the symptoms, we allow the diseases to take root. When a virus first infects your system, it is relatively simple to spot and deal with, but wait until it has trampled through your files and then see how easy it is to remove. Prompt action is the key to successful computer housekeeping.

From now on, you are the master. Make a vow that nothing will go on inside your computer without your permission. Your programs and data are yours alone and no one else has the right to access them unless you say so. Tell yourself that your computer is nothing more then a big lump of metal and plastic – a mindless machine that cannot crunch a single number until you tell it to. Over the next few chapters we are going to reassert control. We are going to clean up your system and get rid of the gremlins, we are going to build a double-thickness barbed-wire fence around your data and lay a minefield ready for anyone who gets through the fence, and we are going to forcibly eject any snoopers who are already lurking inside your machine so that you get the privacy you are entitled to. So there.

So, now we are clear about who is the boss, we can set about looking for problems to solve. Our greatest enemy here will be complacency. The safest approach is to always assume the worst. We will rely on good old Murphy's Law and its timeless truth that 'Anything that can go wrong will go wrong...' but update it with the essential appendix '...and at the worst possible time'. Equally valid are the immortal words of Pokémon's Team Rocket – 'Prepare for trouble, and make it double'.

Actually, this is a very positive and proactive approach. If we prepare for trouble (and double trouble), we take precautions; we are ready for the worst that can go wrong. Assuming that hackers are going to try to invade our computer-space, we install the locks and bars that can keep them out. If we know that our computer will crash and mutilate essential data, we anticipate trouble by backing up our files. Certain that viruses are waiting to pounce, we inoculate our system against infection. But you get the point.

In this book we are going to creep down into the sewers of cyberia. We are going to meet some of the foulest denizens of those dark depths and discover what they are trying to do to you and how they will try to do it. We will also look at that surprisingly stupid machine you call your computer and examine why it misbehaves so often. We will, however, stop short of suggesting that there is a demon infesting your machine, or that it has its own evil personality. That way lies madness.

Meet Our Cast Of Characters

Before we go any further, I am going to introduce you to some of the characters who inhabit the world we will be looking at. We will be meeting them now and then in the following chapters and seeing how a particular problem or technology is likely to affect them. Of course they are just stereotypes, but surprisingly realistic ones. Most of us will display some of their characteristics and share some of their concerns.

Eugene The Businessman

Eugene runs a successful company, which sells office stationery. He is alive to new business opportunities and embraced e-commerce with outstretched arms. His company has its own website and he uses e-mail to update his salesmen.

So far, Eugene has had no problems with his in-house network. He believes it is under his control. He uses proven business software and never allows his staff to bring their own media into the office.

The worst we can say about Eugene is that he might be a tad complacent – but a tad, in computer terms, is a very large unit of measurement.

Michael The Concerned Parent

Michael knows that without computer skills his much-loved teenage children will be at a serious disadvantage when they start looking for work. He also knows that the web can be a rough place.

He encourages his children to use the family computer for schoolwork and play. Occasionally this brings problems. The kids borrow games from friends at school and bring in the odd virus. But Michael is a patient man. He disinfects his computer and reminds his children to be more careful.

Unfortunately, teenagers being teenagers, they have cruised websites that would horrify their parents. Michael worries about this, but dislikes the idea of censoring their activities.

Maureen The Leisure Surfer

Deep inside, Maureen is shy and quiet, but the web allows her to blossom. She is an avid inhabitant of chat rooms and internet discussion forums where she has made many friends. (Some of these friends are not what they seem and have distinctly unpleasant intentions.)

Maureen was quick to sign up for a high-speed internet connection. She needs it for the hours she spends online each day. Like many computer users, she has taught herself to be highly competent within her own little world, but has not bothered to learn the skills she might need to protect herself and her machine.

Soon, some of those not so nice friends will come calling, and Maureen's world will turn upside-down.

Peter The Computer Hater

Peter just knows that the whole world and everything in it hates him. He takes it all very personally. His computer contains an evil demon, which loves to torture him by crashing just before he saves an entire evening's work.

Peter never even wanted a computer, but his company gave him one and told him to use it to process his sales figures and write his reports. Every time he switches it on, he is waiting for it to let him down.

And it does, usually because Peter's processing technique involves a frenzy of key-punching and screaming at the monitor when the computer objects to his rough treatment.

RatZnuTZ The Cracker (Artist's Impression)

RatZnuTZ (real name Justin Longbottom) is proud to call himself a hacker. (Genuine hackers despise his kind, calling them 'script-kiddies'.) Just 19, he considers himself the arch-wizard of the internet, cruising the hackers and warez[1] sites looking for rogue code that he can use to mess with other people's systems.

RatZnuTZ cuts a solitary, faintly nerdish figure. Unless he is sitting behind a keyboard, he exudes impotence. He belongs to a group that calls itself The DooMSlayerZ (*sic*) that specializes in hacking into proprietary software to cripple the routine that asks for the registration number. The DooMSlayerZ website then distributes these hacks to others who prefer not to pay for their software.

Gordon The Young Professional

Gordon simply adores technology. As the most junior partner in an inner-city law firm, he sees it as his duty to spread the gospel of computerization to the older, more conservative colleagues around him.

---

[1] This is not a misspelling. For some unknown reason, the script-kiddy type has tHiZ coMpuLziOn 2 tYpe like tHiZ. This may be a good thing, since it can act as a warning sign to others.

When interviewing clients, Gordon doesn't take notes: he scratches on the screen of his Personal Digital Assistant (PDA). All his records are stored on his computer and he prefers DTPing his letters rather than dictating them to his secretary.

Gordon's computers form the centre of his universe. He has three – one at work, one at home and a laptop to carry between them. But he worries that technology is passing him by. Should he invest in a newer, faster machine? In Gordon's case, the answer is always 'yes'.

Susan The Student

Susan the Student is a harmless computer user. She has no real interest in technology beyond a kind of half-hearted acceptance that it might help her to get a job after university.

Her parents bought her a computer to take to college and she diligently uses it for her assignments, but she doesn't trust it. Her friend, Dave, is constantly being summoned to repair this and explain that. (Dave doesn't mind, because he quite fancies Susan.)

Apart from the college work, Susan's machine is loaded with all sorts of odd software her friends have found or borrowed. Her hard drive contains a seething mass of viruses and rogue code all competing to cripple her machine. Occasionally, Dave will clean it up for her, but within days the infections will be back.

Dennis The Porn Peeper

Dennis is a man of two halves. By day he works in a bookshop, earning an honest wage to support Christine and his three young children. But late at night, when Chrissie and the kids are asleep he trawls the web looking for enormous bosoms. (It is strange how enormous bosoms have come to dominate Dennis' thoughts in recent months.)

While this activity is quite legal, it preys on Dennis' mind. He knows that it would upset Christine. He looks for ways of concealing his hobby and hiding his trophies from casual scrutiny. Of all our characters, he alone exhibits the first symptoms of paranoia.

We will be meeting these characters later and examining how they negotiate or, in most cases, fail to negotiate the minefield of computer activity. With our cast waiting in the wings and our paranoia starting to brew, we must turn our attention back to the computer. At the start of this chapter, we considered it as a machine. Now we need to think about what we actually mean by computer security and why it is important.

Thinking Secure Thoughts

Computer security means peace of mind. Do you ever feel a twinge of anxiety when you switch on your machine? Are you afraid that it won't start or that the files you saved last night won't be where you left them? If you are, this is good because it is the start of that essential paranoia which will compel you to prepare for trouble. Security, as I mentioned earlier, is mainly about taking control. Expect resistance – there will be times when you feel that your computer itself is fighting you, but trust me, you will win through in the end.

Most offices, colleges and other organizations seem to feature at least one person who is totally relaxed about his or her computer operations. When things go wrong, he (or she) calmly puts them right again. Unexpected crashes, virus infections or security breaches don't phase him in the slightest. He twiddles with his software, downloads the latest patches[2] from the internet, whips the back off his computer and makes adjustments in complete confidence. He is the man that others turn to when they are flummoxed. By the end of this book, you will be that person.

I want you to develop a secure way of thinking; a security mindset. Whether you are starting fresh on a new computer, or correcting bad behaviour on an old one, you should start by telling yourself that you are in charge. However messed up and disorderly your machine is, there is nothing that cannot be put right with care and patience. At this point we don't care if your computer is awash with viruses, open to alien invasion or crashing every few minutes. We are going to put everything right.

Let's get ourselves ready to go by recognizing some of the problems we will be facing.

---

[2] I will be using footnotes throughout this book to define technical terms. I will try not to do it too often. When a programmer finds an error in his work, he will often release a small correction to a program in the form of an executable file. Download that file from the internet and run it to patch up the error. Thus 'patches'.

Operating System Alert

It is a mistake to sell a computer as 'user-friendly' or 'idiot-proof'. Nothing is idiot-proof. An experienced idiot can be relied upon to turn the simplest process into a complete pig's breakfast. Nine times out of ten, the phrase 'my computer has stopped working' can be translated as 'my own stupidity has mashed things up'. Computers demand care and attention to detail. Learning to use them requires dedication and commitment. And the most helpful response to those endless calls for help is RTFM (Read The F*****g Manual).

Let's look at the situation from a new angle. That thing which we call a computer is not just a big, plastic box filled with electronic circuitry. Unless it is to be used as the world's most badly designed paperweight, it also requires programs and data – software. The term 'software' covers a multitude of different elements. There is the operating system, which is, in effect, the master control program for the computer. It handles the computer's internal functions, as well as allocating processing time and resources.

Overlaying the operating system is the Graphical User Interface (GUI), which is the software that represents computer functions as the icons, buttons and menus that you see on screen. Figure 1.2 shows Windows Explorer with all the key elements of the GUI – buttons, icons and menus. Then there is the application software; the word processor, database, video editor or graphics package which allows you to create

Figure 1.2 The Windows GUI in action

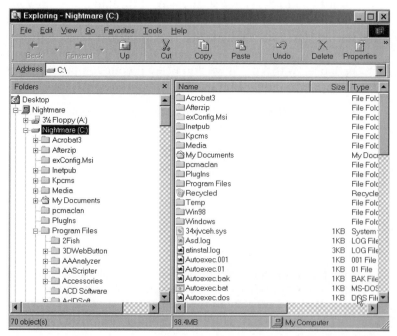

documents, images and other data. Finally there is the data itself, your lovingly created digital pictures, your letters and business notes, your home videos.

Between these easily identified elements are a host of largely unseen programs which allow the major elements to work together. There are device drivers, which let the operating system access your disk drive, scanner, printer, etc. There are utilities, which run constantly in the background to tidy up after you and warn you of problems. Most of these little programs remain invisible, as they are intended to do, but they all add to the complexity of a computer's internal operations. It requires a genius to work out exactly what is happening inside that box at any one moment. Any application which you deliberately fire up, can start a plethora of other software to provide essential support functions and to mesh it into the operating system.

With so much happening at any one time, it is hardly surprising that things go wrong. Software programmers are fallible and make mistakes in their code. Most applications are not concrete – they are crazy paving, cracked and flawed with odd patches jammed in as repairs. A minor coding error and the program grinds to a halt, but a major error illustrates the house of cards principle and brings the whole operating system down. Most computer users are very familiar with the famous Blue Screen Of Death (BSOD) with its comical suggestion that by pressing a key, the faulty application will terminate and the system recover. It almost never does! Experienced computer operators measure their success by the number of times they have to reboot the system each day – the fewer the better.

To provide the extensive list of services we demand, the modern personal computer (PC) has traded off stability for flexibility. The most common platform, the so-called 'Wintel' machine (running the Windows operating system on an Intel (or similar) processor), is intended to run any software which complies with a set of integration rules defined by an API (Application Program Interface). An API is a piece of software, which provides the functions and resources that programmers require to access the operating system. By writing software to conform with a Windows API, the programmer knows that his application can take advantage of standard menus, dialog boxes, keyboard commands, etc.

APIs are valuable. They simplify the learning process by ensuring that programs look and respond in a standard way. They foster the familiarity that encourages us to try out new software. The problem is that the more extensive the API, the more the operating system is exposed to abuse. Most people will have had the experience of a newly installed program producing strange results on screen. Icons transformed into garbage, windows refusing to close, menu choices that produce unexpected results, even the much-loved Blue Screen Of Death can all result from the poor implementation of an API. People often whine about Windows, but despite all the moaning, it is a good operating system. It is attractive, easy to use and fairly stable. But any operating system is worthless without application software, and it is almost always the bugs in the application software that bring your computer crashing down. We will be looking in detail at the problems of software and data management later in this book.

Peter The Computer Hater

Our model of inadequacy here is Peter. All the time he is using his computer, he is waiting for it to break down. He tries to write files to a CD-ROM, and while that application is running, he also tries to open a memory-hungry word processor. Faced with this over-use of resources, the OS desperately tries to portion out CPU[3] time and thus slows operations down to a crawl. Peter is convinced that his system has frozen and starts pressing keys and clicking buttons. Each of these sends a new signal (an interrupt) to the CPU, which slows the system still further. Eventually Peter gives up and restarts his machine, losing most of his work in the process. Peter is not known for his patience.

For now, remember that the sensible user always expects trouble. He closes one heavyweight application before opening a new one. He waits for one process to terminate before starting something else. He avoids overloading the operating system with resource-heavy instructions. But most users are click-crazy. They expect their computers to cope with anything that is thrown at them, then throw things that no computer could be expected to cope with. Even a computer with an ultra-fast processor and bags of memory is still finite in capacity. Load enough activity and the system will slow down and eventually retire in exhaustion.

Watch Out For Relatives, Friends And Colleagues

While researching this book, I interviewed any number of computer technicians and systems support staff. Almost without exception they identified the well-meaning amateur as the greatest danger to system stability. I myself have lost count of the times when some anecdotal solution ('I found that the best way to deal with that is to do this') has brought down a complete network. Here are just a few of the ways in which your friends are your enemies.

➤ Your brother sends you an e-mail, which carries an attached document file. Unknown to him, the file is infected with one of the familiar Word macro

[3] CPU – the Central Processing Unit refers to the internal storage, processing and control circuitry that sit at the heart of the computer and handle computer operations. Processing functions are controlled by the microprocessor chip – usually an Intel Pentium processor (or similar) but there are still some older devices in use. The sensible user knows that any microprocessor more than a year or two old is pretty much obsolete and avoids stressing it with too many tasks at any one time.

viruses. You read the file, because it comes from your brother, and guess what, your computer is infected.

➤ One of your programs starts acting strangely. Your colleague at the next desk tells you that she had exactly the same problem and explains how she fixed it. You try her solution, but because she has misread your symptoms and misremembered her remedy, your whole system locks up and takes a nosedive. You will spend the next two days reinstalling all your software.

➤ A friend at college recommends a site on the web. Of course he doesn't know that the site is a hacker refuge which nasty people use to gain access to your computer. You trundle in and download a program (a Trojan, of which, more later), which opens a backdoor into your system. Now you can be used as a launching pad for a whole range of criminal activities.

In computing, your friends are your enemies. However well intentioned, it is wise to suspect their advice.

The Balanced Approach To Computer Security

The lesson of this chapter is to prepare for the worst and then prepare some more. The sensible user does not just cover his arse. He covers it, then clads it with foam rubber, then armours it in Kevlar, then sets his arse in concrete and guards it with a machine gun. And even then he will worry that he has not taken adequate precautions. Let's illustrate this approach with a simple example. Take a look at Table 1.1 which suggests different levels of precautions you might take to safeguard an important document.

In this example, is our Level 5 user going over the top? You might wonder if the report is important enough to justify this degree of caution. But at least the report is safe and the additional work involved has only added perhaps five minutes of machine time to the hours it took to complete. The time has come to assess the data held on your own machine and estimate how long it would take to recreate it after a catastrophe. How many hours of thought went into that book you are writing? Could you ever reassemble the cast for that digital family photograph? Even if Level 5 is excessive, the fact remains that almost nobody takes data security as seriously as they should.

To close this chapter, I propose the following set of principles, which we will apply to all the problems, dangers and anti-social activities we will meet in the rest of the book.

1 Always assume that the worst is going to happen.

2 Question everybody's motives.

3 Nothing is free – there is always a catch of some kind.

4 Protect, then protect the protection.

5 Never trust anybody to do what they say they will do.

6 Never postpone taking a precaution.

7 Never take chances with computer data.

8 Proactive is always better than reactive.

9 Everybody is out to get you.

10 These principles are not sufficiently paranoid.

Armed with these principles, we can now face our computer activities with a degree of confidence.

Table 1.1 Levels Of Security

Security level	Action taken
1 Innocent	A user types an important report on his computer. He saves it to disk and goes to bed.
2 Cautious	A user types an important report on his computer. He saves it to disk but also prints it out.
3 Protective	A user types an important report on his computer. He saves it to disk and prints it out. He also saves a second copy to a back-up drive on his computer.
4 Paranoid	A user types an important report on his computer. He saves it to disk, prints it out, and saves a second copy to a back-up drive. He also saves a third copy to floppy disk.
5 Massive overkill	A user types an important report on his computer. He saves it to disk, prints it out, saves a second copy to a back-up drive, and saves a third copy to floppy disk. He also saves a further copy to an online drive on the internet and, when he goes to bed, he takes the floppy copy with him, so that if his computer catches fire it won't take the floppy with it.

At the end of each chapter, I will be providing a Security Checklist to remind you of the key points we have covered and the action you should take. Here is the first one:

Chapter 1 – Security Checklist

1   Start thinking of your computer as an open system which is constantly under attack. These attacks can come from outside (hackers, viruses, etc.) or from inside (rogue code, hardware failure, etc.).

2   Cultivate deep-rooted paranoia. Assume that everything is out to get you, that you are the target for outside attack and that your computer is permanently on the point of breaking down.

3   Tell yourself that you are the master of your computer and that it will do nothing without your permission.

4   Watch out for the well-meaning assistance of friends, relatives and colleagues. They can be a major source of bad advice.

5   Read through and repeat often the set of principles listed above. Tattoo them on your arm. Teach your children to chant them after supper. Paint them on your wall in big red letters.

'... If You Buy A Computer, Don't Turn It On!'

In This Chapter

➤ A mish-mash of mismatched machinery

➤ Causes of hardware failures

➤ Acts of God (and the Electric Company)

➤ Doing it yourself

➤ Is your computer out-of-date?

➤ Buying a machine with security in mind

A Mish-Mash Of Mismatched Machinery

The title of this chapter, added to the title of Chapter 1, make up Jeff Richard's famous Laws of Data Security. To quote them in full:

➤ Don't buy a computer.

➤ If you buy a computer, don't turn it on.

The point, of course, is that it is never possible to implement total computer security. This isn't strictly true. If you are prepared to lay out a lot of money and an enormous amount of time, you can achieve almost total security, but one of the costs is constant vigilance. In this book, we are concerned with developing a realistic risk management strategy, which means balancing the value of your data and your privacy against time and cost factors. We are going to start this analysis by considering your hardware.

When we talk about a computer, we normally use the term to include all the assorted bits and pieces that sit on (or under) your desk. Strictly speaking, the term 'computer' refers to the electronic circuitry and components that actually handle the data processing. Everything else – the monitor, keyboard, disk drives, etc. – are integrated or peripheral devices – integrated if they fit inside the case, peripheral if they are attached with wires.

A computer has been defined as 'a machine that can follow instructions to alter data in a desirable way'. (Note the 'desirable' bit!) For simplicity, we can consider all computer activity as the process illustrated in Figure 2.1. This diagram shows that a computer is a system which accepts data from a variety of different hardware devices, processes that data according to rules defined in software or in response to user input (via more hardware), then outputs that data to another (or the same) hardware device. Why is this important? Because it illustrates how the computer's hardware is involved at every stage of the process. It is true to say that the security of our data relies on the security of our hardware.

The core workings of the computer itself are not intended for human intervention. There is no way in which even the maddest enthusiast can modify the processor itself or rewire the bus which moves data around the system. But apart from that core, out in the peripheral zone, computers are built as open systems. They are designed to let users add new devices, increase memory or upgrade components. This open configuration is essential – otherwise you would be locked into an ageing system with no means of improving it – but it is also terribly dangerous. Ham-fisted amateurs can wreak havoc on sensitive circuits. Electronics are tricky at the best of times. A computer relies on sound electrical pathways down which signals can travel. If these pathways are damaged, or if components cannot make good contact with the circuits, signals can't flow and the computer stops working.

Figure 2.1 A simplified look at computer processing

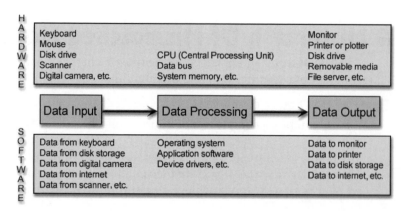

Hardware manufacturers encourage you to upgrade your machine, but any computer repairman will tell you that 90 per cent of his work comes from putting right what inexperienced users have put wrong. A wise person knows his or her limitations. If you are not totally confident of your own abilities, ignore the salesmen's proclamations and get an experienced computer engineer to undertake your upgrades. (If you are determined to DIY, check out the section below entitled **Doing it yourself**.)

Michael – The Concerned Parent

Michael is under constant pressure to upgrade his computer. His children nag him for the latest hardware to allow them to play the latest games. As a result, he is constantly installing new graphics cards and hardware drivers. Michael is a careful technician, but he is still only an amateur and he makes mistakes. Cards are misaligned and only make intermittent contact. Sometimes he forgets to reconnect cables. As a result, the family computer is often out of action.

Michael's life would be much simpler if he stopped botching and sat down with his family to agree a computer configuration which would answer everybody's needs. He could then do one major upgrade, or send the machine to a qualified technician to do it for him. After that, he should leave it alone for a few months until changing demands suggest that the next major upgrade is required.

Causes Of Hardware Failures

Like any other piece of equipment, computers do break down. Breakdowns don't usually result from any failure in the components themselves, but from two unavoidable sources – heat and movement. Heat is a by-product of most electrical and mechanical activity. Standard IDE hard drives can get quite warm and you can sometimes fry an egg on a SCSI drive. Your microprocessor and circuitry get hot when they are working hard. Modern processors are usually equipped with a heat sink or a cooling fan to handle heat dissipation. Although your computer's case is equipped with another fan, remember that both of these fans just move the heat around, they don't do any actual cooling. One upgrade always worth considering is adding a second fan.

We won't get bogged down in acronyms, but since I have just used a couple of them, here is what they mean. IDE stands for Integrated Drive Electronics and is the standard hard disk interface supplied on most computers. SCSI (pronounced *scuzzee*) stands for Small Computer Systems Interface and is an interface which accepts a range of peripheral devices including hard disks. SCSI drives supply data much faster than IDE drives, but are also much more expensive.

It is worth remembering that computers (like any electrical equipment) work better at cooler temperatures – the cooler the better, within limits. In fact, the fastest computers contain an integrated refrigerator to keep all the components nicely chilled. Most of the components on a circuit board are generating a small amount of heat, and this heat, added to that coming from the processor and disk drives, builds up inside the case. Unfortunately, an optimal temperature for a computer would be far too cold for the poor human sitting at the keyboard. We prefer to work in nice warm rooms which don't suit our computers at all. Unless you are a real hothouse flower, try to keep your work space as cool as you can comfortably put up with. Your computer will love you for it.

The second source of problems is mechanical movement (which, incidentally, generates heat as well). Hard drives, not to mention floppy disks and CD-ROM drives, spin at high speeds. The platters which actually store the data are mounted on a bearing which rotates around a central shaft at thousands of revolutions per minute and eventually, these bearings start to wear out. Moving across the platters, and looking rather like the arm on an old record player, are read-write heads which transfer data to and from the platters. These heads are designed to float just above the platters, but occasionally they fail and grind into them, making a spectacular noise and permanently destroying the drive. Luckily, modern hard drives are extremely reliable and very seldom fail, but accidents do happen.

A computer has a working life of only a few years before it becomes obsolete, so the chances are that you will replace your machine long before any of the moving parts begin to wear out. The chances are ... hmm, time to consider that risk management strategy I mentioned. At every stage of this book you need to pause and think about the value of the data stored on your computer. Yes, the chances of a hard disk crash are extremely remote, but it does happen, and if it does you are unlikely to be able to recover anything from the disk. Already we are beginning to see the need for storing back-ups of all our critical data, but many better reasons are still to come!

The other parts of your computer which are prone to mechanical damage are easier to replace and will not cause any serious harm to your data. Keyboards are relatively flimsy things. They suffer from being dropped, having things dropped on them, and the occasional shower of coffee. Few keyboards can survive an encounter with coffee, so, if you have an accident of that kind, expect to junk the thing. Keyboards are relatively cheap to replace. Mice are also semi-disposable. Here the problem is not usually wear, but a build-up of muck clogging the small rollers which measure the activity of the mouse ball and translate it into electrical signals. It is possible to strip down the mouse and clean all the moving parts with isopropyl alcohol, but eventually most mice become erratic and are best replaced.

This might be hard to believe, but sometimes a drink-splashed keyboard can be repaired by washing it! Remove the keyboard and hold it under a tap for a few minutes. Shake off the droplets of water, then stand the keyboard upright in a warm place with good ventilation for several days.

My apologies to smokers, but it must also be stated that smoke is a killer of computers. Look at the ceiling in an old bar, and you will often see a slick yellow film discolouring the paintwork. This is tar – the same tar that sneaks into your computer and coats its internal workings. If you must smoke – and who am I to tell you what to do – you should consider using an extractor fan to suck the fumes out of the room. Better still, invest in an air conditioning unit and chill the room at the same time.

One single act is more likely to harm your hardware than anything else I have mentioned and that, believe it or not, is turning your computer on. Engineers will tell you that more equipment fails at start up than at any other time, and the reasons are not hard to find. Without power, your computer is an idle lump of plastic and metal. Bang on the power and every mechanical and electronic process is jump started – disks spin, electrons flash down circuitry, warning lights flicker and voltages surge. What you have done is applied a major shock to the system by jolting it into life.

If your data is critical (risk management strategy again!) consider leaving your computer switched on and allowing its own power management features to switch off the monitor and power down your disk drives. A sleeping computer uses very little electricity and is considerably more stable than one which is constantly being switched on and off.

Acts Of God (And The Electric Company)

Some of the greatest perils to your hardware are outside your control. Computers need electricity to function of course, but that electricity must be delivered at a constant voltage. We need to be concerned with three types of supply failure – loss of power, power spikes and power surges. Each of these brings its own dangers.

Power losses can last from a fraction of a second to several hours or even days, but the effect of even the shortest loss of supply can be catastrophic. To understand why, look at Figure 2.2

While data stored on your hard disk is vulnerable in other ways, it is at least safe against power loss. Hard disk storage is **non-volatile**, which means that the particles on the magnetic surface of the platters which actually store information remain polarized even if power is interrupted. When you access or create a file, the data it contains is transferred to Random Access Memory (RAM). (You can think of RAM as

Figure 2.2 Data security during data processing

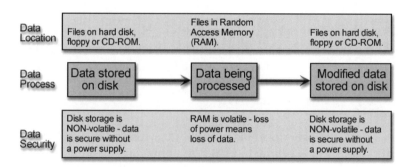

the workbench of the computer.) But RAM is **volatile**. If the power fails – even for an instant, the microscopic electronic capacitors which actually store the data promptly forget their charge and all the data held in RAM is lost forever. In practical terms, this means saving your work often. As soon as data is stored back to disk, it is safe against power loss and if you do suffer a power cut, all you will lose is the changes you have made since the last save. (And sometimes not even this since some applications auto-save your work every few seconds.)

Spikes and surges, on the other hand, can do much more than just lose your data. An electrical spike is an increase in power which usually lasts less than a millionth of a second. A surge lasts longer, usually a few millionths of a second. They can be caused in several ways, but the most common are lightening strikes on the supply network or equipment failure at the electricity supply stations.

Sometimes you can spot a spike by a brief brightening of your lights, but usually they go undetected by humans – not, unfortunately, by computers. Surges and spikes can travel down the power lines into the transformer which supplies the low voltages your computer runs on and produce a voltage high enough to fry the main board and all the other circuitry. The result is a seriously dead computer. Never plug your computer directly into the mains. Invest in an extension block with surge protection – they are not very expensive, and you will protect your machine against all but the most lethal spikes and surges.

There is a second way in which electrical spikes can get in and it accounts for a frightening number of fried computers each year. Most people still rely on the telephone lines for their internet access. If you are one of those who tend to leave their modems plugged into the telephone socket, you could be in for a nasty surprise. Lightening is happy to use the phone lines to blast your hardware, so unplug your modem cable whenever you are not online. (Honesty forces me to admit that I have lost two computers like this.)

Doing It Yourself

Let me repeat my advice. Unless you know your way around the insides of a computer and are confident of your technical abilities, leave upgrades to a qualified technician. But if you are competent, or incredibly pig-headed, there are several things you can do to improve your chances of performing a successful operation. Before we look at a logical approach to computer DIY, there are two particular dangers to be aware of.

First, remember that you can cause some quite impressive electrical spikes yourself. Slide around on a nylon carpet for a few minutes and you can build up a sizable static charge – quite enough to damage delicate computer circuitry. Before you touch any components inside your machine, it is necessary to earth yourself and lose your static charge. The best way to do this is to ignore the classic advice about unplugging your computer before attempting to work on it. The rule is: switch your computer off before you start work, but leave it plugged into the mains. The power lead provides a handy route to earth.

Mains voltage only travels as far as the power supply – the metal box in your computer which accepts the mains lead on the outside and is festooned with coloured wires on the inside. The power supply converts mains voltage into the much smaller voltages used by the electronic circuitry. This means that you cannot get an electric shock from any of the internal components. The computer's metal chassis and all the brackets and braces which support the drives and boards are earthed. By touching these before you start work (and occasionally while you are working) your personal charge is dispersed.

The second major problem is the hazard of bringing metal tools into contact with electronic components. Always remember how fragile components are and how easily they can be damaged by a misplaced screwdriver or even a screw dropped onto the motherboard. Some components carry a residual charge even when the power is off. Any piece of metal can cause a short-circuit and short-circuits are not good news. Use all tools with great care and if you are forced to fish about for lost screws, your fingers are much safer than pliers.

Keeping these two potential disaster areas in mind, we can now formulate a logical upgrade plan. Most upgrades follow a similar path, so let us assume that you intend adding a new expansion card to your computer. A sensible approach to upgrading is demonstrated in Table 2.1.

Table 2.1 A Sensible Approach To Upgrading

Step	Action
1 Prepare your tools and your workspace	➤ Before you touch your computer, make sure you have everything ready. Fish out any manuals you will need, assemble your tools and unpack the parts or cables you will be installing.
	➤ Most new circuit boards are supplied in anti-static bags. Leave them in these until you need them. Earth yourself once more (see above) before unpacking boards and only hold them by the edges.
	➤ Make sure that you have plenty of space to work in and that the workspace is well lit.
	➤ You'll probably need a torch for those dark corners and a small mirror is often useful.
2 RTFM	➤ Read the f****** manuals. Go through the installation instructions carefully, noting any special tools or techniques required. You may need to go back to Step 1 at this point.
	➤ If there is anything you don't understand, call a halt to the whole job until you do. Don't assume that all will become clear as you go along. You might find extra help on the web or by asking someone who knows what they are doing for advice.
	➤ Some upgrades require you to install the software before you install the hardware. Follow the printed instructions to the letter.
3 Prepare your computer.	➤ Switch off your computer but leave it connected to the mains.
	➤ Move the box (or lay it on its side) so that you can get to the screws which hold the cover on. Remove the screws and place them in a safe location. (You might end up with lots of different screws, so keep them in separate batches.) Remove the cover and earth yourself by touching the metal chassis.
	➤ Reposition the computer and possibly your light source so that you can see and access the insides. Computers are built in all sorts of different patterns, but always try and work with the motherboard parallel to the tabletop.
4 Plan the job.	➤ Without touching anything, work the job through in your own mind. Decide which screws will have to be removed, which

cables will need to be disconnected and how you will make certain that they are replaced correctly.

➤ If there is likely to be any confusion, consider marking cables and other components with labels. (You might even note down the whole procedure as a series of steps to be ticked off when completed.)

➤ Look for potential trouble. How easy will it be to connect a cable between two close-fitting boards? Are you likely to drop a securing screw if you attempt to work from a particular angle? Plan solutions to possible problems.

➤ If anything is not clear, go back to the manuals and look for help.

➤ If you cannot plan the job from start to finish, stop at this point, replace the cover and retire defeated. (There is no shame in this!) Look in the phone book for a qualified computer technician ...

5 Carry out the work.

➤ Following your plan as best you can, carry out the procedures as they are described in the manual(s). Try to work in a slow, methodical way. You will need to improvize when things don't go as intended.

➤ Connect components and cables with great care, applying only just enough pressure to ensure a good connection. Never force anything. If something doesn't want to fit, pull it out again, check that you are inserting it the right way round and try once more. It often helps to get a different view of the problem, so try looking at the connection from a different angle, or use a mirror.

➤ Most parts and cables will only connect one way, but there are exceptions. Use your labels and notes to make sure that everything fits as it is supposed to. Most ribbon cables have a red stripe down one edge and this edge always goes to Pin 1 on a connector. If you look closely (torch and even magnifying glass!), you will often find that Pin 1 is marked on the connector itself.

➤ When you are finished, check that there are no bits left over – except for the screws that secure the cover, of course.

6 Test the upgrade.

➤ Reconnect any wires and cables that you have removed, but don't close the case.

Table 2.1 *continued*

Step	Action
	➤ Power up your computer and make sure the new parts work as they are supposed to. Windows will usually spot any additions to the hardware and start up the New Hardware Wizard to help you install any drivers that are required. You may find that your new hardware's manual is at odds with Windows' approach to the installation. If there is a conflict, always follow the manual and ignore Windows. Your hardware manufacturer should know what he is doing.
	➤ Once your new device is fully operational, shut down the computer and screw down the cover. Power up the computer once more as a final check.
7 After the event.	➤ Don't lose the manual or any of the notes you made during the installation. Store everything in a safe place in case you need to refer back to it.

This approach might seem long-winded, but it takes longer to itemize than it does to follow. If you adopt the procedure suggested above, you remain in control of your installation and are unlikely to encounter any serious problems. Above all else, stay calm!

Is Your Computer Out-of-date?

Yes it is! All computers are out-of-date five minutes after they leave the store. There is nothing more annoying than investing in a state-of-the-art machine, only to find that within a matter of weeks, something faster and more powerful is available. Older machines are almost valueless. There are no trade-in facilities like there are with cars, and if you try to sell a second-hand computer, you will probably find that it is worth a tiny fraction of its retail price. Sometimes schools or charities will offer homes to old computers.

People often complain about this cycle of obsolescence, but it is built into the system. For the most part, the computer industry is hardware-driven. Processor manufacturers are continuously producing faster chips around which the computer companies build faster machines. Ferocious marketing tries to persuade us that we need to constantly replace older computers to take advantage of performance improvements. In fact, nothing could be further from the truth.

If you buy a computer that is competent to handle a particular set of tasks, there is no reason to change computers unless those tasks change. Some computer activities do require phenomenal performance and massive data storage – video editing is a good example, but for most common tasks, a newer, faster machine will bring no advantages whatsoever. Most home users have limited processing requirements. They want internet access, e-mail and messaging facilities, word and data processing and, perhaps, some limited graphics handling. None of these needs a particularly fast processor or a lot of memory or disk storage. Money spent on an ultra-fast system that is never going to be used to capacity is money wasted. The exception, of course, is computer gaming. Games manufacturers are always pushing hardware to the edge. The latest games usually require the fastest processors, the most advanced graphics cards and bucketfuls of memory. The dedicated gamer will be constantly buying new cards, downloading updated drivers for his hardware and configuring his system for ultimate performance.

The rest of us can soldier on with yesterday's machinery, but eventually we will need to get something better. Often the best solution is not to buy another machine, but to improve the one you already have. This is usually cheaper than replacing an existing computer since we do not need to spend money on the usable hardware we already have. Do you really need a new keyboard, for example? Table 2.2 below, lists some of the most useful upgrades.

Table 2.2 Some Useful Upgrades

Hardware	Possible reasons to upgrade	Notes on upgrading
Memory	To speed up data processing. To handle more tasks simultaneously. To allow you to use new software or later versions. To allow you to upgrade your operating system.	It is always worth adding more memory, up to the maximum that you can afford and your computer can support. Increasing memory is usually more productive than any other upgrade, including a faster processor. You will need to check which type of memory your computer uses and make sure you buy the right modules.
Disk drives	To allow you to store more data. To allow you to implement a more intensive back-up strategy.	If your hard disk is filling up, you can either archive a lot of files on removable disks or CD-ROMs or you can upgrade your drive. One sensible solution is to add a second drive to your computer and use that for data storage. (See

Table 2.2 *continued*

Hardware	Possible reasons to upgrade	Notes on upgrading
Disk drives *continued*		Chapter 4 for details of different drive configurations.)
Monitor	To improve picture quality. To handle graphics at a higher resolution. To enlarge your desktop to cater for more or larger open windows.	Most monitors are plug-and-play which means that an upgrade is just a question of plugging the new monitor in and letting Windows handle the software configuration.
Processor	To handle new software that requires a particular processor. To speed up data processing.	It is not worth upgrading your processor unless you have a specific need for one. You will probably require a new motherboard as well, and this means a major refit rather than a simple change of components. See below.
Modem	Better internet connection speeds. Faster communications.	Despite the growth of broadband internet connections such as Digital Subscriber Lines (DSL), ISDN and cable, most people still use the traditional modem. Internet content is moving towards multimedia and interaction, which require faster connections. Before upgrading your modem, you need to make sure that broadband cabling is available. (I look at this in more detail in Chapter 14.)
Graphics card	Improved graphics handling and display. Better gaming performance.	New graphics cards are constantly coming onto the market and often provide remarkable improvements in graphics handling. Graphics cards are simple enough to replace. They slide into an expansion card slot on the motherboard.

CD/DVD-ROM drives	To provide a back-up system. To play audio/data/multimedia disks.	Modern computers are always equipped with a CD-ROM or DVD-ROM drive, and often with a CD writer. As we will see in Chapter 9, a CD writer is an excellent tool for backing up your data and is well worth fitting for this reason alone.
Mouse/ Trackball	To improve accuracy when handling on-screen elements.	The new optical mice prevent the old problem of muck clogging up moving parts. A trackball provides fine control if you are working on graphics or multi-media projects.
Motherboard	To provide additional or specific types of slots for expansion cards. To permit a processor upgrade. To allow more or faster memory to be fitted.	Changing a motherboard involves stripping the entire computer down and rebuilding it. This is not a job for the amateur, although care, rather than technical ability, is the essential skill.

Buying A Machine With Security In Mind

If you do intend investing in a new computer, approach the purchase with care. Treat a salesman's recommendations with a pinch of salt – his agenda is not necessarily yours! You are buying a computer to handle a specific range of tasks. He might be looking to offload an end-of-line machine, to meet his monthly sales target, or even to get off to lunch early! It is a depressing fact that far too many high street computer sales staff are inadequately trained in the technologies they are expected to sell. If you are not technically competent, find a friend who is and take him shopping with you.

Go into the store with a specification in mind – better still, write down your minimum requirements and hand the list to the salesman. Do not make compromises – there are plenty of other stores to visit. Look at any machine which is offered to you in terms of its suitability for the tasks you have in mind. If it passes this test, consider its ergonomics (see the box overleaf). Is the keyboard comfortable to type on for extended periods? Is the monitor large enough with a high contrast display and no annoying flicker? Ask the salesman if you can use the machine for a while and see how it fits your standards of comfort.

Ergonomics is the science of designing machines and work environments so that they are both comfortable and healthy. Recently there has been a lot of concern with RSI (Repetitive Strain Injury). It is now accepted that continually working at a computer can cause damage to wrists, elbows and even the spine. To avoid this, medical professionals suggest arranging your work environment so that your arms and wrists are properly supported and you sit in a comfortable upright position. They also urge you to take regular breaks. Some computer products are specially designed to reduce the risks of RSI. Take a look at the special keyboards, mice and accessories available from www.kinesis-ergo.com for examples of these.

Above all, be aware of the need to purchase a system which can provide a secure environment for your computer activities. Ask yourself (and the salesman!) questions like these.

➤ Will this machine allow me to upgrade components easily?

➤ Does this machine provide adequate disk storage for me to implement a secure back-up strategy? (A 60-gigabyte drive is sufficient for most purposes, but see the notes on drives in Table 2.1 and in Chapter 4.)

➤ Does this computer have adequate memory to allow me to run the additional software my security measures require? (128MB is an absolute minimum – 256MB is better.)

➤ Does this machine include a CD writer for removable back-ups?

➤ Do the manufacturers provide adequate online and telephone support for their products?

➤ What happens if something goes wrong?

You might consider adding a list of suitable questions to your specification sheet.

Do not be swayed by the bundle of goodies offered with the computer. It might seem very attractive to buy a job lot with scanner, printer, speakers and digital camera thrown in, but the chances are that the devices on offer are not the best ones for your particular requirements. It might cost more, but in the long run you are better off buying the peripherals you need using the same controlled approach I am proposing for your computer purchase. Software bundles are equally suspect. You need an operating system, of course, but application software should be chosen to suit your needs, not because it is thrown in with the computer.

There are times when the high street stores are not enough. If data security is a serious consideration, you might need to go for some heavy-duty hardware, which will probably not be available on an off-the-shelf machine. Consider buying direct from a manufacturer such as Dell, who build machines to order. One well-established back-up strategy involves what are known as mirrored drives – two separate hard disks each of which stores an identical copy of your data. To implement this, you will also need special mirroring software – PowerSync from LinkPro Technologies or PeerSync Pro from Peer Software are proven examples. Still more secure, but more appropriate to mainframe computers is the RAID, or Redundant Array of Independent Disks, which uses a range of different drives to store duplicates of your data.

The golden rule is not to buy anything unless you are totally satisfied that it suits your needs. Even if you find an apparently ideal machine, it is worth holding back for a few days in case you can find something better. Don't rush. Get it right first time.

If you need more than a high street special, the places to start are the computer manufacturers' websites. www.dell.com, www.compaq.com and www.gateway.com are all well-designed sites which will allow you to examine a series of models and find one which suits your needs. If you wish to buy components and upgrade your computer, good places to start are www.dabs.co.uk or www.jungle.com both of which offer a range of components at excellent prices.

Chapter 2 – Security Checklist

1   Try to work in a cool environment and keep smoke away from your computer.

2   If your data is critical, consider leaving your computer switched on all the time to avoid the stress that power-ups impose on your hardware.

3   Save your work regularly to minimize lost data if there is a power cut.

4   Invest in an electrical extension cable with surge protection and plug your computer into that rather than the mains.

5   Always unplug your modem from the telephone socket when you are not online.

6   If you are bent on handling upgrades yourself, beware of static electricity and of the dangers of metal tools contacting delicate circuitry. Plan your repairs, read the manuals and work logically through the procedures.

7   Upgrading your computer is often a better solution than buying a new one.

8   Approach buying a new computer with caution. Start with a written list of requirements and check what is offered against that list. Beware of bundles – the peripherals offered are seldom the ones you really need. If you are unsure, take a friend who understands computers.

9   If the high street stores cannot meet your needs, look at the computer manufacturers' websites for advanced models.

SOS (Save our Operating System)

Pity Your Operating System

Spare a tear for the poor operating system – it has a really miserable life. Like a police officer on traffic duty, its job is to control the flow of operations within your computer, and when the traffic backs up or even jams solid, it gets all the blame. For most of us, the operating system means some variety of Windows®. Ask the Windows-haters why the product has come to dominate computing across the globe and they will scream about unfair marketing and abuse of monopolies, but they are wrong. The reason why Windows has become so prominent is that it is a very good operating system which most people are comfortable using.

Figure 3.1 The MS-DOS prompt window

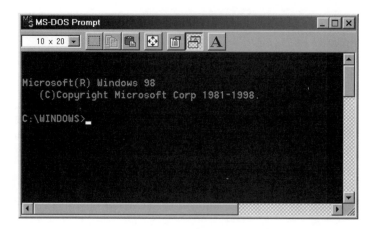

Those who have started using computers in the last few years – and that means most people – have never experienced the uncertainties of the old Command Line Interface (CLI). Microsoft's® original operating system was known as MS-DOS (Microsoft Disk Operating System) and like its predecessors UNIX and CP/M, it allowed you to control your computer by typing in instructions on a command line. Until the most recent Windows distributions, DOS was still accessible from the desktop. Clicking the MS-DOS prompt icon, brought up a window looking like Figure 3.1.

Here you could type in your instructions, using the old DOS commands like *dir* (list the contents of a directory) or *cls* (clear the screen). Before Windows, this was how all computing was handled and very unfriendly it was too. An operator needed to remember (or keep looking up) a host of commands and type them in without errors. As an example, here is a typical command to copy a file from one folder to another:

copy c:/windows/myfolder/myfile.txt c:/media/myotherfolder/

In the latest versions of Windows, Microsoft has removed access to DOS altogether, which is a shame because the old CLI can still be useful on occasions.

For most of today's users, pre-Windows computing would be a cold and worrying experience. The introduction of the Graphical User Interface (GUI) meant that all the objects on your computer – files, folders, applications, etc. – were represented by little on-screen graphics known as icons which could be double-clicked to open or dragged from place to place. This made the computer experience much more friendly, but more importantly, it made it intuitive. If you are looking for a file called *myfile.txt*, there it is clearly visible on your desktop with a cheerful little picture to show you what it contains.

We are inclined to think of Windows as nothing more than the GUI which allows us to interact with our computer, but the operating system is much more than this. In essence, the OS controls the way in which a computer's software interacts with the

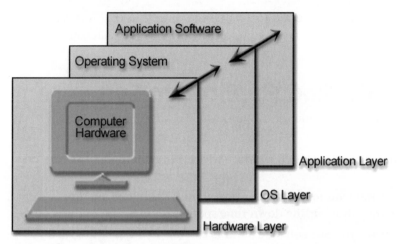

Figure 3.2 The operating system in action

hardware (thus *DISK* Operating System). In simple terms, we can represent this as shown in Figure 3.2.

When you fire up an application – let's say your word processor – it might need to access several hardware devices. For a start it must open a file from your hard disk, then it must display that file on your monitor, it must accept commands from your keyboard and mouse, and eventually print it on your printer. Some of these devices might also be doing other things at the same time. Your monitor is displaying your desktop and any files you have opened previously, your mouse must register movement and clicks in any part of the screen, and so on. The job of the OS is to handle all of this in a logical manner, portioning out processing time and the use of hardware resources between all the different demands. In simple terms, the OS acts as the interface between your hardware and the programs that run on your computer.

In the diagram above, I have referred to the hardware layer, the operating system layer and the application layer. These are not vital to an understanding of how the operating system works, but if you are technically minded, you might be interested in this concept. Layers are often used to describe computer activities where certain procedures are insulated from other procedures – rather like your skin prevents the air from getting at your internal organs. In this case, the OS layer stops applications from getting direct access to the hardware. Would you really want your word processor to seize control of your printer and refuse to let any other applications use it?

What is clear from all this is that the operating system is critical to the operation of your computer. If it stops working, your computer halts at once and you will almost certainly need to reboot your system. I said at the start of this chapter that Windows is almost always blamed when things grind to a halt, but the truth is that it is very seldom at fault. To understand why, we need to consider the factors that cause things to crash.

The Windows OS And Application Software

Let us begin by declaring our confidence in Windows! We can sum up its benefits like this.

➤ It provides a friendly and intuitive interface which most computer users are now familiar with.

➤ It encourages software authors to produce programs which look and operate in much the same way, thus cutting down time spent ascending the learning curve.

➤ Because of its open structure, software authors can use well-established sub-routines to access hardware devices such as disk drives and printers.

➤ Unless interfered with by rogue code or user errors, it is a relatively stable platform.

➤ It is well-supported with reliable upgrades and patches to fix any bugs that do emerge.

The sheer volume of code which comprises the Windows OS is now so vast, that it inevitably has some flaws in it. Each release of Windows incorporates new features and thus increases the likelihood of bugs. Software programmers are only human, after all. Frankly, I am constantly impressed at how stable it really is.

Of course, without application software, Windows by itself is almost useless. The distribution does come with a few applications, but any serious user will need to install a raft of other programs if he or she wishes to become productive. It is nearly always the programs we install which cause the operating system to fall over. There are several issues that need to be considered here. The first and most obvious is the question of software compatibility. Not only must the software you are planning to use be compatible with the OS, which is pretty obvious, but it must also be compatible with the version of the OS that you have installed. Windows has gone through several revisions and one major leap – the change from 16-bit to 32-bit operation (see the box below).

Don't get bogged down in bits. A 16-bit operating system processes two bytes (16 bits) of data at a time; a 32-bit system processes four bytes (32 bits) at a time. Bits and bytes are explained in more detail in Chapter 6, but for now it is enough to generalize that a 32-bit system is twice as fast as a 16-bit system.

Although the 32-bit distributions (Windows 95 and onwards) can still handle 16-bit software – a feature known as **downwards compatibility** – processing speeds can be slowed dramatically and can create serious conflicts. Luckily, there is very little 16-bit software still around.

Assuming that the software in question is happy to work with the OS, the next question is: has it been written to make proper use of the operating system? To answer this, we need to take a look at the OS's own software interface – the Windows API.

How Application Software Integrates With The OS (The Windows API)

Before looking in more detail at how application software operates within the Windows environment, we need to understand the basics of the Windows Application Programming Interface, or API. In the same way that the OS itself insulates hardware from the demands of applications, the API insulates the operating system from the software running on the computer. It forms a software interface that is used by other programs. You are familiar with the Windows GUI. This is the software interface which allows you to interact with the programs and data stored on your computer. The API performs a similar function by allowing application software to interact with processes, graphical elements and hardware.

Different operating systems offer different APIs which, incidentally, is the main reason why Apple Macintosh programs cannot run on a Windows system. Apple's own API uses different 'calls' from the Windows API. In simple terms, Windows cannot understand what Apple software is asking for.

So what does the API actually do? First, it handles hardware operations such as displaying data on a monitor and providing access to the disks and the printer. It also provides all the common graphical elements that we are familiar with. It generates the dialog boxes such as the **Open** and **Save** boxes which are common to all Windows applications. It handles warning messages, drop down menus, configuration settings – in fact all those elements which make up the Windows interface. It is because programmers make use of the API that all Windows software has a similar look and response.

The API is, for the most part, stored in the Dynamic Link Library (**.dll**) files, most of which can be found in your Windows system folder. The operating system makes these files accessible to application programs which can use their functions freely. There is certain to be a huge number of **.dll** files installed on your computer, but the key files here are:

➤ **User32.dll** which provides user interface functions;

➤ **Kernel32.dll** which provides operating system functions;

➤ **Gdi32.dll** which provides graphical interface functions; and

➤ **Shell32.dll** which provides Windows shell functions.

Because Windows makes these functions freely available to other programs, it could be said to be an open system. It this very openness which can cause problems. Just because someone lends you their car, it doesn't mean that you know how to drive it. Bad programmers can make a complete pig's breakfast of integrating their code into the Windows API, using faulty function calls which not only crash their own programs, but also bring down the whole operating system. To take two very unlikely examples, a programmer could accidentally instruct a monitor to print a file or call for a dialog box as big as a house.

If an application tries to do something stupid, Windows is usually clever enough to stop it before it causes a major problem. You should see a warning box similar to that in Figure 3.3. Nobody but a hard core programmer can make much sense of the details provided, but note the phrase 'general protection fault'. This is Windows' way of telling you that it has stopped the application to protect the operating system. People are all too ready to blame Windows when this happens, but they have got it the wrong way round. Nearly always, the fault is in the application and Windows has acted out of self-preservation!

Knowing The Weaknesses In Windows

Perhaps the heading of this section is a little unfair. As I have admitted earlier, Windows does contain its fair share of bugs but most of the weaknesses we will be considering in this section are the inevitable results of its open architecture. We have already noted that poor programming can cause problems by not interacting properly

Figure 3.3 Windows warns you when a program does something illegal!

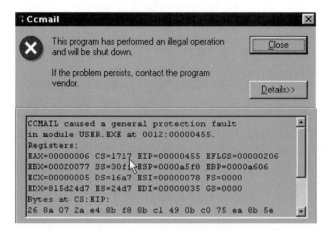

with the API, but this cannot be blamed on the OS itself. From the outset, Windows, unlike some other operating systems, was designed to support third-party programs. If this is its greatest weakness, it is also its greatest strength and the reason why it has come to dominate global computing.

Anyone with even the most meagre grasp of programming can write software that works under the Windows operating system. The major software manufacturers, the Adobes, Corels and Macromedias of this world, have vast teams of programmers who are not only masters of their languages but also fully understand how to integrate software with the Windows API. But some of the most innovative and useful software comes from tiny companies or even individuals who spot a specific requirement and write a program to meet it. Much of this software is released as try-before-you-buy shareware, and much of it, unfortunately, is of very poor quality. We will look at software problems in more detail in Chapter 7.

As a piece of software, Windows is never really finished. In the same way that technical developments drive the hardware manufacturers into developing faster computers, so Windows is constantly being modified to reflect the demand for new functionality. Microsoft is often accused of bringing a new distribution to market before all the bugs have been ironed out. There is some truth in this, but Windows is developed to meet consumer demands, and consumers are not known for their patience. When a new Windows distribution is launched some bugs are inevitably exposed, but the OS is then installed on thousands of different computer configurations and subjected to all sorts of strange uses that cannot be tested for. In general, the best option is to wait until the second or third version of a new distribution is released, by which time most of the problems have been sorted out.

Responding To Windows Error Messages

One thing that it is hard to forgive Microsoft for is the relative unhelpfulness of Windows' error messages. We met one example above that makes no sense to the average user. There are far too many error messages for this book to cover them all, though most of them are explained on Microsoft's website (www.microsoft.com). Table 3.1 lists some of the most common ones, what they really mean and what you can do about them.

There are many other error messages you might see and there are some you won't see, but should, if Microsoft had a sense of humour. Figure 3.4 shows some of the best suggestions available on the internet.

Table 3.1 Error Messages

Message	What it really means
'This program has performed an illegal operation and will be shut down. If the problem persists, contact the program vendor.'	Don't worry about the 'illegal' bit, no laws have been broken! Your application is trying to access a function, file, memory area or other resource that it shouldn't. This is usually because the resource in question is being used by another program, but sometimes it has become corrupted or is reserved for another purpose. When you click **OK**, the program is shut down, but it is usually quite safe to start it up again. If the 'problem persists', and before you 'contact the program vendor', try deleting the program (**Start > Control Panel > Add/Remove Programs**) and reinstalling it.
'Error starting program. There is not enough memory. Quit some programs and try again.'	This can be quite confusing if you have a lot of memory installed! Often the problem has nothing to do with the amount of physical memory installed and everything to do with the system's User Resources, which are explained in detail in Chapter 7. Closing programs will usually solve the problem, but not all the programs running are visible on your Task Bar. There are also resident programs, some of which load at start-up without your knowledge. To find out what is running, press the **Control** (Ctrl), **Alt** and **Delete** keys at the same time. (This is also explained in detail in Chapter 7!) Some programs are bad at releasing memory when they are closed down, so if nothing else helps, you might need to restart your computer. Finally, this message can also indicate that your hard disk is filling up. When it runs out of physical memory (RAM), Windows stores data in a special area of your hard disk known as the swap file. Emptying your Recycle Bin or deleting a few unnecessary files can often solve the problem.

'Error Reading Drive [Disk drive letter].'
'Data Error Reading Drive [Disk drive letter].'
'Serious Disk Error Writing [Disk drive letter].'
'Seek Error – Sector not found.'

Any one of these messages can indicate a serious problem such as a damaged disk drive, although they might mean no more than corrupted data on the disk. Try accessing the disk from Windows Explorer and if it is visible, run a disk repair program such as ScanDisk. (Right-click on the drive letter and click the **Tools** tab.) Use the 'Thorough' option and ScanDisk will mark any bad sectors so that they are not used for future data storage. Of course if ScanDisk finds too many bad sectors it is time to back up your files and buy a new disk.

'[Disk drive letter] is not accessible. The device is not ready.'

Obvious this one. You have tried to access a drive without a disk in it. Insert the disk and try again or click **Cancel**.

'Missing Shortcut: Windows is searching for [something]. To locate the file yourself, click Browse.'

This usually appears when you click on the shortcut to a file that is missing or has been moved to another location. Windows will try to find the file, but it is often easier to **Browse** for it instead. If you have deleted the file, delete the shortcut as well. If you are not sure which file the shortcut points to, right-click on it and choose **Properties**. The **Target** textbox will give you the name and path of the associated file.

Updating Your OS From The Internet

As I explained earlier, Windows is always being modified to correct bugs and improve performance. Whether you buy your distribution as part of a computer package or as a software product to install yourself, you should expect to be constantly updating it. Luckily Microsoft makes this easy to do via the Windows Update system which is installed with the OS. In most cases, Windows Update will appear on your **Start** menu. If you can't find it there, open Internet Explorer, and click on the **Favourites** menu, Windows Update is listed in the **Software Updates** category. Whichever option you use, you will be taken to the Windows Update section of Microsoft's website which will look something like Figure 3.5. Clicking on the Product Updates link will generate a page of proposed updates specially tailored to your own computer. These are divided between essential updates and useful ones you might consider installing. Look in particular for bug fixes, security patches and the customer service packs, all of which should be downloaded.

Windows Update not only downloads the updates for you, it also verifies and installs them. This process seldom causes any problems unless your internet connection

Figure 3.4 Error messages we would like to see!

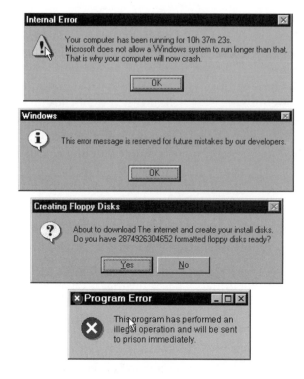

Figure 3.5 Microsoft's Windows Update page

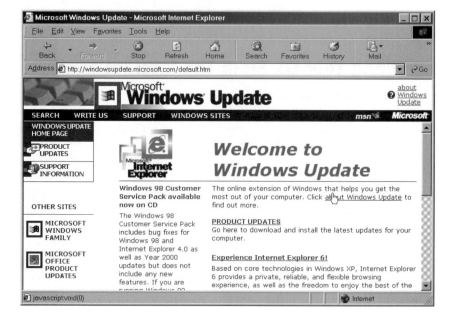

collapses halfway through, in which case you will have to start all over again. Microsoft claims that the whole process is managed without any information about your computer being passed across.

There is a second Update section which is equally useful. You will find it at www.microsoft.com/security If Windows Update is aimed at the regular customer, the security section is intended more for the advanced user (you, for example) who is aware of the importance of good computer security. Here you will find a whole range of security patches to plug the various holes in Microsoft software. I would advise visiting this address on a regular basis and downloading and installing any patches which are appropriate to the software you are running.

Configuring Your OS For Stability And Security

The final part of this chapter is concerned with what you can do to make your operating system more stable and more secure. If, like most people, you have bought your computer with Windows preinstalled, you are probably looking at the standard default installation. This is almost certainly not the ideal configuration for you. In Chapter 7, I will be looking at how you can take control of software operations including managing the programs which start automatically. For now we will be content with organizing one or two operating system functions.

Many OS functions are managed via the Windows Control Panel (**Start** > **Settings** > **Control Panel**). Clicking this sequence brings up a window like Figure 3.6. From here

Figure 3.6 The Windows Control Panel

*Figure 3.7 Windows
System Properties Device
Manager section*

you can control the workings of much of your hardware, such as the keyboard, mouse, monitor, etc., you can add new hardware and software and control a wide range of system settings. Most changes you make via the Control Panel are written to the Windows Registry (see Technical Talk on page 48) where they are stored and accessed as required.

With one or two exceptions, Control Panel settings have little effect on your system's security. The exceptions are **Network** which we will consider in detail in Chapter 13, **Internet Options** – reserved for Chapter 14 – **Add/Remove Programs** – Chapter 8 – and **System**, which we will look at now. If you double-click the **System** icon a new window will open with four tabbed sections, **General**, **Device Manager**, **Hardware Profiles** and **Performance**. The **General** tab provides some basic, but useful information about your computer. Click the **Device Manager** tab and a window looking like Figure 3.7 will open.

This window lists all the devices attached to your system and notifies you if any of them are experiencing problems. In Figure 3.7, you will notice a question mark against **Other devices**, indicating that Windows has spotted some hardware attached to the computer, but has not been able to make it work. Your first job is to work down this list, clicking the little crosses against each device type and making sure that the entries represent hardware that is actually present. If your computer was extensively tested before you bought it or if other peripherals were attached at any stage, you might find unnecessary entries in the list. These should be marked with question marks or red crosses, but this is not always the case. If you find any devices listed that you know are

Figure 3.8 Windows System Properties Performance section

not present, click them, then click the **Remove** button. If you accidentally remove something that does exist, don't worry. When you restart your computer, Windows will redetect the device and correct the entry. Sometimes the OS wants you to update your drivers. You will either need your original distribution disks or new drivers downloaded from the internet. Follow the Wizard to install them.

Now, click the **Performance** tab and look at the window which opens (Figure 3.8). Here you can check that your computer's file system is operating correctly. Ensure that your file system is operating at 32-bit. If it is operating in MS-DOS Compatibility Mode, your computer will be very sluggish. You need to read the error messages associated with the entry and, if possible, correct the problem. Where MS-DOS Compatibility Mode appears, it often means that you have inherited trouble, possibly from an older device driver which is being loaded when your computer starts up. Your Virtual Memory should also be running at 32-bit. Virtual Memory is an area of your hard drive which Windows uses to supplement physical memory. Leave the **Advanced settings** alone unless you know what you are doing!

It is well worth getting familiar with the **System Properties** window at this early stage. It is a useful resource to check the way in which Windows is handling your hardware and gives you the opportunity to correct errors and improve performance. We will be returning to this subject several times in later chapters.

The Windows Registry is the heart of the operating system and we will return to it time and again during the course of this book. Essentially, the Registry is a storehouse for all the data which is required for your computer to operate properly. It is contained in two files, **system.dat** and **user.dat**. The first stores settings which relate to your system configuration and the second stores settings specific to a particular user. If either of these files become corrupted, there can be serious consequences for computer operations. Windows guards against this by storing a back-up of the Registry every time it boots successfully. If, for any reason, it subsequently fails to boot, it can then revert to this back-up. Because the Registry is so important, it is vital that you make a back-up before attempting any operation which might modify its contents. Instructions for doing this are given on page 49.

Using third-party system configuration utilities

There are several third-party programs which allow you to configure certain aspects of the operating system. TweakUI® is a Microsoft utility which was supplied with earlier versions of Windows but can still be downloaded from Microsoft's website. TweakAll® is a more advanced version of the same thing. But the undoubted master of the OS tweakers is X-Setup from Xteq Systems. This utility is almost an essential for the security-minded computer user, so go and download it right now! It is completely free for individual use, and, in the words of the old cliché, once you have used it, you will wonder how you ever did without it!

*Figure 3.9 X-Setup from
Xteq Systems*

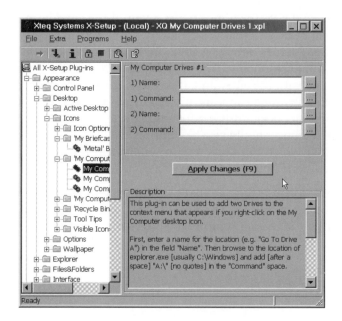

Once you have installed X-Setup, fire it up and you will be presented with a window similar to the one shown in Figure 3.9. X-Setup works by providing a series of 'plug-ins' – individual control panels which allow you to modify aspects of the operating system. When you click the **Apply Changes** button, each change is written to the Windows Registry. Sometimes you will need to restart your computer to see the effect. We are interested in improving Windows' stability and security, so the X-Setup plug-ins which handle appearance are not relevant here – although you might like to play with them and see what they do.

TweakAll is available free from the curiously named www.abtons-shed.com X-Setup can be downloaded from www.xteq.com Xteq X-Setup requires the Microsoft Scripting Engine (MSE) to work properly – this component is installed by default in Windows 98 and upwards. You can also download the MSE for free from: www.microsoft.com/msdownload/vbscript/scripting.asp Before downloading TweakUI, check your Windows CD-ROM and see if it is there. If you are running Windows 95 or 98, you should be able to save yourself the download. Otherwise look on www.microsoft.com

Now pause for an essential precaution. You are about to make changes to the Windows Registry, so before you do anything else you must make a back-up of the existing Registry settings. From the X-Setup menu bar, click **Programs > Regedit**. This will open the Windows Registry Editor. Now click **Registry > Export Registry File** and save a copy to a secure location. (You should do this every time you intend modifying the Registry.) In the unlikely event that you do something catastrophic, you can restore your original Registry settings with **Registry > Import Registry File**. X-Setup itself will warn you if you attempt to use a plug-in which has the potential to damage your computer's operation. As a general rule, do not use any plug-in which throws up a warning. None of the settings in the table overleaf will do so.

To modify the OS configuration, work through the table. Note that the X-Setup window consists of three panes. On the left, and looking like the folder hierarchy you will find in Windows Explorer, are the various plug-ins grouped by type. Paths to the relevant plug-ins are in the first column of the table overleaf. The top right pane is the area in which you make changes, and the bottom right pane provides explanatory notes, although these are sometimes not as helpful as they might be. In each case, consider making the change suggested in the second column of the table after reading the notes in the third column. The first suggested change is shown in Figure 3.10, by way of an illustration. After making each change, make sure you click the **Apply Changes** button.

Figure 3.10 Changing the Computer Role setting

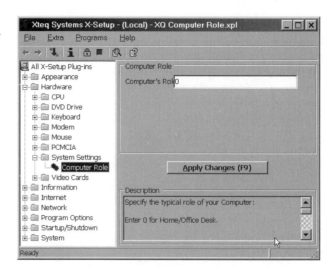

Table 3.2 Some Suggested Changes

Path to the plug-in	Suggested change to make	Notes
Hardware > System Settings > Computer Role	Change the Computer Role to *3 for always on.*	We have noted in Chapter 2 that the most dangerous time for hardware is during start-up. Change this setting and leave your computer switched on permanently. You can then use Window's own power management settings (available by right-clicking the desktop, then clicking *Properties > Screen Saver > Settings*) to turn off your monitor and power down your system after a pre-set period of inactivity.
Startup/Shutdown > Shutdown > Windows 9X/ME > Shutdown Options > AutoEnd Programs	Ensure that *AutoEnd Hung Programs* is checked.	For a number of reasons relating to data security, you require Windows to shut down seamlessly. Normally, if Windows detects a hung program, it will halt a shutdown and ask your advice on what to do. This plug-in allows the OS to bypass this process and automatically shut down any hung programs. (If this doesn't make sense at this stage in the book, relax! It will do so later.)

Startup/Shutdown > Startup > Windows 9X/ME > Boot Menu > Advanced Options	Ensure that *Enable Logging (BOOTLOG.TXT.)* is checked.	This plug-in ensures that when you boot up your system, a text log is created which details the process. You can use this log to sort out any problems with the way in which your computer starts up. The log is created in your root folder which is usually *C:*.
Startup/Shutdown > Startup > Windows 9X/ME > Boot Menu > General Options	Ensure that *Enable F4, F5, F6, F8 and Shift keys while booting* is checked.	This setting allows you to interrupt the boot process by pressing one of these function keys as Windows starts to load. Microsoft removed the display of the Startup Menu from Windows Millennium Edition (Me), but most of the boot options are still available if you press the relevant function key when the message 'Windows is starting' is displayed. Here are what these function keys will do.

F4 boots the previous version of MS-DOS (from 6.00 up to 6.22).

F5 boots in Safe mode without network support, bypassing *config.sys* and *autoexec.bat* entirely.[1]

F6 boots in Safe mode with network support (if you have a network connection), bypassing *config.sys* entirely.

F8 boots in Logged mode (*bootlog.txt* is created in the root folder of the boot drive, usually *C:* – see note above).

Shift + F5 boots in Safe mode to the CLI command prompt. No devices, drivers or resident programs are loaded and *config.sys* and *autoexec.bat* are bypassed entirely.

Shift + F8 boots via a step-by-step confirmation of all entries in *config.sys* and *autoexec.bat*.

[1] We will be looking at *config.sys* and *autoexec.bat* in detail later in the book. For now it is enough for you to note that these files are throwbacks to the older incarnations of Windows which are still included in the boot process to ensure backwards compatibility. Both of these are text files which control how the OS starts up. They are used to set certain system parameters, such as the keyboard configuration, and to load device drivers and some start-up programs.

Table 3.2 continued

Path to the plug-in	Suggested change to make	Notes
System > Advanced System Settings > Windows 9X/ME Options	Ensure that *Log application errors to FAULTLOG.TXT* is checked.	This plug-in ensures that errors caused by applications are logged to the file *faultlog.txt* in your Windows directory. Like *bootlog.txt* explained above, we can use this file to sort out problems with our application programs.
System > File System > CD Autostart > Autostart Data CD	Ensure that all these entries are unchecked, except *Allow autostart for fixed drives (HD)*.	Our policy is that we will control what happens on our computers, and if unchanged, these settings allow CD-ROMs to start up automatically. This is a potential security breach, since when CD-ROMs start, they can run programs without our permission.

Note that if you activate AutoRun for removable devices or network drives, Windows will check these drives every time you open Windows Explorer or a file is requested by an application. Because this takes some time, this check can be really annoying! |
| *System > Memory > Swap File Usage* | Provided you have at least 128MB of memory, ensure that *Use maximum available physical RAM...* is checked. | Real memory (physical RAM) is considerably faster than virtual memory (the Windows swap file). It is also more secure because sensitive data previously stored in a swap file can sometimes be accessed, while data in memory disappears completely when a computer is shut down. This plug-in ensures that your computer uses all the real memory available before it resorts to virtual memory. |
| *System > Security > Common > Script files* | Ensure that all the options are checked so that all script files open in Notepad rather than run when double-clicked. | A full explanation of this is given in Chapter 5. Script files can contain potentially dangerous code or even carry viruses. This plug-in ensures that if you double-click a script it opens as a readable file in Notepad instead of running as an executable file. |

We will be returning to X-Setup later in the book and using some of its more advanced functions. For the moment, we will leave the Windows operating system in what you might call a semi-secure state and turn our attention to other areas. Chapter 4 looks at the possibility of building your own secure computer platform.

Chapter 3 – Security Checklist

1   Avoid installing a brand new Windows distribution as soon as it is launched. Wait for the second, or even third, release, by which time most of the bugs and security holes will have been sorted out.

2   Take a note of any error messages that are thrown up by the operating system. While these are often mysterious, the most common ones are listed in Table 3.2 above along with suggestions on how to resolve the problem indicated.

3   Microsoft provides a Windows Update system which allows you to download and install updates to the operating system from the internet. Make use of it to keep your computer's OS in good shape. It is also worth checking for any new security patches available from the Microsoft website.

4   Uses the Windows Control Panel to ensure that your hardware is working properly and that your file system is operating in 32-bit mode.

5   Always back up the Windows Registry before attempting anything which might modify its contents. Remember how critical it is to the smooth running of your computer.

6   Download X-Setup from Xteq Systems and use it as described in this chapter to configure certain aspects of your operating system for additional stability and improved security.

Building A
Secure System

In This Chapter

➤ Do-it-yourself computer building

➤ Designing your own hardware platform

➤ Planning your disk drive configuration

➤ Choosing the right software

➤ Organizing your computer work space

➤ A quick look at other operating systems

Do-it-yourself Computer Building

This is a chapter for the technically competent – or the absurdly over-optimistic! In previous chapters we have considered the risks that come from computer hardware and the Windows operating system. Most computer users are doomed to those risks, because they buy a ready-made system from a dealer with the hardware preordained and the software preinstalled. In such cases, securing a system often means undoing what has already been done and reconfiguring much of the software to plug holes (which is what most of this book is about, if you think about it!) The alternative – though not one for the nervous – is to build your own system from scratch.

The first thing to note is that however secure a system you end up with, the home-build process is not likely to save you money. This seems unfair, but you will be buying at retail prices the components that the major manufacturers buy in bulk. You might be able to save a bit by cannibalizing old systems for a keyboard, a case and other less time-dependent parts, but the core components – motherboard, memory, processor, etc. – will need to be bought new, and that's where your money will go.

Note also that this chapter is not intended to provide detailed instructions on how to put a system together. If you need such instructions, you really shouldn't be attempting the job in the first place. What I am concerned with here is looking at the key components from a security perspective and suggesting how to select and install the right hardware and software to ensure you end up with a stable system.

I will divide this process into four sections as follows.

➤ Designing your own hardware platform.

➤ Planning your drives.

➤ Choosing the right software.

➤ Organizing your computer work space.

Before we start, there are one or two things to keep in mind. In Chapter 2, I included some general advice on handling hardware modifications. If you skipped this the first time around, I suggest you go back now and work through the notes to minimize the chances of your damaging fragile components. Before you pick up a screwdriver, there are two things you should do. First, RTFM[1] and RTFM again, and second, keep a pen and paper to hand and religiously write down everything you do. Here is a simple checklist. You should always write down the following.

➤ **The reference information printed on any component you are going to install**. This means any part numbers, technical data, jumper or switch settings, etc. In this way, you will avoid the irritating business of having to remove a part later to check what is printed on it. Note also that some manufacturers stick wiring or setting diagrams to their hardware. It is also worth copying these onto a sheet of paper.

➤ **Any changes you make to physical settings on a component**. If, for example, you need to set jumpers or move switches, note down what you have done. Drawing a little diagram of the new settings often comes in useful.

➤ **Any cable connections you make**. Again a diagram might help. I would even advise attaching a paper label to each wire and marking it with its function. If you need to get back inside the box once all the parts have been assembled, it is often difficult to see where cables come from.

---

[1] RTFM: In case you missed it earlier, RTFM is the best advice there is. RTFM means Read The F****** Manual.

With our manuals read and our notes made, we can proceed to consider the hardware requirements for a secure computer system.

Designing Your Own Hardware Platform

Building a secure computer is not difficult if you are technically competent and go about it in a logical way. But it is not something you should do on the spur of the moment. You will need to decide in advance the specifications you require and put together a shopping list. The table below proposes one approach and includes security implications where relevant.

Table 4.1 A Shopping List

Component	Security considerations
Case	Some cases provide a lock option which allows you to physically secure your system so that the computer cannot be started without a key. While the lock is fairly primitive and can easily be wired around, it does provide some degree of security against the casual snooper. Other cases cannot be opened without a key and thus prevent physical tampering. Depending on your circumstances, these features might be worth considering.
Motherboard	There is a wide choice of motherboards available and most offer some rudimentary security measures. Using the system BIOS – if you don't know what this is, you certainly should not be building your own computer – it is possible to password-protect some of your system settings, but the protection offered is at a very low level. Again some BIOS systems offer simple anti-virus protection, but this cannot be relied on and is no substitute for a good AV package (see Chapter 5). In general, go for the best motherboard you can afford and make sure it supports the processor and memory configuration you are planning.
Processor	A secure system is inherently more processor-hungry than a standard one because you will be running more background applications. It makes sense to buy the fastest processor you can afford, but be warned: there was an uproar in 2000 when it was discovered that some Intel chips carried a secret code which could be used to identify a particular computer. These codes can now be disabled, but it is worth checking to make sure that you are not being labelled in this way. Remember that one aspect of security is personal privacy.

Table 4.1 continued

Component	Security considerations
Memory	You can't have too much memory. Aside from the more obvious reasons of speed and efficiency, if you have limited memory installed, Windows will need to use more **Virtual Memory** – in fact an area of your hard drive – for temporary data storage. Although Virtual Memory is theoretically cleared after use, in reality, data once stored there can sometimes be retrieved with specialized tools. If you are dealing in sensitive data, try to reduce your dependence on Virtual Memory by installing plenty of the real thing.
Hard disk drive(s)	There are three schools of thought here. School one is that you should buy a large hard disk so that you have ample storage space and room to save back-up copies of all your important data. School two is that you should buy two hard disks and use one to mirror the other. (I looked at mirrored drives at the end of Chapter 2.) School three is that you should buy a smaller hard disk, thus forcing yourself to constantly move data onto a removable storage media such as CD-ROM. The most secure option is undoubtedly number two, but this is also the most expensive and the most complicated to set up. School one is the least secure since all your virtual eggs are in one basket.
Floppy disk drive	You might ask if you really need a floppy drive at all. As far as security is concerned, the floppy drive does pose a threat since it is the classic way in which computers were infected with viruses (see Chapter 5). Certainly, floppies are now useless as far as back-ups are concerned. They are simply too small to store modern data files. On the other hand, if your computer does get sick and you cannot get it to start from your CD-ROM drive, the humble start-up disk might prove a lifesaver.
CD-ROM drive	Standard CD-ROM drives are essential these days since nearly all software is distributed on CD, but consider the advantages of buying a CD-ROM writer/rewriter. This will greatly simplify the process of backing up data, and is one of the most vital parts of a good security strategy (see Chapter 9).
Graphics card	There are no security considerations here.
Sound card	Or here.
Network card	Unfortunately, once installed, a network card will open big holes in your system security. But if you need to access a network, you will

have to have one. Most network cards are very similar in design and function.

Back-up devices   If you choose not to go the CD-ROM writer route, it is essential that you have some form of back-up device. Zip/Jazz drives, tape drives and micro-drives all have their advantages and disadvantages. You will need to consider storage capacity and price of course, but make sure you have some means of storing data off your computer.

Peripherals   Keyboard, mouse, monitor, printer, etc. None of these components pose any security questions, so you can get whatever you can afford. (There are keyboards which are designed to read your thumbprint and refuse access to unauthorized thumbs, but we are trying to remain on this planet!) For modems, refer to Chapter 14.

Use this checklist by all means, but do not let it prevent you from buying the components you need to handle the tasks you will be attempting. Above all else, a computer is a tool, and you must ensure that it is the right tool for the job. It is worth writing out a detailed specification which lists everything you want the computer to do and using it to source the right components. It might be useful at this point to look again at the notes on buying a computer at the end of Chapter 2.

Planning Your Disk Drive Configuration

One aspect of your system is particularly relevant to your security and that is your drive configuration. Before you go out and buy anything, you should decide how you will set up your data storage space. On most purchased systems (laptops are often different) the physical hard drive is formatted as a single logical drive[2] – usually identified as the C:\ drive by the operating system. While this is certainly the simplest arrangement, it is by no means the only one. Nor is it the most secure configuration.

Let us first consider how we might use two hard drives rather than one. As we noted at the end of Chapter 2, heavy-duty systems often use two separate mirrored drives where the contents of one drive exactly match the contents of the other. This, of course, is a very secure arrangement since if one drive crashes the other can take over with no loss of data. It is also an expensive set-up because it effectively renders half of your total storage capacity unusable.

---

[2] There are physical drives and there are logical drives. Physical drives are actual hardware, while logical drives are physical drives divided into separate partitions in software. Windows treats both types in the same way by assigning them drive letters (C:\, D:\ etc.) and you will see them listed in Explorer like this.

Techno Talk

In case you have ever wondered why the hard drive is nearly always identified as the C:\ drive, here is the explanation. The earliest PCs had no internal hard drive, just a floppy drive through which you first loaded the operating system and then your application software. The first floppy drive was therefore identified as the A:\ drive. This meant a lot of fiddling about. When you finished with an application, you were obliged to eject its floppy and reload the OS floppy before continuing. (Well do I remembering monitoring my activities on an early Osborne computer, and finding that in one hour I changed floppy disks no less than 43 times!)

To make life easier, some manufacturers started equipping their machines with a second floppy drive so that the OS could stay loaded. This drive, naturally enough, was identified as the B:\ drive. When internal hard drives appeared, they were awarded the next vacant number – thus the C:\ drive. Next on the scene was a CD-ROM drive and that usually becomes the D:\ drive – and so it goes!

Gordon The Young Professional

You will not be surprised to learn that Gordon uses a mirrored drive array in his law office. The data on his firm's computers is not only highly sensitive, it is also critical to the success of his legal practice. (Late at night in the local wine bar, Gordon has been known to boast that if a hacker could get into his office system, he could blackmail half the businessmen in town.)

Mirrored drives are essential where loss of data is of prime importance, but they must be set up properly and used correctly. Of course, Gordon never makes a mistake, but some of his elderly partners are less competent.

Where data security is not so critical, a better solution is to use the two drives for different purposes. Drive C:\ might be allocated to the OS and application programs, while drive D:\ might be reserved for data. There are obvious advantages to separating data – which cannot be restored except by using a back-up – from programs – which can be reinstalled from CD-ROM or other storage media. In this configuration, drive C:\ would get much more of a hammering than drive D:\ and would therefore be much more likely to develop faults.

But if, like most computer users, you are restricted to a single drive, you might consider formatting the drive into two or more partitions which will be seen by the OS as logical drives and awarded their own drive letters. While this does not provide the security of a back-up drive, it does at least move your data away from the applications that use it. This not only makes the process of backing up data that much easier to organize, but also moves critical information away from Microsoft's preferred folder locations (My Documents, My Pictures, etc.) which are often targeted by hackers and snoopers. This is looked at in greater detail later in the chapter.

In the previous chapter, we used X-Setup to modify some aspects of our system configuration. Another very handy plug-on allows us to change Microsoft's default data folders to our own preferred ones. A suggested folder 'hierarchy' – a tree of folders – is proposed later in this chapter in the **Organizing your computer work space** section. If you choose to implement these suggestions, you can then use X-Setup to point some of your software to these folders rather than their default locations.

Now go away, buy the bits, build your computer and come back here ...

Choosing The Right Software

Once you have built your system, you need to install the software, and choosing the right software is every bit as tricky as choosing the right hardware. I assume that you will be running the Windows operating system which means buying and installing the latest distribution, but you need to proceed with caution. Windows is a massive OS with a vast range of features and functions – many of which you might not need and some of which open worrying security holes.

At all costs avoid the 'Typical' installation offered by Windows SetUp. In this configuration, the choice of which components are installed is made for you, and although it is nice to sit back and drink coffee while the installation rolls along, this is definitely a bad idea. Instead, select the 'custom' option which lets you decide the installation set. If you subsequently find you need to add or remove components, this is easily managed from the **Add/Remove Programs** function in Windows Control Panel. Of course you will have no choice about the Windows core components. These will be installed automatically, but work carefully through all the optional components and install only those which you know you will need. If there is anything doubtful, or which you do not understand, choose not to install it.

Some of the Windows components described in Table 4.2 have serious implications for your system and should not be installed unless you have a very good reason for doing so.

Once Windows has been installed, you will then need to consider application software. I have no intention of telling you which programs to install. Your choice will be based on your needs and your preferences – and quite right too! However I am including some notes that you might like to consider when selecting software. Here they are.

➤ If you are using Microsoft's operating system (Windows), there is a lot of sense in selecting Microsoft's application software. (Already I can hear shrieks of rage and

Table 4.2 Windows Components To Avoid

Name of component	Reasons for not installing
Windows Scripting Host (Accessories)	This component provides an environment in which scripts can run, and scripts can carry malevolent code and even viruses. The WSH is discussed in detail in Chapter 5.
Dial-up Server (Communications)	This provides a connection to your computer via a modem. It also provides a route by which unwanted intruders can get into your machine. Unless you intend using your computer to serve files to the internet, leave it out of your installation set.
Direct Cable Connection (Communications)	Allows you to connect two computers together via a parallel or a serial cable. Again this could provide an access point for an intruder.
Microsoft Chat (Communications)	Allows you to 'chat' – in reality to send text messages – to other people via your computer. Chat software has come under a lot of fire as you will see in Chapter 19 and the Microsoft version has raised questions about security. Unless you need it to be compatible with others, leave it off.
Microsoft Wallet (Internet Tools)	This component is intended to provide a secure location in which you can store personal details. In my opinion, the security offered is not adequate. We will consider this in Chapter 19, but until then leave it uninstalled. There are better ways to protect sensitive information.
Real Audio Player (Internet Tools)	There is a major question mark over Real Networks and the various internet tools they provide. Certainly their products are highly invasive, and they have been accused of 'spyware' – storing information about your habits and transmitting it to commercial interests. Spyware is considered in detail in Chapter 19.
Online Services	I advise against installing any of the online services provided. These are all commercial concerns interested primarily in signing you up for their internet services. If you do pursue any of the links these components install, you may well find them very difficult to get rid of. I look at this in detail in Chapter 14.

accusations of corruption!) I have no financial interest here, but consider the facts. Your OS handles all aspects of the way in which your software integrates with your hardware and other programs on your computer, and who will understand the Windows operating system better than Microsoft programmers? The simple fact is that Microsoft application software performs better on a Microsoft platform than the offerings of other application providers. In my opinion – and it is just an opinion – Microsoft Office® makes better use of the Windows API than any other business suite. Of course you must decide on which products offer the functionality that you require, but when all things are equal, the safest choice would be the Microsoft offering.

➤ Of course, there are excellent free programs and appalling commercial programs, but there is a lot of truth in the old cliché about getting what you pay for. If you decide on a free or low-cost alternative, do not expect the range of functions you get from the expensive package.

➤ You should also consider the support offered. The larger software manufacturers stand over their products by providing upgrades and telephone or online support. You cannot expect this degree of service from a one-man programmer working from his spare bedroom.

➤ Resist the temptation to add in software which you think might prove useful at some time in the future. (The problems with installing software are detailed in Chapter 7.) Try to adopt the logical approach of determining a need, identifying the product which best services that need, and obtaining and installing your preferred application. There is nothing that wrecks a stable system faster than the indiscriminate installation of buckets of suspect software!

Application software can be roughly divided into four categories. The categories I am using are fairly arbitrary, but they can be useful when deciding which software you should install. Table 4.3 describes how my system works.

Organizing Your Computer Work Space

Tracking down and installing software is a continuous process. You will be constantly spotting a better program to replace an existing one. But as soon as your basic software set is installed, and before you jump into action, it is worth deciding how you are going to organize your work space. Your work space is the environment you set up within your computer to manage your activity. Windows itself sets up a rudimentary work space. It creates a folder called **My Documents**, and possibly a series of second-level folders called **My Music**, **My Pictures**, etc.

There is one very good reason why you should not accept this arrangement, and it is this. Almost every Windows-based computer on this planet has a folder called **My Documents**, so this is often the first place a virus looks to find documents it can

Table 4.3 How My System Works

Category	Explanation	Examples	Notes
The operating system	Oh, come on! You know what an operating system is.	Windows, MacOS, Linux.	Most of this book assumes you have gone with the majority and chosen Windows. There are some brief notes at the end of this chapter on other operating systems.
Major applications	These are your key applications; the software which allows you to be productive and creative on your computer.	Business suite (word processor, database and accounting package), graphics software, web design program.	Expect to buy these programs from a computer store. They will usually be expensive and too large to download – although there are exceptions. Because each of these applications represents a major investment, it is critical to choose the right product from the outset. Expect good customer support and readily available upgrades.
Utility programs	These are smaller, more specialized programs which enhance and expand your abilities and provide your computer with additional resources.	Internet browser, software firewall, internet download manager, enhancement filters for your digital imaging software.	These programs you will probably obtain from the web or magazine cover disks. Try not to buy them as packaged software, since they might be out-of-date. Most programs here will be sold as shareware or even freeware. Most of the 'wasted' software that clogs up the machines of the unwary comes in this category!
Single-function tools	These are small programs which handle one job that is usually too specific for the major manufacturers to be interested in.	A program which synchronizes your computer's clock with an internet-based chronometer, a program which converts one image format to another.	These tools usually consist of small programs available from the internet or from magazine cover disks. Each one will solve a particular problem, but it is good practice to first identify the problem and then find a solution rather than the other way round!

Figure 4.1 Modifying Microsoft Word's file locations

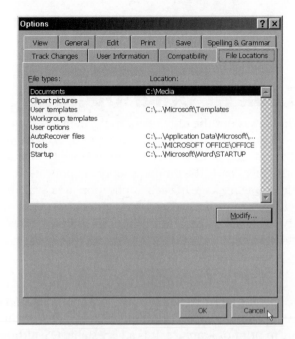

infect. Of course, if you have installed a second hard disk for your data, or divided your primary disk into two or more logical drives, you have already stepped away from the Windows model. This is a good thing to do.

A badly organized work space slows up efficient computer operating and can often result in lost files. Since almost all of your applications will try to install in sub-folders of the Windows-generated **Program Files** folder, it makes sense to follow this practice when organizing your data files. I suggest you generate a top-level folder called **Data** or something similar. Every data file you create will now be installed in a sub-folder of this. This will often mean configuring your applications to use your chosen folder, rather than the default, but this is usually a straightforward operation. You will not be surprised to learn that our old friend X-Setup will handle most of this for you, but where necessary you can specify default storage folders from within each application. Figure 4.1 shows an example of how this is done from within Microsoft Word (**Tools > Options > File Locations**).

The sub-folders you create will of course depend on your computer activities. You might choose to name them **Photographs**, **Graphics**, **Music** and **Words**, for example. But be generous in the number of folders you set up and, where necessary, create a further level of division. **Music**, for example might include sub-folders called **Rock**, **Jazz**, **Dance** and **Folk**.

If you are working on a single hard disk, try to limit the number of top-level folders. You will inevitably have ones called **Windows** and **Program Files**, and, if you follow my suggestion, another one called **Data**, but wherever possible, prevent applications from generating any other top-level folders. This will not only keep your work space neat and easy to manage, it will also help with security as we will see later in the book.

A Quick Look At Other Operating Systems

Of course Windows is not the only operating system available, but, as we have noted, it has come to dominate the market. Other types of OS have their own, sometimes fanatical, followers and, in certain areas, are superior to Windows. The biggest drawback with other OSs is the limited supply of application software. Although there is usually at least one package in each application area available for each operating system, the choice can be limited and can work out expensive. If you are interested in the possibility of breaking away from Windows, here are one or two notes on the viable alternatives.

MacOS

MacOS is the operating system which runs on Apple computers. It is an excellent operating system with a number of unique features, and is still the OS of choice for those working in print or graphics. It is a very stable OS, although this might be due to the limited access it offers to application software. From its beginnings, MacOS has provided powerful network support and good multi-tasking capabilities. The most recent distributions look fabulous, but application software is limited.

Linux

In the last few years, Linux – a free version of UNIX – has become a rival to Windows in some areas, particularly for internet servers. Linux's greatest strength is also what has prevented it from being widely accepted as a consumer product. Linux is basically a DIY operating system. All its source code – the program instructions themselves – are freely available and can be modified by anyone who thinks he or she can improve it. Installing Linux can be a nightmare, although recent distributions from companies like Red Hat and S.U.S.E. have simplified the process for non-technical users. Although Linux now offers a choice of graphical user interfaces, installing and setting up applications still requires tinkering at command-line level and is not for the inexperienced. On the plus side, Linux is extremely reliable and stable and there is a massive range of application programs for it, most of which are free.

There are other operating systems available, but they are not really suitable for domestic use, or are only available on specialized platforms.

If you would like to learn more about the alternative operating systems mentioned above, there are numerous sources of information on the web. For MacOS, the first place to look is on Apple's own excellent website at www.apple.com A good search engine (www.google.com is the best) will track down other resources. You will find Linux everywhere on the web – indeed, it powers much of it, but a good place to start is www.linux.org

Chapter 4 – Security Checklist

1 Before you attempt any DIY computer building read the manuals that relate to the hardware you have chosen and write down any information printed on the components themselves. Make diagrams of connections and jumper settings.

2 When selecting components, consider the security implications listed in this chapter. These might include physical locks, security features and their convenience as back-up devices.

3 Try to plan your hard disk(s) configuration to provide the maximum protection for stored data. There are several options here, with the securest being a pair of drives each of which store all your essential data. If this is not viable, at least try to physically separate your programs from your data using logical drives.

4 Be cautious when it comes to installing your operating system. Windows' 'typical' installation can load your computer with utilities you don't need, some of which can be security hazards. Choose the 'custom' option and make your own decisions.

5 Carefully consider the application software you need. Pick software logically to suit your needs and budget. Do not be tempted to load up applications just because they're available or cheap.

6 Organize your work space for ease of use and also with security in mind. Windows, default document folders are the first place a hacker looks for data.

Vicious Viruses, Wiggling Worms And Bouncing Bombs

In This Chapter

➤ What's bugging you?

➤ The low-down on computer viruses, worms and logic bombs

➤ How computer viruses attack your computer

➤ Spotting the invaders in your own system

➤ Tracking down anti-virus software

➤ Dealing with the aftermath

What's Bugging You?

There is one question that keeps bugging me. Why would anyone who is not mentally deranged wish to let loose an electronic demon the sole purpose of which is to destroy other people's work or their ability to work? Viruses, worms and all the other internet diseases have become a fact of life. Originally, contagion was slow since such infections could only be passed on by physically transferring programs from computer to computer, usually by way of floppy disks. The internet, and particularly the rapid growth of e-mail, has provided a whole new field of business for the virus breeder. Now viruses can propagate as fast as electronic signals can pass down a wire.

The first computer virus, called Brain, emerged in 1986. Three years later there were

*Figure 5.1 Milestones in
virus history*

1986	Brain, the world's first boot-sector virus appears.
1987	Enter the Lehigh virus - a memory-resident program which attacks the DOS command processor.
1989	Frodo is the first stealth virus that hides itself away.
1990	An evil genius invents polymorphic viruses which modify themselves each time they infect. Difficult to detect!
1991	The Tequila virus appears - the trickiest one yet. It uses stealth and polymorphic technology to avoid detection.
1995	With Windows 95, most of the old DOS viruses become obsolete. The first Word macro viruses arrive.
1996	The Concept macro virus spreads across the world.
1999	Melissa arrives. It uses an e-mail address book to post itself to other computers via the internet.
2000	Enter the Loveletter worm which arrives as an e-mail attachment using VBScript.
2001	Kournikova and other VBS worms get busy.

still only seven viruses. One year after that there were 80. By the end of 1999, the number had jumped to over 40,000. It is estimated that each month around 1,200 new viruses are created but most of them never get loose or cause real damage. Figure 5.1 shows some of the milestones in the history of viruses. (My thanks to *Personal Computer World* (*PCW*) for suggesting these.)

It is difficult to assess the real danger of viral infection. There are now so many different viruses and variations on a theme that no one can be certain exactly how many are on the loose or how much of a threat most of them pose. (A survey in 1998 suggested that there were in excess of 2,000 varieties, but that 90 per cent of all computer damage was caused by just 10 of them.) Anti-virus software companies often claim that their products can handle over 60,000 different viruses, but the Wild List, which only logs active viruses spotted on at least two different sites, suggests that the actual number of genuine threats is much lower. In August 2001, for example, the Wild List included just 232 viruses.

One of the reasons for the dramatic increase in the number of viruses is that they have become so easy to create. Where once you needed heavy-duty programming skills, almost anyone can master the business of writing macros for Microsoft Word® or scripts which make use of the Windows Script Host (see box, right). There are even instant virus makers available on the internet. The VBS Worm generator, for example, allows someone to create a worm with no more than a few mouse clicks. The evidence suggests that things are likely to get worse in the future.

We are going to be talking about scripts a lot in this chapter, so let's explain what they are. Scripts can be thought of as small programs written in the JavaScript or VBScript languages. These are not full-blown programming languages like Java or C++, but they do allow programmers to control or automate certain functions. Scripts cannot run by themselves – they require a host application. One commonly installed application is the Microsoft Windows Script Host® (WHS), which provides a host environment in which scripts can run. (Another host environment is your web browser.) WSH makes objects and services available for the script and provides a set of guidelines within which the script is executed.

But if the threat is difficult to quantify, it still remains very real. Most computer users will encounter a virus at some stage. It is also true that despite the dangers, most computer users do not have adequate anti-virus protection – usually for one of three reasons.

➤ They do not have anti-virus software installed.

➤ They have anti-virus software installed, but they don't use it.

➤ They have anti-virus software installed and they use it, but they don't regularly update the program with the latest definitions.

Susan The Student

Susan the Student remains blissfully unaware of the dangers that viruses pose. In her flat she has a computer on which she types her college projects, and her course includes several sessions each week in the college computer lab. The IT staff there try their best to keep the machines free from viruses, but students are tricky. They bring disks of games in and when the lecturer's back is turned, download all sorts of strange things from the internet. As a result most of the college computers are rampant with viruses. Susan takes her college disks home with her and infects the computer in her flat. One of her computer-literate friends is convinced that the only reason Susan's computer keeps going is that there are so many viruses on it that they keep cancelling each other out.

Virus writers are increasingly resorting to trickery to get their unholy programs into your computer. They make use of victims' gullibility by persuading them that an infected e-mail attachment is an important message or even a photograph. The Loveletter worm, for example, proved irresistible to many people. Could you stop yourself from opening an attachment claiming that someone loved you?

The Low-down on Computer Viruses, Worms and Logic Bombs

Let's get our terminology correct. We tend to use the word 'virus' to describe all sorts of nasty infections, but it pays to be specific. Table 5.1 below describes the different varieties of virus, along with some notes on how they behave.

Table 5.1 How Different Viruses Behave

Type	Description	Notes
Virus	A computer virus is a program which attaches itself to a file and reproduces by spreading itself to other files. When you run an infected program, the virus also runs. According to its code it can now reproduce itself and/or deliver its 'payload'. The payload is the mission of the virus. This might be to delete certain files, to scramble data or program code, or simply to wind you up. The Stoned virus, for example, did nothing but deliver the message 'Your PC is now stoned.' There are also boot-sector viruses which infect the small file which controls how your computer starts up, so they run every time you turn your computer on. Boot-sector viruses are particularly nasty. They can cause serious damage and prevent your computer from starting. Most anti-virus scanners check the boot sector as a computer starts up.	Most viruses attach themselves to *executable* files. These are the programs that actually run on your computer and have extensions like *.exe* or *.com*. Not surprisingly, viruses are usually aimed at programs which run frequently, otherwise they might remain in oblivion for months. Viruses are usually passed on by physically or electronically moving software from machine to machine. A floppy disk, CD-ROM or internet download can harbour a virus which is then transferred to every computer it runs on.

Macro virus	Microsoft Office® includes a useful macro editor which allows users to create small programs (scripts) which automate the production of documents. Unfortunately, it also allows unpleasant individuals to write infections into a macro which is then stored in a document or spreadsheet. If that document is opened on another computer, the infected macro is transferred into the macro pool where it can infect other documents.	Most anti-virus specialists recommend that where a document is to be passed to other machines, it should be saved in Rich Text Format (*.rtf*) rather than as a Word document (*.doc*). Unfortunately, this is not always practical, and RTF files can harbour macro viruses anyway. It is always a good idea to adjust the macro security settings in Microsoft Office to high. I will explain this later in the chapter.
Worm	A worm is a specialized virus that does not need to attach itself to a file. It is designed to seek out holes in a computer system's defences, usually by exploiting weaknesses in network security. Once inside, the worm can reproduce and deliver its payload.	Increasingly, worms are using the web's electronic mail systems to gain access. The infamous Internet Worm, for example, brought down more than 6,000 internet hosts by slowly clogging up data storage space until each host computer ground to a halt.
Time bomb	Most viruses start to work as soon as they enter a system, but time bombs are specialized viruses which sit down quietly and wait for a specific time event. This is normally triggered by the computer's internal clock reaching a particular date. Time bombs can be particularly frustrating because they can hide unseen and give no evidence that an anti-virus program can respond to. This can mean that they are widely distributed while in their dormant state.	Time bombs are usually programmed to watch for a significant date such as Christmas or Hallowe'en. The Michelangelo virus, for example, contains a time bomb that waits until the artist's birthday on 6 March before scrambling your files. One unintentional time bomb was the famous Y2K scare that caused so much grief leading up to the millennium. Much of the world's software makes use of a two-digit date field, so 99 stands for 1999. The worry was that when the date rolled over to 2000, computers might interpret 00 as 1900 and go mad.

Table 5.1 Continued

Type	Description	Notes
Time bomb *continued*		Even today it is not clear whether computers were brighter than we feared or the extensive Y2K proofing solved the problems. In any event the so-called 'Millennium Bug' caused very little trouble.
Logic bomb	A logic bomb is similar to a time bomb but responds to the appearance or disappearance of specific date rather than a time event. A programmer who thinks he is about to be sacked might design a logic bomb to activate if his name disappears from his companies pay roll, for example.	

Note: For information on Trojan horses (Trojans) look at Chapter 23.

There are two other types of virus we need to be aware of. Did you know that there are good viruses as well as bad ones? Some well-intentioned programmers have created saintly varieties that track down and destroy evil viruses or even patch buggy code. One such is the Cheese worm which repairs security holes on certain Linux computers. While the Cheese worm and others like it are well-intentioned, they are still viruses. They enter your computer without your knowledge, modify files without your permission and replicate themselves – just like any other virus.

The other type of virus to watch out for is the hoax virus. There are all manner of false warnings doing the rounds of the internet. These often cause damage by advising you to delete files from your system which are actually useful or even necessary. One well-known example was a widely distributed e-mail which advised users to delete a file called **sulfnbk.exe** if they found it in their Windows folder. This program has a strange name and an equally bizarre icon attached to it, and these facts were enough to convince many people that it was a virus. In fact, **sulfnbk.exe** is a legitimate Windows file which helps manage long file names. If you do receive a virus warning, take the time to check its source and validity before acting on it.

Figure 5.2 Virus payload graphics

How Computer Viruses Attack Your Computer

Most computer viruses are designed to cause trouble, but the extent of that trouble varies from the minor to the terminal. At the bottom end are viruses which are intended to do little more than reveal the skill of the programmer. Like the Stoned virus described in Table 5.1, some of these simply flash a message onto your screen, produce an interesting visual effect or even play tunes through your speakers. Figure 5.2 shows some of the more interesting graphics displayed by virus payloads.

At the other end of the scale are the real villains – viruses which can damage or delete files, scramble programs or even reformat your hard disk to wipe out everything. Most viruses stop short of causing a major meltdown and cause just enough trouble to irritate. In the early days of computing, viruses were often compared to graffiti. They were seen as artistic attempts by undiscovered programmers to showcase their skills. Computers users who have suffered a serious infection would be less charitable. I have heard viruses described as more like car bombs – 'destructive, indiscriminate, and costly'.

All viruses operate in slightly different ways and deliver different payloads. To see how a virus might operate, we will take just one example and track the course of its infection.

Win32.SirCam.137216 – Aka The SirCam Worm

The SirCam virus is a worm which arrives as an attachment to an e-mail message. The message itself can be either in English or Spanish. A typical English version might look like this:

> Hi! How are you?
> I send you this file in order to have your advice
> See you later. Thanks

The middle line is chosen at random from the following list, but due to a bug in the worm's random number checking, the first line is always the same:

> I send you this file in order to have your advice
> I hope you can help me with this file that I send
> I hope you like the file that I sendo [*sic*] you
> This is the file with the information that you ask for

The name of the attachment varies, but will have a double extension such as **sopimus.doc.exe**. The double extension is a recognized way of hiding a file's real nature, since, by default Windows hides the final extension for file types that are recognized by the OS. (See Chapter 9 for full details of how to undo this setting.) Final extension might be **.pif**, **.bat**, **.exe** or **.com** – all executable files. The subject of the message matches the attachment name, except without the extensions, so if the attachment is called **sopimus.doc.exe**, the message would be titled 'Sopimus'.

If the lame English of the message doesn't make you suspicious and you open the attachment, here is what happens. First, the worm creates a file called **SirC32.exe** in your Recycle Bin (**C:\Recycled**) and a file called **Scam32.exe** in your Windows System folder. It then modifies two registry keys:

> HKEY_LOCAL_MACHINE\Software\Microsoft\Windows\CurrentVersion\
> RunServices\Driver32="<Windows System>\SCam32.exe"
> HKEY_CLASSES_ROOT\exefile\shell\open\command="C:\recycled\
> SirC32.exe" "%1" %*"

and creates a third:

> HKEY_LOCAL_MACHINE\Software\SirCam

The first key causes the worm to run when Windows starts, the second causes the worm to be run whenever any **.exe** program is executed and the third establishes SirCam as a legitimate program as far as Windows is concerned.

The worm then checks all the **.doc**, **.xls** and **.zip** files in your **My Documents** folder and selects several at random. It buries a copy of itself into these files and saves the modified files to your **Recycled** folder, adding the second extension to the filename just as before. Next it checks your address book and starts sending messages to addresses it finds. Each message carries one of the modified files as an attachment to start the whole cycle once again. Figure 5.3 shows an e-mail from the SirCam worm. Note that the subject of the message (Sopimus) matches the name of the attachment (**Sopimus.doc.pif**).

Figure 5.3 An e-mail from the SirCam worm.

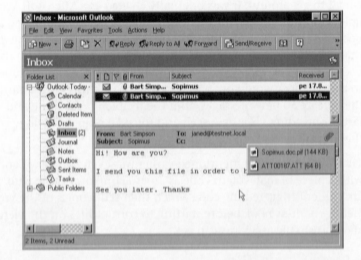

But the worm has a second trick up its sleeve. It now looks to see if any of your drives are shared on a network. If it finds a shared drive with a **Recycled** folder it copies itself there, creating a file called **SirC32.exe**. If the shared drive contains a Windows start-up file called **autoexec.bat**, it adds the line:

   @win \recycled\SirC32.exe

… which ensures that the worm is run every time the computer is started up. Finally, it looks for the Windows system file **rundll32.exe** and replaces it with the worm, renaming the original file as **run32.exe**. When the worm is executed from **rundll32.exe**, it automatically executes the back-up file **run32.exe** to ensure that Windows appears to operate normally.

The worm carries a payload which is intended to delete all the files and subfolders from the hard drive which Windows is installed on (usually C:\), but ironically there is a bug in the code which normally prevents it from activating! However, if one of the worm's files is renamed or modified before it is run, the payload can be activated with disastrous results. (Soothing note: Don't worry if you didn't understand all the technical stuff in this example. I have included all these details just to show how tricky and complex a virus can be.)

Other viruses operate in other ways, but most follow a similar path.

➤ They gain access to your system by some kind of stealthy means.

➤ They establish themselves on your hard disk.

➤ They set up a mechanism by which they can replicate and infect other systems.

➤ They deliver their payload.

As you might expect, most replication today is done via the e-mail system. Like the example quoted above, Melissa, possibly the most successful virus of recent years, used e-mail to get around. It was originally created as a Microsoft Word® document and uploaded to an internet newsgroup. Anyone who downloaded and opened the document would trigger the virus which would then send the document (and therefore itself) in an e-mail message to the first 50 people in that person's address book. Melissa cleverly generated a friendly message that included the person's name, so the recipient would open the document thinking it was harmless. The virus would then create 50 new messages from the recipient's machine and so on. Melissa was the fastest-spreading virus ever seen and forced a number of large companies to shut down their e-mail systems completely.

The Loveletter virus I mentioned earlier was even simpler. It consisted of an e-mail with a piece of malevolent code as an attachment. People who double-clicked the attachment triggered the code which then sent copies of the virus to everyone in the victim's address book before starting to corrupt files on the victim's machine. This is about as simple as a virus can get.

The Melissa virus took advantage of the programming language built into Microsoft Word called VBA, or Visual Basic for Applications. It is a complete programming language and it can be programmed to do things like modify files and send e-mail messages. It also has a useful but dangerous auto-execute feature. A programmer can insert a program into a document that runs instantly whenever the document is opened which is how the Melissa virus was programmed. Anyone who opened a document infected with Melissa would immediately activate the virus. It would send the 50 e-mails, and then infect a Word file called **normal.dot** – the default template Word uses to create new documents. Any file based on this template would also contain the virus.

After these assorted horror stories, perhaps we should close this section by agreeing exactly what a virus can and cannot do. While different viruses can attack your system in many different ways, they cannot harm your computer hardware. Some viruses generate on-screen boasts that they have crashed your hard disk or trashed your monitor, but these are just scare tactics. They can destroy the contents of memory chips and flash memory – particularly relevant to viruses that attack Personal Digital Assistants (PDAs) like the Palm® and the Compaq iPaq®. These devices store data in memory and not on a hard disk.

Most viruses attack data stored on your hard disk, but there are different strains. So-called **polymorphic viruses** not only scramble data, they also mutate before spreading, making detection extremely difficult. A second type, known as **file infector viruses** go for your programs rather than your data. They modify the code within your executable files or your system's operating software (such as damaging Registry files) so that you are unable to launch programs. File infector viruses are particularly troublesome because they can prevent you from running anti-virus software. I have already described **boot-sector viruses**. They attack your start-up files making it impossible to load your operating system and start your computer. Finally, I should mention **retro viruses**, viruses that target your anti-virus software itself.

Spotting The Invaders In Your Own System

Most early viruses were easy to spot since their mission was either to damage their host or to produce some visible effect. More recently, virus programmers have raised their game and are not satisfied unless their products threaten life on this planet! In most cases this means that stealth and replication have become the priorities, with payload delivery lower down the agenda. One result of this new approach is that your own responsibility has increased. Not only must you keep your own computer free from infection, you must also prevent that infection from getting out. If you know you have a virus, you must effectively put your machine into quarantine until it has been thoroughly disinfected.

So, how can you tell if you have a virus? The best way, of course, is to invest in a good anti-virus program and use its AV scanner to check your system. We will be looking at anti-virus software later in this chapter. Otherwise you can watch for symptoms. The following list details some of the possible ways in which viruses reveal themselves. Remember, however, that it is not inclusive – new viruses are emerging all the time, and that the symptoms listed might indicate other problems with your system.

➤ Your computer refuses to start or boots part of the way and then crashes.

➤ Your computer shuts down or reboots unexpectedly.

➤ Your computer slows down or exhibits other unusual behaviour.

➤ Files mysteriously disappear or you find that you cannot save files.

➤ Programs start up by themselves – you might notice your hard disk beavering away when you are not deliberately reading or saving data.

➤ Your hard disk starts to fill up with data.

➤ Your e-mail program uploads or downloads large numbers of messages.

➤ Your computer displays strange visual effects such as characters disappearing from your screen or unusual graphics appearing.

➤ Your computer produces strange audio effects such as a toilet flushing or someone laughing.

➤ You receive on-screen messages such as 'Gotcha', 'Your PC has been stoned' or 'I want a cookie'.

If you are suffering from one or more of these problems, there is a reasonable chance that you have a virus. Whatever else you do, don't panic. Since it is quite likely that the damage has already been done, your job is now to deal with the virus, restore as much of your system as you can and learn from the experience. Read the rest of this chapter – in particular the last section.

Keeping Those Infections Out

For now, let's assume your computer doesn't have a virus and look at ways of making sure it stays that way. Remember that in simple terms a virus is a program like any other program, and cannot do anything unless it is run. This means that you will have to execute it if it is to infect your system. We have already noted different ways in which you can do this, but let us sum them up.

➤ You can start up a virus like any other program by double-clicking its executable file.

➤ You can boot your computer from an infected disk – hard, floppy or even CD-ROM.

➤ You can open an infected Microsoft Office document such as a Word file, Excel spreadsheet, Access database, Power Point presentation, or Project file.

➤ You can run an infected Visual Basic Script or Microsoft JScript, including invisible ones embedded in web pages or HTML-formatted e-mail or in messages posted to internet newsgroups.

➤ You can open an e-mail attachment which contains an infected script.

Of course you will invest in anti-virus software and you will keep it up-to-date, but it is better still if you never need to use it in anger. Here are the golden don'ts and the golden dos. Follow them and you minimize the risk of infection.

Table 5.2 The Golden Don'ts

The rules	Comments and solutions
1 Never open e-mail attachments even if they come from your best friend, your mother or the Pope.	With e-mail now the most common source of infection, it makes sense never to open an attachment when it arrives. Instead, you should save it to disk, scan it with your anti-virus program and, even then, unless you are completely satisfied that it is safe, delete it unopened. It is not enough just to discard e-mail attachments from strangers, since friends and colleagues are quite likely to forward infected attachments, and there are worms, as we have seen that can do this without them knowing anything about it.
2 Never boot your computer from a floppy disk unless you created it yourself and stored it safely where other people could not have got at it.	The easiest way to infect a computer is to inject a virus during the boot process while all sorts of things are happening which are invisible to the user.
3 Never install new software on your computer without running it through an up-to-date anti-virus scanner.	No matter whether the software comes from some disreputable hacker, the most respected software archive or a computer magazine cover disk, you cannot afford to assume it is virus free. For improved safety, consider buying an uninstaller program (I will be looking at these in Chapter 8) which can monitor the installation and reverse it if things go wrong.

Table 5.2 Continued

The rules	Comments and solutions
4 Never open a Microsoft Office document unless your macro security is set to high (Office 2000) or better still, disabled altogether. Macro viruses can be difficult to spot and deal with.	Macro viruses rely on Microsoft Office to activate them. Here is what Office Help says about the security settings available from **Tools > Macro > Security**:

A macro virus is a type of computer virus that's stored in a macro within a document, template, or add-in. When you open such a document or perform an action that triggers a macro virus, the macro virus might be activated, transmitted to your computer, and stored in your normal or global template. From that point on, every document you open could be automatically 'infected' with the macro virus – and if other people open these infected documents, the macro virus is transmitted to their computers.

Microsoft Word offers the following levels of security to reduce the chances that macro viruses will infect your documents, templates, or add-ins:

➤ ***High** – You can run only macros that have been digitally signed and that you confirm are from a trusted source. Before trusting a source, you should confirm that the source is responsible and uses a virus scanner before signing macros. Unsigned macros are automatically disabled, and Word opens the document without any warning.*

➤ ***Medium** – Word displays a warning whenever it encounters a macro from a source that is not on your list of trusted sources (described later in this topic). You can choose whether to enable or disable the macros when you open the document. If the document might contain a virus, you should choose to disable macros.*

➤ ***Low** – If you are sure that all the documents and add-ins you open are safe, you can select this option – it turns off macro virus protection in Word. At this security level, macros are always enabled when you open documents.'*

(Copyright © 2000 Microsoft)

5 Never install the Windows Scripting Host – the application which allows scripts to run. Unfortunately, the WSH is installed by default on most computers, but unless you are developing scripts or have a particular need for it, you are best off without it. If it is installed, get rid of it.

WSH is installed automatically if you choose a standard installation of Windows, install Internet Explorer 5 (or later), or download it from the Microsoft website. To check whether WSH is currently installed, click **Start > Settings > Control Panel > Add/Remove Programs**. Now select the **Windows Setup** tab, select **Accessories** from the list and click **Details**. Scroll down the list and you will see something like Figure 5.4.

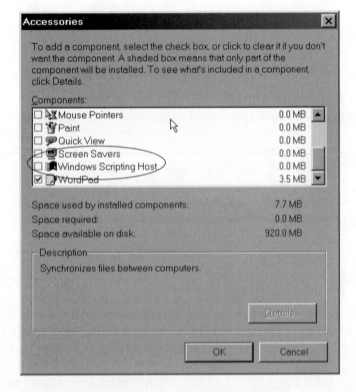

Figure 5.4 Removing Windows Scripting Host

If Windows Scripting Host is checked, uncheck it to remove the program from your system. Click **OK** to return to **Add/Remove Programs** and click **OK** to finish.

Table 5.3 The Golden Dos

The rules	Comments and solutions
1 Buy a current and effective anti-virus program (see the following section). Make sure you keep it up-to-date by downloading the virus updates at least once a week.	However carefully you implement the rest of this strategy, you are still at risk from viruses. Virus writers are a crafty lot and work hard at getting round your security measures. You need a good anti-virus program as your last line of defence. Remember that anti-virus software is always out of date. It is constantly playing catch-up as the ungodly produce new infections. Each time a fresh batch of viruses are detected, the AV software companies release an update to add a new layer of protection to your machine. Updates are free – so download and install them.
2 Regularly check the manufacturer's site for upgrades or security patches for your e-mail program.	Microsoft and other communications software manufacturers regularly post updates and patches on their websites. Most people do not take advantage of this free facility. Since these patches are often designed to block up security holes, it is foolish not to download and install them.
3 Back-up your critical data regularly.	I cover this in detail in Chapter 9.
4 Disable scripting so that if you do accidentally double-click a malevolent script it doesn't run.	There are several ways to achieve this. Some firewalls and anti-virus programs automatically quarantine any incoming scripts they encounter. Xteq X-Setup, a utility we have met earlier in the book, allows you to associate all scripts with Windows Notepad so that if you do accidentally double-click them, they will open in Notepad rather than run. Far and away the best way to control e-mail attachment scripting is to disable it altogether by moving your e-mail client into the 'Restricted Sites' zone. This sounds forbidding, but is simplicity itself. Internet Explorer allows you to apply your own security settings to internet sites by adding them to different zones. You can treat your e-mail program as a website like this: Click **Start** > **Settings** > **Control Panel** > **Internet Options**. Then click the **Security** tab and select the **Restricted Zones** section. You will see a Window like Figure 5.5.

Figure 5.5 The Internet Properties Control Panel

Now click the **Custom Level** button and a Window like Figure 5.6 will open.

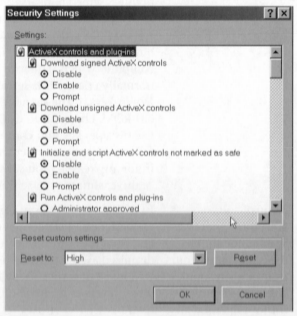

Figure 5.6 Internet Security Settings for the Restricted Site zone

Table 5.3 continued

The rules	Comments and solutions
4 *continued*	Work down the list of Settings and disable everything except the following three which should be set to prompt. ➤ Drag and drop or copy and paste files. ➤ Submit non-encrypted data. ➤ Login – set to **Prompt for username and password**. Now open Microsoft Outlook or Outlook Express and click **Tools** > **Options** > **Security** and change the default security zone to Restricted Sites. Now infected attachments will simply not run.
5 Change the booting-up sequence in your computer's CMOS so that your computer boots from the C:\ drive even if there is a floppy in the A:\ drive.	This also sounds more complicated than it really is. By default, most computers try to boot from the floppy (A:\) drive before they look at the hard (C:\) drive. Normally, you shouldn't need to boot from A:\ unless your computer is ill. The CMOS (Complementary Metal-Oxide Semiconductor) is a small chip on your motherboard which stores the basic system configuration details. To access these, restart your computer and when the start-up BIOS screen appears, press the **Delete** key (or whichever key is specified in your manual). This will open up your system BIOS settings. These vary from machine to machine, but somewhere you will find a setting which tells the computer which sequence of drives to boot from. You can normally change this setting using the **Page Up** and **Page Down** keys. If the sequence is set to something like A, C, CD-ROM, change it to C, CD-ROM, A. Back out using the **Esc** (Escape) key and confirm the changes when you are asked to. Your computer will reboot. If, for any reason, you subsequently need to boot from the A: drive, simply reverse the process.
6 Be suspicious of everything that is sent to your computer. If e-mail comes from an unknown source, consider deleting it without opening any	In particular, watch out for attachments that look as if they are designed to attract your attention. Although .jpg, .gif and MP3 files cannot be infected with a virus, a virus can be disguised as one of these using the double extension trick we looked at earlier. Treat jokes, pictures, graphics, screensavers and movie files with suspicion. These are often used to disguise viruses.

attachments. Even when attachments come from a friend or colleague, if you are not expecting them, you might contact the sender just to make sure everything is genuine.

Ask friends and business colleagues to send e-mail in Plain Text rather than HTML. Plain Text cannot carry hidden code.

7 If you are producing a document which is going to be sent or passed on to someone else, save it as a Plain Text file rather than as a Word **.doc** file.

I admit that this is not always practical since Plain Text cannot carry graphics or any kind of formatting, but if you are simply sending words, this is certainly the safest option. You can select this format from Word's **Save** menu.

Tracking Down Anti-Virus Software

There are loads of comprehensive anti-virus packages available. Computer stores carry them and they can also be downloaded from the web. They all claim to offer total protection from infection, but the truth is that some of them are more effective than others. Rather than just buying the first one you find, it is worth taking some time to investigate their claims. There are several sites on the internet which check the efficiency of a range of AV programs and publish comparative results. Unfortunately, these results never seem to agree with each other, so the best solution might be to visit several and take an average.

My preferred comparison is the one published by the prestigious *Virus Bulletin*. Most months, they check a wide range of virus scanners against all the viruses currently on the Wild List. The check they make is simple in the extreme. Scanners are exposed to all the viruses. They either detect all of them and pass, or miss some of them and fail. The *Virus Bulletin* has been running these tests since January 1998. Here are the results up to September 2001 for the most common anti-virus programs.

Table 5.4 Passing The Test?

Anti-virus program	No. of tests carried out	No. of passes	No. of fails	Passes/tests percentage
CA Vet Anti-Virus	21	10	11	47.62%
ESET NOD32	16	15	1	93.75%
Symantec Norton Anti-Virus	20	14	6	70.00%
CA InnoculateIT	18	10	8	55.55%
Norman Virus Control	21	14	7	66.66%
Sophos Anti-Virus	21	13	8	61.90%
Kaspersky Lab AVP	21	13	8	61.90%
Network Associates VirusScan	20	7	13	35.00%
Command Anti-Virus	19	6	13	31.58%

I am not going to say that this particular comparison is any better or worse than any other one and certainly other tests produce different results. You must make up your own mind. But whatever AV program you decide on, get it, install it and keep it up-to-date.

If you want to compare various brands of anti-virus software, I suggest using a search engine such as Google (www.google.com) and searching for 'anti-virus software comparison'. If you want to check out the *Virus Bulletin* site, go to www.virusbtn.com

Since ESET NOD32 came top in this test, let's use it to illustrate the different facilities a good anti-virus program should provide. There are five essential ingredients to AV security, although some software offers additional resources. The five essentials are as follows.

➤ The AV program must check the system during the boot process to ensure that it is loading free from boot-sector or Windows start-up viruses.

➤ The AV program must provide a resident monitor which starts with your system and maintains a constant watch on computer activity, warning you whenever virus activity is detected. The AMON monitor supplied with ESET NOD32 is shown in Figure 5.7.

➤ The AV program must include an anti-virus scanner which can check your hard disks, floppies and CD-ROMs for viruses. The best software allows you to

Figure 5.7 Nod32's AMON monitor

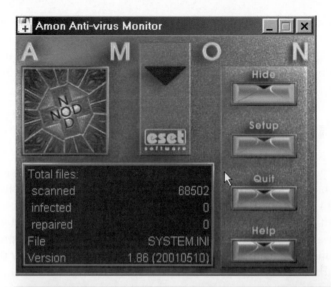

Figure 5.8 The NOD32 Anti-virus program

timetable regular checks without user intervention. NOD32's anti-virus program is shown in Figure 5.8.

➤ The AV program must include a simple and effective way to upgrade virus definitions from the internet.

➤ The AV program must provide an e-mail attachment scanner to spot malevolent code sneaking in on the back of a message.

So, compare products, check features and make your choice. Once you have installed the software, use it and use it constantly. If you use your computer on a daily basis, it does no harm to check all your executable files every single day. Adjust your timetable to suit your usage. Since viruses cannot appear out of thin air, you will remain uninfected if you don't use e-mail, connect to the internet, install new software or use anyone else's removable media. But if you do any of these things, match your anti-virus strategy to your exposure to danger.

Dealing With The Aftermath

This is a short and fairly miserable way to close this chapter. What do you do if you find your computer is infected? The answer depends on the extent of the infection. If you have an anti-virus program which successfully detects the virus and stamps it out, then your immediate problems are solved. Breathe a sigh of relief and start to investigate. Try to work out how the virus got into your system. Did you install new software recently? Is there an e-mail in your system with a suspicious attachment? Did anyone else recently use your computer? If you can identify the threat, warn your friends and colleagues – your IT Manager, if at work. You might even post a warning to one of the internet newsgroups that take an interest in virus activity.

But, as we have seen, there are viruses which prevent your AV software from working, or your computer from starting at all. You can try booting from a floppy disk, booting from your Windows CD-ROM or from a specialized emergency start-up disk such as the one provided with Norton Utilities®. If Windows won't start normally, try booting in safe mode. Hold down the Control (Ctrl) Key as Windows tries to start and pick **Safe Mode** from the menu that appears. If you can get to your Windows desktop, try running your anti-virus software. If all else fails, try to copy your data files (NOT your programs) to a removable disk or back-up drive. Then, at least they are safe.

If your computer has been hit with a macro virus, you will need to scan all of your Microsoft Office documents as well as your document templates. Remember to contact anyone you have shared a document with as they will need to do the same.

Your final sanction against which no virus can prevail is to reformat your hard disk and start again from scratch. This is a depressing last resort, but once you've done it – I have – you will make absolutely certain that you never get infected again!

Chapter 5 – Security Checklist

1   Invest in a good anti-virus program, install it, use it and keep it up-to-date by downloading new anti-virus definitions as soon as they are published.

2   Be vigilant! Watch for symptoms of virus activity on your computer – the full checklist is given earlier in this chapter. In general, be suspicious of any unexpected computer activity. If your hard drive is whirring or your computer does strange things, don't assume everything is all right. Investigate at once.

3   Never open an e-mail attachment unless you are absolutely certain that it is genuine. Remember that your friends and colleagues can inadvertently spread viruses, so a recognized name on the message does not guarantee its safety. If in doubt, delete it immediately.

4   Never install new software without checking it for viruses – and make sure you check it using the most up-to-date set of virus definitions available for your scanner.

5   Watch out for Office macro viruses which can creep in inside documents. Make sure you set your macro security to the highest possible setting.

6   Kill the Windows Scripting Host unless you have a specific need for it and while you are at it, disable scripting by moving your e-mail client to the Restricted Zone.

7   Change your computer's boot-up sequence so that is starts from your hard disk and not from a floppy.

Part 2
Taking Control Of Your Own Machine

In Part 2, your purpose is to take back control of your computer from all the software that tries to impose itself against your wishes. You'll start by looking at how a computer stores information as digital data and how data is made available to your applications. You will also examine where data is stored and how it can be secured against accidental and deliberate damage.

Next you will look at your application software, how it operates within the constraints of your operating system, and how it can crash your system. I outline common causes for software conflicts and ways in which you can recover from the inevitable breakdowns that follow. I also propose setting up a regular maintenance schedule to clean your system up and guard against trouble.

I describe the dangers of installing new software and suggest ways to ensure that problem programs can be completely removed and the system returned to a secure state. Finally, I'll show you the importance of a back-up strategy, making sure that your precious data is safe.

By the end of Part 2, you will understand how a computer stores data, how application software operates and how to manage new programs. You will also have decided on and implemented appropriate back-ups. Your critical data will be secure against any trials and tribulations.

Thinking Digital

Understanding Digital Data

So what exactly is data? Up until now, we have mainly concerned ourselves with securing application and utility software. Unless you are a programmer and write your own, you will have obtained all this software on CD-ROM or as an internet download, so if you have problems, you can reinstall your programs from the original distributions. Data, on the other hand, cannot be replaced so easily. We will define data as the text, numbers, sounds and images stored in a form that can be processed by your computer, but the key point, of course, is that data is the software you create for yourself.

If you are paranoid enough (and by now I hope that you are well on your way to advanced paranoia!) you will consider implementing a rigid back-up strategy to ensure that your data cannot easily be destroyed. We will look in detail at back-up strategies in Chapter 9. This chapter is concerned with the concepts of data, data storage and data security.

Perhaps we should start by considering how computer data represents actual information. As you probably know, your computer is a digital device. Digital is a word that has muscled its way into everyday conversation, but people often use it without understanding what it implies. We know that CDs store music digitally and we know that digital TV is more advanced technically than traditional television. We are often told that digital is good – but why? To answer this, we need to understand exactly what is meant by digital information and how it applies to computer data. This is where it gets a bit tricky.

According to the dictionary, digital implies a form of representing something by using distinct objects or digits. This may not be very helpful, so let's consider what this means in practice. Think carefully about what is implied by this sentence:

> The number '1' is a digital representation of the concept of a single item.

Pick up your pen. If I ask you how many pens you are holding, you will answer 'one'. But the number 1 is not the pen itself. It is a representation of the number of pens you are holding, expressed as a digit. To put it another way, the concept of a single item is not a mathematical object. It cannot be added to or subtracted from another mathematical object. The digit '1', on the other hand, can be manipulated. You can calculate the result of the term '1 + 3' and produce another digital representation, the digit '4'.

The alternative to digital representation is analogue representation, where something is represented by a changing value. To understand the difference between these two forms of representation, think of car speedometers. In a traditional analogue speedometer, a needle moves constantly up and down a dial to indicate an infinite range of speeds from zero up to the maximum limit. Note that because we are talking about an infinite range, the needle could point to any value within that range. A modern digital speedometer can only indicate a preset range of speeds – a range limited by the number of segments the display is capable of lighting up.

Figure 6.1 illustrates the difference between analogue and digital devices. The analogue speedometer on the left represents the speed using a needle and a dial. Because the needle can move infinitely small distances, the actual speed shown here might be something like 73.49987659304 miles per hour. The digital speedometer on the right, however, represents the speed as specific digits, in this case 73.50 miles per hour.

Computers are digital devices, but instead of using the ten digits from 0 to 9 that we are familiar with, they operate with binary numbers. Binary arithmetic uses only the digits '0' and '1' to represent numbers – which means that all the information stored

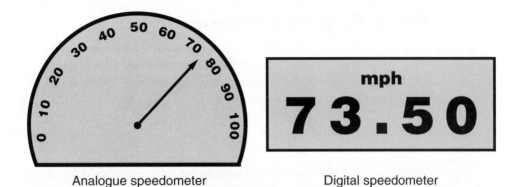

Analogue speedometer   Digital speedometer

Figure 6.1 Analogue and digital speedometers

on your computer is represented by a pattern of zeroes and ones. You may already be familiar with the concept of binary arithmetic. If not, Table 6.1 below shows how ordinary numbers can be rendered in binary format.

Table 6.1 Binary Numbers

8s	4s	2s	1s	4-bit binary number	Calculation	Decimal number
0	0	0	1	0001	$0 \times 8 + 0 \times 4 + 0 \times 2 + 1 \times 1 =$	1
0	0	1	0	0010	$0 \times 8 + 0 \times 4 + 1v2 + 0 \times 1 =$	2
0	1	0	0	0011	$0 \times 8 + 1 \times 4 + 0 \times 2 + 0 \times 1 =$	4
0	1	1	0	0100	$0 \times 8 + 1 \times 4 + 1 \times 2 + 0 \times 1 =$	6
1	0	0	0	0101	$1 \times 8 + 0 \times 4 + 0 \times 2 + 0 \times 1 =$	8
1	0	1	1	0110	$1 \times 8 + 0 \times 4 + 1 \times 2 + 1 \times 1 =$	11
1	1	1	1	1111	$1 \times 8 + 1 \times 4 + 1 \times 2 + 1 \times 1 =$	15

The table above shows how four binary bits can represent numbers from 0–15. Add a further bit (16s) and numbers from 0–31 can be represented. Clearly, the more bits, the larger the number that can be produced. In ordinary decimal numbering, the digit on the far right of a number indicates the number of 1s, the next digit to the left, the number of 10s, then 100s and so on. The number 643, for example, is a quick way of saying 6×100 plus 4×10 plus 3×1. Binary numbering works in exactly the same way, except the columns reading from the right are 1s, 2s, 4s, 8s, 16s, 32s, etc. – each column representing twice the value of the previous one.

Digital Data Representation

Turning numbers – or even colours and musical notes – into the binary code that computers can understand is called digital data representation. Digital data representation means rendering information as computer bits. The bit (**bi**nary digi**t**) is the basic unit in any digital system. Think of an ordinary lightbulb. It has two states – on and off. In the electronic circuitry of a computer, 'on', or 'current high' in computer terminology, would represent the number 1. 'Off', or 'current low', would represent the number 0.

Look back at Table 6.1. You will note that a single bit, as shown in the four columns on the left, can carry only limited information – 1/0, yes/no, or on/off, etc., but series of bits can represent anything we want them to. For example, 2 bits give us four different states, which we can represent as 00, 01, 10 and 11 (zero/zero, zero/one, one/zero and one/one, not zero, one, ten and eleven!) These could represent 0, 1, 2 and 3 or North, South, East and West. In the same way that more bits allow us to represent more numbers in binary, they also allow us to represent more alternatives as shown in Table 6.2 below.

Table 6.2 Alternative Representations

Number of bits	Number of alternative representations	Possible data applications
1 (1-bit)	2	Yes or No, On or Off, Black or White
2 (2-bit)	4	Directions, seasons of the year.
4 (4-bit)	16	Names of players in a rugby team – plus the coach!
8 (8-bit=1 byte)	256	Characters – the full range of upper- and lower-case letters, numbers and symbols.

A byte consists of 8 bits. Having 8 bits allows us to represent a total of 256 different numbers or alternatives, using binary code from 00000000 (0 in decimal numbering) up to 11111111 (255 in decimal numbering). With 256 possible variations, a byte is often thought of as the space required to store a single character – a letter, a number, a punctuation mark or a space, on a computer. You probably know that computer storage is measured in terms of megabytes. A megabyte is roughly a million bytes (1,048,576 bytes to be precise), so one megabyte of disk capacity can store roughly one million characters.

The letter 'A', for example, is usually represented on PCs by the binary number 11000001. But 11000001 does not have to represent the letter 'A', it could just as easily represent one of 256 colours, or a musical note, or a temperature. All that is required is that the computer handling the data understands how it is to use the bits it encounters and interpreting digital data is exactly what computer software does. The same sequence of binary digits turns up countless times in computer operations, but you can trust your machine not to produce a block of colour when you are typing text into your word processor, and not to suddenly play a note when you are creating a drawing.

To sum up, computers are digital devices which operate on a binary number system. Any data can be rendered as binary digits. A binary number can represent a decimal number, a character or any other type of information, provided the handling computer understands how to interpret the data.

Storing Digital Data

So far so good, but now we need to turn these concepts into the realities of data storage. Your computer might well contain thousands of files on its hard disk(s). Some of these files are applications, some are the additional resources the applications need to operate and some of them are the data files which are processed by the applications. To keep track of all this information, your computer maintains an internal filing system, which logs essential information such as the name of the file, its extension and its size. This directory (or a graphical representation of it) is visible in Windows Explorer. In addition to being a very useful tool for copying, moving and deleting files, the disk directory has a profound psychological effect on the user. He can take comfort in the certainty that all his precious files are logged and accounted for. Explorer oozes stability.

Time to let a little paranoia seep back in. At machine level, each hard or floppy disk is divided into clusters, the basic units of data storage. (The actual storage capacity of a cluster depends on how your computer has been set up and is not relevant here.) The operating system maintains a record of these clusters in a hidden and very inaccessible file known as the File Allocation Table (FAT). When a file is saved to disk, it is spread over as many clusters as it requires, but these clusters are not necessarily next to each other, or 'contiguous' in computer terminology. Pieces of your file might be scattered all over the drive, and only the FAT knows how to put them back together.

The actual mechanics of this are simple enough. For each file, the FAT's directory records the address of the first cluster it is stored in. In the FAT entry for that first cluster is stored the address of the next cluster and so on until the last cluster which contains an end-of-file code. If the FAT gets damaged there is no other way of finding out how to reassemble a file. For safety's sake, the OS maintains two copies of the FAT

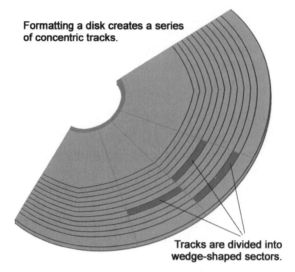

Figure 6.2 How a disk is organized for data storage

Formatting a disk creates a series of concentric tracks.

Tracks are divided into wedge-shaped sectors.

A cluster consists of one or more sectors.

and updates them one at a time. You may wonder why a computer does not store all the parts of a file together and reduce the chances of losing bits of a file. The answer is that computer disks are dynamic media. Files are constantly being created, modified and deleted, and their sizes are constantly changing. If files were all stored contiguously, after a few weeks your disks would appear full, but actually be peppered with groups of empty clusters waiting for files small enough to fit them.

When you consign a file to disk, the FAT identifies the first empty cluster and sends the drive's read-write head to that location. The head then magnetizes particles on the disk's surface to create alignment patterns, which can be interpreted as the ones and zeroes of digital data. Of course, the head can subsequently read these patterns to recreate the stored data so that the CPU can process it. Figure 6.2 shows how a disk is organized into tracks, sectors and clusters.

Programs Versus Data

As we have already noted, everything on your computer is stored as a pattern of '1s' and '0s' and this applies to your programs and the data they operate on. We can divide all the contents of your hard drive into data and programs, although the difference is not always as clear as you might think. If, for example, you download a piece of software from the internet, it is often parcelled up as a Zip file which you unpack using an archiver such as WinZip®. In this instance, the software download itself is the data that is processed by the WinZip program. After it is unpacked, that data becomes a program.

We tend to think that the programs stored on our computer are secure. After all, whenever you fire up your machine, they all appear in your Start menu. As we have seen in the previous section, programs are nothing more than digital patterns held in place by a stable magnetic field on your hard drive. Get a strong magnet and wave it over your C:\ drive, and you will see just how fragile this storage medium really is. Under ordinary circumstances, program software is fairly stable. Most software is designed to resist unauthorized tinkering. You can change the name of an executable file – although the operating system will warn you that doing so will interfere with its operation, but it is considerably more difficult to get inside it and alter its contents. Difficult – but not impossible!

Unfortunately, the executable file is not usually the complete program. As we noted in Chapter 3, to work within the Windows operating system, the executables rely on a whole series of other files such as DLLs (Dynamic Link Libraries), INI files which tell the program how to start up, data logging files which store the current state of that program's data, help files and so on. Many of these files are not proofed against interference. How can they be, when they need to change as the program runs?

Let's take a typical INI file as an example. I run a utility called Typograf, which helps me to manage the ridiculous number of fonts I have installed. When it starts up, Typograf reads its INI file to determine how it will operate. Here are the current contents of its INI file:

[Uninstall]	Height=845	[Info]
Icons=C:\WINDOWS	Left=13	FCounts=2
\Start Menu\	Top=8	
Programs\Typograf	maximized=0	[Katalog]
	AnzeigeSubDir=0	IDWertX=0
[Ansicht]	KurzHilfe=1	
XWidth=0	TipDesTages=1	
WriteTest=0	SortAfterChDir=0	[History]
1=	SortType=1	0c:\program
2=	SortItem=0	files\typograf\=x
Xid=182240565	StartAnz=2	
MaxTag=0		
Width=1248		

While I can hazard a guess at the function of some of the entries, I have no idea what most of them mean – it doesn't help that some of the entries are in German. But I can open this file in a simple text editor and change the contents at will. If I modified the line **Xid=182240565** to read **Xid=ripe bananas** and then started the program, it would quite possibly have an impact on the way in which the program operates – if it operates at all. The point here is that the operation of a program can be disrupted very easily – in this case by using a simple text editor.

If a program becomes damaged, either because an internal computer error has corrupted it or because some outside influence has deliberately messed with it, it is usually possible to restore it from the original software distribution. This means reinstalling the software from the supplied CD-ROM or re-unpacking the Zip archive it is stored in. (This is one of the reasons why any software downloaded from the net should be backed up somewhere.) Reinstalling software usually corrects any corruption but it can also mean that you lose any personalized data stored in program files. If, for example, the 'Width' and 'Height' settings in the listing above were there because I had set the program to operate in a particular size of window, a fresh installation might reinitialize these settings to a default size, which I would then need to reset. OK, this is hardly a major problem, but imagine the annoyance if this INI file stored useful information on every font on my system, and this data was lost by the reinstallation.

Data, of course, is meant to be modified. I am writing this using Microsoft Word®, and every time I add a few lines, I click the **Save** button and change the contents of the file which stores the chapter. If I wanted to secure the data on my computer, I would track down all the files I had created and back them up, but I might easily overlook those equally important support files, which are created invisibly by the program itself. These associated files are often every bit as critical as the data files we create.

Data Storage Locations

There is always a difficulty in identifying which files relate to a particular program. When you install an application, part of that installation might go something like this.

➤ The installer creates a new folder in your Program Files folder.

➤ Within that folder, the installer creates a series of other folders to store components, resources, temporary files, processed data, etc.

➤ In the primary folder it installs the executable file itself along with any additional components that it requires.

➤ It then drops further components into the secondary folders.

➤ The installer then checks Windows' own system folders to ensure that you have any shared resources (such as Dynamic Link Library files) that it requires. If not, it installs them as well.

➤ The installer then places shortcuts to its executable(s) in your Start Menu and sometimes on your desktop.

Unfortunately, most installations do not bother to tell you which files they have

Figure 6.3 Susie's thumbnails window

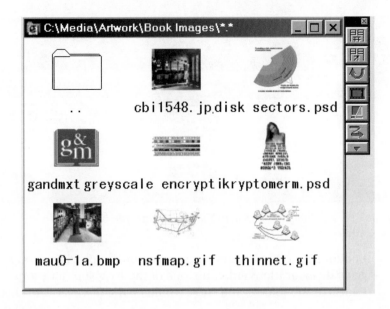

installed or where they have installed them, which can turn backing up your data into a nightmare. To add to the problem, when you use an application, it is likely to store data in an anonymous file that it creates invisibly. Let's look at an example. Because I keep a large number of graphics files on my computer, I need a utility to view and manage them. To do this, I use an excellent Japanese graphics viewer called Susie. Starting Susie opens a small control panel on your desktop and, when I drag a folder full of images onto the control panel, Susie sorts through them and creates a thumbnail image for each graphic in the folder. These thumbnails are stored in a file called **_thumbnl.sue**. (Figure 6.3 shows Susie in action.) When I back up my data, I will copy all my graphics onto a network drive, but I might easily forget to copy the **_thumbnl.sue** file, first because it is not obviously a graphics file and second because I was not advised by the program that it had even been created. If this file gets destroyed, I need to reopen Susie and get her to build the thumbnail catalogue all over again, which can be a time-consuming business.

So, how can you find out where your programs are storing both your data files and their own internal data files? The straight answer is, you can't! It helps that many programs automatically store data in a particular location – usually either a sub-folder of the program's own folder or in one of Windows' default folders. Back in Chapter 4, we noted that Windows prefers you to keep your text files in the **My Documents** folder, which is created by the operating system during installation. This is where Word, for example, will place your **.doc** files unless it is told otherwise. A lot of recent software now follows this model and creates its own storage folders on installation. A quick look through your hard drive might turn up **My Download Files, My**

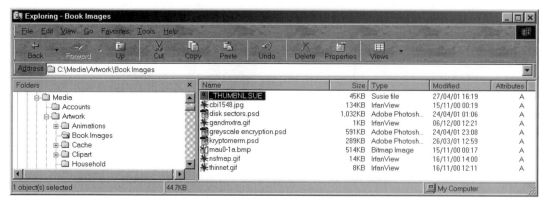

Figure 6.4 The images folder with the thumbnails file highlighted

Bookmarks or **My Images** – depending on the programs you have installed. In general, applications either use one of these obvious locations, or they use their own folders or sub-folders, and these would be the first places to check.

There are some applications however that seem to go out of their way to complicate matters. Many people use Microsoft Office® as their core business software. Part of the suite is Outlook, an excellent e-mail client that also provides a diary, address book, memo pad and a range of other utilities. Not surprisingly, as a security-minded individual, you want to back up the information held by Outlook, but where do you look for it? Eventually you will track it down to a file called **outlook.pst** which, in my case, is stored in the folder **C:\Windows\Local Settings\Application Data\Microsoft\Outlook**. Not, you will agree, the most obvious of locations.

As we will see later on in this book, one way to monitor unwanted activity on your computer is to keep a watch on files that change. (This, by the way, is one of the tests applied by real-time virus protection programs.) Knowing that the OS records changes to files gives us one way of discovering which files are being modified by an application, and thus which files we might need to back up. Let's stick with Susie for an example. As you can see from Figure 6.3, the folder **C:\Media\Artwork\Book Images** contains eight graphic files. After Susie has done her business, it also contains the **_thumbnl.sue** file containing the thumbnail images. Figure 6.4 shows this folder opened in Windows Explorer.

If you look to the right of the illustration, you will notice that one of the columns is headed **Modified**. If you click this heading, the order in which the files are listed will change from the default alphabetical to the order in which they were last modified. The time and date listed below the heading specifies exactly when that last modification took place. In this case, **_thumbnl.sue** was modified at 16:19 on the 27 April 2001. Knowing that this information is stored, we can use it to discover exactly which files have been changed by an application. By clicking **Tools > Find >**

Figure 6.5 Using Explorer's Find tool to track down modified files

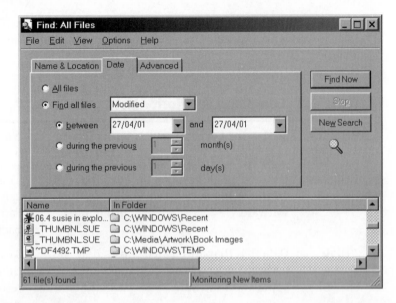

Files or Folders on the Explorer menu bar, and then selecting the tab marked **Date**, we open the window shown in Figure 6.5. You will notice that I have adjusted the settings to search for files modified between 27/04/01 and 27/04/01. In practice, of course, you would set this to today's date. By clicking the **Find Now** button, I discover that 61 files were modified on that date, and in the list, of course, is **_thumbnl.sue**.

By scrolling through this list I can see at a glance both those files that I have created and those which application software and the operating system have modified. Unfortunately, I cannot tell which files should be part of my back-up set without some additional information. If you look again at Figure 6.5, you will see four (of 61) files listed in the bottom pane. The top two, stored in the **C:\WINDOWS\Recent** folder are only shortcuts to files I have been working on, the third one is the actual Susie thumbnail file we have been looking at, while the bottom one is a temporary file which is probably due for deletion. Knowing which files are important and which are not comes partly from experience and from understanding the way in which Windows software operates. We will consider file types in more detail in Chapter 9.

Data Security Strategies

We will finish this chapter by defining the data security strategy which we intend to implement over the next few chapters. Of course, good security practice insists that we will never be certain that our data is safe enough and will always be looking for new security procedures to provide still further protection. The principle aim of our strategy will be to ensure that we can recover all our critical data in the event of a complete hard disk failure. The key word here, of course, is 'critical'. We need to determine from the outset the data that we cannot easily recreate. To simplify the process, we should start by agreeing a priority list to decide which files we need to back up and which files can be left to a software reinstallation. Table 6.3 below shows a suggested list.

Table 6.3 Compiling A Priority List

Priority	Software type	Sample file extensions[1]	Notes
1 Highest	Data files that we have created using application software.	.doc, .txt, .jpg, .gif, .xls, .psd, .html, .mp3	These are the files that we cannot afford to lose. They can only be restored from back-ups.
2 High	Data files that are created invisibly when we use application software.	.pst, .dot, .gid, .bak, .msg	Any important data in these files can only be restored from back-ups, but the files themselves will be recreated (usually almost empty) when we reinstall the application software.
3 Medium	Data files created by a software installation then modified when we run the software.	.ini, .log, .reg, .dat	Losing these files is more of an annoyance than a tragedy since they will be recreated when we reinstall the application software.
4 Low	Application software and its essential components.	.exe, .dll, .hlp, .vxd	These files can be recreated quite simply by reinstalling the original applications or the operating system itself.
5 None	Files that are created by a process such as software installation then never required again.	.log, .tmp	There are surprising numbers of files like this. Since they simply clutter up your hard drive, they can be deleted or destroyed without causing any problems.

[1] The file extensions in the third column are only listed as examples. Depending on how a program operates, a file type might appear under several different priorities. For example, I have included the .html extension in the list of files you might create, but .html could equally well be the extension of a Help file and thus appear in the fourth row.

While this list is not comprehensive, it provides a starting point from which we can develop our data security strategy. The principle aim of this strategy is to secure the data on our computer against accidental or deliberate damage. We should also agree a series of secondary targets, not only aimed at securing data but also ensuring the smooth operation of our computer system itself. This list not only reflects the data security issues we have looked at in this chapter, it also draws on lessons we have learnt in previous chapters. The list might look something like this.

➤ We will take steps to ensure that all our critical data files are identified and regularly backed up to minimize damage in the event of a catastrophe.

➤ We will only install software the origins of which and reliability we can be sure of.

➤ We will only install software that integrates properly into the current version of our operating system.

➤ We will take precautions to make sure that anything we install can be completely removed without damaging the stability of our system.

➤ We will monitor all the processes running on our computer to identify potential problems before they cause breakdowns.

➤ We will undertake routine housekeeping duties to clean out debris and tidy up our system.

Of course, this is just the first of our security strategies. Later in the book we will need to develop others to cope with confidentiality, personal privacy, etc. For now, with a basic strategy agreed, we can take the next step and look at system and application software. We need to find out why programs are often unreliable and unstable, and how rogue software can bring the whole operating system crashing down around our ears.

Chapter 6 – Security Checklist

1 Remember that in addition to the data files that you create, there are other data files created invisibly by your application software. A good back-up strategy requires tracking these down and including the important ones in your back-up set.

2 It is useful to prioritize the importance of your files from critical data which can only be restored from back-ups down to application files that can be restored by reinstalling the original programs.

3 As the first step towards securing your system, draw up a simple data security strategy (or use the one I have provided). This sets targets for your security operations.

The Curse Of Software

In This Chapter

➤ Why software is so fragile

➤ How software operates within the Windows environment

➤ Common software problems

➤ How to deal with software crashes

➤ Emergency brakes – the three-finger salute

➤ Taking control of software operations

➤ Stopping the auto-starters

➤ Housekeeping routines – keeping your system spick and span

Why Software Is So Fragile

Moaning about the unreliability of software has become a feature of modern life. Whenever two computer operators get together, you can almost guarantee that at some point the conversation will turn to how WordPerfect keeps falling over or why Internet Explorer is so unreliable. In most cases, the conclusion reached is that software is not properly tested. Why can't they iron out the bugs before delivering the product to market?

This is a naïve view of the software development process. A major software release from one of the big manufacturers is tested, retested, checked and double-checked. It is then tried out on a wide range of different computer configurations before a pre-market release (a beta version in technospeak) is distributed to a panel of independent testers whose job it is to find as many bugs as possible. Yet even after all this, a new piece of software will still let down a surprising number of users. Almost inevitably, more bugs emerge and are corrected by 'patches' – minor upgrades designed to resolve specific problems in the original code.

The reasons for this lack of reliability are not hard to find. First, it is important to remember that all software is written by fallible human beings, then interpreted by computers with no imagination and no sense of humour. If you and I are following instructions and meet one that is clearly idiotic – I am thinking consumer manuals badly translated from the original Japanese here – we have the common sense to stop and try to work out what is actually intended. Computers can't do this. They just plough on regardless, getting into more and more of a mess until finally collapsing in a heap. With many modern applications running to several million lines of code, it is hardly surprising that programming errors do creep in.

The second thing to remember is that very few programs operate in a vacuum. Instead they are expected to integrate with countless other applications and processes that are running at the same time. They need to work with the operating system which controls their access to hardware and various system operations, and to accept data from a wide variety of different sources. No two computers in the world are exactly the same. Every one is set up slightly differently, is running different programs and makes use of different hardware configurations.

Consider a packet of seeds. Seeds from the same batch are sold to thousands of different gardeners and sown in thousands of different gardens. In some gardens they thrive, in some they struggle to survive, in some they grow then wither, and in some they don't even germinate. Success or failure depends on dozens of different factors including soil fertility, availability of water and the gardener's skill and dedication. Don't blame the seed, blame the environment.

How Software Operates Within The Windows Environment

I hope that in previous chapters I have succeeded in persuading you of the essential virtues of Windows as an operating system. To understand how application software can bring down a mighty OS, we now need to look in more detail at the way in which programs integrate into the Windows environment. Back in Chapter 3, I introduced the concept of the Windows API (Application Programming Interface). You will remember that the API contains a set of functions and resources that programmers can use to create common interface features such as menus, dialog boxes and keyboard commands.

When an application makes correct use of the Windows API, it ensures that users are faced with a familiar set of controls and functions. Most of the Windows API is contained in a few system files called DLLs (Dynamic Link Libraries). There are loads of DLLs scattered around your system and most software installations add even more, but the ones we are concerned with here handle three critical areas.

Most important are the **kernel functions** which manage memory, processes and threads. Then there are **user functions** which look after the user interface and manage operations such as window creation and the display of messages. Finally, there are **GDI (Graphics Device Interface) functions** for drawing graphical images and displaying text.

The Windows API is a very stable environment, provided programmers use it properly. Unfortunately, far too many applications abuse the system, calling up resources they don't really need and hogging them when other programs want to use them. Worse still, when a program closes, it can refuse to hand resources back to the operating system – a system starved of resources will often crash.

 I have mentioned resources several times, so now would be a good time to explain the term. Resources can refer to any facilities available to a computer system, but when programmers talk about resources, they are usually referring to a very specific concept – system resources. System resources are areas of RAM reserved for the Windows User module – the module which deals with window management issues. The User module is responsible for the creation and manipulation of windows, dialog boxes, buttons and other graphical user interface components. These areas are surprisingly small – just 64 Kilobytes, compared to the Megabytes of memory installed.

Common Software Problems

Knowing that applications are fragile and finicky things prepares us for the problems that can arise. Let's begin this section by looking at how the perfect application should behave itself. While this is a hugely simplified explanation, we could say that in an ideal world the following happens.

➤ An application is fired up by double-clicking its executable (**.exe**) file, by double-clicking a shortcut that links to the executable, by selecting a shortcut from a menu or by being invoked by a programming routine from another application.

➤ The application starts up correctly by referring to data in any guide files (**.ini**, **.gid**, etc.) or from entries in the Windows Registry.

111

➤ It negotiates with the operating system for rights to use appropriate hardware devices, such as disk drives, monitors, printer, etc., and for rights to use system resources such as graphical interface components, memory, etc.

➤ The application uses all these devices and resources within the limitations imposed by the operating system, surrendering resources, processing time and access to hardware as the OS demands.

➤ It responds correctly to input, either from the user via hardware such as keyboard and mouse or from other software sources such as programming routines, other applications or internet downloads.

➤ When finally closed, the application also shuts down any opened data or program files and releases all the hardware and software resources it has been using.

Knowing what should happen gives us some insight into what can go wrong. Table 7.1 below uses our perfect world list to explain how applications can misbehave.

Table 7.1 How Applications Can Misbehave

Stage	Problem	Notes
1	Software fails to start up.	If an application refuses to start, the most likely causes are that one or more of its essential files have been corrupted or that it cannot find one or more files that it needs. If this is simply a shortcut that cannot connect with its target, Windows will warn you of this. A few applications are clever enough to reconfigure themselves after a failed start-up and try again using a more basic set-up, but usually you will need to reinstall the application from scratch.
2	Software starts up incorrectly.	This is often caused by missing or corrupted support files or errors in the Windows Registry. If you are lucky, the application will tell you what is wrong and give you the opportunity to fix it, but the chances are that you are heading for a reinstallation.
3	Software cannot access the hardware or system resources it requires.	Problems like these can arise in several different ways. Your system itself might be running short of resources, in which case you can sometimes solve the problem by closing down a few applications. Resources might be tied up because previous applications have failed to release them. Here you will need to restart your computer. You might even have hardware problems.

4	Software abuses the resources it has been allocated.	This is a common cause of programs crashing while they are running. The problems might be caused by any of the situations suggested earlier or they might result in errors in the application's own programming. Try restarting the application. If this doesn't help, try reinstalling the application. If similar problems keep occurring, you might have to abandon the program altogether or try finding an upgrade or later version on the internet.
5	Software fails to respond properly to input.	This could indicate programming errors or hardware problems. Some programs are not configured to handle non-standard input devices such as specialized keyboards and mice, graphics tablets or trackballs.
6	Software fails to shut down properly.	This can be a real pain. If a program simply refuses to close down, the first thing to try is the Windows Close Program dialog box explained below. What can be just as irritating, but almost impossible to spot, is a program which has failed to release the resources it has been using, thus interfering with the running of subsequent applications. If this happens, you will need to reboot to free those locked-up resources.

How do you know when an application is misbehaving? Sometimes, the evidence is unmistakable. Your system will hang – everything on screen will lock up and your mouse and keyboard will not produce any response. Your computer might throw up the famous Blue Screen Of Death (see below) or even reboot unexpectedly. A less serious problem might produce a warning box from the operating system. You might see nothing more than some strange behaviour on your monitor – graphical elements disappearing or becoming corrupt, menus or dialog boxes which refuse to go away. Any combination of these warnings indicate a problem from which an application is unlikely to recover. What can you do? Read on ...

How To Deal With Software Crashes

It doesn't matter how careful you are, sooner or later – and probably sooner – you will suffer a software breakdown. Like most breakdowns, crashes come in different degrees of unpleasantness. At one end of the scale is a simple glitch – a window that refuses to close or an icon that suddenly takes on a strange picture. Such problems often relate to those system resources we discussed earlier or to a momentary conflict between two processes. In many cases it is safe to carry on working or at least to pause for a minute and see if the system recovers by itself. But even these little hang-ups should be viewed as symptoms. They often indicate a more serious problem waiting in the wings.

Peter The Computer Hater

Whatever else you do at this point, don't follow the example of Peter. Peter is a compulsive key puncher. When he encounters a problem, Peter waits for several milliseconds, then starts stabbing buttons. He starts with the Escape key, on the totally erroneous assumption that it will let him escape from the problem. After that he wanders along the function keys from F1 to F12. When this doesn't work. He goes into a frenzy, bashing down combinations of keys and even whole clumps at the same time. *Do ye not likewise*. Remember that unless the system is irretrievably locked up, every key press sends a signal (known as an interrupt) to the operating system. However bad the situation is, it is always possible to make it worse! Patience really is a virtue.

At the top end of course is the fully fledged system hang where everything stops working. This can even result in the famous Blue Screen Of Death (BSOD) which, despite its cheerful suggestion that you might care to wait and see if things improve, really means that you are dead in the water and might as well restart your computer. Between these two extremes are any number of temporary or not so temporary hold-ups.

If you are faced with an application problem, there are only five things that you can do.

➤ You can wait for a few minutes to see if the application or your system recovers and allows you to carry on. To be frank, it probably won't! If it does, consider this as a lucky break – an opportunity to save your work before things get worse.

➤ If you have been presented with a dialog box suggesting how to resolve the problem, try the options offered and see if the problem can be solved.

➤ Shut down the application – either from its own controls or by using the routine described in the following section. Try restarting the program to see if the problem recurs.

➤ If you have system management software such as Norton Utilities® installed, try using its application control routines to bring the rogue program back under orders.

➤ Restart your computer. This returns everything to a clean slate and gives you the opportunity to correct any obvious problems before restarting the application.

Common sense will tell you that an application which continually causes problems should be jettisoned and replaced with a more stable alternative. Fortunately, almost every program has some sort of competitor offering similar facilities.

114

Emergency Brakes – The Three-finger Salute

Built into Windows is a very handy little feature that can solve any number of software problems. It is usually known as the three-finger salute and consists of pressing down the **Control (Ctrl)**, **Alt** and **Delete** keys simultaneously. In the old DOS days, and still on UNIX-based computers, the effect of this was to reboot the system, but Windows has modified this drastic step by using it to open the Close Program dialog box shown in Figure 7.1.

I assume Microsoft's maternal instincts explain why this little beauty is so badly documented. It is, after all, a dangerously powerful tool in the hands of the innocent, but it is also astonishingly useful. In the first place, the box lists all the programs currently running on your system. If you look at the figure, you will probably recognize some of them. **Chapter 07.doc – Microsoft Word** tells you that I am currently writing this chapter in Word. (I have no secrets from you!) You will also notice that **Norton System Doctor** is monitoring my system for me and that I am using **SnagIt** to capture on-screen windows and turn them into illustrations. Some of the programs it lists are more obscure – **Fmempro**, for example, is a memory manager – and some are system processes you might not even know you are running. If you are sitting near your computer, try it now and see what is happening on your own system.

But the real benefit of this little utility is that it allows you to selectively stop programs even if they are hanging. Click on any of the programs listed, then click the **End Task** button. If the program is running normally, it will stop at once (you will lose any unsaved information, by the way). If the program is in trouble, you will see another dialog box telling you that the program is not responding and offering you a choice to

Figure 7.1 Windows Close Program box

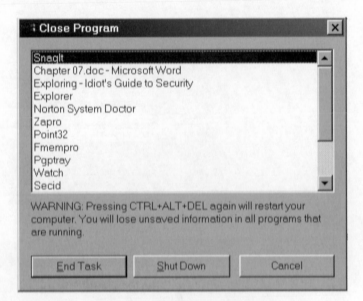

wait and see if it comes back into line or closing it with a bang. Finally, if the whole system has gone sour, you can hit the **Shut Down** key and force your computer to reboot. Note the warning at the bottom of the window. Windows only intercepts the first three-finger salute. Do it a second time and your system will reboot.

The Close Program box also comes in handy if you are suffering from the shortage of system resources described earlier, and as an easy way to check which programs have started without your knowledge. In either case, you will need to know the real name of the program concealed behind the cryptic title shown in the window. One way of doing this is to enter the listed title into Windows' Find utility to track down where it is starting from. Look back at Figure 7.1 and you will see the entry **Zapro**. If I now start the Find utility either from the Start menu or from within Windows Explorer and enter **Zapro** into the **Named** input box, I get the result shown in Figure 7.2.

This tells me that **Zapro** is part of the ZoneAlarm firewall program. Knowing this, I can decide whether to close it or leave it running. (You will also notice that the computer I am working on is called NIGHTMARE. This seems much more appropriate than Microsoft's default name of My Computer!)

You can check all unknown programs like this and free up system resources by shutting down the unnecessary ones. Some of them should be left alone – closing **Systray**, for example, will remove the display of icons from the bottom left of your Task Bar, but none of them are crucial to the running of your computer. The worst that can happen is that you will need to restart your system and that usually solves all ills anyway!

Figure 7.2 Using Windows' Find utility to track down files

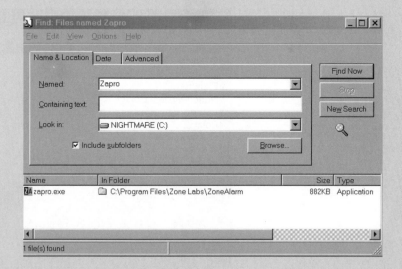

Taking Control Of Software Operations

You will remember that at the start of this book you took a mighty oath to regain control of your own computer? Part of this objective is deciding for yourself which programs are going to load when your computer starts. Some software manufacturers are particularly naughty when it comes to this. They think they have the right to load their own stuff when you boot, and then let it take all sorts of decisions for you. Aside from the ethical question of whether or not they have the moral right to do this, there are three particular dangers here. First, we have already noted that software can be full of bugs and there is no reason to assume that programs which auto-load are free from them! It is also quite possible for two programs that load at start-up to have a serious falling-out and take the rest of your system down with them.

The second danger is potentially much worse. By allowing programs to auto-load, you are effectively granting them free run of your system. Who knows what they are up to? At least when you open a word processor, you can be fairly certain that its purpose is to process words, but ask yourself why an auto-load program needs to sit in memory when you haven't called it. What is it really doing and is it doing it in your best

You may think that I am being excessively paranoid here, but I'm afraid the evidence is against you. Let's take just one example (and by no means the worst one) of what we might call compulsory software and see how it works. I first came across Gator some years ago when it arrived tacked onto a program I bought. Gator purports to be a useful internet utility which sits in your system tray and allows you to enter information into internet forms at the click of a mouse. Of course, before you can use it like that, you are obliged to enter all sorts of information into Gator itself – information like your name and address, phone number, e-mail address and so on – information which, you might think, would be very interesting to a company who wanted to sell things to you!

Here is what actually happens. When you run the Gator installer, it creates entries for itself in the Windows Registry and installs seven executable files including **GatorUninstaller.exe.** So far this is pretty normal, but now it gets strange. Gator runs as a hidden process, not visible to the Windows Task Manager. It has no user interface so you cannot control it. Every time you start your computer, it tries to make an internet connection, and even if you stop it, it remains resident in memory and tries again the next time you boot. Stranger still, the uninstaller mentioned above does absolutely nothing. Run it and no files or registry entries are actually removed from your machine. To sum up, Gator loads every time you boot, does things without your permission and refuses to go away when you tell it to. And Gator is one of the most harmless of these compulsory programs! (What it is actually doing is not relevant here. Wait until Chapter 19 and all will be revealed.)

interests? Finally, remember that everything that starts up is eating away at those precious system resources and slowing down your system for the tasks you actually want it to perform.

Even when they are entirely benevolent, it is still a mistake to allow programs to load just because they want to. I have seen computers where the system tray contains 20 or more icons to indicate 20 or more processes loaded and running. System resources can be reduced to nothing before a single genuine application has even been started! So what can we do to take control here? Fortunately, quite a lot!

Programs can auto-start in a number of ways. These are the three key ones.

➤ They can be started from within system files such as **win.ini** and **system.ini** which are read as part of the Windows start-up process.

➤ They can be started from the Windows Registry.

➤ They can be started from a shortcut in the **StartUp** folder of the Start menu.

We need to look at each of these individually.

Win.ini and **system.ini** are throwbacks to older incarnations of Windows and are due to disappear in future distributions. They are actually text files which can be modified with a simple text editor such as Notepad. Here is part of the **win.ini** file from a computer running Windows 98:

> **[windows]**
>
> **load=**
>
> **run=C:\WINDOWS\SYSTEM\cmmpu.exe**
>
> **NullPort=None**
>
> **device=EPSON EPL-5700L Advanced,EPTMAA1E,\\CABINET\EPSON**
>
> **[Desktop]**
>
> **Wallpaper=(None)**
>
> **TileWallpaper=0**
>
> **WallpaperStyle=0**

Note the lines near the top which begin **load=** and **run=**. These show how programs are started. In this example, the program **cmmpu.exe** is loaded during the start-up.

1 Before you start messing around with system start-up files such as **win.ini** and **system.ini**, always make sure you have a current back-up of the unmodified file. Right-click the file in question, click **copy** then click **paste** in a safe folder. I would suggest renaming the files to, say, **win.saf** and **system.saf**, so you don't forget what they contain.

2 We are going to use Notepad quite a lot from here on in to look at and modify the contents of files. It will save you a lot of time if you add a shortcut to Notepad to the context menu which appears when you right-click a file. If you open Explorer and look in the Windows folder, you will find a sub-folder called **SendTo**. You will find **Notepad.exe** in the Windows folder. Click and drag it to the **SendTo** folder. This will create a shortcut to Notepad – it won't move the file itself. In future, when you right-click a file, glide down to the **Send To** entry on the menu which opens, and you will see Notepad waiting for you.

Programs can be loaded from the Windows Registry in several different ways, but we are mainly concerned with four methods.

➤ **AutoRun Programs** will start programs whenever Windows is fired up.

➤ **AutoRun Programs (Current User)** will start programs when a particular user is logged on.

➤ **AutoRun Services** will start services (system programs as opposed to applications) whenever Windows is fired up.

➤ **AutoRun Services (Current User)** … yes, you've guessed it!

Finally, the **StartUp** folder sits in your Windows folder and contains shortcuts to programs that will fire up immediately after Windows has finished loading but before you can do anything else.

If you look in all of these places, you will probably find a fair few auto-start programs. It would not be a good idea to stop them all since some of them are essential for your system to operate properly and others are running to provide you with active protection. Before we do anything about them, we need to know which are the goodies and which are just wasting space. Table 7.2 overleaf will help you to identify which auto-start programs are worth preserving.

To take control of what starts on our system, we will need to:

➤ find out the names of every program which auto-starts;

➤ investigate each one and discover what it is doing;

➤ prevent those we don't want from starting – this is not always as easy as it should be!

119

Table 7.2 Essential/Non-essential Auto-start Programs

Auto-start group	Program types	Examples	Notes and hints
1 System essentials	User core components, system libraries, hardware drivers, etc.	user.exe comctl32.dll scanregw.exe	Usually located in the Windows folder or the system folder. These are crucial, so leave them well alone.
2 System utilities	Power management utilities, printer environment checkers, task managers, etc.	systray.exe e_srcv03.exe	Usually located in the Windows folder or the system folder, but might also be third-party utilities. These are useful enough to leave alone unless they are causing trouble or you are running short of resources.
3 Essential active protection	Resident anti-virus programs, firewalls, anti-Trojan programs, etc.	zapro.exe nod32.exe lockdown.exe	The name will usually tell you what these are. Unless they have come pre-installed on your machine, you will probably remember installing them. Since these are essential to your security, don't touch them.
4 Useful but not essential	Software monitors, system checkers, internet management utilities, etc.	winpatrol.exe washer.exe fmempro.exe cgmain.exe	A lot of auto-start programs are useful but not essential. Remember that you can always start these in the normal way if you need them.
5 Waste of resources	Music file players, CD writing software, time checkers, back-up utilities, etc.	directcd.exe winamp.exe secondcopy.exe	Why these programs auto-start is a mystery. In some cases they can save you a couple of clicks, but in most cases, they are better off started as and when you actually need them.
6 Unwelcome	Spying and snooping programs.	gator.exe tsadbot.exe	Kill, kill, kill!

Stopping The Auto-starters

Tracking down, investigating and stopping these programs might sound a daunting task, but there are several utilities that will do the job for us. One of them is built into Windows 98 and subsequent distributions, the **msconfig.exe** program. Click on **Start > Run**, then type **msconfig** into the text box and click **OK**. The window that opens will look like Figure 7.3.

The system configuration utility is a very handy little application which gives you a lot of control over what loads during boot and Windows start-up. As you can see, there are six sections to the utility accessible through the tabs along the top. The general tab allows you to decide which of the start-up groups are loaded from, while the remaining five tabs allow you to edit the groups themselves.

Figure 7.3 The system configuration utility

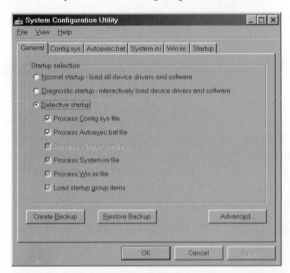

The first two tabs, **Config.sys** and **Autoexec.bat**, will contain very little on a modern Windows-based computer. Like the **System.ini** and **Win.ini** files discussed earlier, they are little more than left-overs from an earlier age of computing and exist mainly to permit backwards compatibility. Despite this, you should check through all four tabs looking for anything that is loaded or run during boot (remember **load=** or **run=**). **Autoexec.bat** is a batch file (thus the name) – a text file containing a series of commands to the operating system. A program can be started from within a batch file, so look out for anything ending in **.exe**, **.com** or **.bat**.

The **Startup** tab is where you will find most of our targets. Click this and a window like Figure 7.4 will open.

All programs which have ever attempted to auto-start get listed in this window. Those with a tick in the check-box are allowed to do so. As you can see, in most cases the box shows the full path to the program which means you can tell at a glance where

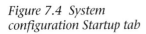

Figure 7.4 System configuration Startup tab

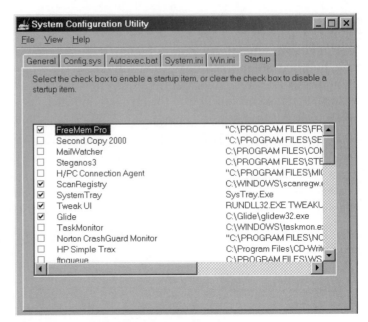

the program comes from. Take a look at the programs listed in Figure 7.4 and note how many have had their auto-start capability chopped off. MailWatcher, for example, is a useful utility for spotting unpleasant attachments to e-mails, but why should you run it when you are not using your e-mail program? HP Simple Trax thinks it will help by providing a continuous facility to back up files. Thanks HP, but I'll decide when I want to make back-ups and how I'll do it.

There are many other third-party utilities which do the same job as Windows' System Configuration Utility. Some provide better control and more information. Unless you have money to burn, I wouldn't recommend buying a program specifically to do this job, but there are several programs which offer it as an additional feature. One of them we have already met in Chapter 3, X-Setup. I have already sung X-Setup's praises, so I won't repeat the chorus here. If you start X-Setup and drill down to **System > Startup > AutoRun**, you will see something like Figure 7.5. Here you will note that the programs are divided into the groups I listed earlier. It is useful to know which programs apply to all users and which to a particular user.

Whichever utility you use, you are now in a position to make a list of all the programs which auto-start. I suggest good old pencil and paper and make sure that wherever possible, you note down the full path to the program. This is an important clue when we come to investigate what each one does.

Figure 7.5 Xteq Systems
X-Setup AutoRun options

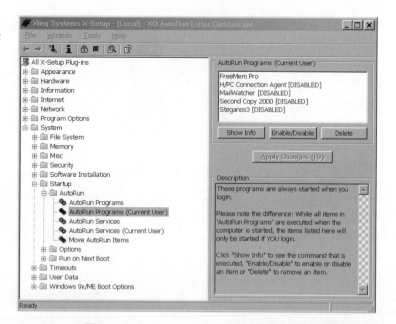

Note that both of the utilities discussed above only check the auto-start situation for the current user. If your system is configured for multiple users, you will need to repeat the process after logging in as each of the registered users. If you have teenage children, this might prove a harrowing experience!

Michael The Concerned Parent

Michael is lucky I remembered this! Although he keeps his own desktop spotless, his kids have their own usernames and passwords and it was only after he checked their work spaces – with their permission, of course – that he discovered all the unnecessary rubbish that was loading each time they logged on. Younger users are notorious for downloading all sorts of fun things from the internet. Some of these might well include unwanted auto-starters. Parents beware!

Armed with this list, we can set about tracking down the auto-intruders and removing their privileges. If you do not have the full path for each program – in other words, if you don't know where they are starting from – you will have to use the Find utility as described in the Tricks of the Trade box earlier in this chapter. The third bit of information we need is who created the program. Unless you are sure of the source,

123

Figure 7.6 An .exe file's properties window

find each program in Windows Explorer, right-click it and select **Properties**. You will see a window looking like Figure 7.6. This window relates to the utility **Fmempro.exe**, which also appears in earlier figures. By clicking on the **Version** tab, then clicking **Company Name**, I discover that the program was issued by Meikel.com. Since I know who they are and remember buying software from them, I can assume the utility is genuine, but do I really want it to auto-start?

Eventually, you should end up with a detailed list showing name, path and source of all your auto-start programs. Grab your pencil and proceed as follows.

➤ Cross out any programs which are starting from the Windows or the System folder and which are distributed by Microsoft. (Note that I am not saying that all Microsoft programs should run unquestioned – only those you don't recognize. It is safest to assume that these are essential system files.)

➤ Cross out any programs which you know are part of your personal or network defence system. By this I mean your virus checker, your firewall, etc.

➤ Cross out any programs that you want to auto-start. Far be it from me to interfere in the way you run your computer. But do remember my comments earlier in the chapter about soaking up system resources. For each item you cross out here, you should ask yourself: do I really need this running all the time or is it easier to start it when I want it?

Now what's left? If nothing, congratulate yourself on having preserved a nice clean computer, but if there are still entries in your list it is time to get serious. Fire up **msconfig** again and prepare to kill a few unnecessary processes. Find each of the remaining entries on your list under the relevant tab – **Config.sys, Autoexec.bat, System.ini, Win.ini** and **Startup**. Against each is a check-box. In most cases, unchecking the box will ensure that the process will not start automatically, although there are some programs which will simply create a new **Startup** entry in the list. You might find these as shortcuts in your Windows **Startup** folder, so knock them out of there as well. Once you have finished modifying the entries in **msconfig**, close the utility and restart your computer. Now you can check once more to see that all is as you intended it to be.

Housekeeping Routines – Keeping Your System Spick And Span

The final section of this chapter is concerned with computer maintenance. Left unattended, your system will slowly clog up with unwanted files and other debris. To keep your work space tidy and your computer in peak condition, it is a good idea to establish a regular housekeeping routine. Here is my suggested list of chores. I propose that once a week you …

➤ … clean out any temporary files that applications have failed to remove. Many programs create some sort of temporary files while they are working. These are often stored in your default temporary folder, usually **C:\Windows\Temp**. With all your applications closed down, you can safely delete any files left in there. Some applications are less co-operative and create temporary files elsewhere. Use the Find utility as described earlier in the chapter to track down any files with a **.tmp** or .bak extension and delete them. (Note that some applications use other file extensions for temporary files. You will have to find these for yourself!)

➤ … empty your Recycle Bin. When you delete a file, it is not actually removed from your hard disk. Instead the first letter of the file name is changed to mark it as deleted and the space it occupies on your drive is reserved to the Recycle Bin. This means that if you subsequently realize that you need the file, it can easily be recovered. If you don't regularly delete files, your Recycle Bin folder can rapidly swell to a surprising size. The bin can be emptied by right-clicking on its desktop icon and selecting **Empty Recycle Bin** from the menu. Before doing so, do check to make sure that there is nothing in the bin worth saving.

➤ … error check your drive(s). In Windows Explorer, right-click on each drive letter, then select **Properties** from the menu that appears. Click on the **Tools** tab and a window like Figure 7.7 will open. From here you can check your drive for errors using the **Check Now** button which will fire up ScanDisk®. You can also use this box to defragment your drive. This means reorganizing the way in which your files are stored so that all their pieces are placed next to each other – contiguous, you might recall. You might not need to do this every week. Once a month might be often enough. (See the box overleaf.)

125

Figure 7.7 Windows drive Properties box, Tools tab

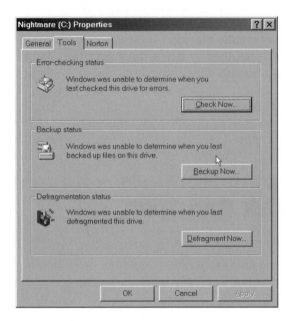

Many people have problems running the Windows defragmenter, and sometimes the error-checker as well. This is because both of these utilities need to run without interruptions. Depending on how your system is configured, you might be running processes which continually write to the hard disk. This can upset the defrag procedure and cause it to start again. If you suffer from this problem, there are two things to try. First, use the Windows Close Program utility we looked at above to stop all the processes running on your computer. (Don't close Explorer or your computer will shut down.) If this doesn't work, reboot your computer in Safe Mode and try again. In Safe Mode, the defragmenter will run very slowly, so it might be a good idea to start it before you go to bed and hope that it is finished before you need your computer again.

➤ ... tidy up your work space to remove any unnecessary icons, shortcuts or files that are no longer required. (Note that I have listed this entry after the '... empty your Recycle Bin' one. Now you have a week to make sure that you haven't tidied up anything you shouldn't have!) Clean up any desktop clutter by sweeping unwanted objects into a special desktop folder – mine is called *The Old Man's Bag*. You might also tidy up your Start menu by sorting all the shortcuts into application categories. Create folders on your Start menu called things like **Graphics, Text, Internet**, etc. and use these to store the relevant shortcuts. There is no point in having a Start menu that is six feet long.

➤ … if you have installed any system management software such as Norton Utilities, run the system checker it provides to clean up your Registry and system files.

The Norton Utilities is a sizable suite of software, best bought boxed from your computer store. To see what it is capable of, check out Norton's website at www.symantec.com Of course there are other system management applications, but Norton's has consistently proved to be the most efficient. If you want to take a look at the alternatives, take a trip to one of the major software archives on the internet (www.davecentral.com or download.cnet.com are excellent) and see what they have to offer.

Now, with your system clean and tidy, and operating as you want it to, we can turn our attention to that source of untold misery – installing new software.

Chapter 7 – Security Checklist

1   Be prepared for software breakdowns. Know the signs and watch out for them. If your applications crash, you can try restarting them or even restarting your system, but be prepared to get rid of applications that constantly misbehave. You should have no difficulty in tracking down replacements.

2   When obvious steps fail to work, rogue programs can often be halted from the Close Program box, generated by pressing down the **Control (Ctrl), Alt** and **Delete** keys simultaneously. The resulting window will show you all the processes running on your computer and give you the opportunity to shut each one down individually.

3   Watch out for programs which load at start-up without your permission. They can use up vital system resources and you cannot be certain they are operating in your best interests. You need to monitor every process which auto-loads and remove those which are not contributing to your needs.

4   Before you make any changes to your system's start-up files, take the precaution of saving back-ups of the originals to a secure location. In addition to saving a copy of the Windows Registry as discussed earlier, you should also save **Autoexec.bat, Config.sys, System.ini** and **Win.ini** by copying and renaming them.

5   It is worth keeping your work space tidy, cleaning out your hard drive(s) and running an error checker on a weekly basis. To do this, follow the steps in the list above. Housekeeping not only makes it easier to find the files you need, it also frees up space on your hard disk and keeps your computer running sweetly.

In With The New And Out With The Old

In This Chapter

➤ Loading up trouble for yourself

➤ How new software installs onto your computer

➤ The hazards of installing new software

➤ How to install new software safely

➤ How to remove rogue software completely

Loading Up Trouble For Yourself

We live in a world where software practically grows on trees. Wherever we look, there are new plums just waiting to be plucked. Every computer magazine has its cover-mounted CD-ROM stuffed with irresistible offerings you can hardly wait to try for yourself. The internet bustles with download sites promising applications you just can't live without. Then there are friends and colleagues at work, all urging you to try out golden utilities that have done wonders for their computing experience. It's all so hard to resist.

Admit it, you are expecting me to tell you to resist it, but you are wrong. New software is the very lifeblood of computing. Unless computing is to be nothing more than a chore, you need the excitement of tracking down new applications and trying them out to see if they add convenience and interest to your experience. Computing, whether at home or at work, should be fun!

By now you are probably wondering why I have called this section 'storing up trouble for yourself'. The reason is simple. It's not installing and testing new software that's the problem. For most people, it's the way that they do it. As we noted in Chapter 7, all software is prone to bugs, but none more so than some of the amateur efforts that make it onto magazine cover disks and into internet download sites. I have nothing but admiration for the small firms that develop programs to fill the cracks left by the major manufacturers, but the simple fact is that they cannot afford the extensive testing supported by the big boys. Their debugging procedures are less rigorous and inevitably their output is more likely to be flawed.

There is a huge number of download sites on the internet. Some of the very best are www.davecentral.com, download.cnet.com, www.tucows.com and www.webattack.com You can find plenty of others through a search engine. While most download sites feature some kind of ratings system, it is important to remember that none of them can guarantee the software they are supplying. Some products might be bug-infested, others might have unfortunate effects on your system, still others might conceal the kind of parasite programs we will be looking at in Chapter 19.

Very few software applications operate in splendid isolation. They have to co-operate with other running processes and make proper use of the operating system to manage hardware resources. Errors on a computer tend to be cumulative. If one bug disrupts its operation – even slightly – the whole edifice is weakened for subsequent bugs and eventually everything comes crashing down.

How New Software Installs Onto Your Computer

Most software companies make use of ready-made installers. They buy a licence which allows them to bolt a proprietary installer onto their programs. The installer then takes over the actual installation of the new software. The best-known installers are probably InstallShield and Wise Solutions, both of which have established excellent reputations for reliability, but all installers operate in a similar way. Fire one up and you are usually greeted with a screen like the one shown in Figure 8.1. Installers are customized by the software manufacturer according to the jobs that are required. They come with their own libraries of options so the licensee can pick and choose the ones that suit the software to be installed. Usually, the installation follows the sequence shown in the list, right, but this can vary and may not require all of these steps.

*Figure 8.1 The Wise
Installation System
wizard, from Wise
Solutions, in action*

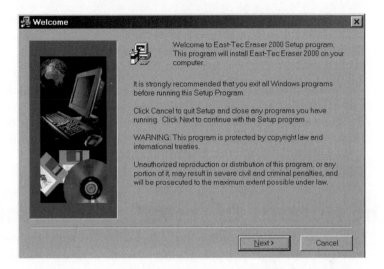

- ➤ The user is greeted, told what he is about to install and offered the option to cancel the installation.

- ➤ The user is shown the licence agreement for the software to which he must agree by clicking a confirmation button before the installation can proceed.

- ➤ The user is asked whether he prefers a predefined installation, a minimal installation or a custom installation in which he can pick the components he requires.

- ➤ The installer checks for previous installations or installed components which might affect the new installation.

- ➤ The installer checks if all the required support components (DLLs, etc.) are available on the system. If not, it can install them, advise the user where to get them or offer to get them for him. (The latter would usually require a live connection to the internet.)

- ➤ The user is asked to confirm where he would like the program installed, either by accepting the default folder – usually **C:/Program Files/Whatever**, or specifying another folder.

- ➤ The installer compiles an installation set which defines which files are to be installed, and where they are to go.

- ➤ The user is asked to confirm the installation set and verify the decisions he has already made. (A good installation routine will usually offer him the option at this point to go back and make changes.)

- ➤ The installer unarchives (decompresses) the required files and installs them on the hard drive. Most files will be placed in the program's own folder, but others may go to the Windows System folder or elsewhere on the disk.

➤ The installer creates Registry entries for the new software and creates shortcuts on the Start menu. (Sometimes the user is asked whether he wants shortcuts placed on the desktop or in his system tray.)

➤ If the new software requires (or wants) to load processes at start-up, the user is prompted to remove any disks from his drives and restart the computer.

As you can see, installation can be a hefty process, although not all installers are this complex. The end result, as far as the user is concerned, should be a new program and support files correctly installed on his computer, accessible from the Start menu and possibly the desktop and system tray.

The Hazards Of Installing New Software

It must be said that most new software installs correctly and causes a minimum of grief. But there can be problems, and most of them come from shared resources. As we noted in Chapter 7, Windows is structured so that programmers can make use of existing system files to interact with other applications, the operating system and system hardware. This is a sensible approach, since it means that programmers do not need to reinvent the wheel and that the size of new installations can be kept down. Imagine the nonsense, for example, of every new program including a different routine to write to a printer. As we have seen, most of these shared routines are stored as DLL (Dynamic Link Library) files, which are made accessible by the operating system.

Like most components of the operating system, DLLs are occasionally upgraded with improved versions, so if you move up to a new version of Windows or use the internet-based **Windows Update**, your old DLLs might well be overwritten with later ones. Windows attempts to protect some of your key system files by giving them read-only attributes (see the box below) but because most DLLs must be available to third-party software, they cannot all be protected like this. A bad installer can overwrite your up-to-date files with older versions, and although Windows tries to prevent this, it is not always successful. Older DLLs might not provide the same functionality as their successors and this can lead to problems when other software tries to make use of them.

Attributes can be defined as system information that a file stores about itself. There are four attributes that can be applied to Windows files: the **Archive** attribute which indicates whether the file has been modified, the **Read-only** attribute which prevents a file from being changed, the **Hidden** attribute which conceals the file in Windows Explorer and the **System** attribute which declares a file to be essential to the operating system and prevents it from being altered. As we shall see later in the book, attributes can be changed or removed entirely.

Figure 8.2 A typical uninstall window

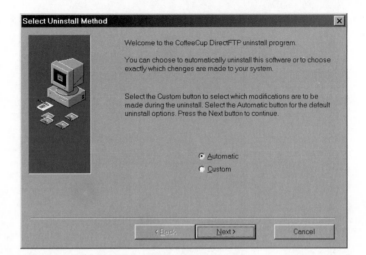

Installing new software can occasionally cause conflicts for other reasons. Badly implemented installation routines can crash the operating system or create problems for previously installed applications. If you find you have installed something which is causing more trouble than it is worth, the obvious answer is to uninstall it, but this doesn't always solve the problem.

Many applications include an uninstaller as part of the suite – one of these is shown in Figure 8.2 – but the approved method for getting rid of a troublesome program is to use the **Add/Remove Programs** utility available in the Windows Control Panel. (**Start > Settings > Control Panel > Add/Remove Programs.**) Opening this will produce a window looking like Figure 8.3. I have never known anyone to use the **Install** button near the top of the Window, but the bottom pane lists all the software currently installed on your computer. Click on an item and the **Add/Remove** button becomes live. Clicking it opens the program's uninstall window. Different programs have different uninstall routines, but in general they follow the same basic procedure, deleting the application, its support files, its shortcuts and any entries in the Windows Registry. From the uninstall window that opens it is simply a matter of following the instructions to remove the software – or at least it should be!

Several factors interfere with a clean uninstall. The first, and most devilish, is when the programmer intentionally designs the software not to uninstall properly. We saw one example of this in Chapter 7. Gator is deliberately designed NOT to uninstall, but to remain on the system despite your wishes. Less offensive than this are those programs which are designed to leave one or more residual files on your computer so that if you reinstall the software or even a later version, your earlier installation can be recognized.[1]

[1] This is not always done with evil motives. Some shareware, for example, is written to allow you to try it for a limited period after which it stops working. An old, and rather dishonest, trick was to then reinstall it and get another free trial period. A residual file can spot this and prevent the software from working for a second time. I've said it before and I'll say it again – play fair with shareware. Try it for the suggested time, then buy it or uninstall it.

Figure 8.3 Add/remove programs

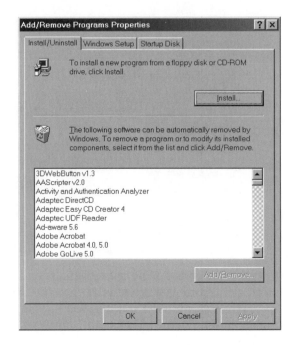

Gordon The Young Professional

Our bad example here is Gordon. Combined with his fascination with new technology is an irresistible urge to try out every new piece of software he comes across. Gordon is convinced that somewhere out there is a program to cure all ills. He has only just got the hang of one business program, when he finds another one which promises even more functions. On to his hard disk it goes and damn the consequences. His Start menu is bursting with shortcuts to programs he hasn't used in months.

If your Start menu currently scrolls off the monitor, you are probably suffering from Gordon syndrome. My advice: find an application which answers your needs and stick with it. If your needs change, find another and uninstall the old one.

Files which are currently in use by the operating system or by another application cannot be uninstalled while these are running. Usually, such files are marked for deletion when your computer is restarted, but with shutdowns and start-ups being such delicate times, this can sometimes go wrong. Uninstallers are also very bad at deleting folders and shortcuts. These can often remain until you spot them and delete them manually.

134

How To Install New Software Safely

The first and most important rule when installing software is to only install one program at a time and test it thoroughly before installing something else. The temptation, when you get a new magazine-cover-disk full of interesting applications, is to load them all up at once. If you do this, and one of the programs causes problems, it will be almost impossible to tell which one is the culprit. Practise patience and it will repay you.

It is also worth checking that the software you want to install is compatible with the version of Windows you are running. These days this isn't much of a problem since Windows makes great efforts to accommodate older software, but the change from 32-bit code to 64-bit code is underway and will render a lot of current programs obsolete. It is also worth temporarily disabling any anti-virus software you are running. Although most virus scanners are intelligent enough to recognize and not interfere with a new installation, they can sometimes interrupt the process. Some installations modify existing files and this is usually what a virus scanner is programmed to watch for. Be safe and switch them off.

Before proceeding with the installation, it is worth taking a moment to think about what you are about to do. At present, I assume, you have a working system. You are about to make changes which might, in the worst case, stop your system from working. Ideally, what you need to do is to take a snapshot of your system as it stands before the installation. If things go sour on you, you can roll back all the changes so things are exactly as they were. It is possible to do this manually. Since the installer will not tell you what it is about to do, this means copying all your critical files – effectively most of the operating system – to a secure location so that if the worst comes to the worst, you can copy them all back again. You will also need to take a copy of the system Registry, which almost all installers will change to some extent, ready to copy that back as well.

As you might imagine, this would be a massive undertaking and 99 times out of 100 would also be a complete waste of time. A quick fix is to back up your entire **Windows** folder, but this is not always practical. The Windows folder and all its sub-folders can be very large and even a compressed back-up will take up a lot of space. Of course, some bright programmers have got there before you and there are several excellent uninstallers on the market. Of those available, one is so good that Microsoft have licensed part of its code and incorporated it into Windows itself. I can recommend CyberMedia's UnInstaller® without hesitation. Install it and it will drop a little utility called the CyberMedia Agent into your system tray which monitors any attempt to install new software. When an installer starts working, up will pop the little box shown in Figure 8.4, asking if you wish to monitor the installation.

*Figure 8.4 The
CyberMedia Agent
Copyright 2002 Networks
Associates Technology,
Inc. All rights reserved.
Used with permission.
CyberMedia® and
Uninstaller® are
registered trademarks of
Networks Associates
Technology, Inc.*

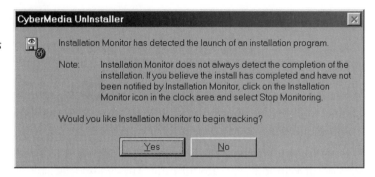

CyberMedia UnInstaller is available from www.McAfee.com The package includes much more than just the installer we have looked at. It also offers useful features like a hard disk clean-up utility, an archiver and a program for moving software from place to place so that the operating system does not lose track of its location. Alternatives include Add/Remove Plus from www.aurelitec.com For other uninstaller software, try one of the major download sites.

Of course, you say yes, and the UnInstaller holds up the installer for a few moments while it carries out all those tasks described above. Once it has completed taking a snapshot of all your system files and settings, the installer is released and the software is loaded onto your computer. When the installer has finished, up pops the UnInstaller once more to take a note of all the changes that have been made. It then asks you to name the 'backtrack' archive it has created. If you subsequently decide to remove the program, you can select the relevant backtrack archive and the UnInstaller will return your computer to exactly how it was before the installation. Simple and foolproof.

Most uninstallers operate in a similar way, but they do have their limitations. Although they can store archives from dozens of installations, realistically they can only roll back the machine to the state it was in before the most recent one. Not surprisingly, they cannot cope with changes to changes to changes. Once again, the sensible rule here is to install one application and test it thoroughly before installing something else. A second limitation is that by using the new software you have installed, you might well further alter system files and settings and, of course, these changes are not recorded in the roll back archives. Despite these drawbacks, I recommend using an uninstaller every time you install new software.

If you choose not to, there are certain steps you should take before installing a new program. One option, as mentioned earlier, is to back up your entire Windows folder. If this isn't practical, first, you should back up your Registry. As you know, the Registry is the core of the operating system and its continuing good health is vital.

136

Figure 8.5 Windows
Registry Editor

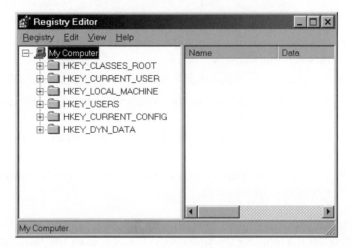

Click **Start** > **Run** > **Regedit**, and a window like Figure 8.5 will open. Click **Registry** > **Export Registry File** and save a copy in a secure location. Second, you should save good copies of those Windows start-up files which might be modified by an installation. These, you will remember from before, are **win.ini** and **system.ini**, which you will find in your **Windows** folder, and **autoexec.bat** and **config.sys** which you will find in your root folder (usually *C:*). Third, it is worth preparing for a complete catastrophe such as your entire system going to hell, by making sure that all your critical data files are securely backed up. (We look at this in detail in Chapter 9, so it might be worth reading this before proceeding.)

When you perform the installation itself, do not hurry it. If you are offered options, think carefully about the choices before deciding on one. If one of those options is a 'custom' installation, always select this. While you will not be able to influence the core software components, you can at least control which additional components are installed. Always remember that you might have to uninstall, if the software proves flawed or useless for your purpose.

How To Remove Rogue Software Completely

The final section of this chapter looks at removing software. As we noted above, the best method of removing unwanted programs and rolling your system back to its previous state is to use an uninstaller. The second best option is to use the **Add/Remove Programs** function from the Windows Control Panel. The third best choice it to use the uninstall program provided with the application itself, although not all software offers this. If there is an uninstaller, you will find it in the application's folder and it will usually be called **uninstall.exe** or, if the program has made use of the Wise installer, **unwise.exe**. Only as a last resort should you consider simply deleting the folder with the program in it.

137

To remove all traces of a program from your system requires the following steps.

➤ Removing the program and its support files and the application's own folder and sub-folders.

➤ Removing any support files the program's installer has dropped in other places.

➤ Removing any entries in the Windows Registry or Windows system files that refer to the application.

➤ Removing any shortcuts or entries in the Start menu that point to the application.

➤ Undoing any other changes that the application has made to your system's configuration.

While a good uninstaller will handle all five steps, the other techniques listed will often fail to complete the process. At the very least they will leave the application's folder containing a few stray files on your hard drive along with orphaned shortcuts and even odd Registry entries. While none of this debris is likely to actually harm your system, it bloats your Registry – a lean, mean system is always the most efficient.

Decision time! If you decide to remove an application, you have two choices. The first is to employ the **Add/Remove Programs** function from the Windows Control Panel and leave it at that. This is undoubtedly the safest option, but, over the course of time, your system will become cluttered up with orphaned files and Registry entries. Your second choice is to clean up manually after the uninstall routine has done its job. This will involve manually deleting some files and folders, which is not a problem, and then editing the Windows Registry – not a job for the faint-hearted! Remember that the Registry is the core of your operating system and if you damage it, this will have serious repercussions.

So, let's assume you are going to take the bull by the horns and do a comprehensive uninstallation. First you will follow the standard procedure and use the **Add/Remove Programs** function. Then you will open Windows Explorer and manually delete the dead application's folder and any sub-folders it contains. Next you will search through your Start menu and on your desktop for any relevant shortcuts and delete these as well. Should you now go ahead and face the awesome task of digging through the Windows Registry? Well, before you go any further, you should be aware of what you are facing.

The Windows Registry is a textual representation of an enormous range of configuration settings for all the software installed on your computer. These settings are organized into various groups which probably make sense to hard core programmers, but not to the rest of us. The language used to describe the settings is equally impenetrable. Let me give you an example.

Assume that I wish to uninstall an application I use called SnagIt manufactured by the

TechSmith Corporation. I can fire up my Registry Editor as before by clicking **Start > Run > Regedit**, and after making that vital back-up of the Registry,[2] I can use the editor's Find function (**Edit > Find**) and search the Registry for 'SnagIt'. By continuing the search after each entry is found (using the **F3** Function key) I end up with a total of 35 entries. Here is just one of them.

HKEY_CURRENT_USER\Software\TechSmith\SnagIt Name=(Default) Data=(value not set)

Should I simply delete each of these entries (or 'keys' as they are called)? The answer has to be no, because I do not know exactly what each of these entries actually does. I am not a Windows programmer, and I am sure you're not either. My advice is to leave the Registry alone unless you know exactly what you are doing.

Just for the record, the one entry that I know I can safely remove is the key that relates to the uninstall function. I can find this by working down the folder hierarchy in the left-hand pane as follows: HKEY_LOCAL_MACHINE > SOFTWARE > MICROSOFT > WINDOWS > CURRENT VERSION > UNINSTALL. Here I will find a list of programs that can be uninstalled. I can see an entry for TechSmith which I can right-click and safely delete. But all I have done is deleted a few of the 35 entries and saved a tiny amount of space. Is this really worth the bother?

And that's quite enough about software operations for the time being. In Chapter 9, we will be looking at one of the most critical areas of computer security – backing up your data.

Chapter 8 – Security Checklist

1   If you are installing new software from any source, do not assume that it is free from bugs. While the major manufacturers can afford extensive pre-release testing, smaller companies and individual programmers cannot. Remember that badly written programs will not only crash and burn, they can also damage your operating system.

2   Sometimes an installation routine will try to overwrite existing system files with older versions. These might not offer the same functionality and can cause other applications to crash. Normally Windows will spot an attempt to do this and warn you. In most cases, the safest option is to keep the later versions. If this means that the application you are installing will not run – this does happen occasionally – you are probably better off without it!

---

[2] Never, never, never, never skip this step!

3   If you decide to install trial applications, make sure you only add one at a time. The best option is to install a program, then thoroughly test it for several days before deciding whether or not to keep it. Only after you have approved it or rejected and removed it from your system, should you install another application.

4   Before installing any new software, it is sensible to back up your system files. Better still, you might back up your **Windows** folder (including all its sub-folders), but this can take up a lot of space on your drive. An excellent solution is to invest in a software uninstaller which will take a snapshot of your system before and after the new installation and can roll everything back if necessary.

5   Uninstall routines often fail to clean up properly. They can leave a lot of debris behind to clutter up your hard disk. Using good-quality uninstaller software can solve this problem, but otherwise you will need to resort to manually removing files, folders and shortcuts. There will often be orphaned entries left in the Windows Registry, but you should not attempt to clean these up unless you really know what you are doing.

Back-ups –
Computer
Lifesavers

In This Chapter

➤ The terrible risks to stored data

➤ You are backing up your data – aren't you?

➤ The advantages and disadvantages of different back-up media

➤ Deciding on a back-up strategy

➤ Using Windows' back-up utility

➤ Save disk space with a compressed back-up

➤ Third-party back-up software

The Terrible Risks To Stored Data

In a perfect world, data stored on your hard drive would be 100 per cent safe. But there ain't no justice, so it ain't! As we have already seen, data is stored by polarizing magnetized particles to represent digital bits. While this method retains the patterns when power is switched off (non-volatile, you will recall), it is susceptible to environmental damage. The main culprits when it comes to data loss are magnetic fields, heat, dust, mould and, I have to admit, cigarette smoke. Time itself can also play havoc with stored data. Over the months, magnetic media gradually lose their charge and stored data eventually disappears. Experts usually recommend making fresh copies of long-term files at least every two years.

Then there is mechanical failure. Hard drives do crash occasionally, and while it is sometimes possible to retrieve data from damaged disks using specialized equipment, the process can be formidably expensive. Finally, there is always accidental or deliberate damage. You, yourself, can overwrite important data by mistake, while viruses or unauthorized intruders can mash it up on purpose.

Only you can decide just how valuable your data is. You may think it is fairly unimportant – a few notes, some family photographs, nothing you couldn't live without. This is not the right way to assess its value. Instead, ask yourself how easy it would be to recreate that data. If the answer is more than the few minutes it would take to back that data up, then the answer is obvious!

Susan The Student

Did you really expect Susan to bother to back up her data? College life is frantic enough without one more chore. Susan comes from a generation to which computers are no more unusual than TVs and microwaves. She expects all her gadgets to be hassle-free, and back-ups to Susan definitely come in the hassle category.

It is a pity that Susan cannot be bothered. For the last few months, she has been working on a major college project – a key component of her degree. Her project, her notes and her references are all stored on her hard drive. Something else is stored there too – a particularly destructive virus knocked up for a laugh by one of her friends from the IT department. A few days from now, virus and college work will meet and Susan will be tearfully explaining to her tutor why she has no project to submit.

You Are Backing Up Your Data – Aren't You?

If you are the average computer user, the answer, unfortunately, is probably not. Most people don't and a surprising number of them live to regret this. For home users, data loss is annoying, possibly even infuriating, but for a business it can be disastrous. Remember, your bank keeps all your account records on computer. Would you want to wake up one morning to find that your savings had disappeared without trace? Of course banks and other professional institutions use heavy-duty systems to safeguard their files. They back up, then back up the back-up, then back up the back-up of the back-up (let me know if I'm getting too technical) using the RAID array technology we met earlier. You do not need to be this conscientious!

Remember also, that apart from the obvious files that you consciously create in your word processor or spreadsheet program, your computer is continuously storing other, less visible data. Here is a list of just some of the things you will lose if your hard disk dies.

➤ The e-mail addresses of your friends and business contacts.

➤ All the software for which you do not have distribution disks – internet downloads, for example.

➤ The preferred settings for your applications.

➤ The favourite sites you have bookmarked in your web browser.

➤ Your internet connection settings.

➤ Any web pages, images or documents you have downloaded for off-line browsing.

➤ Any modifications you have made to your desktop – background images, screen-savers, etc.

➤ Any updates to your system software that you have brought down from the internet.

➤ Your usernames and passwords. (You didn't write them down and stick them under your keyboard, did you?)

Give me half an hour and I could list a dozen more …

Why people are so resistant to backing up their data is a mystery. Back-ups are neither complicated nor time consuming. They can easily be automated so the user doesn't even need to remember to do them. They save heartache and occasional financial collapse. Yet data recovery specialists estimate that only three out of ten people ever back up their critical files, and that only one in ten backs up regularly. You are about to join that lonely one.

The Advantages And Disadvantages Of Different Back-up Media

There is a wide range of different media which can be used to back up data. Table 9.1 overleaf lists the most common ones, along with some notes on their advantages and disadvantages.

You can make use of this table to decide which media, or combination of media, is most suitable for your own back-up strategy. You should certainly consider price and convenience – the cheaper and easier you can make the process, the more likely you are to stick with it. Remember also that some media are inherently more secure than others. A copy of your data burnt onto a read-only CD-ROM is safer than a copy on floppy disk, since floppies, like hard drives are susceptible to magnetic fields. If your data is critical, you should also consider two further steps. It might be a good idea to physically distance your back-ups from the originals so that a serious accident – a fire,

143

Table 9.1 Media To Back-up Data

Media	Advantages	Disadvantages
Floppy disk	Compact, easy to store, can be used in most PCs, cheap.	Very small storage capacity, easily damaged, very slow to write to and read from.
Zip, Jaz or similar disk	Compact, easy to store, viable storage capacity (depending on type of disk).	Expensive, requires specialized hardware, relatively slow to write to and read from (compared to hard disks).
CD-ROM and CD-RW	Very cheap, large storage capacity, can be used in most modern PCs (CD-RWs require special reader software), resistant to damage.	Relatively slow to write to (compared to hard disks).
Tape drive	Very secure, large storage capacity, writing speed can be fast (depending on type of hardware).	Almost obsolete on modern equipment, requires specialized hardware.
Secondary hard disk	Fast read and write, very large storage capacity (depending on capacity of disk).	Can be caught up in the same calamity which overtakes the primary hard disk – fire, for example.
Network server	Fast read and write, very large storage capacity (depending on capacity of disk), data stored remotely from primary drive.	Dependent on network for file retrieval.
Virtual internet drive	Large storage capacity (depending on configuration), data stored remotely from primary drive, data is private.	Dependent on internet for file retrieval, data can be fragmented by broken connections (requiring a fresh download).

for example – would not destroy both copies. And for total security, perhaps you might make two back-ups – one local and one remote.

Deciding On A Back-up Strategy

Whichever back-up media you decide on, the important thing is to establish a practical back-up strategy that is appropriate to the value of your data and to implement that strategy right now. The strategy should be based on your answers to the following questions.

➤ How often is your critical data modified?

➤ Do you wish to implement an automated back-up or will you back up your data manually?

➤ Which files do you need to back up?

Remember too that your back-up strategy must be flexible. Your computer usage will undoubtedly change over the months and the value of your data might also change. You might, for example, decide to automate your tax return or your bank account which would increase the importance of regular back-ups. Be prepared to adjust your routine accordingly.

Deciding On A Back-up Strategy

How often should you make back-ups? Figure 9.1 suggests a simple routine which would be adequate for anyone who is not handling highly critical data. If you are considering adopting a strategy like this, ask yourself how bad it would be to lose one day's work. If the answer is 'unbearable', back-up more often. If, on the other hand, you only create the occasional data file, it might be enough to make back-ups once a week. Only you can judge the value of your data and assess how often you need to secure it.

Two notes! In the diagram I have shown the back-up device as a network file server, but the same principles apply if you are securing your data to a CD-ROM, a virtual internet drive or any other back-up medium. I also suggest keeping two distinct back-ups and overwriting them alternately. Not only does this improve security, it has the added benefit that a recent unaltered copy of your work is also saved just in case you've changed something you subsequently wish you hadn't.

Figure 9.1 Deciding on a back-up frequency

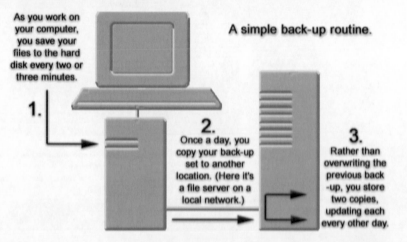

A simple back-up routine.

1. As you work on your computer, you save your files to the hard disk every two or three minutes.

2. Once a day, you copy your back-up set to another location. (Here it's a file server on a local network.)

3. Rather than overwriting the previous back-up, you store two copies, updating each every other day.

Whatever back-up frequency you decide on, the most important thing is to stick to it. It will do no harm to back up more often, but never go beyond your timescale. You can be quite sure that the night disaster strikes will be the night you haven't bothered to make a back-up.

Identifying Files To Back Up

The most difficult decision is exactly which files should be backed up. This ought to be obvious, but it seldom is. The problem here is that not only should you back up your precious data files, but also those containing applications settings, personal information, passwords, etc., and these are likely to be scattered all over your hard disk. The most complete, but also the most time-consuming, back-up strategy is to copy all the files on your computer which have been modified since your last back-up (or in the last few days, if you have never made a back-up before). As you can imagine, this strategy involves moving a huge amount of data, but is relatively simple to achieve.

Windows includes a useful Find utility which can track down any files whose content has changed during a given period. You can access this from Windows Explorer by clicking **Tools > Find > Files or Folders**. Figure 9.2 shows the Find utility in action. As you can see, it has been configured to find all files modified during the previous six days, and has found 101 of them. They are listed in the Find window and could simply be dragged from there to a new location – **Edit > Select All** would bundle them up for you.

If you are using very few applications and have not made many changes to the system's configuration, this might be an ideal back-up solution, but it has its drawbacks. First, you would inevitably be backing up files that do not need it. Some

Figure 9.2 Finding modified files

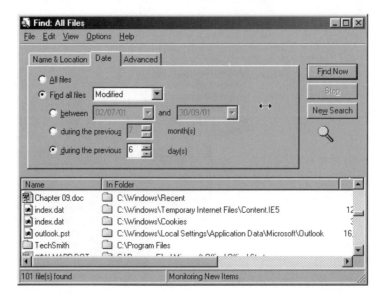

files are modified every time an application starts, or every time Windows is fired up. This does not mean that they necessarily contain critical data. Second, although the back-up set in this example isn't massive (101 files), in most cases it would be much larger and contain a number of very big files.

Let's look at better ways of deciding on a back-up set. Whether you are using Windows default folders and saving your files to **My Documents** or you have specified your own folders, you should not have any difficulty in tracking down the data files, you have created. If you have allowed your applications to store files wherever they pleased, you may need to spend some time finding them all. This might mean drilling down through Windows Explorer and looking in all your application folders for files you have created. If you didn't take the hint earlier in the book and disabled Windows' habit of turning off the extensions for registered file types, I suggest you do so now. In Windows Explorer, click **Tools > Folder Options > View**, then uncheck **Hide file extensions for known files types**. This will make file extensions for data file types such as **.doc** and **.jpg** visible in Explorer and make your search much easier.

As you find individual files or folders you need to back up, write down their names and full paths – **C:\My Documents\Private\Letter to Bank.doc**, for example. I admit that this can be a time-consuming operation, but it only needs to be done once. After you have compiled your list, take a look at it and decide if now would be a good time to reorganize your work space. I suggested this approach back in Chapter 4, but if you ignored me then, I shall have another shot at persuading you now. If you gather all your data files into a single location, back-ups become much easier. Here is what I do, but feel free to modify my set-up to suit yourself.

➤ I create a first-level folder called Media (**C:/Media**).

➤ Inside that folder, I create second-level folders to distinguish between the different types of data files I am working on. At present, these are called Art, Words, Web and Finance. (**C:/Media/Words**).

➤ Within these folders, I create third-level folders to contain the data for individual projects. Third-level folders can have fourth-, fifth- or even sixth-level folders within them. For example, Figure 9.2 above is currently stored on my computer as **C:/Media/Words/Books/CGI Computer Security/Graphics/09.2 finding files.tif**.

You see the advantage. When I need to back up my data files, all I need to do is copy (or synchronize – of which more later) a single folder and its sub-folders, to know that all my work is safe.

If you do decide to adopt this model, stop now and reorganize your work space. Then, working from the list of data files you have compiled, move them all into the relevant folders. Now you can throw away the list knowing that all your data is stored under a single folder which is easy to back up. I really am trying to make life easy for you!

So much for work files. The next step is to track down all the other important files which need to be backed up, and this is a much more involved operation. The first and most important thing is to back-up your Windows Registry. Registry information is contained in two files – **System.dat** and **User.dat**, and it is possible just to copy these files to your back-up media. For simplicity, it makes more sense to use Regedit's (The Windows Registry Editor) own back-up utility. Click **Start** > **Run**, type **regedit** into the box and click **OK**. When Regedit opens, click **Registry** > **Export Registry File** and save it to your back-up media. While you are at it, you might also consider backing up the Windows start-up files we looked at in the previous chapter.

The next consideration is operating system configuration files. Windows is not terribly consistent in where it stores information. This makes a comprehensive back-up quite complicated. If you don't wish to back-up the entire Windows folder, you should still consider securing those folders which contain important personal records and data which relates to how your operating system has been configured. This information will not be recreated if you reinstall Windows; you will need to reconfigure or enter it all again! The table, right, lists those folders which I think are worth backing up along with some notes on what they contain. Depending on how your system has been set up, you will find all or most of these as sub-folders of your **Windows** folder.

Many of these sub-folders contain third- or fourth-level folders which also store key files. Your Windows configuration might also be very different and include other, equally important, folders. All the other critical data is in the Windows folder itself. You must decide how much or how little of this you need to back up. Losing all of the files and folders in this list will not prevent you from getting your system back online. You can reinstall Windows, reinstall all your applications, then set about reconfiguring all your software. Eventually you will have everything as it was before the catastrophe. But backing up all, or most, of the Windows folders listed above will save you an enormous amount of time.

Now you need to consider your applications and this can be a long or a short job depending on how much software is installed on your computer. As we have noted earlier, applications often depend on support files which store configuration settings and information about the data files you have created. You will have to decide how important this data is and if it is worth the time and trouble of tracking down and backing up the files which contain it. Susie, the example I used in Chapter 6, creates thumbnail files which are clearly worth securing, but other applications may do no more than simply record your preferred window size and the last few data files they accessed.

Work down through Windows Explorer, checking all your application folders. To see which files have been modified, you can click the **Modified** column heading in the files pane which will list all the files according to the date they have been modified – see Figure 9.3. In this figure I am checking an application I run called Second Copy – this is a back-up utility which I will be discussing later in this chapter. I ran the

148

Table 9.2 The Folders To Back up

Name of folder	Contains
All users	Application data and information on your default desktop and start menu.
Application data	In a perfect world, this would be where all software manufacturers store their configuration settings. Of course, it isn't.
Cookies	If you like to hang on to your cookies – see Chapter 17 for my opinion of the pesky little things – you had better back up this folder.
Desktop	All the shortcuts which currently litter your desktop.
Favorites	Shortcuts to the websites you have bookmarked (along with a load of other ones that Microsoft thinks you should have bookmarked!)
Fonts	All the fonts installed on your computer. If you make do with the fonts which Windows installs by default, you needn't bother to back up this folder.
History	A record of all the websites and network addresses you have visited in the last two weeks. (There might be very good reasons for not backing up this folder.)
Local settings	Microsoft application data relating to a single user. This, for example, is usually where you will find the Outlook® file which stores all your e-mails, contacts and engagements.
Recent	Shortcuts to all the data files you have recently accessed.
Start menu	Shortcuts to all the applications which appear in your Start menu.
System	Core operating system files including most of your DLLs and hardware drivers, plus a lot of configuration files. The majority of this folder would be recreated following a reinstallation of Windows, but the bit you would lose could prove irritating.
System 32	As system above but intended for 32-bit drivers.

application, on 5 November. If you look at the list of files, you will notice two, **profiles.dat** and **log.rtf**, which were modified on that date. This suggests they contain configuration information or data relating to my use of the application. All the other files are older and probably date back to the original installation or an earlier use. I might well decide that it would be worth including these two files in my back-up set

Figure 9.3 Checking in Explorer for modified application support files

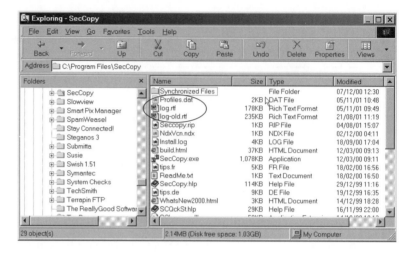

on the grounds that if I ever needed to reinstall Second Copy these files would help me to return the application to its current state.

I am afraid there are no shortcuts in this process. The only consolation is that once it has been completed, you will not need to change your back-up set unless you install new applications. Eventually, you will end up with all the files and folders you think it worth securing listed on a piece of paper. The thought of copying these one by one to your back-up media would be enough to put anyone off, but relax, you don't have to.

Enter Windows Backup.

Using Windows' Back-up Utility

Windows comes with a fairly substantial back-up utility, imaginatively called Backup. This is not actually a Microsoft product, but has been written by Seagate, which is better known for manufacturing disk drives. Since Backup is not always installed by default, the first thing to do is to check if it is loaded onto your computer. Click **Start > Programs > Accessories > System Tools**. If it is not listed, you will need to install it from your Windows CD-ROM, using **Start > Settings > Control Panel > Add/Remove Programs > Windows Setup**.

While Backup is fairly basic compared to some proprietary software, it does an excellent job. Basically, it allows you to specify a back-up set – this, of course, is the list of files and folders you have just made – and to store that set on your choice of media. Start Backup and you will see the window shown in Figure 9.4. You will notice that the application's window is overlaid with a dialog box which starts a Wizard. I prefer to handle my back-ups personally, so I suggest closing the box by clicking the **Close** button and working with the utility directly. As you will see from Figure 9.5, Backup's main screen allows you to check any files and folders you wish to include in your back-up set. If you look at the area called **What to back up**, you will notice that it

150

*Figure 9.4 Windows'
Backup utility*

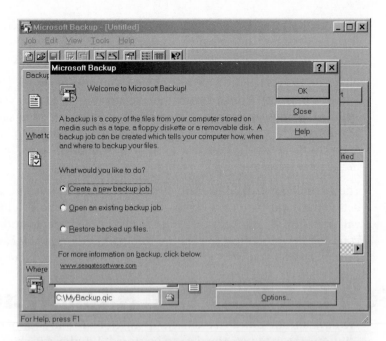

*Figure 9.5 Specifying a
back-up set in Backup*

resembles the layout in Explorer except that each folder (in the left-hand pane) and
each file within each folder (in the right-hand pane) has a check box next to it. Now
you can work through your list, checking all the items you wish to secure. In the
Where to back up box, you can specify the media you wish to back up to. (Note that

151

if you are using a CD writer, you will need to have a formatted CD-ROM ready to receive your files.) You can also browse to a folder on a second drive or a network drive. Once everything is ready, click the **Start** button and your data will be backed up.

I have not forgotten the final area marked **How to back up**. The default option here is **Verify, Compress, Prompt** which means that all the files in your set will be checked against the originals for errors, the set will be compressed to save space and you will be prompted to answer any questions the utility might have. In general, this default option is the most appropriate, but it does have one major drawback that is discussed in the next section.

The second tab, marked **Restore**, is pretty much a reverse of the first one. Here you define the name of your back-up – back-ups have the default extension **.qic**. Backup will then display a list of all the files stored in the back-up and ask you which ones you wish to restore. You can restore these to their original locations or elsewhere and decide whether you wish to overwrite existing files or rename the backed up versions.

Save Disk Space With A Compressed Back-up

We have already noted that a back-up might consume a lot of disk space. An obvious solution is to compress the data to be stored. Windows Backup (discussed above) uses its own data compression system, while proprietary back-up software (described in the following section) sometimes makes use of other compression systems supplied by third parties. The best-known file compression software is WinZip® – a utility which is widely available from magazine-cover-disks. There are many others such as NetZip, WinRAR (my preferred choice) and StuffIt Expander.

However you compress your back-ups, there is one serious drawback. If your Windows system crashes, you will not be able to access the software required to decompress the files until your system is operational. (I am acutely aware of this problem, since I was once caught out in this way.) If, for any reason, you think you might need to get to your back-ups while your Windows OS is out of action, avoid compressing them and store them in full under their original file names.

Third-party Back-up Software

If you require something more sophisticated than Windows BackUp, a very wide choice of back-up software is available on the internet. I have tested a fair cross-section and most of them are similar in terms of functions and usability. You can check out what is available from any major download site on the web. At present, my preferred program is Second Copy 2000, published by Centered Systems. Like several of its competitors, Second Copy allows you to define a series of 'profiles'. These are back-up sets along the lines of the one we looked at earlier in the chapter. Figure 9.6 shows some of the profiles I use as part of my own back-up routine.

Figure 9.6 Second Copy 2000 listing a series of back-up profiles

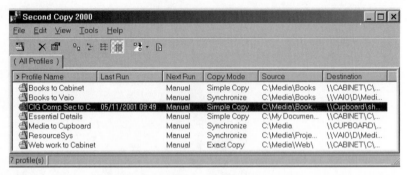

If you look at the profiles listed here, you will see references to several back-up devices. **Cabinet** and **Cupboard** are both network file servers, while **Vaio** is my laptop computer. Each profile is given a distinctive name, and where there might be confusion – as in the first two entries which both back up books I am writing, I include the name of the device each profile is saved to. So the highlighted entry, called **CIG Comp Sec to Cupboard**, tells me that the book you are currently reading is being backed up to the Cupboard file server. The rest of the entry informs me that the back-up is run manually (rather than automatically), that it is a simple copy where modified files replace the saved ones, and that files are copied from my **C:\Media\Books\CIG Computer Security** folder to **\\Cupboard\shelf 3\CIG Computer Security** – a folder on the network drive.

Most back-up software operates in a similar way. You:

➤ create a new back-up set, giving it a unique name;

➤ specify the files to be included in the back-up set;

➤ specify a location where the back-up is to be saved;

➤ specify how often the back-up is to take place;

➤ specify how the back-up is to be made – there is often a range of options here, but they boil down to two basic choices: either all files are simply copied to the back-up location replacing any older versions already stored there or files are synchronized between the two locations with newer versions replacing older versions in either direction.

To see how this works, let's generate a new profile in Second Copy 2000. Since there is ample room on the **Cupboard** network server, I am going to back up my entire **Windows** folder. My first step is to open the New Profile Wizard by clicking **File > New Profile**. The window that opens offers me a choice of **express** or **custom** setup. Since this is a simple back-up, I select **express**. The screen that now opens is shown as Figure 9.7. Here I have specified the source folder – in this case **C:\Windows**, and confirmed that I want to include all this folder's sub-folders. The **Next** button takes me to a similar window where I can specify the location in which to store my back-up. Here I have browsed to **\\Cupboard\shelf 4\Windows Back-up**.

Figure 9.7 Second Copy's Profile Wizard – What do you want to copy?

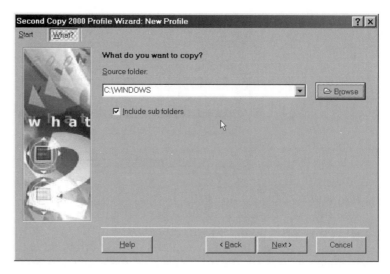

Another **Next** button takes me to the window shown in Figure 9.8, where I can define very precisely when I want the back-up to take place. I can configure the program to operate after a specified number of hours, on certain days of the week, at start-up and/or shutdown and not before a certain date. If you were using Second Copy, you would be sensible enough to specify the timescale to suit the preferred frequency you established earlier in the chapter. Unfortunately, I am something of a control freak and don't like anything happening behind my back. I set the Frequency option to **manual** and run the back-up whenever I want to. To quote an ancient proverb: do as I say, don't do as I do!

Clicking **Next** brings up a final window asking me to name the new profile. After I have done this, the profile is added to my list. If I had wanted greater control of the

Figure 9.8 Second Copy's Profile Wizard – When do you want to copy?

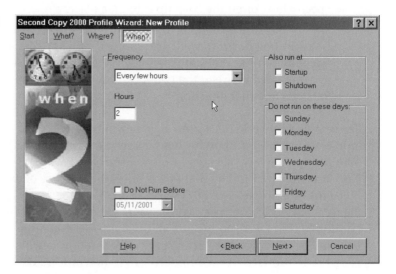

process, I would have used the **custom** setup. Here I could also have specified the exact file and folder set to back up and defined how the back-up should be handled.

So, now you have three options. You can:

➤ back up by simply copying files from your hard disk to your back-up media;

➤ use Windows' own back-up facility; or

➤ load up some third-party software to handle the job.

Whichever route you go, you cannot start your back-up strategy too soon.

Second Copy 2000 can be downloaded from www.centered.com To compare the various compression utilities discussed above, look on one of the major download sites. Try to avoid those that describe themselves as 'adware'. They will display advertising while you are using them! WinRAR can be obtained from www.rarsoft.com It handles all the current compression systems and the superior RAR compression which seems to have fallen out of favour.

Chapter 9 – Security Checklist

1 Start off by assessing the importance of the data stored on your computer. Ask yourself the question: how long and how much effort would it take to recreate it – if, indeed, it can be recreated? Your letters, photographs and e-mails might have no commercial value, but they probably represent hours of personal effort. Back-ups are vital!

2 Don't delay working out and implementing a back-up strategy. Although setting one up initially can take a lot of time, once the folders and files you wish to secure (your back-up set) is decided, back-ups can be handled quickly and smoothly. They can even be automated to take place in the background with no user intervention at all.

3 You will need to decide on the back-up media to use. There are several options listed in Table 9.1. Consider such criteria as price, read and write speed and storage capacity. A good choice for many people is a CD writer, although regular back-ups might get through a lot of CD-ROMs.

4 Establishing a good strategy implies deciding which files you need to back up, how often you need to back them up and whether you will handle back-ups manually or automatically. Your strategy must also be flexible to cope with changes of circumstance.

5 To establish your back-up set, you need to consider not only your data files, but also operating system and application files. This process might involve a lot of scouring your hard drive and noting down all the files and folders worth securing, but it only has to be done once unless you add new applications to your computer.

6 If you have not already done so, consider reorganizing your computer work space so that all your data files are stored in sub-folders of a single data folder. By backing up this folder, you know that all your data files are secure.

7 Once you have decided on your back-up set, you can consider the best means of organizing your back-ups. Windows includes a basic utility called Backup or there is a choice of third-party solutions which offer more features. Whichever way you go, you will need to tell the software which files and folders to secure and where you want them to be stored.

Part 3
Going Cryptographic

Part 3 is mainly concerned with securing your secrets. You'll look at why data encryption is important and why it is a useful technology for everyone. I describe in detail the background to encryption and how it works. I show you how to evaluate different encryption methods and how to pick one that is appropriate to your needs. You will also look at the strength of data encryption and how resistant it is to being broken.

Next I describe three different levels of data security and how they might apply to your own needs. I'll show you the software needed to provide each level of security and suggest ways of hiding your own confidential files. Finally I describe file deletion and ways in which snoopers can recreate apparently deleted files. I'll help you to compare different ways of securely deleting files against both software and hardware recovery tools.

By the end of Part 3, you will have decided on a security level that suits the confidentiality of the data you are handling. You will have implemented a comprehensive security strategy and will be familiar with the techniques required to ensure that unnecessary files are completely deleted from your drives. Now your hardware, software and data should be safe.

What Have You Got To Hide?

Cryptography is nothing more than a mathematical framework for discussing the implications of various paranoid delusions.

Don Alvarez

Your Right To Privacy

Ask yourself this question. Is there anything stored on your computer that you would prefer other people not to see? Before you say, 'No, I have nothing to hide!' think more carefully. Is your full postal address somewhere on your hard disk? Would you like a direct marketing company to know that? How about your credit card number or your bank account PIN number? Have you ever drafted a letter to an old boy or girlfriend? Innocent enough perhaps, but how would your present partner react? Are you storing business statistics which would be of interest to a competitor? Would your employer approve of that letter of resignation you have been working on? How about those slightly naughty pictures you downloaded after that late-night drinking session? I could go on, but I think the point has been made.

The fact is that everybody has something they want to keep private, and most people – including the European Convention on Human Rights – believe that privacy should be everybody's right. Here is what the Convention says in Article 8(1):

> *Everyone has the right to respect for his private and family life, his home and his correspondence.*

Privacy refers to an individual's wish to preserve what has been defined as his or her 'intimate sphere of existence' from the knowledge of other people. It is a concept which has never been properly defined, but as far as your computer activities are concerned, it must cover such elements as the right to:

➤ pursue your private activities and interests;

➤ secrecy in electronic correspondence;

➤ store personal data and protect that data from other people;

➤ be protected against the misuse of information technology.

Before the use of computers became widespread, your rights to privacy were protected by specific legal provisions such as the inviolability of your home and your

Figure 10.1 Encryption means rendering data to hide its content

correspondence, and your right to professional secrecy. In the last two decades, these rights have been threatened by a number of new technologies such as the electronic interception of correspondence, telephone tapping and remote recording of conversations. To counter some of these threats, member states of the European Union (or European Economic Community, as it was) signed the Data Protection Convention in Strasbourg on 28 January 1981. This convention, which came into force on 1 October 1985, sets out a series of principles designed to govern the protection of privacy. Member states were obliged to bring in legislation to conform with those principles. In short, and in the words of a recent report to the European Union:

> *The protection of privacy is properly enshrined in national and international legal orders as well as in Community law.*

One difficulty with interpreting such law is deciding how far it should be applied. Would you, for example, extend such protection to burglars or anarchists? How about terrorists or child pornographers or drug smugglers? Here we are entering stormy waters. Is it right that a thousand innocent people should have their private communications exposed, if that process secures the arrest of one paedophile? Should a good citizen be prepared to give up the right to privacy in the interests of law enforcement? Or national security? Or accurate government statistics? You will have to make these decisions for yourself, but before you dismiss your rights too quickly, stop and think.

RatZnuTZ The Cracker (artist's impression)

Would you extend that right to privacy to RatZnuTZ? His time online is spent trying to break into other people's systems to instigate his own brand of electronic anarchy. Most of the data stored on his computer has been obtained by theft and fraud. European law requires the authorities to try to protect us from the attentions of RatZnuTZ and people like him. It can be argued that in his own small way he is holding back the development of the internet and online commerce, much as the old-time highwaymen prevented people from using the roads.

When you come to analyse it, most of us in Western democracies have very few rights to privacy left. Our elected representatives have quietly taken most of them away, and we have done surprisingly little to stop them. Even your home is no longer 'inviolable'. (The water boards, to take a rather depressing example, have a statutory right of entry.) Your mail can be opened if the police believe it to contain incriminating details. Your telephone can be tapped and your conversations taped. Bugs, high-powered microphones and surveillance cameras are no longer reserved for the security services. They are an integral part of domestic police operations today.

Turning once more to European law, we find that in all member states the supposed right to privacy has been watered down to suit national requirements for security, national defence, crime prevention and anti-terrorism campaigns. For example, the interception of communications by national police forces is authorized, although this is supposed to comply with strict rules intended to protect the privacy of the innocent. The European Union is bound by the European Convention on Human Rights which obliges member states not only to combat unlawful interceptions, but also to prevent lawful interceptions being used for any purpose other than the authorized one.

There are other laws too which impact on your individual rights. In many countries there is a supposed right to free expression, but of course that expression must not offend anybody. Insult someone and you can be hauled into court for libel. Insult someone's beliefs and, in come countries, you could face a charge of blasphemy – surely the most absurd and archaic statute still on the books. Complain loudly and demand action and you may find yourself charged with inciting a riot or that old UK favourite, threatening behaviour likely to cause a breach of the peace. And woe betide you if anything you say can be interpreted as racist or sexist. What we are left with is a seriously limited right to free speech; we can say whatever we like as long as it conforms to everybody else's opinions and upsets nobody.

To sum up, your computer is no more private than any other form of communication. If the police or security services suspect that you are storing information connected with criminal activity or in some way threatening national security, they can obtain a warrant, seize your computer and your storage devices, and search through your private files as they please. In Britain, you cannot even protect your data from official intrusion by using encryption. The Regulation of Investigatory Powers Act (RIP – rather aptly), which came into force in 2000, compels you to hand over your passwords and if you refuse, you can be fined or sent to prison for two years. This law does not require you to have committed any other crime – keeping your passwords private is now a crime in itself. For the FBI's opinion, look at the box below.

The potential use of commercially available encryption products by a vast array of criminals and terrorists to conceal their criminal communications and information poses an extremely serious threat to public safety and national security. Law enforcement fully supports a balanced encryption policy that satisfies both the commercial needs of industry for robust encryption while at the same time satisfying law enforcement's public safety and national security needs. Robust, commercially available encryption products, which include some type of recoverable capability that allows for immediate, lawful access to plaintext is clearly the best method to achieve the goals of both industry and law enforcement.

Encryption: Law Enforcement. 3 June 1999.

Possibly the gravest danger to your right to privacy is the assumption that because you are in possession of encrypted data, you are automatically indulging in illegal activities. This viewpoint prevails in totalitarian states and it is worrying to see it now being expressed quite often by our politicians and policemen. There is a further problem. To secure your data, you require some form of encryption software. The very existence of such software on your computer might persuade the authorities that you had something illicit to hide. The security services have access to some very efficient code-breaking programs. If you intend to lock up your secrets, you will need equally effective encryption techniques to defeat them.

Scrambling Your Secrets

After you have picked your way through this moral maze, you come up against a simple decision: are you going to encrypt your data or not? There are many reasons for doing so and some of them are listed in Table 10.1, overleaf.

Since the publishers of this book do not limit its sale to upright citizens, your interests might lie above or below the dark band on the table. But it is almost certain that some of the information held on your own or your company's computers fits into at least one of these categories. The trend is towards more confidential data rather than less. The growth of internet banking and online shopping inevitably means that more personal financial information is stored on disk. More and more people are using computers as diaries, databases, stock inventories, etc. Whatever the views of the authorities, encrypting your critical data is not just the paranoid approach: it is plain common sense.

Of course, there are different methods of concealing data. If the best place to hide a book is in a library, the best place to hide a computer file is in a folder filled with other computer files. We can identify several ways of doing this, including:

➤ hiding a data file among other data files;

➤ hiding the existence of the file;

➤ scrambling the data within the file by using encryption software;

➤ hiding the data within another data file (steganography).

The remainder of this chapter looks at these methods in more detail and explains the background to data encryption.

The Mechanics Of Data Encryption

Let's start with some definitions. **Encryption** is the process of rendering data in such a way as to hide its content. **Decryption** is the reverse – transforming encrypted data back into an intelligible form. Both encryption and decryption require that a software process known as an algorithm (a mathematical process which applies a set of rules to

163

Table 10.1 To Encrypt Or Not To Encrypt?

Type of data	Examples
1 Data which it is illegal to possess.	Intellectual property stolen from another computer, material which incites racial hatred, certain types of pornography.
2 Data which relates to criminal activity.	Money-laundering records, a list of people you are supplying with drugs.
3 Data which represents a genuine threat to national security.	Plans for a terrorist bombing campaign.
4 Data which is important to your business and which might be useful to your competitors.	Customer records, plans for new products.
5 Data which you are ethically bound to keep confidential.	A doctor's medical records, a solicitor's correspondence with clients.
6 Confidential data, access to which is intended to be limited to specified individuals or groups.	Government-held personal records, criminal records, credit agency records.
7 Data which you would prefer other members of your family/ business colleagues not to see.	Personal correspondence, the first draft of that novel you always wanted to write.
8 Data which might offend other people.	Candid reviews of other members of staff, smutty pictures, political or social opinions.
9 Personal or business financial data.	Credit card numbers, PIN numbers, bank records.

solving a problem) is applied to the data and that this process is only accessible to someone with specific knowledge. That knowledge is usually a password or pass-phrase, sometimes referred to as a key.[1] In most cases, the same key is used for both encryption and decryption, but some software takes a more secure approach and requires both a lock and an unlock key. Where a single key is used, this is known as **symmetrical encryption**; where two keys are used, it becomes **asymmetrical encryption**.

[1] There can be a degree of confusion about this terminology. Some encryption software authors use the term 'key' to refer to the password or pass-phrase used to encrypt and decrypt data, but some apply the word to the random selection of numbers and digits used by the encryption algorithm to scramble the data or to generate the key.

The difference between symmetrical and asymmetrical encryption is quite important. Symmetrical encryption is fine when the data is to be locked and unlocked by the same person – as in the case of files stored on a local computer. But if the data is to be transmitted or made accessible to a third party, the key must also be passed over. This raises the possibility that the key itself will be intercepted and the security of the data compromised. In this and the following chapter, we are only concerned with securing local data, so symmetrical encryption is adequate, but in Chapter 18 we will return to the subject and look in more detail at the asymmetrical encryption of transmitted data.

The use of encryption to lock up data assumes that the data would be of interest to unauthorized third parties. It should not be assumed that the data is confidential by definition. You should have the right to encrypt a photograph of your mother-in-law, if that is your wish. Unfortunately, as we noted earlier, many law enforcement agencies appear to presume that anyone encrypting data is attempting to hide something illegal. This is not the case and the presence of encrypted data on a computer should not be sufficient to justify a demand that the data be unlocked for public scrutiny.

Before we look at the process of encrypting data, we should take a moment to consider exactly what we are attempting to achieve. In Chapter 6, we noted that all data stored on a computer is represented by a pattern of ones and zeroes. Although a digital computer is happy to process such data, it is effectively meaningless to a human being. What, for example, does ...

0100101001110101 0101000101101010 0010100100111101

... actually tell us? Binary numbers also grow in length very quickly. For example, the decimal number 256 requires three characters but its binary equivalent, 100000000, requires nine characters. To render data understandable, computer programmers usually represent binary data in hexadecimal format.

Working in hex is complicated. Instead of counting in tens, as we normally do, hex counts in sixteens. Here are the first sixteen 'numbers' in hex listed against their everyday equivalents:

0 1 2 3 4 5 6 7 8 9 10 11 12 13 14 15

0 1 2 3 4 5 6 7 8 9 A B C D E F

When data is extracted from your computer it is usually represented in hex. Figure 10.2, for example shows part of a photograph stored on my computer as reported by the Encase® software used by many law enforcement agencies. (The highlighted digits, hex value FF, represent the binary number 11111111, or the decimal number 255. Note the eight binary digits – this is 8-bit data.) From this apparently meaningless string of characters it is possible to recreate the image – in this case, you would see my daughter sitting in her high chair.

Figure 10.2 Computer data represented by hexadecimal numbers

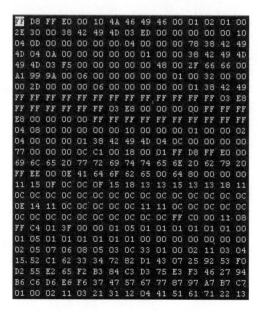

How a computer translates a series of digits into an image or a document is a complex subject and not relevant to this book. We are concerned with storing those digits in a format that only a computer under our control can understand. Implicit in this is the acceptance that other people may gain access to the encrypted data either by using the computer or by getting to it over a network. Otherwise, we could simply remove the hard disk from our machine and lock it up in a safe!

Cryptology, the science of encryption, dates back thousands of years. A cipher is defined as 'a secret or disguised way of writing' (*Oxford English Dictionary*), and ciphers have played an important part in the history of the world. To create a cipher, you apply a process (an algorithm) to each character in a message. A simple cipher might involve replacing each letter in a message with the next letter in the alphabet, so the message:

MEET ME BY THE POST OFFICE

would be rendered as:

NFFU NF CZ UIF QPTU PGGJDF

This sort of cipher is simple to decode, as the frequency with which letters appear in written English is well known. In our message, the letter 'e', the most common letter in written English has been replaced by the letter 'f', which occurs five times. With this as a starting point, a cryptologist (code breaker) would have little difficulty in working out the rest of the message. More complicated letter transposition schemes are also easy to crack, particularly with a computer to help.

Encryption software converts data into cipher text by means of an encryption engine –

the computer program which applies the algorithm. How the program operates is determined by the encryption method (a fixed function), but the output varies because it depends on a piece of information (the encryption key), which is decided by the user. The actual mechanics of the encryption process is known as a cryptosystem. The most secure cryptosystems make use of several different methods of encryption, with the method chosen for a particular encryption process being dependent on the key. It goes without saying that the output obtained by using the decryption key to decrypt the cipher text must be identical to the original data.

Digital data, of course, present an interesting problem for cryptology. Since all data is stored as ones and zeroes, any encryption process at machine level can only either leave each digit in its correct state (1=1 or 0=0) or replace the digit with its inverse (1=0 or 0=1). In fact, encryption software usually operates at a higher level by modifying the representation of the digital data rather than the digital data itself.[2] To do this, it applies an algorithm – remember, a logical procedure for solving a problem. All computer programs use specific algorithms to perform their tasks. You use them yourself, every time you make a shopping list, for example.

There are any number of different encryption systems available – many of them on the internet and some of them free to download. Systems vary from the extremely feeble to the (currently) unbreakable. I say 'currently' because code breakers are a resourceful lot. Time and again, unbreakable codes have been broken, sometimes by discovering weaknesses in the cryptosystem employed, but more often by the so-called 'brute force attack' which involves trying every possible key until you find one that works. Computers make ideal tools for brute force attacks. Once the encryption method is established, they can apply millions of different keys in successive or simultaneous attacks and check whether the results are intelligible or random data.

How successful brute force attacks are usually depends on the size of the key space associated with the cryptosystem. The key space refers to the number of characters, which make up the key. A useful rule of thumb is that the average time required for a successful brute force attack is half the number of possible keys multiplied by the time required to test each key. If the key space is small, then the cryptosystem is vulnerable to a brute force attack. But if a cryptosystem has a very large key space then a brute

---

[2] At first sight, this might seem strange, but think back to Chapter 6 and our examination of digital data representation. At machine level, the patterns of zeroes and ones stored on a hard drive are quite meaningless unless the computer can identify the relevant application software to decode them. To put it another way, if someone designed a piece of software, which stored data according to a completely unknown algorithm, that data would be undecipherable until the algorithm was recreated. When you think about it, this is exactly what encryption software actually does!

167

force attack is not feasible and so any weakness, if it exists, must be sought elsewhere in the system.

Choosing Your Passwords And Pass-phrases

Passwords have become endemic to computer usage. I have just checked my own list of passwords (encrypted, of course) and here is a selection of those I might require for a session on my computer.

➤ The BIOS password to change basic computer settings.

➤ A log-on password to access my home network.

➤ A password to unlock the secure disk where I store my bank account details.

➤ An encryption password to access confidential files.

➤ Passwords to change the settings on some of the application software I use.

➤ A log-in password to access the internet.

➤ An FTP server password if I wish to add new pages to a website.

➤ An e-mail server password to see if I have any new messages.

➤ A password to protect the file where I list all my other passwords!

It does not matter how clever the algorithm used to scramble your files, if your password can be guessed then the cryptosystem is useless. A data security specialist once told me that, in his estimation, over 50 per cent of all secure systems could be broken into by trying the Christian name of the user; his or her date of birth; the names of any children, wives, girlfriends or pets; or the word 'secret' (as in 'my password is secret'). He added that most people write down their passwords and that the first place to check is the underside of the keyboard. A recent survey found that less than 10 per cent of those asked used complex or cryptic passwords. It sounds so obvious, but as soon as you commit your password to paper, your security is compromised. Good practice demands that your passwords are never written down.

Clearly, the more complicated the password, the harder it is to guess. Table 10.2 looks at different styles of password and how they might stand up to a brute force attack.

I emphasize that the cracking times in the last column are only estimates. They could be shortened dramatically by employing a series of computers to mount the attack. Despite this, the lessons are clear. First, a password should not consist of a single word since these are easier to crack by trying keys from a dictionary. A random sequence of words and numbers makes this approach impossible. Second, the longer the password, the safer it is. Fill up the available key space with random characters and your password becomes almost uncrackable by brute force methods.

The sensible computer user always anticipates trouble, and the next possible problem is remembering your passwords. One solution is the 'key chain' approach offered on

Table 10.2 Time Taken To 'Crack' Passwords

Password style	Examples	Range of possibilities	Estimated time to crack using a computer to enter sequential keys
Christian name	John, Sarah	Around 3,000, available from a dictionary of names	2–8 hours
Single word	Globe, vegetable	Around 70,000, available from a dictionary or a computer spelling checker	4–10 days
Two words combined	Sausagetrouser, deadsandwich	Around 4,900,000,000	500–1,000 years
Combination of random letters and numbers	Jh75g9jsuf23kid2l	Around 3,900,000,000,000,000	1,200,000,000 years

Apple computers. In practice, this means storing all your passwords in a single location and then protecting them with a further password, which is both secure and easy to remember. Let us say you wished to encrypt three files. You might consider creating a simple text file like this.

My password file.

➤ The password for file_one is 12hfye890923jasaj020

➤ The password for file_two is hhg65gaj923j0dkq0kql

➤ The password for file_three is hjkafu831ji9casdf990

You could then encrypt that file in turn but instead of using the random character approach, choose as your password the first line of a poem or a complicated sequence of characters which only you would remember – your middle name, followed by the date of your oldest child's birthday, followed by the name of the first house you bought, for example. To access your files, you would then decrypt your text file and copy and paste the keys into the decryption software's dialog boxes to unlock the originals. Simple, but secure.

Hiding The Existance Of Data (Steganography)

In certain circumstances it might not be enough to simply scramble the contents of a file. Security might require us to hide the very existence of the file itself – a concept known as 'steganography'. The word itself is derived from the Greek for 'covered writing' and refers to a wide range of secret methods, which are intended to conceal the very existence of a message. If the underlying message is also encrypted, steganography adds a second layer of security. Before the advent of computer communications, steganographic tricks included invisible inks, microdots, the special arrangement of characters and what are known as 'spread-spectrum communications' where, for example, a radio message masks a second message on a different frequency.

Steganography has been used countless times in the history of communications. The ancient Greeks sent messages on wax tablets. It is recorded that during the wars with Persia, Greek military commanders would scrape the wax away, write the message on the wood underneath, recover the tablet with wax and write an innocent message on that. Invisible inks were widely used by professional spies as recently as World War II. Common invisible inks are milk, vinegar, fruit juices and urine, which all darken when heated. A message would be written in one of these liquids and the paper dried to conceal the text. Then an innocent message would be added between the now invisible lines.

Another technique, and one which points the way to computer steganography, is the use of 'null ciphers' or unencrypted, innocent messages used to conceal the real message. A German spy sent the following message during World War II:

> Apparently neutral's protest is thoroughly discounted and ignored. Isman hard hit. Blockade issue affects pretext for embargo on by products, ejecting suets and vegetable oils.

The key here is to take the second letter in each word, which produces:

> Pershing sails from NY, June 1.

Although invented in the 1870s, it was during World War II that German scientists perfected the microdot – a photograph no bigger than a full stop (period), which can be enlarged to the size and clarity of a typewritten page. With microdots, steganography actually replaces encryption since the message is neither hidden nor encoded. It is just so small that it passes unnoticed.

Since the end of the war, technology has brought a whole range of new steganographic techniques. Messages can now be concealed in images, using colour patterns or other elements to carry a message. Figure 10.3 shows an example, which uses the standard 256-tone grayscale[3] to carry the message 'james bond lives'. This type of cryptosystem would be impossible without a computer since the human eye is

Figure 10.3 Using grayscale to encrypt a message

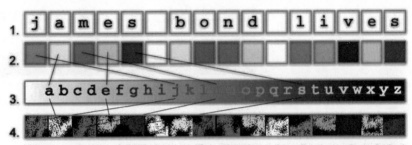

The message appears in the top row. The second row shows its greyscale equivalent using the shade behind the letter in the third row. The fourth row contains the same message, but this time the shades have been randomly airbrushed onto a black square.

not sharp enough to distinguish between the shades of grey. Look at the colours used to encrypt the letters 'o' and 'n' in 'bond', for example.

Steganography can make use of almost any communications media to conceal a message, and by applying modern computer technology even more sophisticated techniques become possible. Using a computer, we can conceal one file inside another file. We can, for example, hide a message within an image or a photograph within a document. We can render files invisible to the operating system. We can even split off parts of our storage media and make them effectively disappear. In Chapter 11, we will be applying some of these techniques to the process of hiding your own confidential data.

Encryption Algorithms – The Tricks That Frighten Governments

We will close this chapter by taking a brief look at the encryption algorithms that are currently available. Now we are entering the realm of the spooks! From the 1950s onwards, the US Government's National Security Agency (NSA) has monitored the worldwide development of encryption technology. Concerned in case unbreakable encryption should ever be used against US interests, the NSA has persuaded the State Department to adopt the International Traffic in Arms Regulation (ITAR), which defines cryptographic devices, including computer software, as munitions or weapons of war.

This means that all encryption software produced within the US requires an export licence from the State Department. The State Department in turn will not grant a licence without NSA approval, which means that ultimately policy decisions over exporting cryptography rest with the NSA. This export policy has been challenged by several different groups including the Software Publishers Association who claimed that it was harming their trade. As a result of these challenges there has been a slight

[3] The term 'grayscale' refers to the colour model used on most computers and non-colour printers to produce images. It refers to the 254 shades of gray between white and black.

*Figure 10.4 SafeHouse's
User Guide reveals that it
conforms to US rules on
exporting encryption*

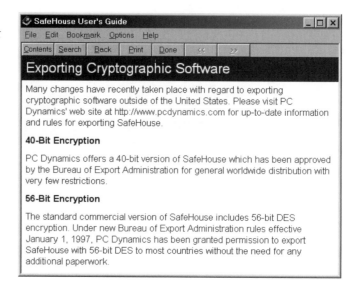

easing of restrictions to allow the export of certain encryption software with a limited
key-space. As we noted earlier, this will render such encryption easier to crack. Figure
10.4 shows an extract from the SafeHouse encryption suite's User Guide, which tacitly
admits that the software uses low-security algorithms which ensure an export licence.

One rather amusing way that encryption software authors have used to get
round these restrictions is to publish their source code as a book. US
government agencies cannot ban the export of a book, because a book is
defined in law as a form of free speech, and free speech is protected by the
first amendment to the United States' Constitution. This trick has been
tried, among others, by the publishers of Pretty Good Privacy (PGP), the free
asymmetrical encryption software that is widely used to encode e-mail and
other transmitted data. We will be looking at PGP in Chapter 18.

One encryption algorithm that the NSA has approved is the Data Encryption Standard
(DES) algorithm. DES is a cipher that encodes 64-bit data blocks using a 56-bit secret
key. The cryptosystem involves both permutation and substitution and is widely used
by the US government. There has long been a suspicion that the NSA influenced its
designers at IBM to ensure that while it was strong enough to withstand most attacks,
it was not strong enough to stand up against the NSA's own highly advanced
computers. Certainly IBM's original design proposed a 768-bit key which, after
intervention by the NSA, was subsequently reduced to a mere 56 bits. Cryptologists
have cracked DES encryption on several occasions, and the cipher is no longer
considered to be secure.

Peter Gutmann, a lecturer in computer security at the University of Auckland, has devised a complicated formula to assess the value of DES as an encryption standard. He calculated the number of computer chips and the time it would take to crack the key and costed these elements in dollars and cents. He estimates that it would cost no more than 8 cents to crack DES, and his conclusion? 'If your secret is worth more than 8 cents, don't encrypt it with DES.' His paper on the subject can be found at www.cs.auckland.ac.nz/~pgut001

The RSA algorithm uses an asymmetrical cryptosystem for both encryption and decryption. Designed in 1977 by Ron Rivest, Adi Shamir and Leonard Adleman, it uses two large prime numbers to generate both lock and unlock keys. Over the years, RSA has proven to be surprisingly powerful, although recent developments in computer technology have delivered new methods of deducing the prime numbers involved in the process. These could then be used to discover the keys.

In 1990, Xuejia Lai and James Massey proposed a new encryption standard, which subsequently became the International Data Encryption Algorithm (IDEA). IDEA operates on 64-bit data blocks using a 128-bit key. To date, IDEA has withstood all conventional attempts to break it. Although similar to other ciphers in operation, it makes use of some unusual mathematical techniques to both 'confuse and diffuse' data. Despite its strength, few encryption programs use the IDEA algorithm. Unlike others, the cipher has been patented and must be licensed for commercial applications.

Stronger still, and considered by many to be the most secure cryptosystem available, is BlowFish, originally designed in 1993 by security guru Bruce Schneier. Like IDEA, BlowFish is a symmetrical cipher that operates on 64-bit data blocks. Unlike IDEA, it uses a variable key space between 32 and 448 bits. For commercial operators it has the advantage of being unpatented and licence-free. It is also much faster than both DES and IDEA.

The new kid on the block is a close relative of BlowFish called TwoFish. TwoFish uses a faster encryption engine than BlowFish. It operates on 128-bit data blocks and offers three different levels of security with 128-, 192- or 256-bit keys. Like BlowFish, it is unpatented so can be freely used without paying royalties. Although designed to be both highly secure and highly flexible, TwoFish has not been subjected to the same degree of cryptanalysis as its predecessors, but it is looking good and might well become the standard encryption algorithm for the next few years.

It is only sensible to treat all claims about the invulnerability of a data encryption system with some suspicion. There are agencies and individuals who spend all their time attacking cryptosystems and there are considerable rewards for those who succeed. Cryptology, by its very nature, is a clandestine business and it is usually in the interests of the code breakers not to admit it when they have cracked a system. In Chapter 23, for example, we consider this aspect from the point of view of unscrupulous businessmen who would certainly prefer their competitors to continue using a cracked cipher.

For now, we need to look at how encryption can be applied to your own privacy requirements and that deserves a new chapter.

Chapter 10 – Security Checklist

1   Look closely at the data stored on your own computer and decide how much, if any, needs to be encrypted. Remember that you cannot assume that your computer is secure. Friends, relatives and colleagues at work can sit down at it, and if you have a network or internet connection, hackers can access it remotely. If you store any kind of critical data on your machine, encryption is vital.

2   While Chapter 11 looks at applying encryption to your own data, you might start to consider suitable passwords or pass-phrases. Long and unpredictable are the golden rules. Always avoid single words or phrases that might be guessed by someone who knows you. Select multiple words or a mixture of random letters and digits. And remember *never write your passwords down anywhere*.

3   There are circumstances in which you might wish to conceal the very existence of certain files. This process is known as steganography. Files can be hidden within other files or made to look like something they are not. Steganography plus encryption is the most secure way to store highly sensitive data.

Locking Up Your Secrets

Choosing The Right Level Of Security

In Chapter 10 we considered encryption techniques and looked at how and why a computer user might choose to employ them. Let me recap by stating that unless you are a very exceptional person, the chances are that you will be storing some kind of data that should be encrypted or at least made inaccessible. As I said in Chapter 10, employing encryption techniques does not imply illegal or anti-social activities. Most computers are accessible to other family members or colleagues at work. There are many entirely innocent reasons why you might not wish your children or friends to see something you are working on. Encryption is a sensible approach to preserving the privacy to which you have a legal and moral right.

This chapter looks at practical techniques for securing your data. The first stage of this process is for you to decide on the level of security which is right for you. Table 11.1

below, shows three levels of security – basic, serious and advanced. These levels are fairly arbitrary and elements from each could easily be moved up or down the table.

Table 11.1 Levels Of Security

Level	Encryption and security techniques involved	Notes
Basic	Concealing the nature of files or making them difficult to find on your storage media. Slowing access to the machine itself with relatively insecure techniques such as screen saver passwords.	Easy to do, but very insecure – more an obstacle to intruders than a level of security. However, this level might be appropriate to a home computer used for nothing more than occasional word processing and the odd spot of web cruising.
Serious	Encrypting individual files, then making the encrypted files invisible. Locking your computer desktop in your absence. Locking the computer's BIOS to prevent access by booting from a floppy disk.	This level of security would be appropriate for data the existence of which was recognized, but its content was confidential – doctor's records, for example, or for a business computer storing sensitive data which would be worth stealing.
Advanced	All of the above, plus encrypting files within encrypted media, then making the media them-selves invisible. (This level would include hiding the tracks which indicate that such files have been created and hiding the very existence of encryption technology on your computer. These aspects are covered in Chapter 12.)	As secure as you can get. Not only are your secrets hidden, but the fact that you have secrets is hidden as well. We have entered the realms of the secret service. One possible drawback at this level is that if a law enforcement agency found any evidence of this type of encryption, it might well assume that you are hiding some kind of illegal activity. This is not only the correct security level for highly sensitive data, it might also suit criminals, terrorists and hard-core pornographers!

We will look at each of these levels in turn, considering their advantages and disadvantages, and the software and hardware required to implement them.

Level 1: Basic security

Level 1 security is almost no security at all. Of course, if you do nothing to secure your data, every file on your hard disk or removable media[1] is accessible to anyone who takes the trouble to look for it. Implementing this level of security will at least make your data a little more difficult to find. Despite this, Level 1 security might be adequate for someone who never stores sensitive or confidential data on his machine and who is concerned only with stopping a passer-by from snatching a look at the odd personal letter.

The biggest advantage with this level of security is that it does not require you to invest in any additional software – everything you need is already built into the operating system. (This, of course, is also a disadvantage since the Windows OS is so well known that almost everyone knows how to bypass its locks.)

Susan The Student

Minimal security is all that Susan the Student requires. Her computer sits in her bedroom in the flat she shares with other students. She has no internet access and uses the machine only to write up her college assignments and the occasional letter asking her mum for some money. Sometimes her letters home might include caustic remarks about her flatmates, so she would prefer them not to be read by someone dropping into her room. Some of her wierder friends have been known to amuse each other by slotting offensive comments into Susan's college work. This, Susan could well do without.

The first precaution at this level is to lock the screen-saver so that if you leave your machine switched on, but unattended, the casual passer-by cannot see what you have been doing. Screen-savers in Windows are accessed from the **Display Properties** of the Desktop. Right-click on your computer's Desktop, select **Properties** from the menu which appears, then click the **Screen Saver** tab and you are presented with the window shown in Figure 11.1. From here you can select any of the screen-savers installed on your computer, decide whether you wish to password-protect them, change the password and specify a time after which the screen-saver will activate.

---

[1] Removable media: just so there is no confusion, by removable media I mean every data storage device that can be separated from the computer. In the early days this just meant floppy disks, but today it would include CD-ROMs, Iomega® Zip and Jaz disks, tape drive cassettes, PC card hard drives, memory sticks, flashcards, portable hard drives and others. While some of these store data using proprietary algorithms, the data's accessibility to snoopers is much the same in every case.

Figure 11.1 Adjusting Windows' screen-saver properties

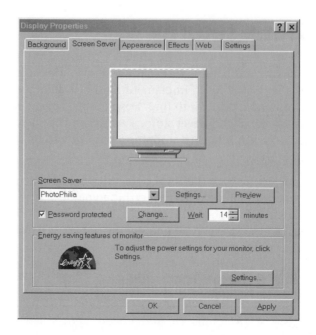

Beyond its irritation value, a password-protected screen-saver offers no real security since anyone who switches the computer off and on again can easily bypass the password. Of course this takes time and might discourage a passer-by who doesn't wish to be caught messing around with your machine.

Equally insecure is the Log-in to Windows procedure which appears after you specify different users for the computer (**Start** > **Settings** > **Control Panel** > **Users**). To be fair to Microsoft, this was never intended to be a security measure, only to allow individual users to set up their desktops and document folders as they wished. If a snooper is confronted by the log-in box, simply cancelling it opens up the default[2] desktop from which the whole computer is accessible. (Of course, to the most casual of amateur snoopers, the mere appearance of a log-in procedure might be enough to deter them.)

Marginally more secure is the concealment of individual files. Let us assume that you have used Notepad (Windows' basic text editor) to draft a letter you would prefer no one else to read. You have saved the letter as **secret.txt**. Like most programs, Notepad has a default storage location where it will save your documents unless told otherwise. In this case it is the **My Documents** folder which Windows creates

[2] Default settings are those things that happen when nothing different is specified. When you open your word processor and start typing, words appear on screen even though you have not defined a font, text size, etc. The word processor is using its default settings, which will continue to be applied until you specify something different. When a dialog box opens on screen, there is almost always a default setting (usually the button outlined in a darker colour). Hitting the **Enter (Return)** button on your keyboard selects the default.

178

automatically on installation. Instead of accepting this folder, you could decide to store it elsewhere on your hard disk. If you chose a system folder such as **Fonts**, at least this would not be the first place a snooper would look for text files. Of course calling the letter **secret.txt** is a bit of a giveaway. A better name would be something less obvious and preferably misleading. **install_log.txt**, for example, would look like a text document created when a program was installed on the computer.

Better still, conceal the type of file. To do this, we need to understand how the OS identifies file types. Most Windows file names consist of two parts – an identifier and an extension. The identifier is the actual name of the file – in the example above **secret**, and the extension comprises the sequence of letters after the dot (period) which specifies the type of file – in this case **txt**, a text file. Windows relies on the extension to determine which application is used to process the file; so double-clicking **.doc** files will open them in Microsoft Word®, **.html** files will open in your default web browser, etc. (Note that this behaviour does not apply to Mac or UNIX computers, where information contained in a branch of the file itself specifies the correct application.)

Let's return to that embarrassing letter. Instead of calling it **secret.txt** and saving it in the **My Documents** folder, we will save it as **hammer.cur** and store it in the **Cursors** folder. (Like **Fonts**, **Cursors** is a system folder created by Windows when it installs. It is a sub-folder of the **Windows** folder.) We can either do this when we initially save the file by specifying this name in the **Save As** dialog box, or subsequently by changing its name within Explorer (right-click on the file and select **Rename** from the menu which appears, or select the file and press the **F2** button). If this generates a warning box from the operating system, just ignore it and continue.

You might find that some programs will not allow you to save files without adding the correct file extensions. Most digital picture software, for example, will not let you save a JPEG image as **naughty_picture.cur**. If you try, you will probably find the file has been renamed to **naughty_picture.cur.jpg**. In this case it is better to save the file with the correct extension and to modify it later manually.

If you open Explorer and look at the **Cursors** folder, you will see a whole series of .cur files which contain the various mouse pointers available on your system. Of course, **hammer.cur** will not actually contain a cursor. Normally, to open a file it is only necessary to double-click it. In this case double-clicking it will open a new dialog box asking you to specify which program to open it with. If you like, you can select Notepad from the list of programs, but make sure you uncheck **Always use this program to open this type of file**, otherwise all your cursor files will be permanently associated with Notepad. You might prefer to reverse the process by renaming the file to **hammer.txt**, after which, double-clicking it will once more open it in Notepad.

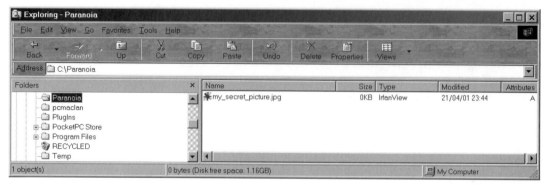

Figure 11.2 Looking up a file in Windows Explorer

Of course none of these procedures qualifies as encryption – the data itself is unchanged and freely accessible to anyone who knows how to track it down. A further problem here is that software exists which can check that a file type conforms to its extension. So let us add in one further trick – our first look at steganography as defined in Chapter 10.

Windows allows a user to define how a particular file type is handled. Let us assume that you have a photograph called **my_secret_picture.jpg** stored in a folder called **Paranoia**. If you look in Explorer, using the **Details** view (selected from the **View** icon on the toolbar), you might see something like Figure 11.2. In the right-hand pane, you can see the file's name, its size and the date it was last modified. It also shows the type of file – in this case it lists IrfanView, the picture viewer used on this computer to handle JPEG images, and it add's IrfanView's icon to the left of the file name to inform you visually that **.jpg** is a registered file type as far as the operating system is concerned.

To hide this and any similar files, I can create a new false file type, then order Windows to handle it in a different way. Within Explorer, if I click **Tools** > **Folder Options** > **File Types**, I open up the File Types window shown in Figure 11.3. Here I can create my own file type by clicking the **New Type** button. This opens the window shown in Figure 11.4. Creating my false file type requires four steps. First, I click the **Change Icon** button and select a random icon from the ones that are offered – I have chosen a meaningless globe. Next I create a spurious type description **Java script file** and define the Content Type as **text/plain** from the drop down menu. Finally, I create a new extension for my file type. I have chosen **.pjp** after checking in the window shown in Figure 11.3 that this extension is not currently in use – it is important to do this. If I now close down these boxes, return to Explorer, change the name of my picture from **my_secret_picture.jpg** to **my_secret_picture.pjp**, and confirm in the warning dialog box that I don't mind if the file becomes **unusable**, Explorer's view of my file changes to that shown in Figure 11.5.

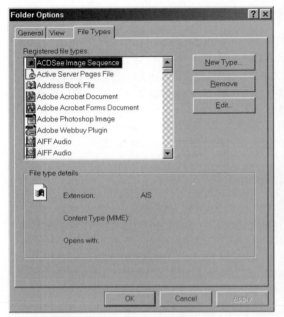

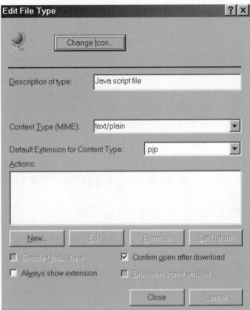

Figure 11.3 Configuring files types in Explorer's Folder Options window

Figure 11.4 Creating a false file type using the Edit button

Note that my new **.pjp** file type is completely legitimate as far as Windows is concerned. It has its own icon and description and appears in every way to be what it pretends to be. More useful still, if I change the extension of any other file to **.pjp**, they too will appear with the globe icon and the 'Java script file' description. Of course, the content of the file is unchanged and if anybody attempts to open the file from within a picture viewer it will display as normal. As with our embarrassing letter above, double-clicking the file will no longer open it in our chosen graphics viewer. We will have to name it back to **.jpg** for this to work. If we wish to conceal the content itself, we need to move up a level of security and look at data encryption software.

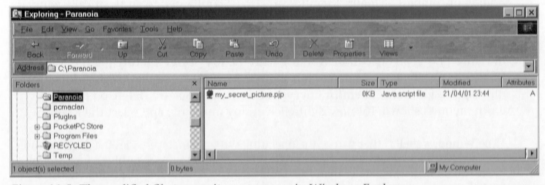

Figure 11.5 The modified file type as it now appears in Windows Explorer

Level 2: Serious Security

As noted in Chapter 10, encrypting a file means applying an algorithm to the contents so that they are scrambled to anyone who does not possess the correct key – usually a password or pass-phrase. To do this, we need to obtain encryption software and install it on our computer. There are any number of encryption programs available; check any of the major software archives on the web, and you will find a good selection. As ever with mainly home-brew software the quality varies wildly. Some encryption programs offer a very high level of security while some are almost useless.

Eugene The Businessman

Level 2 security would be appropriate for Eugene. Eugene would never pretend that the files he stores on his office computer are of earth-shattering importance, but he knows they would be of great interest to his competitors. After all, office stationery is a cut-throat business. Eugene's premises are open-plan which means that any visitor walking through the office can easily look at most of the company's computers. Currently, Eugene is deep in negotiations with an Eastern European paper manufacturer whose products are so cheap and so revolutionary that they could open up a whole new market for Eugene's company. He doesn't want his competitors, or even his staff, to read his correspondence with his new partners. Simple encryption might save him a lot of sleepless nights.

At this level of security, ease of use is also a factor to be considered. Since we are concerned with encrypting and decrypting single files and we are not otherwise hiding their existence, an obvious solution is software which installs a shortcut into the menu which opens when we right-click on a file. One of the most efficient of these is Kremlin®. Kremlin consists of a range of utilities to help you secure your data. Files are encrypted using some of the most secure algorithms including BlowFish, DES, IDEA and RC4, and the suite also includes utilities that securely erase sensitive data from your computer. Finally, Kremlin can also be configured to automatically wipe sensitive areas of your hard disk and erase all records of your activities when you log off your computer.

In Figure 11.6, I am once more working with the **my_secret_picture.jpg** file. When Kremlin is installed, it integrates with the Windows shell,[3] so that right-clicking on a file displays additional **Kremlin Encrypt** and **Kremlin Secure Delete** on the drop down menu as shown. If I now right-click on my image file and select the **Kremlin**

---

[3] The Windows shell is that part of the operating system which provides the graphical user interface (GUI) – icons, menus, dialog boxes, etc. – that many people think of as Windows itself. You, of course, are wiser than that and recognize Windows as the comprehensive operating system it really is!

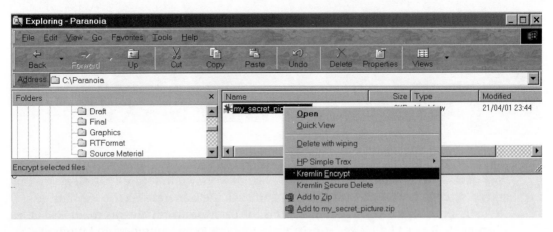

Figure 11.6 *Encrypting a file by calling Kremlin from the right-click menu*

Kremlin is a shareware[4] program published by Mach5 Software and available from www.mach5.com If you obtain Kremlin outside of the United States, you might find that the strongest encryption algorithms are not available. (See the final section of Chapter 10 which explains this.)

Encrypt option, I am presented with the dialog box shown in Figure 11.7. Here I can enter and verify a suitable pass-phrase and instruct the software to delete the source file. This leaves me with an encrypted file called **my_secret_picture.kgb**. Of course this file now shows in Explorer as a **Kremlin encrypted file**. I could use the steganographic process described in the previous section to change this to something much more innocent!

To decrypt this file and restore it to its original form, I simply need to double-click it. This opens the dialog box shown in Figure 11.8. I enter my pass-phrase and, if I wish to, delete the source (encrypted) file and **my_secret_picture.jpg** is restored. One of Kremlin's greatest virtues is its simplicity of operation. Add to that the strength of the encryption algorithms it employs and you have an excellent all-round encryption program.

Similar to Kremlin, but slightly more complex in operation is TwoFish encryption. Using TwoFish requires you to generate a secure key which is then used to encrypt

[4] Just in case you've forgotten or have skipped earlier chapters, shareware is basically try-before-you-buy software. You install the program and try it out for a preset period, usually 30 days. If you like it, you pay for it – most authors now accept secure online payment using a credit card, and receive a registration code which unlocks the software by removing the on-screen reminders to pay and, often, provides additional features.

 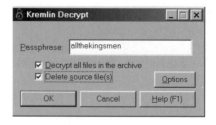

Figure 11.7 and 11.8 Kremlin's Encrypt and Decrypt dialog boxes

your data. Starting the program opens the window shown in Figure 11.9. Here you can enter a suitable key phrase (pass-phrase) and click the **Generate Secure Key** button. (Note that the Secure Key more than fulfils the password requirements we looked at in Chapter 10. It is a 43-digit key consisting of random letters, numbers and symbols.) With the key in place, clicking the **Encrypt File** button allows you to browse to the file to be processed. You can name it anything you wish and give it any file extension you like, which removes the drawback with Kremlin mentioned earlier.

 There are many other programs, some offering stronger or weaker encryption than Kremlin. Most of them can be downloaded free from the web. Try any of the software archives I have referred to previously. A feature-limited version of the TwoFish encryption program described below is available free from www.stealthencrypt.com

Unlike Kremlin, double-clicking the encrypted file does not open a decryption dialog box. Instead you need to re-open TwoFish encryption, re-enter your Key Phrase, click the **Decrypt file** button and browse to the encrypted file. You then enter a name for the decrypted file and TwoFish unscrambles it and writes back the original contents.

Figure 11.9 Using TwoFish Encryption's built-in Key Generator to create a secure key

184

Both Kremlin and TwoFish encryption use symmetrical encryption since the same key both encrypts and decrypts a file.

The second security procedure at this level is locking the Windows desktop to prevent unauthorized access. To be useful, you need this lock to operate both when you leave your computer in the middle of a session and when the computer is started up. This will prevent someone from getting round the lock by simply restarting your computer. When your computer starts up, the desktop lock software is loaded towards the end of the boot process. Anyone trying to access your desktop afterwards will be stopped by the lock, but only if the computer has successfully booted through to the desktop. If the boot is interrupted or reconfigured to bypass the lock software, your protection will not be loaded. Before considering the lock software itself, we should look at the various ways in which an intruder might try to get round the protection.

To implement the security countermeasures outlined in Table 11.2, overleaf, we need to understand how a standard PC boots to the desktop. When a computer is switched on, it goes through a series of self-tests to ensure that its key components such as memory, keyboard, etc. are working properly. This routine is known as the Power-On Self Test (POST) and often beeps at you when it is finished to let you know that all is well. Once the POST is completed, the computer looks at its Basic Input Output System (BIOS) to find out how to proceed. BIOS settings are stored on a special chip on the computer's motherboard, known as the CMOS. They cannot be stored on a disk because the BIOS actually tells the computer which disk to boot from. BIOS settings are volatile. This means that the BIOS chip must be continuously powered otherwise the settings are lost, so a small rechargable battery is used to keep a current flowing.

There is a wide variety of BIOS settings, most of which are irrelevant to this chapter, but we are concerned with the setting which tells the computer where to look for the files which boot the system up to the desktop. BIOS settings can only be modified at boot time, usually by pressing the **Delete** key while the initial boot screen is displayed. (Check your computer's manual if this doesn't work.) This brings up an options menu. The actual layout of the menu depends on the BIOS installed, but somewhere within the settings you will find an option to set the order in which the system should check its disks for the boot files. This is usually displayed as **A,C,CD-ROM** or **C,A,CD-ROM**, etc. We need to set this so that the C:\ drive is first on the list. We then need to find the option that protects the BIOS with a password and enable this too. (Of course we apply the password guidelines detailed in Chapter 10.)

Next, we need to configure Windows' boot options so that an intruder cannot interrupt the process. There are several ways of doing this but we will consider just two, using the software we first met back in Chapter 3. To complete this part of the process you will need either TweakUI or TweakAll. Once you have one or the other installed, we can continue.

Both TweakUI and TweakAll offer controls to turn off the Function keys which allow

Table 11.2 How An Intruder Bypasses Desktop Lock

What an intruder can do to bypass a desktop lock	What we can do to stop him
1 He can interrupt the boot process by pressing the Control (or F5 and F8) keys as Windows starts to load. This will offer him the option of booting into DOS from where he can access your files directly.	We need to disable the Function Keys which allow this to happen, thus preventing an intruder from getting to the DOS command line.
2 He can access the BIOS and reconfigure it to boot from the A:\ (floppy) drive. By using a bootable floppy disk, an intruder can load an unprotected operating system, thus bypassing your desktop lock.	We need to configure the BIOS to prevent the computer from booting from the A:\ drive. Then we need to lock the BIOS to stop this settings from being changed.
3 He can disconnect the BIOS battery. After half an hour (or so) the CMOS chip 'forgets' your settings and returns to its default settings which are configured with the A:\ (floppy) drive as the first bootable drive. He can then proceed as in **2** above.	Frankly, we can't do much to prevent this, but this level of intrusion requires extended access to the computer. This is no longer casual snooping but serious infiltration which requires a higher level of security procedures to withstand.

Check This Out... TweakUI® is a Microsoft utility which was supplied with earlier versions of Windows but can still be downloaded from Microsoft's website at www.microsoft.com. (Check your Windows CD-ROM before doing this.) TweakAll® is a more advanced version of the same thing. It is available from www.codeforge.co.uk

the user to modify the boot process. The relevant windows are shown in Figure 11.10. In TweakAll, on the left of the picture, the relevant control is marked **Enable function keys at startup**, in Tweak UI it is labelled **Function keys available**. In either case, the option should be disabled by clicking in the check-box to remove the tick.

By doing this, we have laid down a further layer of protection, but it is a fairly weak one. As shown in the table above, there always remains the option of powering down the BIOS so that it reverts to its default settings. We are however making things more difficult for a casual

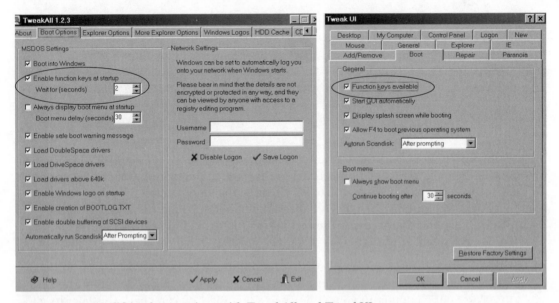

Figure 11.10 Modifying boot settings with TweakAll and TweakUI

snooper and that it all that this level of security is intended to do. With our BIOS settings properly configured we can now look at installing a Windows desktop lock.

There are any number of desktop locking programs available on the internet. In addition, the facility is often provided as part of another application. Symantec's pcAnywhere, for example, which allows you to access your computer remotely, includes such a feature. If you don't want to invest in a complete suite such as Norton Security, I suggest you visit one of the major software archives on the web and compare the features and prices of the standalone utilities before deciding which application suits you best. Of the many available, Windows Security Officer offers an excellent range of features at a reasonable price.

In addition to locking your desktop, Windows Security Officer enables you to restrict access to a wide range of other system settings. You can also assign separate system profiles to different users, providing each with his or her own custom desktop, and you can disable Start menu items, hide particular drives, disable the DOS prompt and hide individual desktop icons. If you are a parent with computer-mad offspring, you can even set an access timer for each user which determines when and how long computer access will be allowed. (We will be looking at Windows Security Officer's role as a virtual policeman in Chapter 20.)

187

To look at the facilities available from Norton, visit www.norton.com. To compare different desktop locking programs, try a download site such as www.davecentral.com, download.cnet.com or www.tucows.com Of the programs mentioned below, Windows Security Officer is available as a shareware download from www.mybestsoft.com, ScreenLock from www.screenlock.com and Windows LockUp from www.softheap.com

Firing up Windows Security Officer opens the window shown in Figure 11.11. You will notice the range of User Options listed in the pane to the left. I have selected the **Lock Desktop** entry, which allows me to specify how the lock operates and enter an access password. The installer also drops a special Lock Desktop icon onto your desktop. Double-click this and access to the computer is barred to anyone without the correct password.

Other desktop security programs operate in a similar way. ScreenLock is an excellent utility which offers fewer functions. In addition to the lock, it also logs any attempts to access your computer in your absence to a text file. You can check this later to see who has been at your computer. Windows LockUp is another which has established a reputation for reliability. It starts automatically with Windows and optionally locks your desktop as soon as it loads. Like Windows Security Officer, Windows LockUp allows you to define a schedule and duration for each user or to restrict access to your PC during certain times.

Figure 11.11 Locking the Windows desktop with Windows Security Officer

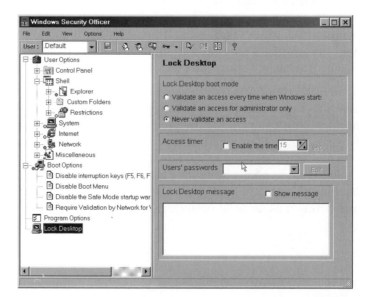

188

Level 3: Advanced Security

We start this level by assuming that you are going to implement all the procedures already covered. Now we are going above and beyond these measures to build a level of security which is enough to defeat the most dedicated hacker or even the might of the law enforcement community. At this advanced level, you risk being seen as a threat to national security – yes, I know this is ridiculous, but current legislation in both the US and the UK supports this statement. Your system will not only employ the strongest encryption available, it will also use stealth technology to hide the existence of that encryption. Why you should need this level of security is, of course, none of my business!

Let's begin by looking at the steps required to implement total security. We are going to:

➤ encrypt data using industrial-strength algorithms;

➤ store those encrypted files on secure media – in effect, on encrypted drives;

➤ disguise those encrypted drives so they appear to be normal files.

We have already covered step 1 in the previous section. We will make a condition, however, that you only use one of the most secure encryption algorithms. I suggest that you install encryption software that offers either BlowFish or TwoFish. As things stand at present, these are the most secure cryptosystems available.

Dennis The Porn Peeper

Advanced-level security is perhaps appropriate to Dennis, the seediest member of our cast. While Dennis' activities in hunting down smutty pictures is not illegal, their discovery by his wife would have serious repercussions. Aware of this, Dennis has become quite paranoid in his attempts to hide his hobby. Dennis has nightmares about police officers raiding his house and finding numerous bosoms hidden on his computer. To help him sleep, he needs to know that his security is at the highest possible level. While we need not have much sympathy for Dennis – after all, he has only himself to blame – the security he demands is appropriate to other, less ridiculous, but equally sensitive, files.

Step 2 requires us to download some very specialized software. Again, there are different choices available, but only two are both secure enough and easy enough to use to fit our requirements. The first of these is Jetico's BestCrypt and the second is Scramdisk from the strangely named Aman and Useful Utilities. BestCrypt is a full commercial program with excellent online support. It allows you to create what are called 'containers' – essentially heavily encrypted folders on your hard disks or

Figure 11.12 The main Scramdisk window

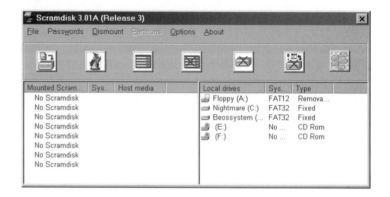

removable media. Once a container has been mounted – for this you need to enter a password – it appears in Windows Explorer as a virtual drive with a drive letter, and behaves like one as well. You can drag files to and from the container or open files and programs from within the container. Close the container – you can do this in a hurry by hitting a hot key combination – and the virtual drive disappears from your computer. Once closed, a container appears as an ordinary file.

Scramdisk is similar in operation, but smaller and faster and free. This explains why it is so popular with those who have secrets to hide! Firing up Scramdisk opens the window shown in Figure 11.12. From here, you can create a new container, enter your password to mount an existing container, dismount a container or control a range of other options. Since both BestCrypt and Scramdisk operate in a broadly similar way, we will use Scramdisk to illustrate how this type of software functions.

From Scramdisk's **File** menu, click **Create Container**. This opens the window shown in Figure 11.13. The wizard, which you have started, guides you through the process of

Figure 11.13 Using the wizard to create a new Scramdisk container file

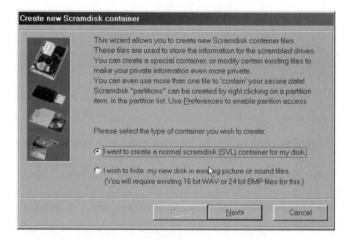

creating a new encrypted container on your hard disk. Note the two options at the bottom. You have the choice of either creating a container which will appear to your operating system as a normal file (the default setting creates a container with a **.svl** extension) or applying steganographic techniques to hide that file within an existing picture or sound file. (BestCrypt does not offer this option.)

Follow the wizard to the next windows and you are then asked to name the file. You can call it anything you like, but common sense will tell you to avoid something like **secret_pictures.svl**. You do not even have to use the **.svl** extension, so a name like **household_accounts.pjp** (remember **.pjp** from earlier?) might be enough to scare snoopers off. You are also asked how large you want the container to be. It can be any size up to 4 Gigabytes.

The next screen asks you to enter and confirm a series of passwords – the wizard suggests four passwords to maximize security, but this is probably overkill. Hit the **Next** button once more and the window shown as Figure 11.14 opens. This one puzzles a lot of users. Scramdisk uses random data – basically a string of unrelated letters and digits to scramble the container. To create this data, you wave your mouse pointer about over the window and keep on clicking the **Random** button until both indicator bars fill up and the **Next** button is enabled. After this, the container is created and appears on your hard disk.

To access the container, you click either **Passwords > Enter a disk password** or the **Passwords** icon on the tool bar. Once you have entered your password(s), clicking **File > Mount Container File** allows you to browse to your container which then opens as a virtual drive. From there, you can use it in the same way as the BestCrypt container I described earlier.

Scramdisk has one distinctly steganographic element which lifts it above similar programs. It treats all files on your computer in exactly the same way regardless of whether they are encrypted containers or not. This sounds obscure, so let me explain.

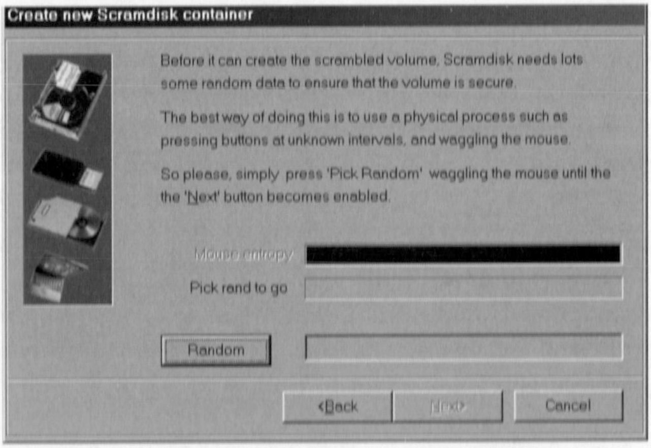

Figure 11.14 Creating random data in Scramdisk

Create new Scramdisk container

Before it can create the scrambled volume, Scramdisk needs lots some random data to ensure that the volume is secure.

The best way of doing this is to use a physical process such as pressing buttons at unknown intervals, and waggling the mouse.

So please, simply press 'Pick Random' waggling the mouse until the the 'Next' button becomes enabled.

Mouse entropy

Pick rand to go

Random

<Back   Next>   Cancel

You can drag a container file onto the Scramdisk window and, provided you have entered the correct password(s), Scramdisk will mount it. If you have not entered the password(s), Scramdisk will ask for them, but it will do this regardless of whether the file is a container or something completely innocent. This means that, at a visual level, there is no way that an outsider can tell which files on your computer conceal encrypted containers and which are ordinary data files.

So now we have encrypted files which we can store in encrypted containers which look like normal files – three levels of security which should be enough to defeat any intruder. One additional precaution might be to remove our encrypted containers from our computer altogether, which means storing them on removable media. An encrypted container on a rewriteable CD-ROM, which can be mounted, accessed, dismounted and stored in a safe location is about as secure as you can get. (If you are storing secrets vital to the nation's security, keep your CD-ROM's in a microwave by your bed, and when you hear the agents of a foreign power breaking down your door, give the disks a quick roast at full power. I guarantee that nothing will ever be retrieved from them.)

Of course there are lots of other little tricks you can play to improve your security. You might consider storing not only your data files but also the software you use to access them in encrypted containers. This means installing the programs with the containers mounted and instructing the installers to load the applications onto your virtual drives rather than the default **C:\Program Files**. You can use the false file type trick we looked at earlier to make your containers look like legitimate Windows files. In fact, you can mix and match any of the techniques described in this chapter to confound the snoopers.

The final aspect of total security is to wipe out all our tracks so that no one suspects there is anything to find. I look at this in detail in the following chapter.

Chapter 11 – Security Checklist

1   Once you have decided that the data on your computer is worth encrypting, you should decide on the level of security which is appropriate to your needs. At the basic level, you might do no more than make your confidential files difficult to find and setting up a password-protected screen-saver to prevent casual passers-by from scanning your disk. At the top level you can not only encrypt your data, but also store it in encrypted containers masquerading as ordinary files. You must decide how secure you need to be.

2   Locking your screen-saver so that the desktop cannot be accessed without a password is a simple precaution to prevent snoopers from looking at your work while you are absent from your computer. It can easily be defeated by restarting your computer.

3 A simple way of hiding individual files is to store them in a folder which is not normally used for data, and/or to change their extensions so that they appear to be different types of files. A more complex, but much more effective, technique is to create a false file type which appears to the OS to be legitimate and to change each file's extension to match the new type.

4 A higher level of security requires the use of proprietary encryption software to render a file unreadable to anyone who does not have the correct password or pass-phrase. Kremlin is an example of this type of program. It integrates with the Windows shell to provide an entry in a file's right-click menu which allows you to encrypt its contents.

5 You will also benefit from securely locking your desktop. Before installing a locking program, it is sensible to reconfigure your system's BIOS to prevent an intruder from getting past your lock. After this, you can install an application such as Windows Security Officer or Windows LockUp which will deny access to anyone without the correct password.

6 The final stage involves storing your encrypted files in special containers, which can be unlocked and mounted as virtual drives. This also requires special software such as BestCrypt or the free program Scramdisk.

7 A further refinement would be to create your encrypted containers on removable media which could be securely stored away from your computer. Using rewritable CD-ROMs is a good way of doing this.

Wiping The Slate Clean

The Tracks You Leave Behind

At the end of Chapter 11, I left one vital aspect of your security hanging in the air. This chapter deals with just one subject: removing files and other traces from your computer. You might think that this is an insignificant subject to devote an entire chapter to, but it gets worse. There is another chapter coming – Chapter 17, as it happens – which deals with much the same subject, only this time it is cleaning up the tracks from your internet browsing. So, two whole chapters on slate wiping. Why is this so important?

To answer this question, we need to look at the way in which your computer handles data files. Let us assume that you are writing a highly sensitive document – we'll call it **Top Secret.doc**. You open your word processor, create this document, and, when it is complete, you follow the security procedures we looked at in the previous chapter and encrypt it. The document is safe, and no one knows it is there. Well, unfortunately not. Microsoft might be pretty good at designing software, but they are not so good at preserving your secrets. Click your **Start** button and check the menu entry marked **Documents**. There is a shortcut to **Top Secret.doc** which tells any snooper that the document exists. Now open Windows Explorer and drill down to **C:\Windows\Recent**. Oh look, there it is again. This is the folder which stores the shortcuts for your **Documents** Start menu entry.

Now, open your word processor and click the **File** menu. Unless you have changed the default setting, there you will find yet another shortcut to **Top Secret.doc**. Of course, none of these shortcuts will enable a snooper to actually read your file which remains safely encrypted. But very often your security will depend on concealing the very existence of sensitive data, and already we have found three signposts pointing to it.

This is still not the end of the story. While you were working on the document, there would have been at least one copy of it stored in memory. If you have sufficient physical memory, this copy will have disappeared when you closed down your word processor, but if memory was running short, Windows will have stored the working copy on your hard disk in virtual memory – the Windows swap file. There is specialized software which can recover data from the swap file. There's more to come. Your word processor will have created a second copy of the document as a temporary file on your hard disk. It will probably have been called **~$p Secret.doc** – note the tilde (~) and dollar signs at the start of the name to identify it as a temporary file. This file should have been deleted when you closed the document, but the fact that it was once stored on your disk means that a determined snooper might still be able to recover it.

Take a look at Figure 12.1. This shows Explorer's view of the folder in which I store the chapters for this book. I am currently writing Chapter 12. Look in the pane on the right and you will see a file called **~$apter12.doc**. This is the temporary copy which Microsoft Word has created. Now look below this at the file called **~WRL0002.tmp**. The date listed under the **Modified** column heading shows that this file was last accessed four months previously. It is another temporary copy which was not deleted

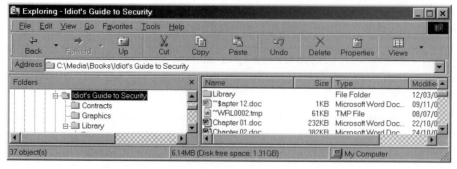

Figure 12.1 Windows Explorer's view of the chapters for this book

as it should have been – possibly my computer crashed before Word had a chance to clean up. Of course I could (and should) have deleted it manually, but I deliberately left it there to illustrate the point that you cannot always rely on your applications to tidy up their own mess. I don't know what **~WRL0002.tmp** actually contains, but I can open and read it in Word, and the same will apply to stray copies of your own sensitive files.

Most modern applications not only store a list of recently opened documents, they also pass the details on to the operating system to include in its Recent Documents list. So the next person to use your computer can fire up your graphics viewer and discover that the last photograph you looked at was **Nudeblonde.jpg** – which could prove embarrassing. So let's consider the steps you need to take to clean up your tracks.

First, we need to remove that list of recently opened documents from the Start menu. Since these are stored as shortcuts, one way would be to open the **C:\Windows\Recent** folder in Explorer and simply delete all the contents. Of course this would just move them to the **Recycle Bin**, where they can still be seen. Holding down the **Shift** key while you delete them will prevent this, and we will be looking at permanently deleting files later in this chapter. We can also call on some old friends to solve the problem. TweakAll, the utility we have looked at earlier in the book, provides a setting to clear the recently used documents list at shutdown. X-Setup goes one better and allows you to remove the **Documents** entry altogether. As you can see from Figure 12.2, drilling down to **Appearance\Start menu\Visible Items\Visible Items** presents you with a list of Start menu entries which can be unchecked. You will see that I have disabled **Documents**, thus solving this problem. Of course you will still need to remove the shortcuts from the **C:\Windows\Recent** folder.

Figure 12.2 Using X-Setup to hide the Documents entry in Windows Start menu

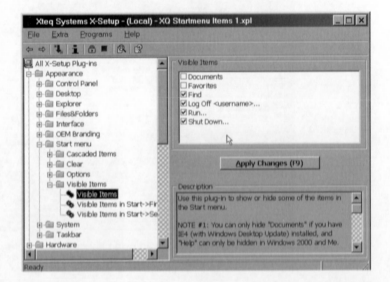

Figure 12.3 Deletion
that doesn't work

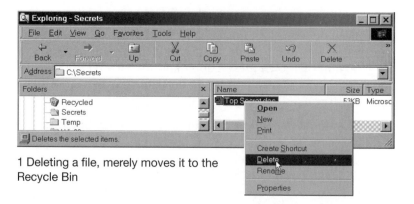

1 Deleting a file, merely moves it to the Recycle Bin

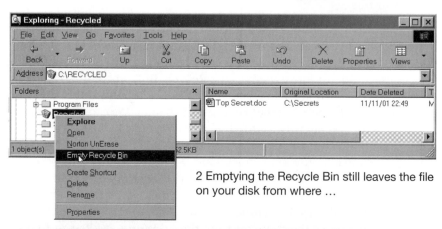

2 Emptying the Recycle Bin still leaves the file on your disk from where ...

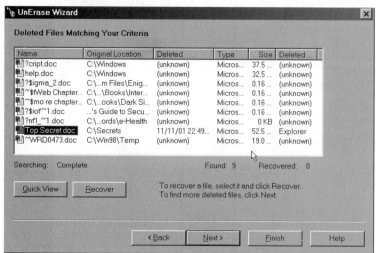

3 ... it can easily be recovered using specialist software such as Norton Utilities' UnErase program

With two signposts removed, we now need to consider the list provided by the applications themselves. This is a harder nut to crack because, unlike the operating system, applications don't store these settings as shortcuts which can be deleted but within their own support files. There is software that can handle this problem. Evidence Eliminator® – a program we will be looking at later in this chapter and in more detail in Chapter 17 – can accept a series of plug-ins for applications which remove these entries. A simpler, but rather tedious solution involves opening enough non-sensitive files from within the application to knock your particular file off the list. So if an application records the last four documents it accessed, you will need to open four innocent documents. Some programs allow you to remove the list of recent files entirely or to limit the number of entries it displays. Look in the applications **Options** settings to see if this facility is available.

The Delete That Doesn't Delete

You might think that the safest way to dispose of sensitive data that you no longer require would be simply to delete it. As an astonishing number of criminals have discovered to their cost, you would be completely wrong.

Microsoft is playing a trick on you. If you select a file and click the **Delete** button, or right-click a file and select **Delete** from the drop down menu, your intention, presumably, is to delete that file from your computer. To protect you from your own mistakes, the brains behind Windows decided that they would give you a chance to change your mind. The Delete command is nothing more than the Move command, but with a single destination folder, the **Recycle Bin**. Look in the **Recycle Bin** and you will find all your deleted files waiting for you to pardon them and return them to their source folders.

If you empty the **Recycle Bin** or hold down the **Shift** key while deleting files, you might expect those files to disappear forever. Wrong again. Windows simply changes the names of the files by overwriting their first characters, removes the File Allocation Table's 'pointer' to the start of the files and marks the space they occupied on your hard disk as available. Until you save something to disk and overwrite them, they remain on your disk in their original form. They can easily be recovered using any of the undelete programs which are currently available. Figure 12.3 illustrates the Delete that doesn't.

I noted earlier that the inability to delete files had confounded criminals in the past. There have been several high-profile cases in the last few years where law-breakers have taken their computers in for repair, thinking that records of their illegal activities had been safely removed from their disks. Instead, computer engineers have resurrected their files and provided the police with enough evidence to convict their surprised clients. Some commentators have claimed this to be a breach of trust, but whatever your opinion, it is important to recognize how hard it is to permanently remove files from your computer.

Before we look at solutions to the problem of permanent file deletion, there is one further complication we need to understand. Magnetic remanence is defined (by the US Navy, of all people) as 'the residual magnetic or electrical representation of data that has been in some way erased or overwritten'. When you delete a file, or even overwrite that file with new data, magnetic traces of the old file remain on the disk. Specialist equipment exists which can read this residual information and can sometimes allow the original data to be reconstructed. This process is both expensive and time consuming, so would normally only concern those dealing in highly classified information. For most of us, overwriting data files would provide adequate data security.

One step up from deleting files is the process referred to in government circles as 'sanitization'. Sanitization refers to a file-cleaning process which renders data totally unreadable. It is used, for example, within government departments when old computers are disposed of. Three techniques are commonly used for media sanitization:

➤ overwriting;

➤ degaussing; and

➤ physical destruction.

Overwriting and degaussing are the methods recommended for the disposal of highly sensitive information. Let's look at each of these in turn.

Overwriting Existing Data

In most cases this is a perfectly secure method of cleaning data from magnetic media. Overwriting uses a program to write a random pattern of data into the locations on the disk where the file to be sanitized is stored. The number of times the data is overwritten determines the effectiveness of the deletion. As described earlier, it is important not to confuse overwriting with deleting the file. Deleting a file merely removes the file's location from your computer's File Allocation Table (FAT) and does nothing to alter the stored data itself. We will consider overwriting in more detail in the next section.

Degaussing

To degauss (pronounced dee-gouse) means to demagnetize. This method magnetically erases data from storage media by applying a strong magnet or an electrical degausser to the disk. This is not a technique available to the ordinary home computer user since it cannot be applied to specific files, only to the entire disk, rendering all data useless. Degaussers can be bought commercially and might be suitable for a company intending to replace its existing computers, which needs to make sure that all sensitive data is removed from the old ones before they are scrapped.

Physical destruction

This is the final, and most drastic, solution to data removal. Again this is hardly appropriate for the home user's hard disk, but it might be applied to media such as floppy disks and CD-ROMs. Snapping a CD-ROM into small pieces or shredding the media from inside a floppy disk's casing is an obvious and highly effective way of making sure that data is destroyed. Better still, throw them into a fire!

I am going to close this section by listing the four steps required to ensure that sensitive data is completely destroyed. These could form the basis of a data security program for a company or an individual dealing in highly confidential information.

➤ Windows' file deletion functions are not adequate to remove sensitive data since they only remove the 'pointer' to a file leaving your data still recoverable.

➤ Any media such as floppy disks, tape back-ups or CD-ROMs which contain sensitive information must not be allowed outside of your control without appropriate sanitization.

➤ When data is removed from storage media, every precaution should be taken to remove duplicate versions that may exist on the same or other storage media, back-up files, temporary files, hidden support files or extended memory.

➤ Any storage media on equipment to be scrapped or transferred outside of your control should be thoroughly sanitized.

Deleting Your Data Completely

Having considered more drastic solutions, let us now look at how we can securely delete individual files. It might seem that by simply overwriting a file with new data, that file would be erased, but this is not always the case. To guarantee that no data from the file can ever be retrieved, we need to undertake the following steps.

➤ File data must be overwritten several times (see below for information on how many passes are required for different levels of security).

➤ The 'file slack' associated with a file must also be properly overwritten. (*Note*: Windows uses fixed-sized clusters on a hard disk to store data. An entire cluster is used even if the data being stored does not fill the cluster. The space between the end of the file and the end of the cluster is called the file slack and can contain sensitive data. If a cluster is filled with data, and then the cluster is only partly overwritten, the data in the file slack space might still be recoverable. (This is illustrated in Figure 12.4)

➤ Any free space on your hard disk must be wiped. Free space – that is space currently unallocated by the file system – can contain previous or temporary versions of your file. Free space is also used by Windows as virtual memory.

➤ The file name as referenced by the operating system should also be scrambled.

201

Figure 12.4
Understanding file slack

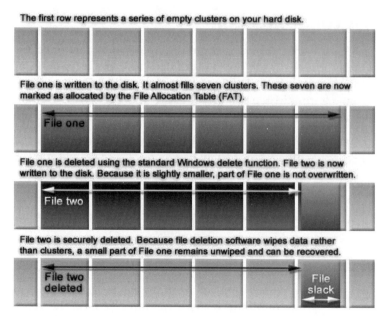

The first row represents a series of empty clusters on your hard disk.

File one is written to the disk. It almost fills seven clusters. These seven are now marked as allocated by the File Allocation Table (FAT).

File one is deleted using the standard Windows delete function. File two is now written to the disk. Because it is slightly smaller, part of File one is not overwritten.

File two is securely deleted. Because file deletion software wipes data rather than clusters, a small part of File one remains unwiped and can be recovered.

How many times should we overwrite sensitive data? (These are known as 'passes'.) A recognized expert in this area is Peter Guttman, designer of the Guttman Method of file deletion (see Table 12.1 below). His recorded view is that each time data is overwritten it becomes harder (and therefore more costly) to recover, but that regardless of the number of passes, data can never be totally deleted. In his own words '...it is effectively impossible to sanitize storage locations by simply overwriting them, no matter how many overwrite passes are made or what data patterns are written.' Despite this, we can render files **almost** unrecoverable. Table 12.1 below describes various recognized methods of secure file deletion, along with some notes on where each method might be appropriate.

Table 12.1 Recognized Methods Of Secure File Deletion

Data deletion method	How method works	Notes
Single pass method	The data area is overwritten once with either 1s, 0s or random data patterns.	Most authorities accept that the single pass method is sufficient to stop standard software recovery tools. It would not, however, withstand the tools used by government agencies. This method is fast but not very secure and cannot be used to wipe data stored on compressed drives. (See note below table.)

Two pass method	The data area is overwritten twice. (The first pass might be with random data and the second pass with zeroes, for example.) Passes should be checked to confirm that data has been overwritten.	This method adds more security against professional software recovery tools. It can also be used to delete files stored on compressed drives.
DoD method	The data area is overwritten up to seven times, using three alternating passes of 0s and 1s followed by one pass of random data. This method is designed to both 'clear' and 'sanitize' a 'rigid non-removable disk'. To clear a disk, the method requires you to 'overwrite all addressable locations with a single character.'	This method is proposed by the US Department of Defense for both governmental and industrial file deletion. It is based on standards outlined in the Department of Defense's National Industrial Security Program Operating Manual (NISPOM). This method is supposed to stop hardware recovery tools such as electron-tunnelling microscopes, but there have been suggestions that the DoD proposes this method, knowing that their own tools are sophisticated enough to defeat it. Some see the hand of the US National Security Agency (NSA) at work here!
'Beyond DoD' method	A secure (but slower) 13 pass wipe method. The first three passes are with random patterns, the next seven passes are the standard passes from the DoD standard and the last three passes are with random patterns. The last pass is checked.	This method exceeds the Department of Defense (DoD) standards. It is a proprietary method used in secure deletion software such as CyberScrub (see below) and is intended to defeat even the recovery tools available to government agencies. It can be used to wipe data on compressed drives.

The ultra-paranoid might also like to worry about the fact that even if a file is never saved, but only printed, it might still be possible to recover the data in the original document. When you send a file to a printer, that file is 'spooled' (spool stands for 'simultaneous peripheral operations online'), which means that the data is copied to the hard disk before it is passed to the printer. This means, of course, that the data it contains will remain on the disk until it is overwritten.

Table 12.1 Continued

Data deletion method	How method works	Notes
Guttman method	Very slow, but very secure. The data area is overwritten 35 times using specialized patterns of random data which take into account the different encoding algorithms used by various hard drive manufacturers. These include RLL (run length limited), MFM (modified frequency modulation), PRML (partial response, maximum likelihood).	A highly secure method, based on Peter Guttman's paper 'Secure Deletion of Data from Magnetic and Solid-State Memory'. The method is designed to erase data regardless of the disk's raw encoding. It effectively removes the magnetic remanence from the disk, thus preventing even the best hardware recovery tools from finding data. It can be used to wipe data on compressed drives.
Custom method	Specify your own number of passes and the patterns of data used to overwrite your files.	Some of the best data deletion software allows you to define your own wiping methods.

Note: If you want to wipe a file located on a compressed drive, the selected wipe method must have at least one pass that uses random data. A random data stream cannot be compressed, therefore you are assured that the entire file is properly overwritten.

Deciding On Data Deletion Techniques

As noted above, there is at least one authority that believes that a file can never be completely deleted. Certainly, it has been established that deleted files can be recovered, even after secure deletion tools have been used. By now you might well be wondering is it possible to delete a file (and its temporary versions, spooled versions, file slack, etc.) so that it cannot be restored? When I tell you that there are rumours that certain government agencies have the capability to recover data that has been overwritten as many as 21 times, you might be forgiven for thinking that this whole chapter has been a complete waste of time. I think you should relax. Are you really likely to be deleting files that compromise national security?

As always, our task is to find a balanced approach to the problem. Ask yourself how sensitive your data really is and who is likely to be interested in recovering it? Table 12.2 might help.

Table 12.2 How Sensitive Is Your Data?

Sensitivity of data	Who might be interested	Appropriate file deletion method
Personal files such as letters, plans, risqué photographs, etc.	Casual snoopers, members of your family, colleagues at work, etc.	A single or double pass method would defeat anyone without specialized recovery tools.
PIN numbers and passwords, credit card details, bank account details, etc.	Criminals – casual and professional, unscrupulous businessmen, hackers, etc.	The seven pass DoD method would withstand most snoopers working at this level. Beating this method would require equipment and resources beyond the means of most crooks.
Sensitive professional records, critical corporate information, new product designs, etc.	Industrial spies, black-mailers, corporate competitors, etc.	You should consider using a method strong enough to resist even hardware recovery tools – perhaps the Guttman Method. Alternatively, a customized process involving 20 or more passes would probably be sufficient.
Illegal material, evidence of criminal activities, plans to bring down the government, etc.	Law enforcement agencies, national security services, etc.	If you are really a terrorist or a criminal mastermind, you need to look to a method as strong as the Guttman Method, and hope that MI5 or the CIA aren't more advanced than you think!

You can interpret this table as meaning that once you have determined the value of your data, you should choose a method which is both appropriate and practical. Time is one consideration since applying techniques such as the Guttman Method will tie your computer up for an extended period. After all, that photo of Aunty Nelly showing her backside on the beach is hardly likely to interest Interpol. Whichever method you decide on, you will need to invest in proprietary data deletion software. There is a wide choice available from the internet.

As always, I recommend that you check out the tools available before deciding on the one that fits your needs. You might consider downloading a selection and trying them out. The four programs which I have found most effective are Jetico's BCWipe, Kremlin Delete, Evidence Eliminator and Beyondsec Technologies' CyberScrub. Each of these programs have things to recommend them. BCWipe is part of the BestCrypt suite that we looked at in Chapter 11. It is also available as a standalone utility which can be downloaded for free. It can be integrated into the Windows' shell, adding secure deletion to a file's right-click menu, and can be run from the command line – a handy feature which means that BCWipe commands can be added to a batch file. You can specify most of the wiping parameters including how many passes and if file slack should also be cleaned. All in all, BCWipe is an excellent little tool and well worth downloading.

Kremlin has already been discussed in some detail. You will remember from the previous chapter that it also integrates with the Windows shell to allow you to securely delete files by right-clicking them. Evidence Eliminator is an old faithful – a secure deletion program that has earned an excellent reputation. It is much more than just a file wiping tool. It also cleans up all sorts of tracks and traces. My only concern with it is that (at the time of writing this chapter) it has not been upgraded for many months.

My preferred tool at the moment is CyberScrub which I am unable to find fault with. Its main window is shown in Figure 12.5. Deleting files is simply a matter of dragging them into this window. You will see that I have done this to our old friend **Top Secret.doc**. I can set the deletion method using the **Options** button on the toolbar. I then click **Erase All** and the file is securely deleted. To ensure that all the shortcuts are also wiped, I would use the Find Files function in Windows Explorer, searching for a pattern such as ***Secret.*** This would track down any shortcuts and temporary versions of the file, all of which I could then drag into CyberScrub's deletion window.

Figure 12.5 also illustrates some of the other features offered by CyberScrub. You can securely eliminate files in your **Recycle Bin**, clear up your internet traces (we will look at this function in Chapter 17) and also wipe your deleted e-mails – a facility missing from most other secure deletion programs. Perhaps CyberScrub's most impressive feature is the option which allows you to define your own wiping method. Figure 12.6 shows this in detail. From this box, you can select one of a series of different wipe

Figure 12.5 CyberScrub's main window

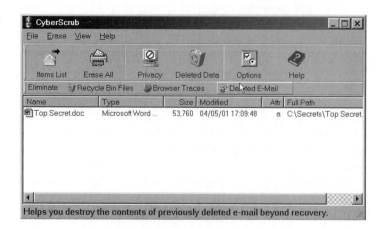

Figure 12.6 Modifying CyberScrub's wipe method

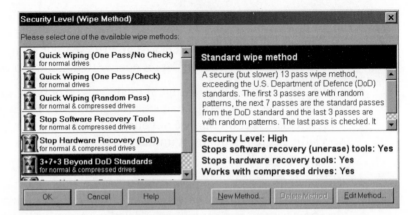

patterns, edit a pattern to suit your own requirements or even create a new method altogether. To do this, you specify the number of passes and the overwriting pattern for each pass, choosing between a fixed pattern (0s, 1s, etc.), a text pattern – CyberScrub suggests 'Censored by Me!', or a random data stream.

Whichever program you choose, make sure you use it correctly, and don't forget to configure it to clean up all the file traces that are left behind on your system.

We have now dealt with securing your data and are ready to take look at an entirely new aspect of computer security. Chapter 13, moves out of your computer altogether to examine network security and eventually the greatest network of them all – the internet.

To investigate options for secure file deletion programs, look on one of the web's major software archives. Evidence Eliminator is available from www.evidence-eliminator.com CyberScrub can be downloaded from www.cyberscrub.com For Kremlin and BCWipe, see the Check This Out ... box in Chapter 11.

Chapter 12 – Security Checklist

1   When you create or edit a file, all sorts of traces of that file are also created. Some of these are shortcuts to that file, intended to help you find it quickly. Others are references to that file within the application which created it. There are also temporary versions of the file created by the application. Secure file deletion requires that all these traces are erased from your computer.

2   Always remember that Windows **Delete** functions do nothing of the sort! They fail in two ways. First, when you perform a standard delete, all that happens is that the file is moved to the **Recycle Bin** folder, from which it can still be accessed.

Second, even if you delete by emptying the **Recycle Bin**, or holding down the **Shift** key while deleting, file data is not actually removed from your disk. Instead, the FAT's pointer to the file is erased and the space it occupies is marked as available. Until the physical data is overwritten, a file can easily be recovered.

3   Once data has been overwritten, it might still be possible to recover it using specialist tools to read the 'magnetic remanence' – a magnetic residue of the data which remains on the surface of your hard disk. This technique requires highly specialized equipment and is unlikely to be of concern to the ordinary home computer user.

4   There are three techniques available to securely delete computer data. The first is to overwrite it with random data. The number of times this is done (passes) determines the effectiveness of the deletion. A second possibility is degaussing. A strong magnetic field is applied to the disk which scrambles the magnetic charges. This is hardly a technique appropriate to the home user. Finally, there is the physical destruction of the media by brute force or even fire. This is a good way to dispose of sensitive data on floppy disks or CD-ROMs.

5   The number of times you overwrite file data should be determined by the file's sensitivity. One pass would be sufficient for a mildly confidential file which is unlikely to be of interest to anyone else. At the other end of the scale, the so-called Guttman Method which proposes 35 passes would render even the most hazardous files unrecoverable.

6   Secure file deletion requires the use of specialist wiping software. Many suitable tools are available from the internet. Check out the features and costs of several before installing your preferred program.

Part 4
Networks, From LANS To The Internet

In Part 4, I expand the perspective beyond the standalone computer to look at what happens when you attach your machine to a network. I sum up the background to networking technologies and help you to understand the serious security problems they bring. I describe attacks from inside and outside a network, and show you how a reliable network security policy can be implemented.

Next I turn to the mother of all networks – the internet itself. I show you how the internet and the world wide web have grown from their humble beginnings to dominate modern computing. I enumerate the many dangers to your personal security that the internet introduces and look at how to set up your internet connection to maximize your control.

I detail the efforts of those who use the internet to ensnare the unwary and look at the threats from active web technologies such as scripting and ActiveX controls. I show you some ways to bomb-proof your computer or your local network and how to use additional software to overcome the shortcomings of your web browser. I help you to consider the advantages of browsing anonymously and ways of cleaning up the tracks you leave behind while cruising the web.

E-mail is one of the greatest threats to your security. I show you how e-mail works and how the unscrupulous can use e-mail attachments to invade your system or spread viruses. I also take you through shopping on the internet and how to ensure that online commerce is secure. You'll go on to consider the dangers from unrestricted access to web content and look at ways of keeping children away from unsuitable material.

After completing Part 4, you will have a secure and controlled internet connection. You will know how to avoid attempts to railroad you to certain sites. You will be able to browse the web anonymously without leaving tracks that others can read. You will have secured your e-mail system against intruders and know how to keep your children safe online.

Networks And Network Security

Data Railways – The Growth Of Computer Networks

If you are working through these pages logically and ring-fencing your system as you go, you should, by now, be reasonably satisfied that your local computer and the data stored on it is secure. Provided you now keep your machine in complete isolation and apply our agreed security strategies to every change you make to your system, you can even afford to relax slightly. Unfortunately, all of this smugness melts away as soon as you connect your local machine to a network. At this stage we are not concerned whether that network is a local office net (a LAN or intranet) or a wide area network (a WAN or the internet itself). The risks are essentially the same.

The reality is that as soon as you plug a connecting wire into the back of your beautifully secure machine, you open it up to outside abuse. The whole point of a

network is to share resources. The hardest thing is to make sure you only share resources with authorized users. Network protocols can be devilishly complex and the more complex they are, the more likely it is that they contain holes through which unwelcome intruders can creep. Networks can be logistical nightmares. Some are constructed to allow users to access a single printer, others so that they can swap files or pull information from centralized databases. But whatever the objectives, a network, almost by definition, compromises computer security by providing a whole series of new access points to stored data.

To understand why networks have developed as they have, we need to take a brief detour through the history books. In fact, we need to go right back to the 1940s. The earliest computers were monstrous machines – huge constructions of wires and tubes that easily filled complete rooms. For example, ENIAC (the Electronic Numerical Integrator Analyzer and Computer) was built in 1945. It was 100 feet long, eight feet high and weighed in at 30 tons.

ENIAC and its immediate offspring were slow, cumbersome and extremely temperamental. They were forever breaking down, particularly if dust particles got into their works. Small wonder that their operators became paranoid about cleanliness. To protect them from pollution, early computers were isolated in dust-free laboratories and nursed by men in white coats. This model of computers as sensitive machines which had to be guarded from abuse was widely adopted by both manufacturers and end-users.

In the 1950s other companies began to develop cheaper and more useable computers. Towards the end of the decade, the transistor replaced the vacuum tube as the essential logical element. Transistors are faster and much smaller than tubes which meant that a computer could be packed into a box instead of filling a room. IBM (International Business Machines) and DEC (Digital Equipment Corporation) started producing computers for businesses – earlier machines had been so expensive that only governments could afford them. At first companies were suspicious of the new technology. Possibly worried by a steady stream of Hollywood schlockers in which machines tried to destroy mankind, businessmen viewed computers as dangerous and unstable. It was to take a further decade before the 'Frankenstein' syndrome was finally laid to rest.

As the 1950s gave way to the 1960s, a new style of computing was developing. Business users had very different requirements from governments. Company managers wanted computer access for various departments within their organizations. They wanted their accounts staff to automate invoicing, salesmen to be able to check product availability and enter orders and management to have access to the latest business statistics. But many of these people were not computer literate. In the opinion of the managers, they could not be relied on to handle the core hardware and software, which was still seen as the function of specialized computer staff.

What was needed was a way of providing computer access to company staff while still guarding the valuable data and programs which made up the core of the system. The solution, of course, was the network. The model adopted became known as client/server computing. Applications and files were stored on a central server which could be locked away and protected with passwords. Lesser staff were given basic workstations, sometimes known as dumb terminals, which were hardwired to the server. These were known as 'clients' and could only access the programs and data that the server allowed them to. Until the 1980s client/server computing was the dominant model.

Techno Talk One advantage of the client/server model was that processing time could be allocated to a number of users simultaneously. Instead of a single user having access to the complete computer, processing power was doled out in segments according to the software model. This system, known as 'time-sharing' dominated early computing, and still does on mainframe computers. Of course, the processing power of the central computer itself does not change, so during periods of peak usage, response time is noticeably reduced. Furthermore, the more operational workstations you attach to a network, the less processing power is available at each terminal.

The Growth Of The Low-cost PC

Things began to change in the early 1980s when low-cost integrated circuits became available. Although the integrated circuit (IC) was first developed in the late 1960s, it took twenty years before the price fell sufficiently for it to be applied to consumer electronics. The IC allowed a large number of transistors to be built into a single silicon wafer. A few years later, the large scale integrated (LSI) circuit and subsequently the very large scale integrated (VLSI) circuit gave birth to the microprocessor – several thousand transistors etched into a single silicon substrate. VLSI microprocessors packed enough processing power for a personal computer small enough to sit on a desk top. As IC prices fell, PCs became affordable. The age of mass computing had arrived.

When processing power is available on the desktop, time-sharing is no longer useful, but networking is still required if users are to share printers or access each others' data. A new style of networking, known as peer-to-peer networking (P2P), became the dominant model. P2P networks do not require a central server which deals out processing to its clients. Instead processing power is spread between all the machines on the network. Like client/server networking, resources are shared according to 'privileges'. One user might be permitted to change the contents of a file, a second user might only be allowed to read the file, while a third user might be denied access to the file altogether.

Figure 13.1 shows two configurations for a simple peer-to-peer network. The three computers at the top of the illustration use bus 'topology', where each computer connects to a single continuous cable known as a data bus. The three computers at the bottom use a star topology, with each connected directly to a routing device called a hub. Most modern networks use star topology.

Figure 13.1 Computer networks

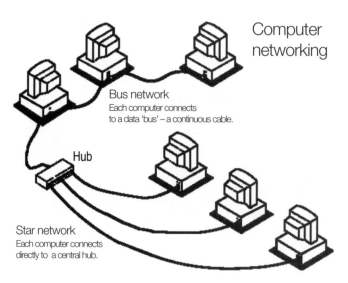

Computer networking

Bus network
Each computer connects
to a data 'bus' – a continuous cable.

Hub

Star network
Each computer connects
directly to a central hub.

As networking became cheaper and easier to install, networks became a standard feature of computing. They also grew larger. The earliest networks connected machines within a single location. This arrangement became known as a local area network (LAN). But many companies operated from more than one location and it proved useful to link different locations together into a wide area network (WAN). The biggest advantage to industry and commerce was that network resources such as printers and centralized data storage could then be shared by a number of users.

Today, of course, office networks are a feature of business life and without them most companies would cease to function. They have also spread into the home as users discovered the advantages of linking all a family's computers to share a single printer or internet connection. But with the convenience of the network arrived a range of new security problems.

Network Security

From the earliest days of networking, administrators were forced to consider network security. In the beginning, most computers were the property of government departments or the military which, quite naturally, felt obliged to protect the data they were storing from unauthorized access. The system which was developed and still remains the dominant model for network security, was to protect each resource with a password and to ensure that each approved user only knew the passwords for those resources he was allowed to access. This would appear to be a relatively secure system, but in fact it has a number of inherent weaknesses.

In the first place, people tend to forget passwords. To prevent this, many users write their passwords down on paper and as soon as someone else sees the paper, security is compromised. Since we considered the question of password security in Chapter 10, I will not return to it here. Research into network security has frequently exposed a second weakness. While individuals tend to be fairly careful when protecting their own property, they are noticeably less so when it comes to corporate property. Users who forget their own access passwords are very likely to borrow those of other members of staff. Like virginity, once a password has been given up it can never be reclaimed.

Any unauthorized intrusion into a computer network is defined as an attack, and attacks can take one of two forms. A passive attack occurs when an intruder only observes data, while an active attack occurs when an intruder attempts to modify data. Either form of attack compromises network security and can cause serious problems. Let's take a moment to agree some terminology which is relevant to network security.

➤ **Access control** means restricting access to resources on the network. These might be computers, printers or individual file folders. All of these can be defined as 'shares'. Access control protects against unauthorized reading or modifying of documents.

➤ **Authentication** means proving your right to access network shares. Normally this involves providing a password to establish your identity, but modern technology such as fingerprint or retina scanning has provided more secure authentication methods.

➤ **Integrity** refers to the stability of data and reflects its ability to resist unauthorized alteration. Preserving data integrity is one of the key functions of network security procedures.

With this in mind, we can now establish a set of guidelines for establishing a secure computer network.

➤ A network must be protected against unauthorized intruders.

➤ Once logged into a network, an authorized user must only be able to access those shares he has permissions for.

➤ Data on the network must be protected against deliberate or accidental damage.

You might wonder why an attacker would be bothered with your system when there are so many more tempting targets. Here are just a few of the reasons why you are under threat. Unless you secure your system, an attacker can …

➤ … get hold of your credit card information and use it to buy goods and draw cash;

➤ … take control of your computer to attack other, more profitable, targets;

➤ … use your network to send thousands of junk e-mails to solicit business or to spread a Trojan program to all your friends and contacts;

➤ … access your and your family's personal information on a home network or your business records on an office network;

➤ … sell (or even give away) your confidential corporate plans to your competitors;

➤ … prevent you from being able to service your customers.

Building a Secure Network

The actual mechanics of installing and configuring network hardware is beyond the scope of this book. There is a wealth of information on the internet and any number of books dedicated to the subject. Like most advanced computer operations, this is not something you should attempt unless you know what you are doing. I would suggest that in addition to the network cards, cables and hub, you consider investing in some specialized items to improve your network security. We will consider this security from two angles. First, we need to protect your network from outside intrusion. I assume that your network will be connected to the internet – if not, you can skip the next section. Second, we will look at securing your network against internal troubles – authorized users who accidentally or deliberately attempt to damage your resources or would-be intruders who sit down at a networked computer.

Securing Your Network Against Attacks From The Internet

Your first layer of protection should be an internet router with an in-built switch. This will transfer the process of establishing an internet connection to a separate device, freeing resources on individual computers and making them harder to access from outside. A switch is a device that establishes a direct line of communication from your network to a destination on the internet. It provides additional security by making it difficult for an attacker to 'sniff' traffic on your side of the switch. (A sniffer is a program that allows an attacker to see the traffic on a network.) Routers also hide your network computers by providing a process known as Network Address Translation (NAT). All computers on your network require an IP (internet Protocol) address – this applies even if you are not connecting to the internet! Just like a postal address, an IP address tells your system where to deliver packets of data. NAT allows all your IP addresses to be transformed (mapped) to a single IP address which is presented to the internet.

Note that an internal network must use IP addresses reserved by the Internet Assigned Numbers Authority (IANA) for private networks. These addresses are: 10.0.0.0 to 10.255.255.255, 172.16.0.0 to 172.31.255.255, or 192.168.0.0 to 192.168.255.255. Your router's manual will advise you on configuring your network to use these addresses. You might even find that your router will automatically assign addresses to your network computers.

There is a wide choice of internet routers available, but make sure that you get one which works with your national telephone system. Linksys and Netgear offer well-respected devices suitable for the American market, while the WebRamp range might suit a larger network. My own preference is the Eicon Diva – a well-designed and compact router which is particularly easy to set up. All of these routers are configured via your web browser and most include advanced features for filtering internet access and for logging inbound and outbound activity.

Your second layer of protection should be a firewall installed on each computer in the network. If an attacker gets past your router, your firewall is the next line of defence. I don't want to discuss firewalls in any detail here since Chapter 23 is devoted to them. All we are concerned with at this stage is that the firewall is capable of blocking all inbound ports unless specifically told to leave them open. To put it more simply, no one should be able to get into your computer without your permission. If you need to know more about firewalls at this stage, I suggest you turn to Chapter 23 and come back when you are finished.

Your third layer is your anti-virus software. Of course this will not prevent access – if an attacker has penetrated your router and breached your firewall, it is too late for this. We are now concerned with minimizing the damage he can do. You already know all about AV software, so I won't repeat the information here beyond reminding you to keep your protection up-to-date. One of your major concerns as a network administrator will be securing your system against Trojan horses – those nasty little client/server programs which allow outsiders to take control of your computers. I am leaving Trojans until Chapter 22. It goes without saying that you should be making regular back-ups of your critical data.

Eugene The Businessman

Eugene's company network has been running for several years without any major problems. It allows his staff to access customer records and to share office printers and scanners. Because it has proved to be so reliable, Eugene has avoided updating his network software. This might prove to be a costly mistake. The dangers to network security have never been greater and all the evidence is that these dangers are increasing. As computer literacy increases, so does the number of those ill-intentioned types who use their skills to crack into business networks to steal and damage data. Next year, Eugene intends to upgrade his internet connection to broadband. This means that his network will be permanently connected to the telephone system and the risks will once more increase. Eugene needs to implement a comprehensive network security policy along the lines we have discussed.

Should an attacker break into our network, the only way we can prevent him from infecting our system (active attack) or from accessing our confidential data (passive attack) is by controlling access to our data folders. Once he has got through our outer defences, the outsider becomes an insider and the precautions discussed in the next section are relevant. Even after our anti-virus software has cleaned up any infections, it is possible that the attacker's 'back door' will remain on our system. Often the only solution is to shut down the network, clean and disinfect each computer and, if necessary, reload all the system software from the original installation disks. For a small home network this might be a nuisance, but for a company that relies on networking to service its customers or carry on its business, it can prove disastrous.

Network security is not just about protecting your own system. In a small way you are also responsible for the safety of the entire internet. We have already seen how hackers can use your network as a base for launching further attacks. If you give them a safe house by not protecting your network, you might be accused of aiding and abetting their activities. One hacker trick is to mount an attack on a web server by choking its bandwidth with small packets of data. This is known as a Denial of Service (DoS) attack and has already brought down some of the largest internet sites. Once an attacker is inside your system he can, often without you even knowing it, add your

218

network to his DoS resources. Innocent you may be, but your system is now a key component in disrupting the workings of the internet itself. (I will be looking at Denial of Service attacks in detail in Chapter 21.)

Finally, you should always remember that you can make use of the ultimate security tool – one which is guaranteed to deny attackers access to your network. You can simply pull the plug on your internet connection.

 If you run a web server on your network, you will need to take special care. You might not even realize you are doing so. A web server is a piece of software which allows others to access files from your computers, so if you are using a share tool such as an MP3 distribution program, you are, in effect, running a web server. Since a web server must accept connection from the internet, you are inevitably making your network more vulnerable and open to attack. There are several ways in which you can reduce the dangers. If possible, store the files you are serving on a second hard drive or at least another logical drive. Don't store system files or sensitive personal files alongside shared material. Use good passwords on all file shares. Don't share whole drives, but limit sharing to the folders containing the files you are serving. (In Windows Explorer, you can right-click on a folder, and select **Sharing** from the drop down menu.)

Securing Your Network Against Local Attacks

Hardware routers and software firewalls can protect you against remote attackers using the internet to access your network, but there is another source of danger much closer to home. Most networks are created to provide shared resources to a number of users, and those users can create as many problems for a network administrator as a remote hacker. We can identify three specific dangers we need to guard against.

➤ The authorized user who accidentally damages shared data or other network resources.

➤ The authorized user who deliberately damages shared data or other network resources.

➤ The unauthorized user who gains access to our network for any nefarious purpose.

Our first task is to restrict access to only authorized users and to do this we need to employ some kind of user authentication. Access to any Windows network requires a user ID (a log-in name) and a password. You are probably familiar with the dialog box shown in Figure 13.2. Authentication methods vary between different Windows distributions. Windows 98 networks are configured so that while an intruder can bypass this log-in by clicking the **Cancel** button, he will still be prevented from

Figure 13.2 Logging on to a Windows network

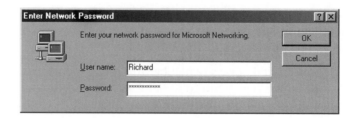

accessing any network shares. (Administering a Windows NT network is too complicated a subject for this book, but Windows 95 and 98 assume that if a person is authorized to use a computer, he is also authorized to access the network that computer is connected to. This is a definite security weakness!) To authorize a new user in Windows 9x,[1] click **Start > Settings > Control Panel > Users** and follow the instructions in the Wizard. After the process is completed, the new user can log-on using his user ID and password and gain access to any available shared resources.

It must be said that the network log-in procedure offers only very basic security. Anyone who can gain access to your computer can create a user profile for himself and thus access your network. If you require any degree of serious network security, you should consider installing Windows NT, Windows 2000 or Windows XP – all of which provide real protection.

As you can see, Windows 9x offers only minimal authentication control. There are several proprietary programs on the internet which provide better security, but only by pepping up the strength of the log-in procedure. Remember that Windows 9x is intended primarily as a PC operating system with network components coming second. Microsoft's philosophy is that a simple peer-to-peer network should be an open system, with authentication controls being applied at the computer log-in rather than the network log-in. From a security perspective this seriously limits our ability to control access to the network. Let's see if we can do better by controlling access to resources.

Our next job is to decide how we are going to control access to network resources – specifically to folders containing files we wish to share with other users. Windows 9x provides two methods of doing this using share-level access control or user-level access control. To adopt one of these methods, either right-click your Network Neighbourhood icon and select **Properties** or click **Start > Settings > Control Panel > Network**. From the Network dialog box which opens, click the **Access Control** tab and you will see a window like Figure 13.3. You can now select which type of control you wish to apply. Two notes are relevant here. First, you will have to set up this

[1] You have probably seen this shorthand before, but when I refer to Windows 9x, I mean both Windows 95 and Windows 98. I assume that most readers will have Windows 98 installed.

220

*Figure 13.3 Setting the
Access Control method
for a network*

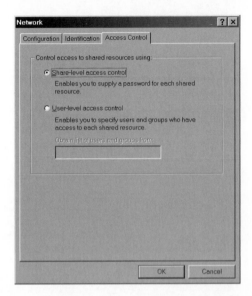

configuration on every computer on your network. Peer-to-peer networking implies
that all computers on a network are of equal importance. Second, you must remember
to enable **File and/or Print Sharing** from the **Configuration** tab, otherwise nobody
will be able to access the resources stored on the computer.

Share-level control is the easiest and probably the only option available on a small
network. As the note below the check-box explains, after you have set this option in
the Network dialog box (and probably restarted your computer) you can then open
Windows Explorer and work through the various folders, right-clicking and **Sharing**
those you wish to make accessible to your network users. Each resource can be
password protected. The other setting, user-level access control, is more appropriate to
a network connected to a Windows NT or Netware server which can supply and verify
a list of users.

Provided it is configured correctly, share-level control can be highly effective, but
getting it right can be a time-consuming process. Look at the dialog box shown in
Figure 13.4. With **File and Print Sharing** enabled, I want to give my network users
access to the **My Documents** folder. I have therefore right-clicked the folder and
selected **Sharing** from the drop down menu. I now check the **Shared As** option,
leaving the **Share Name** as the original folder name, although changing this might be
a more secure choice. So far this is simple enough, but it is the rest of the options that
I need to get right. In **Access Type**, I can decide whether network users can simply
look at the files in the folder (**Read-Only**) or modify their contents (**Full**). I can even
go one better and decide that their access rights will depend on whether they have
been given read-only or full access passwords (**Depends on Passwords**).

221

Figure 13.4 Sharing a folder over a Windows network

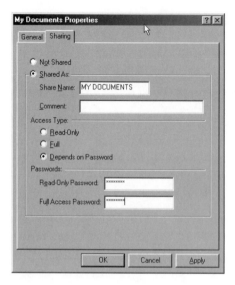

Let's approach this logically using a series of steps to ensure that our network access is as secure as we can make it. For each networked computer under your control, you should:

➤ Decide which folders you are going to share. Do not make the mistake of simply sharing your whole drive – this is asking for trouble. Where possible, store all the files to be shared in a single folder and make only that folder accessible.

➤ Draw up a list of authorized users and decide which of them will have read-only rights to each shared folder, and which will have full rights. You might end up with a table like this.

Table 13.1 Rights of entry to shared folders

	Shared Folder 1: **Business correspondence**	**Shared Folder 2:** **Customer records**
George	Full access. Password: topdog34	Full access. Password: 34senior
Ann	Read only. Password: downboy7	Full access. Password: 34senior
Tom	No access	Read only. Password: 90bottom
Eileen	Read only. Password: downboy7	No access

Note: Windows will only allow you to use eight-character passwords.

➤ Now work through your folders setting up sharing and access passwords according to your table.

➤ Advise your users of the folders they can access and the passwords they will need. (It might also be a good time to remind them that passwords are confidential and should not be written down!)

Provided your users are reliable and honest, this type of access control provides quite reasonable network security. By restricting full read and write access to the absolute minimum, you are also going some way towards protecting the integrity of your key files from accidental or deliberate damage. In the table above, for example, only George can make changes to your business correspondence. Ann and Eileen can only read it and Tom can't get to it at all. Now you just have to make sure that you can trust George! Of course, the best way to ensure against damage to your files it to make sure that they are regularly backed up to a folder which is not shared with anyone – not even George.

Network security is a complex subject and I have only been able to cover the basics in this chapter. As I mentioned earlier, if your network is a vital component of your business, you should be using a secure network operating system rather than Windows 98. Now it is time that we moved on and looked at the biggest network of them all – the internet.

Chapter 13 – Security Checklist

1   Always remember that as soon as you connect your computer to a network, you expose it to a new level of risk. A network connection implies providing access into and out of your computer, and there are plenty of people who will abuse that access.

2   Network security depends on authenticating users, normally by means of a typed in user ID and password. Our agreed rules on passwords are of crucial importance here. We need to watch out for both passive attacks, where an intruder attempts to read data, and active attacks, where an intruder attempts to modify or damage data.

3   We need to enforce three security rules.

➤ A network must be protected against unauthorized intruders.

➤ An authorized user must only be able to access those shares he has permissions for.

➤ Data on the network must be protected against deliberate or accidental damage.

4   Damage to a network can come from outside or inside. Outsiders will use your network's internet connection to try to gain access to your systems. Precautions here include installing a router and setting up a firewall. Insiders will already be within your firewall. Their activities can be controlled by authentication and carefully managing their access to stored files.

5   To control access to network resources, work out a detailed resource management strategy. Decide which folders you wish to share, who will have access to them and what form that access will take. Where practical, restrict access to read only. This prevents users from modifying files. They can, of course, copy those files to their own computers and make changes to the copies.

The Internet – Data Sharing Goes Global

In This Chapter

- ➤ Enter the internet and the world wide web
- ➤ The origins of the internet
- ➤ ARPANET
- ➤ NSFNET
- ➤ The world wide web
- ➤ The development of the world wide web
- ➤ The internet as a communications medium
- ➤ Controlling your connection to the internet
- ➤ Internet hardware
- ➤ Internet software
- ➤ Modifying your dial-up connection settings

Enter The Internet And The World Wide Web

The time has come to turn our attention to the mother of all networks, the internet itself. Nothing in the history of human communication has frightened the authorities more than the explosive growth of the internet. Here, for the first time, was a means of disseminating information completely outside the control of state, church and business. It is also true to say that the internet caught our political masters with their trousers down. The system developed and expanded so fast that they were left quivering in its wake. It is only now that the authorities are attempting to take control of the superstructure and impose their inevitable rules and regulations.

Consider the problem from authority's point of view. Authoritarian states have always survived by limiting their citizens' exposure to subversive information, but anyone who can create a connection to the internet can access uncensored data from around the world. Governments are obliged to appear to be tough on crime, but here is a medium which allows criminals to exchange information in secret while remaining relatively safe from the long arm of the law. Since the web itself is fundamentally an anarchy, it is not surprising to find anarchic and anti-establishment opinions expressed everywhere. Unfortunately, what all this means is that a zealous official can easily find evidence of every kind of aberrant human behaviour, and then use that evidence to justify demands that the web should be regulated.

To understand why the internet and its friendly face the world wide web developed as they have, we need to take another excursion into recent history.

The Origins Of The Internet

It is ironic, but the internet itself came about as the result of a need for security. Back in the 1960s, it was the time of the Cold War and the US government was worried about the effects of a nuclear attack by the Soviet Union. Military chiefs in The Pentagon knew that the electromagnetic pulse produced by a thermonuclear explosion would destroy any traditional network and with so much essential information stored on computers, it needed a way of safeguarding its records.

The problem had already been considered by The RAND Corporation, which, at the time was America's most respected think-tank. RAND's Paul Baran oversaw the research and his team came up with an idea that was both brilliant and simple. Stripped to its basics, the RAND proposal was to duplicate all that essential data and store it on a series of computers in different parts of the country. No one computer would be in charge of the system because a central computer would be an obvious target for missile attack. The concept therefore stepped away from the client/server approach discussed in Chapter 13. Every computer, or node, on the net would be both client and server as necessary. Baran is responsible for an excellent quotation. His network would be 'designed from the beginning to operate while in tatters.' All the nodes would be networked together, but rather than using a traditional 'star' network with connections radiating out from a central hub, they would be connected by a whole series of data lines. If one line was knocked out, information could be routed around the break. A simplified illustration of this principle is shown in Figure 14.1.

But this was only half the solution. Data travelling down a line could still be

Figure 14.1 'Bomb-proofing' a computer network

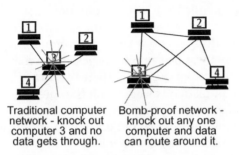

Traditional computer network - knock out computer 3 and no data gets through.

Bomb-proof network - knock out any one computer and data can route around it.

disrupted. To safeguard delivery, a new method of transmitting information was proposed. Look at the right-hand diagram in Figure 14.1. If computer 1 is instructed to send a file to computer 4, the obvious way might be to squirt it down the diagonal line, which connects the two. Knock out the line and the data is lost. Take the same file and break it down into smaller 'packets', then add a header[1] to each packet explaining where the packet fits into the complete file. Now squirt all the packets down every possible connection. The order in which they arrive at computer 4 doesn't matter, because the headers explain how the packets fit together. Computer 4 receives the packets, reassembles them in the correct order and makes the completed file available to its operator. This technology is known as 'packet switching' and is still the key to the workings of the internet.

Compared to direct line communications – a telephone connection between two people for example – packet switching is very inefficient. Redundant packets of data are running around the network, taking up valuable bandwidth. Within a network, however, its inefficiency is less important than its reliability. All those packets ensure that the data gets through.

ARPANET

The RAND Corporation's proposal was passed on to The Department of Defense's Advanced Research Projects Agency. ARPA was instructed to develop the idea into a bomb-proof computer network. They set up a trial project, which combined the RAND concept with research from several other sources, including UCLA (The University of California at Los Angeles) and the National Physical Laboratory in Britain. ARPANET, as it became known, originally connected the computer departments of the four universities in the US where much of the technology was developed. Other educational and scientific establishments were quick to join in. By 1971, there were 15 nodes and, in the following year, 22 further nodes latched on. Data transfer speeds at that time were fairly slow, but it was a beginning.

[1] Most computer files carry both information and information about that information, known as meta-information. A good example is a word processed document which contains both the text that has been typed in and data on how to present that text – the fonts, text sizes, colours, etc. Often this meta-information is carried in a file 'header'.

ARPANET had been intended as a private computer network to support national research projects. Over the next few years the system kept getting hijacked by civilians who thought up new things to do with a data communications network. Soon, most of the traffic on the net was personal messages, the exchange of news and ideas or even gossip. Remember, from the outset there was to be no centralized control of the system. ARPANET administrators were helpless to prevent anyone with access to the network from sending anything they wanted to. Eventually the military interests, which had helped fund the original project, grew so annoyed at losing control of their baby that they split off a segment, which became MILNET. This was (and still is) restricted to military use, but it left the fledgling internet for everybody else.

ARPANET itself was unlike any previous network. Although wide area networks (WANs) had existed before, they conformed to the principles described in Chapter 13. Someone was always in control. But any machine could connect to ARPANET as long as it supported the packet switching system.

Before two computers can communicate, they have to agree a 'protocol' – a set of rules for exchanging information. The original internet protocol was NCP (Network Control Protocol) but this was soon replaced with TCP/IP (Transmission Control Protocol/ Internet Protocol). TCP is the software, which breaks data down into packets on one computer, then reassembles them on another. We have already met IP addresses in the previous chapter. You will remember that IP looks after the routing of packets from node to node until they reach their destination. TCP/IP itself was in the public domain; in other words, anybody could access the software and use it to link into the network.

In 1973, ARPANET went international. Connections were established to University College in London and the Royal Radar Establishment in Norway. Over the next few years, the internet just got bigger and bigger as more institutions attached their computers to the system. In 1977 the first operational e-mail system was launched. (It's worth remembering that e-mail still makes up the majority of traffic across the net.) Net legend says that it was in 1982 that the word 'internet' was used for the first time, but no one can say for sure.

NSFNET

In 1984, the National Science Foundation – a US government agency obliged by its charter to offer access to its scientific database to any educational establishment that asked for it, began building the NSFNET. Its regional structure blended perfectly into the existing internet and provided hundreds of dedicated computers permanently connected to the system. In 1986, and again in 1988 and 1990, the whole network received a major overhaul with faster machines and more efficient telephone connections. Commercial companies, who had been dubious of the benefits at first, began to use the internet for business communications. E-commerce was born.

During the 1980s the use of e-mail – person-to-person communication over the internet – became widespread. Colleges began to offer their students e-mail accounts. In 1988 the first internet virus, the so-called internet worm, was launched in the US. Net users panicked when 6,000 of the then 60,000 host computers were temporarily crippled. An emergency response team was formed to combat the menace, but for the first time the internet was seen as creating problems as well as solutions. Hysteria about viruses, worms and Trojan horses has never really died down since. Internet paranoia dates from this time.

ARPANET itself was formally closed down in 1989, but it had served its purpose. The combination of military, governmental and scientific interests, which had first developed internet technologies, had seen the project expand into an international data communications system which was beyond any one organization's control. As long as it adheres to the TCP/IP protocols, any node on the network is as important as any other node. There is no internet policy, no enforced censorship and no charge for the service.

It is important to remember that the internet at the start of the 1990s was nothing like it is today. There was no graphical interface, no way of viewing images or listening to audio files. All input was by typing directly onto the command line and although the information flow was much faster than in the earliest days, it was still nothing like the speeds we expect today. In a word, the internet was unfriendly. But all this was about to change.

The World Wide Web

In 1989, a scientist named Tim Berners-Lee, while working at the European Laboratory for Particle Physics (CERN) in Geneva, Switzerland, developed a system that allowed physicists to share their research results over the internet. He and his colleagues at CERN hacked together a simple way to display information on-screen and to move from place to place by clicking 'hypertext links' – active pieces of text which linked the user to other pieces of information stored on the internet.

The idea of hypertext had been around for quite a while. The name was first coined by a computer scientist called Ted Nelson way back in 1965. He was trying to invent a way to link all the documents in a library and came up with a system where references in one document would lead the reader to connected references in other documents.

The idea was good, but it would be another 20 years before the technology to implement Nelson's ideas became available. In 1987, Apple Computers® launched a simple application called HyperCard®. HyperCards were on-screen documents which resembled the cards in a traditional card index. They could contain text, graphics and sounds, and users could jump from one card to another by clicking underlined links or 'hot-spots'. This style of implementation was quickly adopted across a wide range of other applications. You will find it, for example, in your own computer's Help system. Eventually, it found a natural home on the web.

Figure 14.2 The NCSA Mosaic browser, Version 1

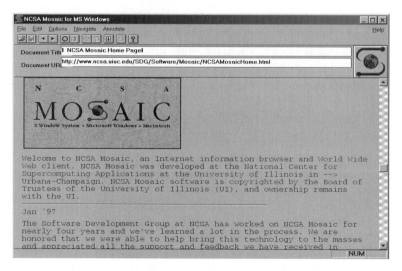

Rather than keeping their ideas to themselves (or trying to make money from them!) Berners-Lee and his team posted their code on the internet, allowing everyone to make use of it. The code allowed users to combine words, pictures and sounds on pages which would display on the internet, but it was another two years before Marc Andreesen and a team of students at the National Center for Supercomputing Applications (NCSA) in Illinois developed the first graphical web browser.

Launched in 1993, Mosaic was the ancestor of all of today's browsers. A screenshot is shown in Figure 14.2. Although it was very primitive compared to the all-singing, all-dancing browsers we are used to, it provided the same basic functions. It used hyperlinks or typed-in addresses to navigate around the internet, downloading and then displaying the pages it connected to. It knew how to present a page written in Hypertext Mark-up Language (HTML), the code in which all web pages are still written. Most importantly, it presented a friendly interface, using the same 'metaphor' of buttons and icons that computer users had become familiar with.

Today's browsers are so easy to use that hardly anybody types in commands to use the internet, as they were obliged to do in the early days. But it is worth remembering that underneath the web browser's graphical interface the internet still exists and internet protocols still do the essential work of moving data from place to place.

The Development Of The World Wide Web

The world wide web is conceived as a seamless world in which all information, from any source, can be accessed in a consistent and simple way.

The quote is from Tim Berners-Lee and sums up the basic concept behind the web. The World Wide Web Consortium (WWWC or W3C) that Berners-Lee and his colleagues founded is the body responsible for overseeing the development of the software which allows the web to function. From its beginnings, the WWWC has adhered to six fundamental principles.

➤ That the web's information system must be able to link data stored in different locations in an arbitrary fashion.

➤ That users must be able move around the web independently without following a predetermined linear path from one computer to the next. (Think of the difference between driving from one village to the next along the roads and walking there across the fields. You will get there either way, but the roads force you to travel in certain directions, while if you walk across the fields, you can twist and turn as you please.)

➤ That the web must work in the same way for every user regardless of that user's make of computer, operating system or native language.

➤ That it must be possible to access information from every type of computer and operating system – including ones that have not yet been developed. (This is called 'future-proofing' and the fact that it was designed into the web at the very beginning explains how the web has continued to grow and prosper despite all the new technologies that have emerged since.)

➤ That users must be able to set up their computers' information systems and use them on the web in any way that they wish. That there should not be one fixed model to which every connected machine must conform.

➤ That updating and correcting information on the web should be a simple and straightforward operation.

From the outset, the web was intended to be independent and uncontrolled. Its architects did not want a formal, rigid structure. Remember that the world wide web was grafted onto the internet which itself had grown up in a fairly random and disorganized fashion. Author Bruce Sterling summed it up perfectly: 'The internet is a rare example of a true, modern, functional anarchy. There is no "Internet Inc". There are no official censors, no bosses, no board of directors, no stockholders.' Although the WWWC has overall responsibility for developing the web's software, it exercises no control over the information that is posted to the web and does not try to influence how it is used.

Almost every day, new uses for the web are discovered. If the original internet was seen as an infinite storehouse for information, the second and third generations of users have taken things much further. In 2000, well over two billion dollars changed hands in the internet shopping malls. 'Vanity sites' – private sites created for their owners' pleasure – are springing up everywhere. (Many of these sites were never intended to be accessible to all and thus contradicted one of the cornerstones of web philosophy.) It seems as if every business in the world, from the tiniest cheese-maker in Cornwall, to the biggest multi-national, just has to have a website. The age of the internet has arrived in style.

The Internet As A Communications Medium

As we have seen, the internet supports the world wide web by providing the hardware and software that stores and transmits information. In a sense, the web is another communications medium, like the press and television. But unlike traditional media, the web is interactive – nothing happens until you connect to the internet and instruct your software to access a website or send an e-mail message. The web also allows you to specifically target the information you are seeking. To find the results of a football match, you might have to buy a newspaper and search through a lot of information you are not interested in before finding the scores you want. Web software permits you to specify precisely what you are looking for and then move directly to that information.

Because of the uncontrolled way in which it grew, the web does not have a particular agenda. Most news media, however independent they claim to be, reflect some sort of political viewpoint and that viewpoint colours the way in which they present news stories. Because the web is not managed by any one organization or government, you will find every possible political, religious and social group represented. And if someone does not agree with any of the views expressed, that person is at liberty to create a presence on the web devoted to his or her opinions.

Fortunately, the web refuses to take itself seriously. For every sincere and dedicated webmaster using his or her site to spread some vital message, there is a wild-eyed lunatic trying to throw a spanner into the works. A quick trawl across the web reveals sites giving advice on how to grow triffids, a translation service from Star Fleet English into Klingon, nude photographs of almost everyone you've ever heard of, hate mail to Posh Spice, a group dedicated to speaking like the Swedish Chef from the Muppets, recipes for whale omelette, and the complete works of James Joyce in Urdu. All you have to do is get in there and dig out what you want.

So the internet is inherently an anarchic system intended, in true hacker style, to spread information freely and without any limitations – and, as we noted at the top of this chapter, this is the aspect which really frightens Big Brother. Information is dangerous and unlimited information can threaten the stability of church, state and business. It is true to say that the history of human communication is a history of censorship. By controlling access to information, repressive governments control the opinions of those they seek to enslave. By preventing their followers from being exposed to alternative theologies, religions ensure that they remain embedded in the 'one true faith'. By restricting the dissemination of ideas and technologies, business interests can maintain their monopoly over certain products in certain markets.

Although the internet and the web are not controlled by any group, there are plenty of groups who would like to control it. Despite almost complete ignorance of the technologies involved, politicians in several countries have called for the regional structure to be, in effect, nationalized so that it can be regulated and policed. Just behind the politicians stands big business, looking at the web as the supreme marketing tool. Business interests would like to buy up pieces of internet infrastructure to enable them to control web content and direct people's browsing to their products and services.

If you are new to the internet, the first would-be regulators you are likely to meet are the Internet Service Providers (ISPs). Some of them like AOL (America On-Line, lest we forget) seem anxious to control your every move, and all of them want to lock you into accessing the web via their portal. Have no fear, we can defeat their foul machinations and end up with an internet connection that works as we wish it to.

Controlling Your Connection to The Internet

It is time to look at the actual mechanics of connecting a local machine to the internet. In all probability, you already have an internet connection, otherwise you would not be reading this book. If your connection is via an office or college network, the chances are that most of the work has already been done for you. You may well find that all the necessary hardware and software has been preinstalled and preconfigured, and all you have to do is to click the right icon on your computer to access the internet. This kind of connection is unlikely to serve your best interests.

If your connection works properly, you might feel unwilling to mess about with the configuration on the 'if it ain't broke, don't fix it' principle. This book is all about taking back control of your system and suspecting the motives behind anything handed to you on a plate. If you have simply installed the internet connection software supplied by an Internet Service Provider, the chances are that your ISP has reconfigured your connection to suit his own ends, which may not coincide with yours. Ask yourself why an ISP would provide you with a free CD-ROM of connection software; why the connection it creates inevitably takes you to the ISP's own portal; and why ISPs make it so difficult to remove the traces of their software from your computer.

If at some stage in the past you have used an ISP's CD-ROM to install connection software and your browser is now permanently painted with their logos and colours, you might want to download the excellent Internet Explorer Personalizer from accesscodes.hypermart.net This will let you customize your browser with your own colours and graphics or simply strip out the unwanted ones.

Later in this chapter, we shall look at several ways of creating and configuring a dial-up connection to the internet. However, before we get down to practical matters, we need to understand exactly how an internet connection works.

Internet Hardware

Most local connections to the internet are still made via the telephone lines, or more correctly, via the PSTN (Public Switched Telephone Network). Alternatives are becoming available using the cable television system, satellite and wireless links. Unfortunately, because these use proprietary software, they are much less open to tinkering, and those who choose these systems will normally have to put up with a preconfigured connection. For the rest of us who are still using traditional internet access, connection settings can be brought under control.

To convert digital output from a computer into the analogue input which can be carried over the PSTN, it is necessary to use a digital-analogue converter at one end and an analogue-digital converter at the other. The converter used for internet connection is known as a modem (short for **mo**dulator/**dem**odulator). A modem receives the digital data output from your computer and converts it into suitable analog audio tones which can be carried by the PSTN – that's the 'modulator' bit. It also converts analog frequencies received from the telephone line into digital input – the 'demodulator' bit. This is shown graphically in Figure 14.3.

Figure 14.3 A modem converts digital input to an analogue waveform

Modems are usually rated according to their transmission/reception speed. A 56.6 Kbps modem can handle up to 56,600 bits of data per second. (Note that modems' speeds are rated in KiloBITS per second and not KiloBYTES – this is a very common error.) You may still see older modems rated at 33.6 Kbps or even 28.8 Kbps, but these are far too slow for efficient data flow.

A more recent development is the ISDN (Integrated Services Digital Network) modem, which requires a special connection to a digital telephone line. A single-line ISDN service provides a 64 kilobits per second connection, but a second line can be added to provide a 128 Kbps connection. ISDN is rapidly taking over from the standard telephone connection and is now available almost everywhere. An ISDN modem – more correctly called an ISDN adaptor, does not require modulation/demodulation circuitry. Instead it uses a device called a DSU (data service unit), which converts the digital data from a computer into a format which can be sent via a digital telephone line. It also requires a further piece of hardware, an ISDN terminal adaptor which is installed by the telephone company.

234

Even faster than ISDN connections are the new broadband connections known as Digital Subscriber Line (DSL). DSL is not yet widely available, although trial systems are being offered in some regions. Like ISDN, DSL is a digital connection, which requires an adaptor to convert the cable signal into computer bits. Unlike ISDN, a DSL adaptor is permanently connected to the internet and provides instantaneous access to the web. This always-on connection brings its own problems, as we shall see in Chapter 21.

Both PSTN and ISDN modems can be either external or internal – meaning they can sit on your desk as a separate unit or can be built into your computer as a plug-in card. In general, external modems are more reliable. They have the added advantage of featuring a series of small LEDs – coloured lights which tell you what they are doing. These will usually indicate when the modem has power, when it is connected to the internet and when it is receiving or transmitting data. These indicators can be very useful if you have problems with your internet connection.

Internal modems are connected directly to the data bus – the electronic pathway that connects the various components within the computer. External modems are connected by a cable to one of the computer's ports. Until recently, this was usually the serial port, but modern modems often use the USB (Universal Serial Bus) port which is faster and 'hot-swappable', meaning devices can be plugged in while the computer is running. To connect a device to the serial port, you need to turn off your computer, plug the device in and then restart the computer. (Note that USB modems do not provide a faster internet connection than serial modems. Internet connection speed is determined by the rate at which data can flow across the PSTN. This will always be slower than the speed at which the port itself can deliver data.)

The final piece of hardware required is a cable from your modem to the telephone socket. ISDN modems are connected in a similar way, but the connector is larger. Installing your hardware is simple enough. Bearing in mind the guidelines outlined in Chapter 7, you should carefully follow the instructions supplied with your modem. In most cases this will involve shutting down your computer. For an internal device, you will need to open the case and plug the modem card into a free expansion slot. With an external device, you will plug the serial or USB cable into a port on the back of the case and then plug in the power supply. Finally, connect one end of the telephone adaptor cable to the modem and the other end to the wall socket. Restart your computer and you are ready to install the communications software.

A final note on modems. Very often, they are left plugged into the telephone socket, even though the computer itself is switched off. Overhead telephone cables are very susceptible to lightning strike and connected modems offer a very convenient pathway for the electrical discharge to fry the insides of your computer. (This has happened to me twice!) Try to remember to unplug your modem from the telephone socket whenever it is not in use. If you can't manage that, at least disconnect it when there is a danger of thunderstorms.

235

Internet Software

None of the hardware described above is of any use without suitable communications software. The first piece of software required is a driver for the modem itself. A driver is a program that provides the computer's operating system with the information it needs to work with a specific device. A modem driver is usually supplied on CD-ROM although Windows comes with some of the most common drivers preinstalled. Follow the instructions provided with the modem to install the driver. Normally this will involve restarting your computer, allowing Windows to spot the modem, then working through the on-screen instructions to install the driver.

With most modern computers, all the internet connection software you need is pre-installed as part of your operating system. You will probably never know it exists, until things go wrong. Both Windows and the MacOS include all the basic software components including at least one web browser – the MacOS supplies two – Microsoft's Internet Explorer® and Netscape Navigator®.

Once your browser(s) is installed, there are several ways of creating the dial-up connection required for your computer to access the internet, but some methods bring their own problems. You can do the following.

➤ Use the connection software supplied by an Internet Service Provider (ISP). This is usually supplied as a CD-ROM, available, often free, from shops and computer stores.

➤ Use Window's built-in Internet Connection Wizard.

➤ Use Dial-Up Networking's simpler Make New Connection Wizard.

➤ Create a new dial-up connection from within Internet Explorer's properties.

We will examine each of these methods in turn, but first a warning note. The rest of this chapter involves setting up and modifying configuration settings and doing so is inherently risky. Make a mistake in the settings and you might be left with a fouled-up connection or even a stalled computer. If you already have a working connection that you prefer not to mess with, or if you are connecting via a network that is pre-configured, I suggest that you consider creating a new dial-up connection, which can always be deleted afterwards. If your computer is part of a network, as most office and college computers are, the correct procedure would be to obtain the network administrator's permission before doing anything.

Even with permission, it is safer not to make changes to any settings without carefully noting down how those settings are currently configured. Then, if there are problems, you can always return the settings to their original values. It is also worth remembering that it doesn't matter what changes you make, provided you click the **Cancel** button to close the settings window. This ensures that the original settings remain unaltered.

Maureen The Leisure Surfer

The internet and the online friends she has made are central to Maureen's happiness. When she first decided to try life online, she was seduced by the TV advertising of one very prominent ISP, and installed their free connection software. This has brought her benefits and problems in equal measure. On the plus side, she received a very simple and easy to operate interface with masses of top-quality content. On the minus side, she found that restrictions were placed on her online activities. The problems really came when she decided to junk her old ISP and transfer to a free service. Try as she might, she was unable to untangle her browser and connection software from the old ISP's tentacles. Eventually, she was forced to clear out her hard drive and reinstall Windows. Yes, it can be that hard to take back control of your internet connection.

Using The Connection Software Supplied By An Internet Service Provider

At first glance, the simplest method would appear to be installing the software provided by an Internet Service Provider. But this approach does have its disadvantages. As we have already noted, most ISPs take considerable liberties with your computer. Some ISP software rewrites your configuration files and makes it difficult for you to change to another ISP. All of them reconfigure your browser so that on connection you are automatically transported to their web portal. Some of them even modify your browser to display their advertising.

Many internet users are happy enough to sit back and let all this happen, but by accepting the default configuration you may not be getting the most efficient internet connection. For those who prefer more control, both Windows and MacOS will allow you to set up your communications software without using any of the software your ISP provides. This, of course, is the most secure approach – never trust anyone to do something for you.

Using Window's Built-in Internet Connection Wizard

If you are running Windows 95 or 98, you can make use of the Internet Connection Wizard, which will guide you through the connection process. Before you start, you will need some information from your ISP. Depending on the ISP you have chosen you might require any of the following.

➤ Your username.

➤ Your access password.

237

*Figure 14.4 Windows'
Internet Connection
Wizard*

➤ One or more phone numbers to dial for access.

➤ Your ISP's Domain Name Service (DNS) address(es).

➤ Other configuration information.

In most cases you can find the Internet Connection Wizard by clicking **Start >
Programs > Accessories > Communications > Internet Connection Wizard**. Some
computers may be set up differently and some might not have the Wizard installed, in
which case you will either have to install it from the original distribution or ask your
network administrator to do so. When you start this Wizard in Windows 98, you will
be presented with the box shown in Figure 14.4.

Setting up the connection using the Wizard is straightforward. You work through a
series of dialog boxes, filling in answers to various questions with the information
supplied by your ISP. The most recent versions of the Wizard actually dial a central
number to identify the various ISPs available to you. When you click **Finish** in the last
box, Windows creates a new **Dial-Up Connection** – a small file which holds the
information required to connect to your ISP. In my opinion, this Wizard is also a poor
way of creating a dial-up connection. The dial-up referral service described above does
not produce all the possible ISPs – only those that are signed up with Microsoft and
after the Wizard has finished, you will still need to enter further details manually.

Your new dial-up connection is accessible by clicking **Start > Programs > Accessories
> Communications > Dial-Up Networking**, which opens a window listing the
various dial-up connections on your computer. This window is shown in Figure 14.5.

238

Figure 14.5 Windows'
Dial-Up Networking
window

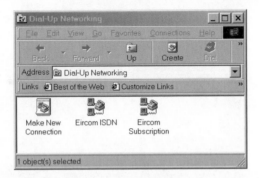

Using Dial-up Networking's Make New Connection Wizard

If you ever need to modify a connection – to change your password, for example – you can right-click on the connection, click **Properties** and make any changes required. As you can see from Figure 14.5, the Dial-Up Networking window also contains an icon called **Make New Connection**, which will lead you through a simpler Wizard than the one described above. The result will be the same as using the Internet Connection Wizard.

Creating A New Dial-up Connection from Within Internet Explorer

There is a fourth way of creating a connection which gives you an even greater degree of control. This method uses the connection settings dialog box available from within Microsoft's Internet Explorer®, the web browser which is bundled with Windows.

Figure 14.6 Internet
Explorer's Internet
Properties window

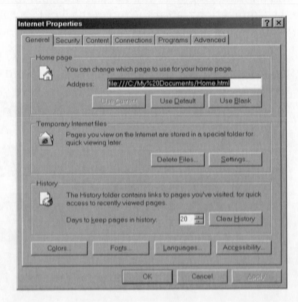

Figure 14.7 The Connections tab in the Internet Properties window

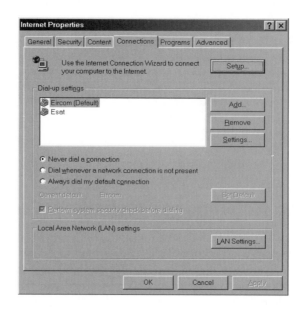

Even if you decide to use a different browser for your web activities, you will not be able to escape from Internet Explorer. At present, IE is an integral part of the Windows distribution and effectively controls the operation of your communications software.

On your Windows desktop, you should find an IE icon, and right-clicking that icon, and then clicking **Properties** opens the window shown in Figure 14.6. (This window can also be accessed from within Internet Explorer by starting the browser and then clicking **Tools > Internet Options**.) The Internet Properties window provides a whole range of settings for managing your internet activities, but for now we are only interested in the **Connections** tab at the top of the window. Click that and a new window will open looking like Figure 14.7.

Look carefully at the various buttons available in this window. The **Setup** button near the top will start the Internet Connection Wizard we discussed earlier. In the box

Figure 14.8 Windows' Make New Connection wizard

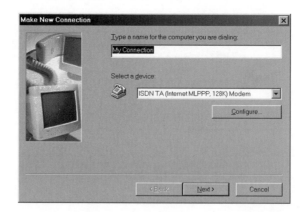

Figure 14.9 Entering phone details in the Connection wizard

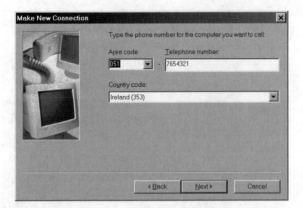

below are listed the dial-up connections that already exist on the computer, with one marked as the default connection. The three buttons to the right of this allow you to add a new connection, to remove a connection or to modify the settings of an existing connection.

Below these are three round check-boxes which determine how the connections are to be made. As shown in Figure 14.7, the most secure choice is always the **Never dial a connection** option and there is a good reason for this. Far too much software these days is configured to connect you to the internet whether you want to or not! Some programs, for example, feature a **Help** button which, instead of opening a Help file on your own computer, takes you straight to the distributor's website. You want to be the one who decides when you will connect to the internet, so check the top box and keep control of your system. (The disadvantage of this setting is that you will need to create a dial-up connection icon on your desktop and use that to connect to the internet. We will return to this later in the chapter.) For now we are interested in creating a new connection, so click the **Add** button and the window shown in Figure 14.8 will open.

The window, which you will now see, is the same Make New Connection wizard which opens when you click the **Make New Connection** icon in the Dial-Up Networking window we looked at earlier. In the first window, you should give your connection a suitable name and ensure that the correct modem is selected. Clicking **Next** opens a second window, shown in Figure 14.9.

In this window, you need to enter the access number provided by your ISP. You will also need to enter an area code, even if the access number is local. Don't worry about this, we can remove the area code later in the process.

Clicking **Next**, completes the Wizard and you will see a new dial-up connection appear. There are still some details to be entered, so the next stage is to highlight the new connection and click the **Settings** button. The window which appears is shown in Figure 14.10.

Figure 14.10 Connection settings window

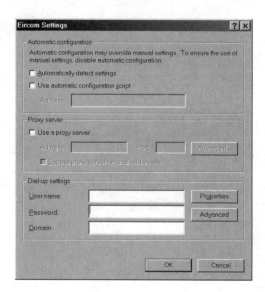

Modifying Your Dial-up Connection Settings

The window shown here is for a dial-up connection called *Eircom*, as you can see from the title bar. In your case the name will be whatever you called your own connection. Now you need to enter the remaining details provided by your ISP. The top section refers to Automatic configuration. Unless your ISP has specifically told you to use a configuration script (these are hardy ever used these days), you should check the **Automatically detect settings** box. (Leaving both boxes unchecked seems to have the same effect!)

The second box is for entering information about Proxy servers. Proxy servers act as intermediaries between a local network and the internet, handling the retrieval of remote files from web servers. (They can also be used to route your internet connection anonymously as we shall see in Chapter 16.) Once again, you should leave this unchecked unless your ISP has given you a proxy address and port number to use. The **Advanced** button, which will become active if the **Use a proxy server** box is checked, allows you to specify proxy addresses for a range of internet functions.

We are more interested in the lowest box in the window, the dial-up settings. Here you should enter the user name and password supplied by your ISP. You are unlikely to require a domain name, but if one has been supplied, enter that as well.

In most cases, this is all you will need to enter, but if your ISP has specified any additional settings, you will need to click the **Properties** button. The window which opens has four further tabs along the top: **General, Server Types, Scripting** and

Figure 14.11 Server Types dialog box in dial-up connection setting

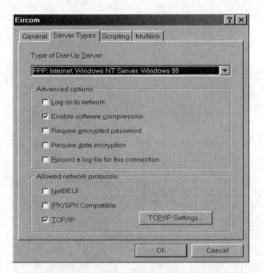

Multilink. The **General** window is useful to correct the access phone number if it changes. You can also remove the dialling code, which the Wizard compelled you to put in if, as in most cases, your access is via a local phone number. As before, you are unlikely to need the **Scripting** section, and you will only use the **Multilink** tab if you are either combining two modems for internet access or using a two-channel ISDN system. It is the **Server Types** tab we need to access. Click this and the window shown in Figure 14.11 will open.

Again, let's take a moment and analyse this window. The **Type of Dial-Up Server** should be set to **PPP: Internet, Windows NT Server, Windows 98**. PPP stands for Point-to-Point Protocol and is the protocol which handles internet access over a dial-up connection. The other protocols available from the drop down list are for specialized network use. In the **Advanced options** section, **Enable software compression** should be checked, and it is usually a good idea to uncheck the **Log on to network** box. Logging on to a network is seldom necessary for internet access and can waste up to half a minute of call time.

In the **allowed network protocols** section, **TCP/IP** should be checked since TCP/IP is the basic internet protocol. **NetBEUI** and **IPX/SPX** are special network protocols used if your internet access is via a local area network and are not required for direct internet connections. With TCP/IP checked, click the **TCP/IP Settings...** button and the window shown in Figure 14.12 will open.

The top section of this window allows us to specify an IP address. IP, you will recall, is short for Internet Protocol – the part of TCP/IP, which handles packet addressing. Normally, with a dial-up connection, each time you access the internet, your ISP allocates your computer its own IP address. This address will change every time you dial in. With DSL however, your IP address is static and this box allows you to enter

243

Figure 14.12 TCP/IP Settings

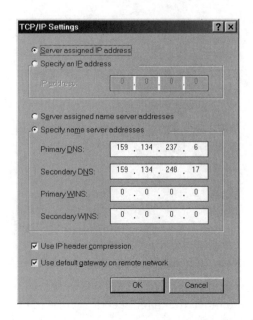

your assigned IP address. In our case, we will leave **Server assigned IP address** checked.

The second section allows us to specify a name server – a special internet server which looks up the internet domain names we type into our browser – www.microsoft.com for example – and maps them to the correct IP address which is a series of four numbers between 0 and 255 separated by full stops (periods). (There are two IP addresses shown in Figure 14.12, 159.134.237.6 and 159.134.248.17.) Some ISPs assign a name server dynamically, so unless you are told to the contrary, the **Server assigned name server addresses** box should be checked. If, however, your ISP has specified Domain Name Server (DNS) addresses, you should check the **Specify name server addresses** box and type the addresses you have been given into the **Primary DNS** and **Secondary DNS** boxes. The two additional settings at the bottom of the window should remain checked.

And that's it as far as settings are concerned. Close all the open windows by clicking the **OK** buttons and return to your desktop. Earlier I said that to simplify connecting to the internet, it would be useful to create a dial-up connection icon on the desktop. To do this, click **Start > Programs > Accessories > Communications > Dial-Up Networking**. In the window that opens, find the icon for the dial-up connection you have created and drag it onto your desktop or taskbar. This will create a copy of the icon which is always accessible.

Your internet connection should now be properly configured, so test it by clicking the desktop icon and making sure that everything works as it should. Clicking the icon will open the connection window shown in Figure 14.13. Make sure that the **User**

Figure 14.13 Internet connection window

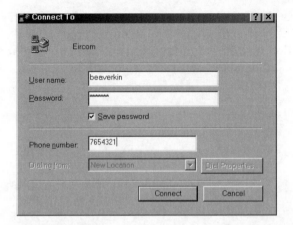

name and **Phone number** values are correct. You won't be able to see your password, but if you have any doubts about it, you can re-enter it now. Click the **Connect** button and a further window will open to tell you how your internet connection is proceeding. When the connection is made, this window reduces to an icon in your system tray and you can then open your browser and access the internet.

Finally, note that if you have configured your system as suggested above, you will also need to close your internet connection manually. The connection icon in your system tray looks like two little computers. Right-click on the icon and then click **Disconnect** to finish your session.

If you have followed the procedure described in this chapter, you now have a connection to the internet which is totally under your control. We will be improving its efficiency in the next couple of chapters. You have ensured that your connection operates as you want it to and not how your ISP wants it to and you have prevented other software from forcing a connection without your approval. Of course it is only once you have made that connection that the real dangers begin. In Chapter 15 we will consider just how vulnerable you are once you fire up your browser and take to the web.

Chapter 14 – Security Checklist

1   Internet connections can be created in several ways. The simplest is to install an ISP's proprietary software, but this will often rewrite your system's configuration to suit the ISP. It is worth taking the extra time to set your connection up manually. In this way you maintain the maximum control over your internet activity.

2   Whichever method you use, you should always configure your internet connection so that it cannot dial into the internet without your permission. A lot of programs these days try to exploit the other settings to contact websites

whenever they want to. To correct this, click **Tools > Internet Options** from within Internet Explorer, click the **Connections** tab and check the **Never dial a connection** box. Do this even if you are using a different browser since Internet Explorer still handles your system connections.

The Unseen Enemies On The Web

In This Chapter

➤ Meet the predators

➤ Understanding HTML

➤ The dangers from active code

➤ Internet traps and snares for the unwary

➤ Software to smooth your browsing

Meet The Predators

We have already looked at the concept of the internet as an anarchy. We know that no one actually controls the internet, and this, in my opinion, is a good thing. In this over-managed world where so many groups believe they have the right to control what we do, say and even think, the internet represents the ultimate home of free speech and free thought. Anyone who can master a few simple tools can create a presence on the web and use it to say whatever he or she likes – and this is how it should be. This level of freedom brings its own dangers.

I am sure that most people create internet content from the best possible motives. By and large, the web is populated with decent people who wish to sell you things, talk you round to their point of view or pass on information. The flipside of the coin is that if we extend total freedom to the decent, we cannot prevent the ungodly from twisting technology to suit their own unpleasant ends. There is a dark underbelly to the web, where unpleasant people do unpleasant things and unfortunately most of them want to do unpleasant things to you!

This chapter looks at the tools and technologies used to ensnare the unwary. There are frightening numbers of them. To understand how web content can be twisted, we need to take a short detour and look at how web pages are created.

Understanding HTML

Pages on the web are written in HTML, or one of its more complex derivatives DHTML or XML. HTML is Hypertext Mark-up Language, and, like a programming language, it consists of a range of text commands that tell your computer what to do. Unlike a programming language, HTML doesn't communicate directly with the operating system. Instead its commands are interpreted by your web browser. Internet Explorer, Netscape (Navigator), NeoPlanet, Opera, NetCaptor, HotJava and every other browser you might find are all HTML-aware.[1] In theory, they all display HTML in exactly the same way; in practice it doesn't quite work like that. Some browsers are much better at displaying web pages than others and some are much more forgiving of mistakes in the HTML code.

HTML is a continuously developing language. The current standard, HTML 4, includes code for a whole range of new features. Unfortunately, because HTML keeps moving forward, older web browsers get left behind. Early versions of Internet Explorer and Netscape (prior to Version 4.0 of each) don't understand a lot of the new code included in HTML 4.0. They either ignore it or make a mess of displaying it. Worse still, the various companies which distribute browser software cannot agree on a common standard. Different browsers offer different features, require different code and even respond to the same code in different ways.

To complicate matters further, HTML itself is now being left behind. DHTML (Dynamic HTML) makes use of scripting languages like JavaScript and VBScript, to create interactive pages which can respond to user input. While this was intended to provide the user with a more interesting experience, it has also exposed web browsing to a whole heap of abuse. The next generation of web pages will be written in XML (eXtensible Mark-up Language). XML offers the web author still more control over his pages by allowing him to move outside the limits imposed by HTML and create his own active content.

Creating a basic web page – that is a page which will display in a web browser – requires no more skill than does using a simple text editor. Provided you can type and enter

---

[1] If a web browser responds correctly to HTML code, it is said to be HTML-aware.

the necessary code accurately, you can create web pages. And there is nothing complicated in writing HTML. A web page consists of the following.

➤ **Content**: the words and images that appear in your browser window.

AND

➤ **Code**: the commands which tell the browser how to display your text, where to place your graphics, when to play your sound files, etc.

Here is a very simple example:

<B>Hello!</B>

The HTML code is **<B>** and **</B>**, and the content is **Hello!** In this case the code tells a browser to display the word 'Hello!' in bold text.

So HTML is simple, but it is also surprisingly powerful. While HTML was not originally designed to handle multi-media or active content, it was designed to handle hyperlinks, and hyperlinks can link to a whole range of different resources. Of course, you are already familiar with hyperlinks; the words and images you click on to move around the web. Hyperlinks make use of HTTP (the Hypertext Transfer Protocol) to bounce you from page to page.

Are you familiar with the concept of a protocol? Before two computers can communicate, they have to agree a set of rules and formats. In computer terminology, an agreed system of communications between two computers is called a protocol. Before the web came into existence, the most common protocol used for accessing remote data on the internet was the File Transfer Protocol (FTP). FTP was too slow for the web and did not allow the additional features that web designers wanted, so a new protocol was developed and christened the Hypertext Transfer Protocol (HTTP).

HTTP adopted the concept of hypertext links, but its protocol includes other features as well. If you think about it, exchanging information on the web requires four distinct message types.

➤ **Connection**: the client (your web browser) must connect to a server (the computer which stores the information you are trying to access).

➤ **Request**: the client must request a resource from the web server. (The request must include the protocol to be used in transferring the resource, the name of the resource requested and information on how the server should respond.)

➤ **Response**: the server must deliver the resource that has been requested or send an error message explaining why it cannot.

➤ **Close**: after the resource has been delivered, the connection between client and server must be shut down.

249

Figure 15.1 A simplified model of client/server computing

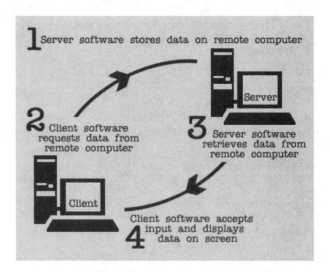

At the end of this process, HTTP has done its job and it is up to your browser (or other software on the client computer) to take on the resource and handle its display or storage.

The web can be looked at as a two-sided system. At the user end (the client, in computer terminology) there are resources to handle the requesting of data, its input and display. Your web browser is the key component here. At the remote end (the server), there are resources to handle storage and retrieval. As we noted in Chapter 13, this approach to handling information flow is called client/server computing. Figure 15.1 shows a simplified model.

There are several reasons why this client/server approach has proved so successful on the web. Because it divides the job of delivering web pages between client and server, the client can concentrate on managing the user interface (the browser), while the server looks after handling requests for data. By storing data on the server, information providers maintain control of their systems and can protect their data, control access to it and keep an accurate record of how often it is requested. To sum up, the world wide web makes use of client/server computing by linking powerful, graphical clients (web browsers) with fast, efficient servers.

Let us imagine that an HTML page on the web includes a link to a music file you want to listen to. Once the link has been made and HTTP has downloaded[2] the resource you have requested, your own computer's installed software takes over. Provided you have an application which can play that type of music file, the application starts up and out comes the song.

[2] Items moved from your own computer (the client) to a remote server on the web are said to be uploaded. Items moved from server to client are said to be downloaded. Strictly speaking, HTTP doesn't handle the download itself, that is the function of TCP.

It is important to remember that most of the web's actual resource handling takes place inside your own computer. You make a link and are connected to whatever server is holding the web resource you have requested. As soon as the resource has been downloaded, you are immediately disconnected from that server. What you see on your screen or hear over your speakers is now stored on your own machine and is handled by your browser, installed applications or plug-in software. (Even audio and video content works like this, although the latest players will start playing the sound or showing the video before it has all downloaded.)

This process is particularly important from our security perspective. A browser is sometimes thought of as a kind of television which passively views remote web content. This is a mistake. The web content you see is temporarily stored on your own computer, and it can bring malevolent scripting with it. By downloading web pages, you are allowing any evils they contain to bypass your defensive layers.

Hypertext is certainly the most powerful feature of HTML. Links can be created to different parts of the same document, to different documents on a website or to documents on a different website altogether. All that is required is that the HTML code points to the correct URL and you will be whisked to your destination as quickly as the internet can manage the transfer.

The Dangers From Active Code

Currently, the trend is for more and more interactive web content. As it changes from an active to an interactive medium, the web becomes more interesting and more responsive. Active code allows designers to personalize your browsing so websites can greet you by name or modify the way in which information is presented to suit your tastes. If you would like to see how easy it is to create interactive content, try the following exercise.

➤ Open Notepad (or any other text editor, for that matter) and type in the following code exactly as it is printed:

```
<html>
<head>
<title>A JavaScript warning!</title>
<SCRIPT LANGUAGE="JavaScript">
<!--
function Warning()
{
    alert ("Never press that button again!");
```

251

```
}
//-->
</SCRIPT>
</head>
<body bgcolor="Black" text="Yellow" face="Verdana">
<H2 align="center">DO NOT PRESS THIS BUTTON!</H2>
<div align="center">
<form>
<input type="button" value="Don't Press Me" onClick="Warning()">
</form>
</div>
</body>
</html>
```

➤ Save this file somewhere on your hard drive, naming it **jstrial.html**

➤ Double-click the file to open it in your browser. After you have pressed the button we have told you not to, it should look like Figure 15.2.

With two minutes of typing, you have created a simple script which produces an interactive effect within your browser. This might be trivial – though kind of fun, don't you think? But the same script could have been used to trigger something a lot less pleasant. With a small modification to the script – the bit between the <**SCRIPT...**> and <**/SCRIPT**> tags, that button could have sent you to a porn site or worse!

Figure 15.2 A simple example of JavaScripting

There are two scripting languages commonly used to create interactive events – JavaScript and Microsoft's own VBScript. They can both be used for good or evil. Although the two languages differ in syntax and usage, from a security perspective, we can treat them much the same. To run, a script needs a scripting environment – basically this means software which can interpret and respond to the script's commands. One such environment is your web browser, another is the Windows Scripting Host I urged you to dispose of back in Chapter 5. If you blinked and missed that bit, take my advice – return to the chapter and remove this threat to your security right now.

Here's a little more detail for technophiles! JavaScript and VBScript can be run wherever there is a suitable script interpreter. This includes your web browsers, where scripts are used to provide dynamic content, such as forms validation, navigation aids, and visual effects; web servers which make use of server-side scripting to perform actions such as interacting with active components on the server (e.g. getting data from databases); and the Windows Scripting Host (WSH) which allows users to write scripts that can interact with active components within Windows to get them to perform customized actions.

After all these warnings, you might be surprised to learn that scripting itself is perfectly secure. A script is nothing more than a piece of text written in a scripting language. By itself, it cannot access your software or cause any kind of damage. It is not until you provide the script with a scripting environment that the danger starts. Most scripts running in a web browser are perfectly safe. Browsers make use of what is known as a 'sandbox' – an isolation facility which prevents scripts from accessing the resources of your computer machine. Where this limitation starts to come apart is when the script is running on an Active Server Page (ASP) or within the Windows Scripting Host (WSH) since both of these environments allow scripts unrestricted access to your file system, Windows registry, and other essential system components.

It was the emergence of the 'ILOVEYOU' worm which really put the cat among the pigeons. This virus, which we looked at in Chapter 5, made use of Internet Explorer's scripting environment to do its dirty work. The Love Bug and other VBS worms exposed serious security weaknesses in Windows' script hosting facilities. Many computer security experts called on Microsoft to block the holes and several patches were issued, but the underlying danger still remains. To quote one security firm 'We have seen very few cases where the VBS Hosting facilities of Internet Explorer have been used for anything other than the spreading of e-mail worms such as Pretty Park, Melissa and similar worms.' The simple fact is that any would-be attacker with minimal programming skills can write a simple script and embed it in a web page. Any computer user who opens that page then runs the script.

Equally dangerous are Microsoft's proprietary ActiveX controls. Like scripts, ActiveX components are small programs embedded in a web page to provide dynamic content.

Figure 15.3 Disabling scripts in IE's Security Settings

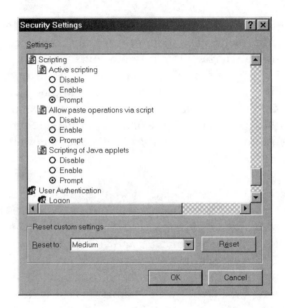

Microsoft uses ActiveX throughout the Windows environment, and very effective the technology is. But once again, in the hands of the ungodly, these controls can be used to turn a user's own operating system into a weapon against his computer or even the whole network to which he is connected. Internet Explorer's default setting is to run ActiveX and scripts with no warning to the user. Although, unlike scripting, ActiveX is monitored by the OS which will attempt to prevent it from causing any serious damage.

The root of the problem is that Microsoft has so thoroughly integrated Internet Explorer into the Windows operating system that anything which happens in the web browser has implications for the rest of your computer. Once you have removed the Windows Scripting Host (this is the third time of asking), scripts can only run within the web browser hosting environment, which offers better controls. You will have to decide if you are prepared to chance the dangers of active scripting in order to receive the marginal benefits they bring to your browsing experience. Disable scripting and many of the most interesting graphic effects of the web will not work. You might also have some difficulties with navigating script-enabled sites. My suggestion is that you reconfigure your browser to prompt you every time a script is encountered. Then, if you are visiting a site you trust, you can allow the script to run, and if you have any worries about the site's integrity, you can disable the script. Here is how to proceed.

From within Internet Explorer, click **Tools > Internet Options > Security**. Select the Internet Zone and click the **Custom Level** button. You will be presented with a dialog box looking like Figure 15.3. Scroll down the list of Settings to the **Scripting** section and check **Prompt** against all three entries. While you are at it, you might as well deal with all the other security settings provided for Internet Explorer. Table 15.1 opposite

254

Table 15.1 Suggested Security Settings

Security settings	Suggested choice	Notes
ActiveX controls and plug-ins		
Download signed ActiveX controls	Prompt	ActiveX controls can be provided with a digital signature which is supposed to ensure that they come from a reliable source. In most cases it is safe to trust 'signed' controls – these usually originate from Microsoft or a reliable software company.
Download unsigned ActiveX controls	Disable	
Initialize and script ActiveX controls not marked as safe	Disable	
Run ActiveX controls and plug-ins	Prompt	
Script ActiveX controls marked safe for scripting	Prompt	
Cookies – these are looked at in detail in Chapter 17		
Java		
Java permissions	High safety	Java (note: this is not JavaScript) is an independent programming language designed to run on all types of computer. Within the browser environment, Java runs in a sandbox and is usually quite safe.
Miscellaneous		
Access data source across domains	Disable	These miscellaneous settings are relatively harmless. I recommend against allowing web-based programs to automatically install items on your desktop.
Installation of desktop items	Prompt	
Software channel permissions	High safety	

lists suggested settings for most of the options provided in this dialog box along with some notes on the effects certain settings might have. I have not listed those settings which are not relevant to your security. From this table, you can make your own mind up as to whether to implement my proposals. Note that because of the browser's integration with the operating system, some of these settings might have an effect on other aspects of your computer's operations. You can, of course always change them back again. Before starting, I would recommend making a note of the original settings. Although the **Reset** button returns everything to its default configuration, this is a heavy-handed way of removing your preferred settings!

After you have made these changes, click **OK** twice and restart your browser to implement them. You will now find that as you visit sites on the web you will often be presented with a little dialog box asking you whether to run a script or an ActiveX control. While this can be a nuisance, it has significantly increased your own security. Another possible solution – although I would adopt it along with, rather than instead of, configuring your browser – is to use proprietary software to control scripts. Among other programs, WebWasher, discussed in the next section, offers this feature.

Internet Traps And Snares For The Unwary

Anyone who, by accident or design, has visited one of the internet's plethora of porn sites will know how difficult it can be to escape from their clutches. In the days of good old static HTML code a visitor had almost complete control over his travels across the web, but the advent of Dynamic HTML (DHTML), Java and scripting has handed a new set of snares to the persistent webmaster. To research this book (and for no other reason) I looked at a number of the most intrusive porn sites – the sort of sites which sucker you in and refuse to let you out again. As you probably know, most web browsers come with a handy utility which lets you examine the source code of the pages you visit. (If this is news to you, click **View** > **Source** in Internet Explorer, or **View** > **Page Source** in Netscape.) Checking the code for some of these sites turned up some brilliantly imaginative use of DHTML. Familiar tricks are to code a page so that when it opens, it triggers a whole series of other windows which explode all over the screen. Nervous users (or porn peepers whose wives are in the next room) can be quite bothered by this. They start closing each window in turn, only to find that a fresh batch of pages are coded to appear by this very action. It is not unknown for the desperate user to turn his computer off at this point.

Pop-up windows are a real nuisance on the web. Even the most respectable hosts often attach them to free websites. If you wish to be rid of pop-ups, you need to equip yourself with some specialized software. As usual there is a wide choice available, and pop-up removal is often one of the features of more complex browsing control software. My preferred tool is the wonderfully named Pop-Up Stopper which does the job brilliantly. It installs as a tiny memory-resident program and refuses to let any

Figure 15.4 Panicware's
Pop-Up Stopper

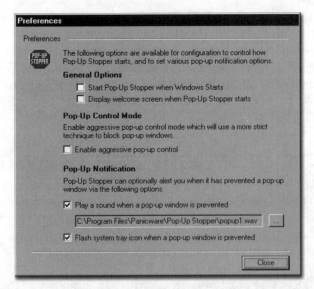

pop-up windows open unless you hold down the **Control** key when clicking a link. It's welcome screen is shown in Figure 15.4. I never browse the web without it!

A newer trick is for an opening web page to reset the user's browser to full screen and turn off the browser controls so that it is impossible to shut it down. This can be a real nuisance. You can try turning it off from the taskbar, usually at the bottom of the screen – right-click the browser's button and select **Close**. If that is impossible, the best solution is the famous three-finger salute we have met earlier in the book. Hold down **Control**, **Alt** and **Delete** at the same time, then select the browser from the list of running programs and click **End Task**. Of course this means restarting your browser, which in some cases implies reconnecting to the internet.

I have never seen any evidence to suggest that this sort of visitor mugging actually sells any more porn. I suppose that some people must be so excited by this blossoming of bosoms all over the monitor that they start clicking links madly, but I suspect that most visitors are so annoyed by the intrusion that they leave at once and make a vow never to visit the damned site again. But this is only my opinion and no doubt the pornographers know best.

As we noted in Chapter 14, the web is intended to be a transparent medium which allows users to travel where they like and at their own speed. Unfortunately, treacherous DHTML (and its even more devious descendant eXtensible Mark-up Language – XML) allow a malicious webmaster to lead a naïve user where he doesn't necessarily wish to go. In web design terms, we talk of dead-ends and teleports. A dead-end is an internet cul-de-sac – a series of links which strands the visitor up an alley with no way back other than by using the **Back** button on his browser. Anyone who has ever played the classic game Doom knows about teleports. Without any warning, they transport you somewhere you never intended to go and strand you there.

Such traps are easy to perform with JavaScript or VBScript. Scripting allows you to trigger links using simple HTML code. Each element on a web page – a graphic, a paragraph or even a single word, can be loaded with what is called an event handler attribute such as **onmouseover**. The simple act of running your mouse pointer across the element fires up the associated script which can open another window on your desktop or transport you somewhere else altogether. So modify your browser to prompt for scripting and take control of your journey.

Software To Smooth Your Browsing

Not only does all this devious nonsense irritate the web user, it also seriously affects internet access speeds. Remember that everything you view on the web has to be downloaded to your computer. This means that all those extra pop-up windows and scripted effects are taking up valuable bandwidth – bandwidth which costs you money in call charges. This also applies to web advertising. No one at present seems quite sure how to make money from the web and a lot of attempts to do so have gone down in flames. Some sites are simply awash with ads, although all the evidence is that most people ignore them completely. There is an ethical question here. Should you be subjected to advertising at all – after all, it costs you money to download the ads – or should you grin and bear it on the grounds that without advertising some sites will close down through lack of funding? You must decide.

One way to dramatically improve browsing speed is to install software which kills off adverts at source. These programs look at each web page you call for and, if they contain content which looks like advertising, they prevent your browser from downloading it. 'How does a program know what advertising looks like?' I hear you ask. Actually this is simpler than it sounds. Take a look at Figure 15.5. This shows some of the configuration options for WebWasher, one of the best programs for dealing with unwanted advertising – and free into the bargain. You will notice that it intends to 'Filter objects by dimension'. In other words whenever it sees HTML code setting up an area on a web page to one of the sets of dimensions from the list, it will automatically kill the contents. It does this by assuming the role of proxy server for your browser. Now I will be covering proxies in detail in Chapter 16, so I won't say too much about them here. For the moment you can think of WebWasher as an in-line filter which accepts content from the internet and delivers it to your browser.

Figure 15.5 also shows some of the other web management features on offer from WebWasher. If you look down the settings to the left of the window, you will notice that among other things it can handle pop-up windows, active scripting, web bugs[3] and cookies, not to mention those irritating animations which seem to clutter up the web. There are several similar programs on the web. AdStopper from Paraben Software

---

[3] Web bugs are small graphics which are sometimes included on pages to track your browsing patterns. I will be talking about these in more detail later in the book.

*Figure 15.5
WebWasher's
dimension filters*

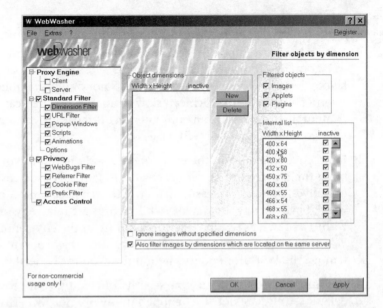

is another option as is AdSubtract's InterMute. But WebWasher, in my opinion, outshines the competition and will cost you nothing.

Another little utility comes in handy if your ISP tends to drop your connection if there is no activity on the line for a certain period. At peak times it is often difficult to reconnect. Stay Connected, a neat little shareware program from inKline Software Labs, can help to avoid this problem. It runs in the system tray using almost no computer resources and constantly simulates online activity to fool your ISP's server into believing that you are beavering away on the web.

There are countless other utilities to smooth your browsing. Many of them duplicate the functions we have already discussed. Others cause more problems than they solve. Your difficulty is more likely to be in correctly identifying the reason for poor browser performance than in finding a piece of software to resolve it. My final advice in this chapter is to keep your browser up-to-date and to download and install any patches which are released to improve its performance or security.

From here we are going on to look at one of the most important aspects of your online security – keeping your internet activities private.

The Pop-Up Stopper is available as a free download from www.panicware.com For WebWasher, visit www.webwasher.com It is available free for non-commercial use only. You will find InterMute at www.intermute.com and AdStopper at www.paraben.com Stay Connected is a shareware program from www.inKlineGlobal.com

Chapter 15 – Security Checklist

1 One of the most important things to remember when browsing the web is that all web content – the words, images, sounds, etc. – is downloaded to your computer before you can view it or listen to it. This not only has implications for your internet access speed which can slow dramatically when carrying bloated page content, it also affects your computer security because malevolent code can get into your computer as part of web page code.

2 Interactive elements on the web not only add interest to your browsing, they also bring their own hazards. Scripts created in languages such as JavaScript or VBScript, or ActiveX controls are easily written into web pages and can, if not controlled, wreak havoc with your system. While scripts are relatively safe when running within a browser's sandbox, scripts running in the environment provided by the Windows Scripting Host are almost uncontrollable. For safety's sake, you should remove the WSH from your system unless you really need it.

3 It is important to maximize the security offered by your browser – Microsoft's default settings are not strict enough in my opinion. Security settings can be configured from within Internet Explorer. You should change any potentially hazardous setting to either disable or prompt. The prompt setting gives you the option of allowing an activity but can prove irritating as confirmation boxes keep popping up when you are browsing.

4 Dynamic HTML uses scripting or ActiveX to generate web pages that respond to user input. This is not always in your best interests. Among the annoying tricks used by some sites are pop-up windows or resetting your browser to suit their content. They can also strand you up a back alley or jump you to somewhere else entirely. You can use proprietary software to stop such anti-social behaviour.

5 To speed up your browsing, consider employing software to filter unwanted content out of the pages you download. Several programs are available which will do this. They can be configured to recognize advertisement blocks from their dimensions, and can often control other annoying web elements such as animation.

Surfing Unseen

The Case For Anonymous Web Browsing

Unless you have an interest in some of the less savoury content available on the web, you might think there is no reason to conceal your browsing tracks. This is very naïve. There is also a view being propagated by many Western politicians that unless someone is engaged in illegal or subversive activities, he has no reason not to have his online movements tracked or recorded. This might sound reasonable until you look at it more closely. The real issue here is your right to privacy. I suspect that you would not wish to have a government webcam in your sitting room recording your leisure activities. You would not wish to fill in a form advising the bureaucrats which books and magazines you are reading. This is not because you have something to hide. It is quite simply none of their business.

There are several reasons why you might want to hide your internet trail. An obvious one is so that other people cannot find out which sites you have visited and this might have nothing to do with illegal activities. If, for example, you are tracking down a new job, you might not wish your employer to know this. If you are looking for Christmas presents for your children, you might prefer them not to know where you are shopping. If you are investigating a business competitor's website, you might want to conceal this from your opposition. To research this book, I have been forced to visit some fairly dubious sites. If my own traces were investigated, a suspicious police officer might well reach the conclusion that I am involved in internet hacking. (I should add quickly that I am not – but I could have some difficulty persuading some humourless official of that.)

Some countries are already implementing draconian anti-privacy laws to ensure that all internet activity – web browsing, e-mail and chat – can be tracked by the police and the security services. The only reason that the system is not yet in place is because the idiots that dreamed it up underestimated the technical difficulties involved. Your Internet Service Provider (ISP) was to have been turned into an unpaid government snooper, logging your activities via a black box and feeding all the information to the security services.

In Chapter 17, we will be looking in more detail at the traces your internet activities leave behind. In this chapter we are concerned with internet privacy – your right to browse the web anonymously. As so often in this book, you have a choice to make. If you are quite happy to have your browsing mapped and logged, you can simply turn to Chapter 17. If, on the other hand, you believe (as I do) that you have a right to browse in privacy, then read on.

The Information Your Browsing Reveals

Before we look at anonymous browsing, we need to understand how an open connection to the internet works. The following list shows a simplified version of the process.

> ➤ Your internet connection software dials the number provided by your Internet Service Provider (ISP).

> ➤ The call is answered by your ISP's server which starts by 'negotiating' with your computer. In other words, they exchange digital signals to establish your name, password, etc.

> ➤ Once your rights have been established, the address of the web resource you have asked for is passed to a Domain Name Service (DNS) server which translates the domain name you have typed into your browser into its four-number IP address.

Figure 16.1 Checking for details at cpcug.org

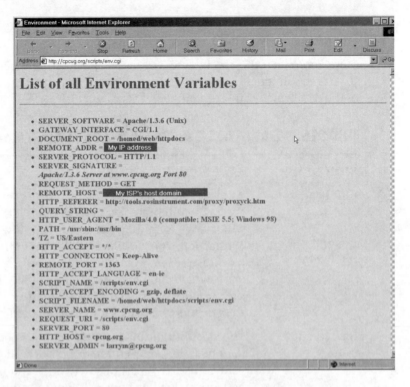

➤ Your request is routed to that IP address via whichever links are available. Traffic across the internet is directed by special computers known as Routers. These control access to the major communication lines sometimes called the internet backbone.

➤ Your request carries a lot of additional information including a return address for the resource you have asked for. The server holding the resource then responds by reversing the process and sending it back to your computer.

➤ The resource arrives at your computer and is displayed by your browser.

Look again at 'Your request carries a lot of additional information.' You might wonder exactly how much information about yourself and your system you are revealing when you browse the web. And, if your request is responded to with a deliberate attempt to obtain still more information, how much can that remote server find out? To answer this question, look at Figure 16.1.

There are several sites on the web which will perform a check on your web request and list the information you are revealing. I have used the environment variables checker at www.cpcug.org and this is the result. Most of the information is not relevant to my anonymity, but the two entries I have blocked out give the IP address of my computer and the remote host name which will identify my computer as part of

263

my ISP's network. These two pieces of information are enough to pinpoint me on the internet – effectively destroying my anonymity.

Much more than this can be discovered. Once you are connected to a remote server, that server can query your system for additional information. Table 16.1 shows some of the data which can be obtained in this way.

Table 16.1 Data That Can Be Obtained From A Remote Server

Information	Explanation
Your IP address.	As explained earlier, this is your address on the internet. If you access the internet via a modem or an ISDN line, your IP address will change each time you log on, but if you upgrade to a DSL connection, your IP address will remain the same. Once it has been discovered, you can kiss your privacy goodbye. Software now exists which can block particular IP addresses from accessing a site, or tailor custom content for them. You have just become a statistic in some marketing man's data files.
Your computer's name.	This does not mean 'Fred', or whatever pet name you call your machine, or even Microsoft's default 'My Computer'. If your computer is part of a network – and that includes the network created by your ISP – your computer will have a host name. This might be something like **p234.as1.hongkong1.myisp.net.**
A referrer's name.	This will be the site from which you linked to the current site. Most browsers forward this information when a link is clicked. It is used to find out where you have been and (where appropriate) which search terms you used to track down the site.
Your browser type and the operating system you are using.	Most browsers send this information if they are asked to. The idea is to tailor page content to suit your particular set-up. Netscape and Internet Explorer, for example, display pages differently and some sites send slightly different pages to suit the user's configuration.
'Trace Route'.	Trace Route is a program which can track your connection across the internet. When you request a web resource, your request hops from server to server across the web until it reaches its destination. Trace Route can list all those hops to discover exactly how your signal arrived and how long each hop took. (*Note:* this is not the same as a list of the sites you have visited.)

Who registered the domain you have come from?	Your computer's name (see left) can be shortened to a simple domain name – **myisp.net** in the example above. This can then be checked on a publicly accessible internet registration database to discover who originally made the registration.
How is your domain configured?	Information on how a domain is set up is stored in a configuration file on the DNS servers. This information is also open for public access.
Who owns your network?	WHOIS is a recognized command which can be sent to the internet registration database to discover who owns a network.

Note: My thanks to Privacy.net for much of the information in this table. Visit www.privacy.net for more information or to see other examples of information that can be extracted without your permission.

You will agree that when you browse the web, the sites you visit can find out a lot more about you than you might reasonably expect. Every time you click a link, you expose your browsing habits to outside scrutiny, but does this matter? You know I am going to say that it does. After all, you have no idea how this information is being used. While I am certain that most site owners are only trying to personalize your browsing by adapting content and presenting information that is tailored to your needs, less scrupulous webmasters can use the same information to target you as a customer or sell your details to other marketeers.

It goes without saying that this same information can – and in some cases, must – be made available to government departments, police authorities and even national security agencies. This brings us back to the start of the chapter! So what can you do about it?

Using Web Proxies To Keep Your Online Activities Private

If you wish to browse the web anonymously, you need to control the information which is passed to a site by your request and to prevent that site from obtaining any additional information by querying your computer. In simple terms this means that your request must be passed through some kind of filter which either strips information away or replaces it with information which doesn't point to your system. This means using a proxy. A proxy is another computer which accepts your requests for web resources, and then fetches those resources for you. We are interested in anonymous proxies which handle this process by substituting their own IP address for yours. A simple diagram of this is shown as Figure 16.2.

Figure 16.2 How a proxy server operates

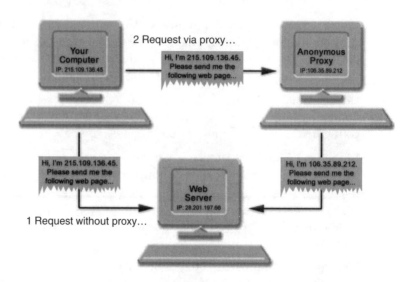

For Request 1, you can see that the request is passed straight to the web server and carries your computer's return IP address. With Request 2, however, the request is routed through a proxy server which replaces your IP address with its own. The web server is not aware that the request comes from a proxy and returns the resources to the proxy server which then delivers them your computer. Of course your anonymity still relies on the discretion of the proxy server which knows your real IP address. You can improve your security by routing your request through a series of proxies, but the first server in the chain will always be aware of your actual identity. For the process to work properly, your first proxy must be discrete.

Dennis The Porn Peeper

You will not be surprised to hear that Dennis always routes his more dubious browsing through a proxy. This stems more from his growing paranoia than from any real need to do so. Dennis thinks that by using a proxy server he is merely protecting his anonymity. He doesn't realize that he is also saving himself from a truck-load of extra trouble. Many porn sites, and other commercial sites as well, log each visitor's IP address so that they can subsequently target them with special offers and sales pitches. Anonymous browsing is not just about privacy, it can also save you from personalized marketing and other invasive business practices (see Chapter 19).

In addition to anonymizing your browsing and protecting yourself from targeted marketing, there are two further reasons why you might want to consider using a proxy server. First, proxy servers can significantly increase the speed of your internet connection. Web resources which are frequently requested are saved by these servers

Your internet browsing can also be routed through a proxy for other reasons. In the previous chapter we looked at WebWasher, the software which strips unwanted content from downloaded web pages. This program, and others like it, are also proxy servers, only they are installed on your own computer. If you access the web via a corporate network, your requests are probably routed via a proxy installed by your company. The same often applies when you use a cable modem.

in special databases called proxy caches. These caches are often of very large capacity and contain not only the resources you have requested, but also those requested by thousands of other internet users. If the resource you are looking for is already stored in the cache, it can be delivered immediately. Second, proxy servers can allow users to bypass the geographical restrictions imposed by some site owners. If you live in Region A and a site in Region B is prevented by, for example, the laws imposed by an unreasonable government from servicing your requests, you can route those requests via a proxy in Region C, where the restrictions don't apply. This technique has often been used by citizens suffering under totalitarian regimes to access information from the free world.

If you are now convinced that using a proxy server is a good idea, there are three ways you can go about it. You can:

➤ track down the address of an anonymous proxy server from the web and configure your internet connection to use it;

➤ install anonymous proxy server software on your own computer and let that take care of your privacy;

➤ use one of the online proxy services.

The next three sections of this chapter consider each of these in turn.

Using An Anonymous Proxy Server From The Web

Tracking down anonymous proxy servers is a simple enough process. Several sites on the web publish lists of free proxies. The list published at www.atomintersoft.com is illustrated in Figure 16.3. It is advisable to be cautious about some proxy servers that claim to be anonymous. A recent survey found that out of 8,000 so-called anonymous proxies, only just over 600 actually concealed your IP address from the sites they accessed for you. Clearly, an anonymous proxy that isn't is a complete waste of time! There is no way of telling whether a proxy server is really anonymous without reconfiguring your connection and then testing it on a checker such as the ones at cpcug.org or www.privacy.net we looked at earlier.

Figure 16.3 A list of anonymous proxy servers can be found at several sites on the web

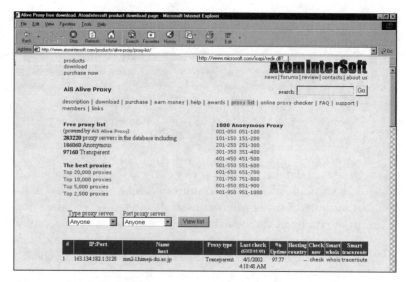

To install a proxy server, start by downloading a list of anonymous servers from the web. I recommend using a search engine to hunt for **list free anonymous proxy servers**. Now go to several of the proxy checkers – there is a list of these maintained at www.privacy.net – and note down the information on your IP address and computer name that is shown. It is always worth checking the results on more than one of these since they don't all operate in the same way and can report different results. Now reconfigure your connection software to use one of the proxies on your list – instructions for doing this follow. You may well find that the proxies are listed in order of speed, so it is well worth trying to use the fastest servers first. With the proxy installed on your computer, go back to the same checkers you used before and confirm that they can no longer discover your details. If they can, or if you can't connect, pick another proxy and try once more.

To install a proxy server, fire up Internet Explorer and click **Tools > Internet Options > Connections**. Click on the connection you intend using via the proxy server and then click **Settings**. This will open a window like Figure 16.4. Check the box marked **Use a proxy server** and type in the address and port number of your preferred proxy. Now click the **Advanced** button and in the box that opens, check **Use the same proxy server for all protocols**. (Subsequently you might wish to modify this setting to use different proxies for different protocols, but this setting will do for the moment.) Now click **OK** twice and close down and restart your browser so the new setting comes into effect.

As you can see, this is a fairly long and complicated procedure. It is also an unfortunate fact that anonymous proxies regularly appear and disappear from the web and their efficiency varies a great deal depending on the time of day and the amount of traffic they are handling. You might well find that a proxy that serves you well for

Figure 16.4 Configuring a proxy server

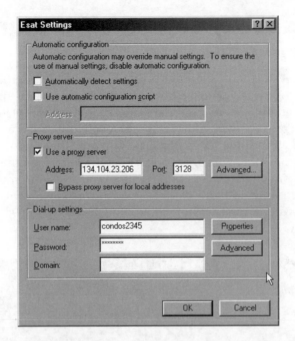

one session on the web will prove worse than useless the next time you log on. If this happens, you will need to repeat the entire process to install a new proxy. Not surprisingly, software designers have come to the rescue and created a number of programs which can take the hard work out of configuring proxies. We will look at some of these in the next section.

You might also like to note that a proxy server can make you anonymous to HotMail, Yahoo! Mail, and other web-based mail servers. This means that you can send anonymous e-mail. When you connect to a server such as HotMail through an anonymous proxy server, your IP address is hidden, and e-mail that you send using the forms on the HotMail server will not reveal your true location. Remember that some services use a secure connection (HTTPS) when you send mail or when you log into your account. You must therefore make sure that your browser is configured to use your proxy for the secure HTTPS protocol. If you configured your browser in the way I suggested above, this has already been set. Otherwise click **Tools** > **Internet Options** > **Connections** as before, select the relevant connection and click **Settings** > **Advanced**. Now enter your proxy address and port number against the **Secure** protocol.

Installing Proxy Software On Your Own Computer

There are several competing proxy programs available from the internet. The two which are most widely used are Anonymity 4 Proxy (A4Proxy) and MultiProxy. Both of these programs operate in similar ways. They come complete with a list of anonymous proxy servers which you can update from their websites. On installation, they handle all the browser configuration for you, thus removing the biggest nuisance with setting up your own connection. When they start up, they check their own listings and fire off requests to some or all of the proxies in their databases. They then assess the responses in terms of speed and efficiency. With this process complete, you can use your browser as normal, leaving the proxy software to take care of your privacy.

Figure 16.5 A4Proxy checking its internal database of anonymous servers

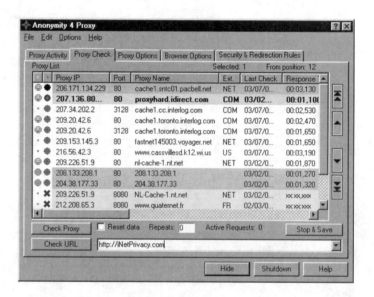

Figure 16.5 illustrates A4Proxy in action. The window shows part of its list of available anonymous proxy servers. The icons to the left of the names indicate whether the proxy is active and how well it is responding. A4Proxy offers any number of options for the expert user, and this can make the program look more intimidating than it really is. In most cases the default options work perfectly and there is no need for further tinkering with the settings.

A4Proxy handles its work in a very professional way. You can use it to monitor outgoing requests from your browser and modify them if you like. In addition, you can block cookies, change the address of your proxy for each request and even use it to send a fake IP address. If you connect to the web over a network, A4Proxy will allow you to share your anonymous connection with other computers on the LAN.

270

Figure 16.6 MultiProxy testing remote proxies

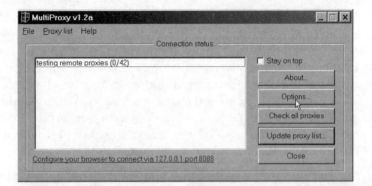

Figure 16.7 MultiProxy's server list

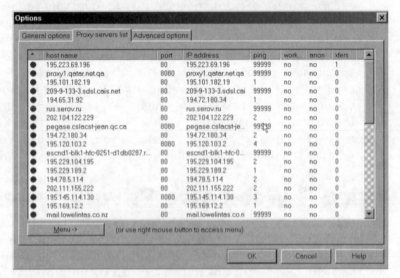

MultiProxy is much simpler to use but does not offer the range of advanced features provided by A4Proxy. On start-up it opens the window shown in Figure 16.6 and proceeds to check all the proxies in its database. With this done, you can fire up your browser and access the web. MultiProxy's most impressive feature is its ability to use several proxies at the same time. If you open more than one browser window, or use other web software alongside your browser, the program will use as many different proxy servers as are needed to ensure an effective connection speed. MultiProxy has the added advantage that it is distributed free of charge. Figure 16.7 shows the list of anonymous proxy servers available from within MultiProxy.

Both A4Proxy and MultiProxy are excellent programs, but I must add a warning. If the proxy settings for your browser are wrongly configured, your internet connection will simply not work. I have known both programs to fail and crash the browser or even the whole operating system. If you are not confident of your ability to dig your way out of possible proxy confusion, you might find it safer to ignore both programs and look at the third alternative described in the next section.

There is one other system we should mention in this section although it is a kind of hybrid between locally installed software and a web-based privacy system. Freedom from Zero Knowledge Systems allows you to create a series of pseudo-personalities, called **nyms**, who replace your own identity when you are browsing the net. These nyms not only have their own IP addresses, they also have names, addresses, e-mail addresses and other personal characteristics. Nym information can be used to fill in web forms and dialog boxes. A Freedom nym can become a complete online character who can visit websites, send and receive e-mail, read newsgroups and participate in chat rooms. Schizophrenia, here we come!

The Freedom system uses its own proxy servers rather than publicly available ones, and the number of Freedom servers used to route your connection determines its security. This has the advantage of ensuring that a server is always available, but the disadvantage that if the nearest Freedom server is some distance from you (in web terms, that is), this can result in a very slow connection. The Freedom suite also allows you to manage a range of other web debris such as cookies. Freedom ought to be an excellent system, but I have to admit that I have never had much success with it. Connections are very slow – this might be because I am not located in the continental United States – and it makes a terrible hash of downloading files. Despite this, you might give Freedom a trial. If it works for you, it should prove an excellent anonymity provider and the software itself is well designed and easy to use.

Using A Web-based Privacy System

Your final option is a totally web-based privacy system. These are subscription services, although some sites do offer a trial version usually with reduced features. To use this type of system, you log on to your proxy provider and type in the first web address you wish to visit. The link is then accessed via the provider's own proxy server(s) which deletes your own IP address and substitutes its own. There are several such systems available, but to illustrate how they work, I'll use Rewebber – a server located in Germany. Figure 16.8 shows Rewebber's home page. Clicking **Login** opens a dialog box where you enter your e-mail address (used as your ID) and your password. After approval, you type a web address into the **URL** box and click **Go!**

Once Rewebber has been activated, each link you click is automatically routed through the proxy. Figure 16.9 shows the Google search engine accessed via Rewebber. Look in the address bar and you will note that Google's web address at http://www.google.com has been modified to http://www.anon.de/surf_encoded/http://www.google.com Rewebber's premium service would go further and replace this anonymized address with a string of meaningless digits. Another useful feature is that you can cut and paste web addresses into the browser address bar. Earlier in the chapter, I visited the environment checker at cpcug.org/scripts/env.cgi If I now replace http://www.google.com at the end of the address in the address bar with the checker's URL, and click **Go**. I will be transported to the browser window shown in Figure 16.10.

*Figure 16.8 Rewebber –
web-based privacy*

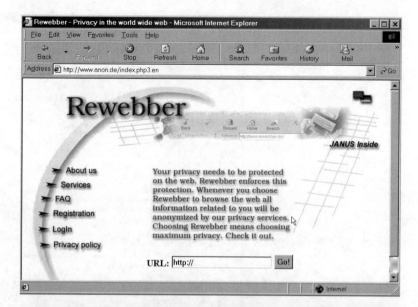

*Figure 16.9 Google
search engine via
Rewebber*

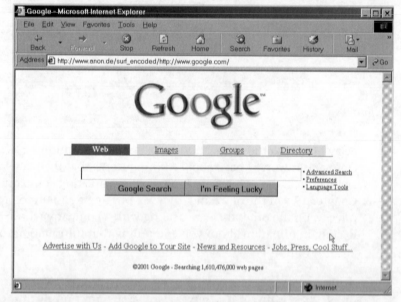

This time I have no need to blank out any of the information. The **Remote Address** shown in line four is certainly not my IP address, and the computer host name is server2.rewebber.com – again nothing to do with me! Rewebber has done its job and privatized my internet connection.

There are other, similar services on the web. One of the best known is Anonymizer which operates in a similar way. Anonymizer offers a free trial (with an annoying

Figure 16.10 The cpcug.org environment checker accessed through Rewebber

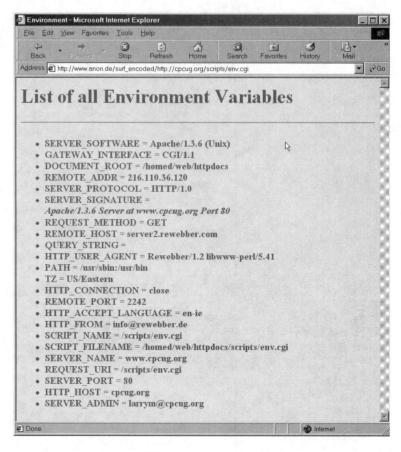

List of all Environment Variables

- SERVER_SOFTWARE = Apache/1.3.6 (Unix)
- GATEWAY_INTERFACE = CGI/1.1
- DOCUMENT_ROOT = /homed/web/httpdocs
- REMOTE_ADDR = 216.110.36.120
- SERVER_PROTOCOL = HTTP/1.0
- SERVER_SIGNATURE = *Apache/1.3.6 Server at www.cpcug.org Port 80*
- REQUEST_METHOD = GET
- REMOTE_HOST = server2.rewebber.com
- QUERY_STRING =
- HTTP_USER_AGENT = Rewebber/1.2 libwww-perl/5.41
- PATH = /usr/sbin:/usr/bin
- TZ = US/Eastern
- HTTP_CONNECTION = close
- REMOTE_PORT = 2242
- HTTP_ACCEPT_LANGUAGE = en-ie
- HTTP_FROM = info@rewebber.de
- SCRIPT_NAME = /scripts/env.cgi
- SCRIPT_FILENAME = /homed/web/httpdocs/scripts/env.cgi
- SERVER_NAME = www.cpcug.org
- REQUEST_URI = /scripts/env.cgi
- SERVER_PORT = 80
- HTTP_HOST = cpcug.org
- SERVER_ADMIN = larrym@cpcug.org

delay built into the connection speed) or a subscription service operating at full speed. One serious worry I have about Anonymizer is that their site is connected with DoubleClick, the deeply invasive internet marketing company I shall be dissecting in Chapter 19. On the one hand, they are offering a system to protect your internet privacy, on the other they are dealing with a company whose business involves logging information about you and selling that information to people who want to sell you things. This must be a cause for concern.

Techno Talk

Using a proxy server also has an effect on the information stored on your computer. If, for example, you do all your browsing via Rewebber at www.anon.de, this web address is the only one which will appear in your **History** folder. Some proxy servers also provide the facility for encrypting the addresses of all the sites you visit. This is the only practical way of hiding browsing information from your ISP which otherwise can log all your internet activities.

This chapter has outlined three ways in which you can use proxy servers to protect your internet privacy. In Chapter 17, we shall look at the information about your browsing that your computer quietly stores away and see how to remove those traces permanently.

A4Proxy is available as a shareware program. A 30-day trial version can be downloaded from www.inetprivacy.com MultiProxy is designed by MishkinSoft and is available as a free download from proxy.nikto.net The Freedom Internet Privacy Suite comes from Zero Knowledge Systems Inc., and can be found at www.freedom.net Anonymizer is available from www.anonymizer.com

Chapter 16 – Security Checklist

1   Internet privacy is your right and has nothing to do with illegal or subversive activities – although this is the suggestion being made by several authorities that wish to monitor your browsing habits.

2   Browsing the web openly allows websites to log a surprising amount of information about you – not least your IP address, your computer's network name and the sites you have browsed previously. This information can be used to build up a picture of your browsing habits either as evidence against you or to target you for internet marketing activities.

3   To privatize your browsing, you can use an anonymous proxy server – another computer on the internet which intercepts your request for a web resource and substitutes its own IP address and other details. In addition to adding anonymity, using a proxy server can speed up your internet access by sending you commonly requested resources from those stored in its own data cache.

4   There are three ways in which you can employ an internet proxy. You can track down a suitable server on the web and configure your browser to route through it, you can install proxy software on your own computer or you can make use of an online proxy service. Each of these alternatives has its own advantages and disadvantages. You should choose the option which best suits you.

5   Whichever option you choose, after your proxy is installed, you should go to one of the checker sites to confirm that your IP address and other details are no longer visible to the sites you visit.

Cleaning Up Your Web Tracks

Who Knows Where You've Been?

This chapter follows on logically from the previous one. In Chapter 16, we looked at the advantages of browsing the web anonymously and how to secure your online privacy. This chapter concerns the tracks you leave behind. Even if you follow my advice and tiptoe rather than stomp around the internet, in some cases you will still leave tracks on your own computer. Both the operating system and your browser maintain records, as do many other web applications you might be using. It is easy to get paranoid about this and assume that these records are maintained for nefarious purposes, but let us try to be charitable. Internet Explorer, for example, stores all the pages and page content you look at in a cache[1] which it then uses to reload those

---

[1] I've mentioned a cache before in different circumstances, so let's define it once and for all. A cache is an area of storage – it could be in memory or on your hard disk – which holds frequently accessed data to speed up retrieval time.

pages much faster should you choose to visit them again. In Chapter 19 we will meet software with much more dubious motives.

In a perfect world, records of your internet activities would only be available to yourself, but we have already seen how easy it is to access data on other people's computers. There is also the chance that these records might be checked by your boss, a colleague at work, a member of your family, a computer technician or, in some cases, a police officer. It doesn't matter if you have browsed anonymously, at least part of your internet route map is still laid out on your machine. There is another, much more practical reason for cleaning up your tracks.

If, like me, you tend to cruise the internet more or less at random, following interesting links just for the hell of it, you inevitably land on sites which are of no interest and to which you will never return. Since your browser cannot distinguish the interesting from the pointless, it continues to cache site content for you and all of this data takes up space on your drive. Figure 17.1 shows part of the data cached in **C:\Windows\Temporary Internet Files**. You might recognize some of the files stored there. They include graphical elements (.**gif** files), style sheets (.**css** files) and HTML documents – all fairly useless and all taking up valuable storage space.

Of course, internet records stored on your computer are as secure as any other data – in theory. In practice, this is not the case. Cookies, which we will be looking at in detail in the following section, are enabled by default and can be accessed without your knowledge by websites through your browser. This process happens quite invisibly unless you reconfigure your internet options. The original concept was that only a site that placed a cookie could subsequently retrieve that cookie, but this has gone by the wayside. Web advertising and promotion companies now place cookies via all the sites they are allied with and retrieve them as they like in an attempt to build up a picture of your browsing habits.

Figure 17.1 Site content cached in the Temporary Internet Files folder

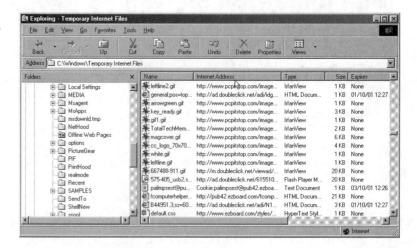

RatZnuTZ The Cracker (artist's impression)

RatZnuTZ, our tame hacker, is most definitely an enthusiast for cleaning up his browsing tracks. This is because a lot of his online activity skates very close to the illegal and he is well aware that others of his kind have been prosecuted for breaking into computers and damaging confidential data.

While we don't particularly like RatZnuTZ, we do have to acknowledge the enthusiasm with which he pursues his solitary hobby. Part of his peculiar ethic is that he refuses to pay for any software, preferring to download cracked versions from the hacker underground. As far as clean-up software is concerned, this does not always work to his advantage.

Software programmers are often as clever as the hackers who try to deny them revenue. I know of at least one clean-up program which, when illegally cracked, keeps a private log of all internet activity and sends it back to the manufacturers. Sorry, RatZnuTZ!

The Data Your Computer Stores Without You Knowing It

There is something slightly uncomfortable about your computer storing information without telling you that it is doing so. I used to teach computing, and wayward students were always amazed that I could tell them exactly where they had been on the internet. There was no magic to this. Look back at Figure 17.1 and you can see that the user in question (me, as it happens) has visited pcpitstop.com and pub42.ezboard.com Scroll down the list and you can see exactly where I have been. By double-clicking the graphics, and ignoring the warning that comes up, you could even look at the images I have been viewing.

So what are these tracks and where are they stored? In fact, five different types of records are kept on your computer. As well as the temporary internet files mentioned above, there are also cookies, entries in your History folder (which also provide the suggestions offered when you start to type in Internet Explorer's address bar), Favorites (Bookmarks) and the internet logs created by other software. All these records are fundamentally different and some represent no real threat to your privacy. To see what's involved, let's take these one at a time.

Cookies

The original idea behind the cookie was probably quite pure. A cookie is a small text file sent by a web server to your browser and stored on your hard disk. It contains personal details that have been collected while you visited a site. These might include your name, e-mail address and the pages you have looked at. When you next visit the site, the cookie is retrieved by the server and used to personalize your experience – by greeting you by name, for example.

Unfortunately, like so much web technology, cookies are now regularly abused by commercial and even criminal enterprises. Here is part of a cookie that was stored on my computer by servedby.advertising.com I have no idea what most of it means, although I do recognize the address of my Internet Service Provider.

99726467

!ee04001000382861000!00000000-00007245-0000ee5e-3ba0a18d-00000000-*109.194.159.238*

servedby.advertising.com/

0

2824103040

29447135

3409667104

29441101

I have never visited servedby.advertising.com, and I don't see what right they have to store information about me on my own computer. I am quite sure that their motives have nothing to do with providing me with a personalized experience and everything to do with targeting me as a potential customer!

Check This Out...

To find out all there is to know about cookies – including some very worrying information on how cookies can be used by unethical organizations – visit www.cookiecentral.com Look, in particular, at their Cookies – The Dark Side page. If you want to see how cookies can be used to target you as a potential customer, visit www.doubleclick.net and prepare to be annoyed.

The most controversial cookie monster on the web is DoubleClick, which uses cookies to target you with unsolicited advertising. When you visit a site which is in cahoots with DoubleClick, a cookie is planted in your system. This cookie is recognized and registered whenever you visit other sites in the DoubleClick system and, bit by bit, their software builds up a picture of your hobbies and interests. At this stage, DoubleClick has a profile, but not a name and address to go with it. Recently, DoubleClick reached an agreement to collect your name, e-mail address and other personal information from some of the websites where you deliberately register – AltaVista, for example. (The jury is still out on whether or not this is actually legal.) Now they can match your name to your profile and target you with personalized advertising and promotions. To my mind this is an abuse of online confidentiality.

Figure 17.2 Disabling cookies in Internet Explorer

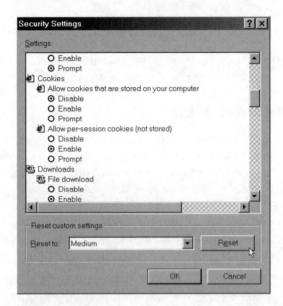

There are, incidentally, plenty of other organizations that do this as well, but DoubleClick is probably the most efficient.

Creating a cookie on someone else's computer is simplicity itself. All a web author has to do is drop a few lines of code into a page's HTML and the job is done. Of course the worst thing about cookies is that the whole process of loading data onto your computer and then subsequently retrieving it is done without your knowledge or permission. Check out your own cookies folder (**C:\Windows\Cookies**) if you use Internet Explorer or track down **cookies.txt** if you prefer Netscape. When you have looked at what has been stored there, delete the lot and reconfigure your browser either to refuse all cookies or only to accept them with your permission. Here's how to do this in Internet Explorer.

➤ Open Internet Explorer and click **Tools** > **Internet Options** > **Security**.

➤ Select the internet zone and click **Custom Level**. You will now see the window illustrated in Figure 17.2.

➤ Scroll down and disable **Allow cookies that are stored on your computer**. (You needn't worry about the per-session cookies since these are not stored.) If you prefer, you can select **Prompt**, but you will then be plagued with pop-up dialog boxes asking your permission to store cookies.

➤ Click **OK** and confirm that you want to change the security settings.

➤ Restart your browser.

Note: Occasionally you might come across a site which genuinely requires cookies to be enabled, usually for secure transactions. If you do find you need them, you can simply reverse the above process, but don't forget to disable them again afterwards.

(*Note*: If you use Netscape, click **Edit > Preferences**, go to the Advanced section, select **Cookies** and then click **Disable cookies**.)

With any existing cookies deleted from your machine and with cookies disabled in your browser, you can pretty much forget about the nasty little things.

Temporary Internet Files

These are the files I looked at earlier in the chapter. They are stored in **C:\Windows\ Temporary Internet Files**, and sometimes backed up to **C:\Windows\Temp** as well. As explained above, the **Temporary Internet Files** folder is a cache containing a mixture of web elements and shortcuts, designed to allow Internet Explorer to quickly recreate a page you have already visited. Of course it also serves as a route map to your travels around the web. To see how this cache is organized, open Internet Explorer and click **Tools > Internet Options > General**, then in the **Temporary Internet Files** section, click **Settings**. A window will open looking like Figure 17.3.

The key setting here is the **Amount of disk space to use**. In the figure, this is set to the Windows default setting of 63MB. To turn off the cache altogether, it should be possible to reduce this to 0MB, but this you cannot do. The smallest setting it will accept is 1MB, which is still enough to store a large amount of internet content. Despite this, I recommend reducing this setting to the minimum and checking the **Never** box in the **Check for newer versions of stored pages section**. I have to tell you that I have not noticed any serious reduction in internet speeds resulting from these settings.

Click **OK** and return to the **General** tab of Internet Options. In the **Temporary Internet Files** section there, you will find Microsoft's approved method of clearing your cache – the **Delete Files** button. Thankfully, this button does not simply tip all

Figure 17.3 Checking the settings for Internet Explorer's cache

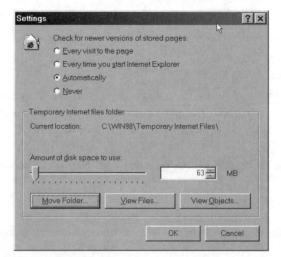

Figure 17.4 Configuring Internet Explorer's History settings

these files into the Recycle Bin – we know already how insecure that is – but neither does it permanently delete them to the standards discussed in Chapter 12. To securely erase these tracks, turn your heavy-duty deletion software on this folder. I'll pick this point up again later in the chapter.

History

This is your official record of the sites you have visited. By default, web addresses from the previous three weeks are stored in the folder **C:\Windows\History**, and arranged into four sub-folders called **3 Weeks Ago**, **2 Weeks Ago**, **Last Week** and **Today**. As with temporary internet files, you can configure your history settings from within Internet Explorer. Click **Tools > Internet Options** and select the **General** tab. You will see a window similar to Figure 17.4. Unlike the previous option, you can set the **Days to keep pages in history** to zero, and this is an effective way of preventing tracks from being recorded. Once again, you can clear any existing history by clicking the **Clear History** button in this window.

Favorites

Unlike the previous entries, the **Favorites** folder does not log entries without your permission. Favorites, or Bookmarks[2] as they are sometimes called, are links to sites

---

[2] A word of explanation here. There was a time when Microsoft and Netscape were in frenetic competition to grab the lion's share of the browser market. Their policy was never to agree on anything so Netscape's use of the word Bookmark to describe a site stored for future reference was overruled by Microsoft's preferred term, Favorite (note the US spelling). Despite this, older internet users still tend to refer to Bookmarks.

that you think you might visit regularly. You actively add their addresses to this folder by clicking **Favorites > Add to Favorites** from within Internet Explorer. Favorites can also be deleted in the same way. The only note of caution here is that, not surprisingly, some of the more aggressive sites make great efforts to persuade you to add them to your list, by including links which do this automatically. It goes without saying that adding to your Favorites a site which you do not wish to be associated with is a foolish thing to do.

Internet Logs

This entry includes any other internet records made by software which allows you to access the web. You might find these in a folder such as **C:\Windows\Internet Logs**, or they might be stored elsewhere on your computer. In many ways these are the trickiest records of all since they can be hard to find, hard to identify and, occasionally, hazardous to delete.

Let's take one example by way of illustration. ZoneAlarm is a personal firewall which is widely used to protect computers from outside attackers. (I look at it in some detail in Chapter 24.) When ZoneAlarm installs, it creates two files called **lamdb.rdb** and **[your computer name].ldb** in the folder **Internet Logs**. These files increase in size every time you access the internet. This has led some commentators to suggest that ZoneAlarm is in fact logging your internet activities for some unspecified purpose. These files are encrypted, so it is impossible for the casual user to know exactly what they contain. Should they be deleted, and, if they are, what will be the effect on the smooth running of ZoneAlarm?

The safest way to deal with unspecified logs is to open them in a text editor such as Notepad, and if they contain readable information about your internet activities, to either delete them or to replace them with a doctored version. Let me explain. Let us imagine you are running a download manager called GetItDown – I have just made this up, so I hope that someone somewhere isn't already using this name! In your **GetItDown** folder, you discover a file called **internet.log**. You open this in Notepad and discover its contents read:

GetItDown log: 1543587

21.12.2001 . 13.54...14.25 . www.findajob.com – application.pdf

21.12.2001 . 14.26...14.45 . www.jobsunlimited.com – CVMaker.exe

21.12.2001 . 14.45...15.10 . www.employme.com etc...

From this, it is pretty obvious that you have been using GetItDown to download files connected with finding a new job. Let us also assume that you would prefer this information not to be available to someone else who has access to your computer – your current employer for example! You might consider renaming **internet.log** to **internet.bak**, thus making sure that if anything goes wrong you can reverse the process, then creating a new file in Notepad reading:

GetItDown log: 1543587

21.12.2001 . 13.54...14.25 . www.microsoft.com – fileupdate.exe

21.12.2001 . 14.26...14.45 . www.somebusiness.com – statistics.pdf etc...

Now save this file as **internet.log**. If GetItDown still runs correctly, you can now delete **internet.bak**, knowing that your traces have been obliterated. You could even save a copy of your doctored file under another name and use it to replace **internet.log** every time you used the program for your own nefarious purposes. I will leave you to worry about the ethics of all this.

To ensure your tracks are deleted, you should look at every program you use to access the internet and ensure that any logs they create are dealt with. Programs worth investigating include download managers, proxy software, internet connection managers, FTP clients, firewalls and even certain multi-media software. If you are running a personal firewall, you should check to see if it stores a record of all the software which accesses the internet since this will tell you which programs need investigating.

If you are comfortable with writing batch files, you might consider automating the clean-up process. Here is part of a batch file which checks if a file (*internet.log*) exists, uses Jetico's BCWipe (described in Chapter 12) to delete it permanently, then replaces it with an innocuous version (*internet.saf*). For this to work, you will need to find a delete program which, like BCWipe, can be run from the command line.

@echo off

if exist C:\progra~1\getitdown\internet.log c:\progra~1\jetico\bestcr~1\bcwipe delete -DoD -NoSwapFile C:\progra~1\getitdown\internet.log

copy C:\progra~1\getitdown\internet.saf C:\progra~1\getitdown\internet.log

How Snoopers Track Your Online Activities

All the information so far in this and the previous chapter assumes that you prefer to browse the web in privacy and not to leave a record of where you have been. It's time we turned this problem on its head and looked at it from the point of view of the potential snooper. If we assume that you have adequately protected your computer or your network from outside intruders, there are only three ways in which a remote snooper can trace your internet pathways.

➤ If you are obliged to make your requests via a server – your ISP's for example, that server's log might contain a record of your activities.

➤ If your browser is set to accept cookies, these can be accessed by websites and used to make a record of some of the sites you visit.

➤ If the pages you download use the technology known as web bugs, these too can return information on your travels. (See the box below.)

Web bugs are a relatively new idea and, as yet, have not made much of an impact on the internet. In simple terms, a web bug is an invisible single-pixel image file loaded to a website by a third party. In theory, these hidden elements can be coded to send cookies and scripts directly to your computer, thus bypassing your browser settings. I have yet to see any hard evidence that web bugs are a very effective snooping technology, although some internet privacy software (see below) is already claiming to deal with them. I suspect that if and when they do become a serious threat, the browser manufacturers will release security patches to sort them out. My advice for the present is not to worry too much about them.

There is nothing you can do about your ISP's internet logs. You have to access the web via an ISP of some kind and you have no control over how they configure their systems. It is worth remembering that when you access the internet, you are just one of many millions. There is some safety in numbers, and the better ISPs do respect the confidentiality of their clients. Hopefully, you have already dealt with the threat of cookies by following the advice earlier in this chapter.

Instead, let us turn our attention to internal snoopers. One of the greatest boom areas in software recently has been in programs to monitor computer activity. The two largest market segments here are employers monitoring their staff and parents monitoring their children. Whether this is entirely ethical or not is not for me to say. Personally, I should hate to work for a company with this kind of Big Brother approach to its employees, but then as a writer, only I am concerned with my own productivity! A typical program here is ABCKeylogger – a free download which is every bit as efficient as expensive commercial products. I have installed it on my computer to illustrate how this type of software works.

Within a program that accepts typed input – for example Microsoft Word, which I am currently using to write this chapter – I type in a word that starts the program. In my case, the word is 'breedersguide'. (It makes sense to pick a word you wouldn't normally be typing!) Without any notification, the keylogger program is now running on my computer, but there are no windows, icons or any other evidence to show me that it is. It is now recording all my keystrokes to a secret log. (It also keeps recording even if I switch to another application – say my web browser.) If I enter a web address, say www.naughtypictures.com, this too is recorded. To view the log, I type in another word to access the control panel, and the word is 'swordfishtrombones'. Figure 17.5

Figure 17.5 ABCKey-
logger's log file

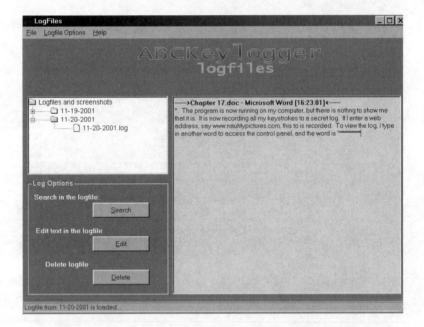

shows the log file I have just created. Note that all my keystrokes (including the error I made typing the fake web address) can be seen in the pane on the right. A log file like this can track all keyboard activity for hours at a time, and provide a snooper with an exact record of his victim's computer usage. Like other programs of this type, ABCKeylogger can also be configured to take regular snapshots of my desktop, so that Big Brother can scrutinize my work (or lack of it).

There are many programs like this available – most of them sold by trading on parents' fears for their children's online safety. There are also heavy duty versions aimed at a very different market. How about this for a sales pitch:

> *Net Detective – 2000 is an amazing new tool that allows you to find out 'EVERYTHING you ever wanted to know about your friends, family, neighbors, employees, and even your boss!' You can even check out yourself. It is all <u>completely legal</u>, and you can do it all in the <u>privacy</u> of your own home without anyone ever knowing. It's even better than hiring a private investigator.*

Among its other features – 'Find out how much ALIMONY your NEIGHBOR is paying' or 'Dig up INFORMATION on FRIENDS, NEIGHHBORS, or BOSS' (spelling errors are a bonus) – Net Detective 2001 also claims to 'Track anyone's INTERNET ACTIVITY to see the sites they visit'. I would not be overly worried about this kind of nonsense.

In an entirely different league is software such as Encase – a product used by law enforcement agencies across the world to drag confidential information out of a computer. You might remember that I referred to Encase earlier in the book. Unlike snooper software which records activity, Encase and programs like it retrieve

287

Figure 17.6 Trapware's Who's Watching Me? Finds the snoopers on your system

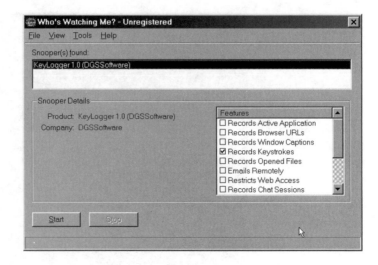

information at a much deeper level. In simple terms, they scan your hard drive for remnants of files – even those files which you think are deleted – and attempt to recreate those files as evidence.

The only way to defeat Encase and its relatives is to make use of software which permanently clears away all traces of your internet activity. (This software is discussed in the final section of this chapter.) As far as snooper programs are concerned, once more the freelance programmers have come to your aid. Who's Watching Me? is a good example of anti-snooper software which checks to see if your boss/parents/ children/spouse are trying to monitor your activities. Fire it up and you will see a window like Figure 17.6. Who's Watching Me? surreptitiously checks all the processes running on your computer to see if any of them are recording your actions. You will notice that it has found ABCKeylogger, the snooper I looked at earlier. Of course it can't disable a snooper, but knowing you are being watched does give you an advantage. If you wish to continue browsing in secret, you will just have to find another computer to work from!

Automating The Clean-up Process

The final section in this chapter moves us into the realms of advanced paranoia. If you feel that your internet activities must be kept completely private, you will need to invest in specialized software that utterly destroys all trace of your browsing. There is a lot of software which handles this type of work. Some programs I have mentioned already. Evidence Eliminator is the granddaddy of them all. CyberScrub, which I used in Chapter 12 to permanently delete files, is one of the late arrivals that I am very impressed with. WindowWasher looks highly professional, while Complete Clean-up looks terrible, but does an excellent job. The trick with all these products is to set them up with great care.

*Figure 17.7
WindowWasher's main
configuration window*

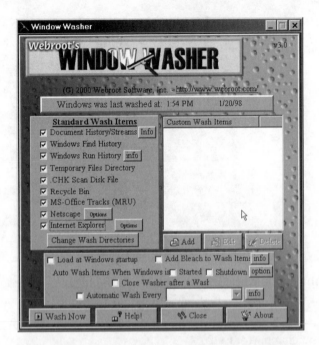

Figure 17.7 shows WindowWasher's main configuration screen. You will notice that its 'washing profile' not only includes **Temporary Files** and **Document History**, but also Internet Explorer and Netscape records. In the right-hand pane you can add your own folders and files to the wash list, while the check-boxes at the bottom allow you to control how and when washing takes place. To ensure that your traces are properly deleted, you should work through every item in this window, ensuring that WindowWasher has correctly identified the correct folders. (Netscape can be particularly difficult to cater for.) Note that WindowWasher will only find the right locations on a computer with a single user. If your system is set up for multiple users, you will need to add their own web records manually. Adding 'Bleach' to the wash – in fact overwriting the data more often – significantly improves your security, and it is always a good idea to check the **Auto Wash Items When Windows is Started** box.

CyberScrub operates in a similar manner, with the added benefit that it also eliminates the Windows Swap File which, as we have already seen, can be the repository of sensitive material. Figure 17.8 shows the configuration options for CyberScrub's 'Browser Traces' and 'Privacy Guard' functions. As you can see from the figure, the program takes care of all the records we looked at earlier, while the second configuration box which appears when you click the **OK** button allows you to add any other sensitive locations you would like wiped.

Any of the programs I have listed will perform an adequate job of deleting your traces, but whether such deletion would stand up against hardware recovery tools is open to question. If your purpose is simply to browse confidentially, I am confident that any

Figure 17.8 Setting up CyberScrub's options for Internet Explorer

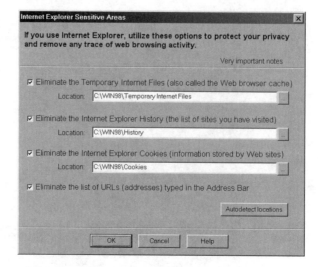

one of them would prove sufficient. If, on the other hand, you wish to browse with criminal intent, then I am afraid you will just have to take your chances!

Our next task is to look at the biggest security wrecker of them all – e-mail! But this deserves a chapter to itself.

A 90-day trial version of Who's Watching Me? can be downloaded from www.trapware.com A 30-day trial version of WindowWasher is available at www.webroot.com and from just about every download site on the web. CyberScrub and Evidence Eliminator, we sourced in a previous chapter.

Chapter 17 – Security Checklist

1 Cleaning up your internet traces is the logical conclusion to browsing anonymously. Your computer stores a series of records of the pages you visit and the content they contain. These records can be used to reconstruct your travels on the web. Removing them does not imply any illicit activity – there are any number of good reasons why you might not wish other people to know where you have been.

2 Browsing records are stored in several different ways. Cookies are small text files loaded onto your computer by a website. The idea is that they can subsequently be recovered when you return to a site and used to personalize your browsing. Unfortunately, they are often used by less scrupulous web marketing companies to build up a picture of your interests in order to sell you relevant products. I

recommend reconfiguring your browser to refuse cookies. If you need to access a site which requires cookies, you can always reverse this setting and temporarily re-enable them.

3   Your **Temporary Internet Files** folder is the cache in which Windows stores all the page content from the sites you visit. You can reduce the size of this cache, but not remove it altogether. Your privacy requires that this cache is emptied which you can do from your browser's Internet Options, but for added security, it is advisable to use a third-party clean-up program which guarantees to remove these traces permanently.

4   Your **History** folder stores web addresses you have visited in the previous three weeks and also provides the prompts that are offered when you start to type a web address into your browser's **Address Bar**. Again, these entries can be cleared from the Internet Options settings, or by using a third-party program. **Favorites** contains only websites that you have chosen to store, but don't be tempted to load it with any addresses you don't want other people to be aware of!

5   There are other internet logs kept by programs you use to access the web. You should check these carefully to ensure that they are not storing records of your browsing. You might check them in a text editor to see if they can be read by others. Where possible, such logs should be deleted or replaced with innocuous versions.

6   You should consider the possibility that your browsing is being monitored locally. If you are using a computer at work, for example, it is possible that your employer has installed a secret logging program which records all your computer activity. There are programs which can check for these so-called 'snoopers' and advise you if you are being watched.

7   To permanently delete any traces of your browsing, you will have to rely on third-party clean-up software such as WindowWasher or CyberScrub. These will flush out all the records stored on your system and overwrite them so that they cannot be retrieved.

E-mail – A Double-edged Sword

In This Chapter

➤ How e-mail actually works

➤ So, who can read your e-mail?

➤ Web-based e-mail accounts

➤ Damned spam

➤ The nastiness that lurks in e-mail attachments

➤ Encrypting e-mails (and other transmitted data)

➤ Sourcing e-mail encryption software

How E-Mail Actually Works

E-mail has taken over our personal and business communications to an extent which would have seemed unbelievable a few years ago. National postal services have even reported an alarming drop in the number of letters they are carrying. Not surprisingly, e-mail comprises the vast majority of internet traffic, and its volume is growing at a remarkable rate. Its appeal, of course, is its ease of use. The whole process of composing and transmitting a message can be carried out without getting out of your chair. Transmission is almost immediate and costs a fraction of the price of a stamp, and you are not tied to postal delivery and collection times. No wonder e-mail is taking over.

E-mail (short for electronic mail) is a message sent electronically from one user to another via a network. Most of us use the internet, but e-mail is also carried on local and wide area networks or via satellite and radio links. A local network will usually incorporate a gateway which allows onward transmission onto the internet. An electronic mail system consists of the software that creates, transmits and receives messages, and the hardware that supports the software and provides the physical links from user to user. Software can be divided into mail client software, packages such as Microsoft Outlook®, Outlook Express® or Eudora®, which allow us to compose, send and read messages, and mail server software, which handles the movement of messages across a network.

The actual mechanics of e-mail are relatively simple. You sit at your computer and compose a message. This can be either in plain text or in HTML, and can carry attachments – files or even programs which travel with the message. All the content of your message is then bundled together using technology called MIME (Multipurpose Internet Mail Extensions). When you connect to your mail server, this bundle is squirted up the wire. The server checks the address it is intended for and forwards it to the server which handles the recipient's mail. There it is stored until the recipient dials in and downloads his or her mail. All e-mail clients can read plain text and almost all of them can handle HTML, so it doesn't matter which client the recipient is using.

Like so many of the technologies we have looked at in this book, e-mail is a mixed blessing. Despite its many advantages, it is not a secure form of transmission. There have been countless examples of e-mails being intercepted and read – and not only by web bandits. Many national governments are now installing systems which allow them to intercept and read electronic mail. There has been considerable resistance by civil liberties groups to keyword recognition software – an automatic process where a computer scans your e-mail looking for particular words. How successful this has proved has not been reported, but you might try sending an e-mail saying 'Terrorists plan to assassinate key government ministers' and see who comes knocking on your door! Figure 18.1 suggests how this might work.

Who Can Read Your E-mail?

Assuming that your e-mail is not encrypted – and we'll look at this later in the chapter – the answer is quite a lot of people. As I mentioned above, e-mail is stored on a mail server and can be read by anyone with access to that server. Although servers are configured to delete messages after they have been downloaded, there have been accusations that in some cases copies of e-mails have been made and sent to government agencies and even commercial interests. Hackers have been known to

Figure 18.1 Word-recognition software alerts the security services automatically

Andy's computer

Hello George, well as you know our plans for an old school reunion are well advanced. I have been talking to some of our fellow students from 1982 and most of them are very keen on the idea. Michael says he can't be bothered. But then he always was a pain in the neck. Do you remember how that science **called him terrorist whe ;et fire to the** then go on for a night on the town. Love to Sally and I hope the kids are all well. Regards, Andy.

E-mail monitor spots the word... **terrorist**

Automatic alert sent to security services....

George's computer

strip e-mail messages out of the internet data stream for their own twisted ends and, of course, anyone with access to your computer can read the e-mails stored there.

The most worrying developments, as I mentioned earlier, have been the measures taken by several national governments to intercept electronic mail. In Britain, for example, the National Criminal Intelligence Service is attempting to implement a plan for a 'data warehouse' which would store a copy of every e-mail that passes through British mail servers and retain it for seven years. The police are justifying this by claiming that it would assist in the detection of criminal and terrorist activities. Certainly there are already agencies such as the National Security Agency (NSA) in the United States and the Government Communications Headquarters (GCHQ) in Britain which have the ability to monitor and read electronic communications. Not surprisingly, these agencies are not inclined to discuss their abilities or the technologies they use, but as any hacker will tell you, intercepting and reading e-mail is a relatively simple process.

It is safest to assume that e-mail is not secure, and not to trust the system with confidential information. At the very least, your e-mail will be accessible to anyone:

➤ who works for your Internet Service Provider;

➤ who works for the recipient's Internet Service Provider;

➤ who receives a copy of your e-mail from your Internet Service Provider;

➤ who operates one of the many internet routers which handle the delivery of your e-mail;

➤ with physical access to the telephone switching equipment, such as those who work for the phone company.

This is hardly a problem if your e-mail consists of messages to friends and family, but raises serious security questions if you use it to transmit confidential business information. Recently, there have been several high-profile cases where company e-mail has been intercepted and passed to competitors. Some businesses are now installing e-mail filters similar to the type describer earlier which alert managers when outgoing messages contain keywords such as 'confidential' and 'strategy', but the safest solution is to make sure that staff understand the risks inherent in unencrypted transmissions.

Web-based E-mail Accounts

The alternative to managing your own e-mail client is to use one of the many web-based e-mail services such as Yahoo, Microsoft's own Hotmail or Mail City. On the face of it, this would seem to make your messages more private because they are stored on a remote server. In reality, web-based e-mail is no more secure than using a local client. The information still has to be sent along a wire, and anyone who has access to that wire can, in theory, open and read your messages. Even mail sent by instant messaging technologies such as ICQ or America Online's Instant Messenger (AIM), is insecure.

Web-based e-mail is very popular among company employees and students at college. The larger services are accessed by millions of clients each day, most of whom prefer the flexibility of a system they can access from any computer. Both employers and college authorities can easily intercept such traffic, with just a little more effort than it takes to sort through someone's Outlook InBox. One technique employed both by companies and, ironically, by hackers to check web mail is the so-called 'sniffer' program which, when secretly installed on a network, can capture not only the text of e-mail messages, but also the addresses of websites visited and even the passwords required to operate the computer or access sites. One of the most controversial sniffers is Carnivore, the FBI's online surveillance system, which is used to monitor the e-mail of people who are under investigation.

The keystroke monitoring software we looked at in Chapter 17 is used by some companies to monitor web-based mail as well as browsing habits. While some employers claim it is not a practical solution because of the resources required to monitor millions of keystrokes, other justify it by claiming that they need to ensure that company secrets are protected, while abusers of their networks are exposed.

One reason why web-based e-mail systems are less secure than local e-mail clients is that your archived e-mail remains online. After you have downloaded your e-mail from an incoming mail server, messages are usually deleted so the only copies remaining are stored on your local computer. With web-based mail, messages can remain on the server for days or even months until your mailbox limit is exceeded or you manually delete them.

Damned Spam

Lack of security is only the first problem built into the e-mail system. The second problem, and one which drives most users to distraction, is e-mail that you don't want, and that goes by the delightful name of 'spam'. Why is it called spam? The joke comes from an old Monty Python sketch where conversation is constantly interrupted by a chorus of Vikings singing 'spam, spam, spam, spam' etc. (This proves that, contrary to public opinion, computer nerds do have a sense of humour.)

Spam is defined as unsolicited e-mail. It is the electronic equivalent of all those special offers that cascade through your letterbox, but it is much more annoying. Postal services around the world accept money to deliver leaflets and they are distributed pretty much at random. Direct mail companies have refined the technique and can now target individuals. But junk mail is easily binned and forgotten. Spam, on the other hand, costs you money. You pay on your phone bill for the time spent downloading messages that you don't want and didn't ask for.

At present, legislators in several countries are considering the legality of spam. In the US, there have been several attempts to introduce legislation dealing with the problem, but, as yet, nothing has been finalized. In Europe, the European Union has decided that spam is a 'legitimate business practice', but that individuals must have the right to opt out. This is naïve in the extreme, since the most intrusive spammers seldom offer this option. The worst spammers hide behind false e-mail addresses and are almost impossible to track down.

To make matters worse, spam is on the increase. Internet marketing has become a recognized science. As we have seen, any number of marketing companies are actively compiling a profile of you from your online activities. They also claim that spamming is a legitimate business practice. When they get hold of your e-mail address and match it to your commercial profile, you can be targeted with waves of messages tailored to what they see as your interests and buying habits. If you reply to spam e-mail – even just to tell them to stop – this is seen as confirmation of your existence. You have admitted to reading their stuff and in all probability the spam flow will actually get bigger.

Not surprisingly, there is a lot of information about spam on the internet. You might care to check out spamcop.net, where they take the subject very seriously indeed. You can actively fight spam at spam.abuse.net or treat yourself to a virtual bite of the real thing at www.spam.com!

Dealing with spam is quite tricky. There are various programs available which promise to deal with the problem, but I have yet to find one which is completely satisfactory. Sometimes the best solution is to change your e-mail address – easy enough if you have an online account with HotMail or Excite or similar, and a fairly small address book; not so easy if you have a business address which is widely advertised. If you are not yet being spammed, I would recommend signing up for a second account with one of the web mail companies and using that address whenever possible online. You can then keep your personal e-mail address for friends and business contacts. Even this is not a long-term solution. Sooner or later the spammers will track you down!

This leaves us with filtering software. Spam controllers all work in a similar way. In

Figure 18.2 Configuring SpamWeasel's filter rules

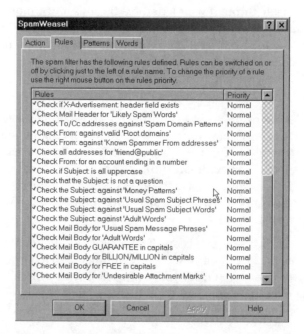

simple terms, you program them with a set of rules and they then check each incoming message against those rules. Two simple rules might be:

If an e-mail contains the words 'free offer', move it to a special folder.

If an e-mail comes from <u>spammy@spam.net</u>, delete it immediately.

The difficulty comes in defining these rules. A friend might e-mail you to tell you about a free offer she has discovered, but your filter would still sling the message into your spam folder.

One of the best spam controllers is SpamWeasel – it also has one of the best names! Figure 18.2 shows the program's set-up window. You will notice that it comes with a whole range of sensible rules preconfigured. You can simply click these on or off to suit your requirements. The **Action** tab lets you specify what SpamWeasel should do with filtered messages. The default setting is to pass the message, but to modify its subject line to 'SPAM – [old subject]' and sling it into a special folder. It will also intercept any messages from a particular address or address pattern. Perhaps its most useful feature is SpamWeasel's ability to check a message for a pattern of words that indicate its 'spamminess'. Figure 18.3 shows some of these patterns. You can add new patterns as required.

SpamWeasel, like all e-mail filtering programs, requires you to reconfigure your e-mail software. For most of us this means Microsoft Outlook or Outlook Express, although there are other e-mail clients such as Eudora or Netscape®. In all cases, the changes are the same. You will need to modify the address for your incoming (POP3) mail server from its current setting to the Local Host setting of *127.0.0.1*. You should not make any changes to your outgoing (SMTP) settings. You will also need to modify your account name by adding **@[your incoming mail server]** to the end. Close and restart your e-mail client so that the changes can take effect.

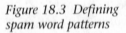

Figure 18.3 Defining spam word patterns

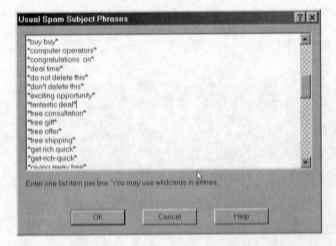

Figure 18.4 Defining Outlook rules

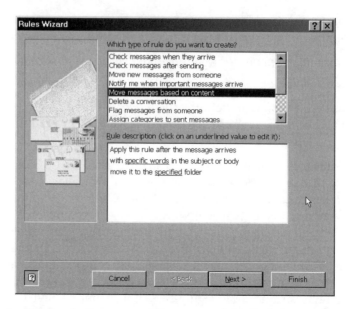

If you do not require this level of spam-proofing, you might find that your e-mail software itself offers adequate filtering. Taking Microsoft Outlook as an example, clicking **Actions > Junk E-mail > Add to Junk Senders List** (or **Add to Adult Content Senders List**) will consign a particular sender to the dustbin and any subsequent messages from the same source will be disposed of. You can also define your own rules for specific message content as shown in Figure 18.4

Using Outlook's Rules Wizard is similar to setting up rules in specialized filtering software. You can select a rule type from the top pane, then modify it in the bottom pane. In the illustration, I am defining a rule based on the **Move messages based on content** template. In the bottom pane, I click on the link marked **specific words**, and enter a phrase such as 'special offer', then click on the link marked **specified** and enter the name of a folder to junk the message in. Most e-mail clients do a reasonable job of filtering messages, but they do not offer the range of features provided by a dedicated filtering program.

SpamWeasel is available from www.mailgate.com and comes with my personal recommendation! Other filtering software can be checked out at any of the major software archives on the web. Quality varies widely, so I suggest testing a few trial versions before spending money on any one program.

The Nastiness That Lurks In E-mail Attachments

I have covered this particular danger in some detail in Chapter 5. If you skipped the section, I urge you to go back and read it now. Even so – and at the risk of boring diligent readers – I am going to repeat one vital point. Several times in this book I have mentioned the importance of modifying the settings in Windows Explorer so that all files are shown with their extensions – the three letters after the dot which identify the file type. If some evil person wishes to damage you with a virus or other malicious code, he needs to trick you into running that code on your own computer. As you know, most programs have the extension **.exe** – thus **virus.exe** is an executable file. With extensions turned off, this will appear on your computer simply as **virus**. Your malevolent chum might send you an attachment called **funnycartoon.gif.exe** – an executable (program) file, but strip off the extension and all you will see is **funnycartoon.gif** – apparently just a graphics file which you might think safe to open. Open it and wallop! The code runs and you have been nuked.

In case you missed it before, here is how to turn on file extensions. Open Windows Explorer and click **Tools > Folder Options > View**. Now uncheck **Hide file extensions for known file types** and click **OK**. This not only enables file extensions in Explorer, but in every other program you run.

E-mail is now the most common source of viruses. If you haven't already followed the suggestions in Chapter 5 for dealing with this danger, you really should do so right now.

Gordon The Young Professional

Gordon's law firm increasingly uses e-mail to communicate with other solicitors. It goes without saying that most of the firm's messages are highly confidential. Should they be intercepted, the firm's reputation will be shattered, and could even leave them open to a law suit. Ironic, that! Leading from the front, Gordon has persuaded his partners to invest in sophisticated encryption techniques to ensure that e-mail is secure, but this has also brought its own problems. There are several different encryption standards available, and Gordon often finds that his firm's methods are not compatible with those used by other solicitors. If you are going to encrypt your e-mail, make sure that the encryption you use will not leave your recipients unable to read your messages.

Encrypting E-mails (And Other Transmitted Data)

It has often been said that the surface mail equivalent of an e-mail is a postcard without an envelope. In other words, e-mail messages are an open form of communication. If such messages are transmitted in plain text, it is safe to assume that they can be read by anyone who can gain access to them. The obvious solution to this problem is to encrypt the message, but it must be said from the outset that the encryption standards offered by the major players (Microsoft, Netscape and Lotus, for example) are not as strong as they might be. It has been established that e-mails encrypted using the methods they offer can be easily read by such authorities as the National Security Agency (NSA) in the US and GCHQ in the UK, although these are probably the only agencies that are able to do so. Anyone who requires totally secure data transmission will need to move beyond such low-level encryption and make use of more complex algorithms. (For an explanation of this and further details on how encryption algorithms work, I refer you back to Chapter 10.)

You will remember that when we discussed encryption techniques earlier I referred to symmetrical and asymmetrical cryptosystems. These terms define whether the same key is used for both encryption and decryption or the system requires both a lock and an unlock key. I made the point that symmetrical encryption was fine when data was to be locked and unlocked by the same person – as in the case of files stored on a local computer – but that if the data was to be transmitted or made accessible to a third party, the key must also be passed over. Clearly, this increases the danger since if the key itself is intercepted, the security of the data is also compromised.

To solve the problem of secure key exchange, new types of cryptosystems were developed in the 1970s. These were known as public key systems and provided for asymmetric keys so that the decryption key is not the same as the encryption key. These systems were intended to solve the problem of secure key exchange. They allowed you to make your encryption key publicly available so that anyone could encrypt a message with it, but no one – not even the sender – could decode that message with the decryption key which you naturally kept secret. This process is illustrated in Figure 18.5.

Like all encryption software, an asymmetric cryptosystem uses mathematical algorithms to generate the public and private keys. The security of the system depends on how difficult it is to crack that algorithm and this is a function of the length and complexity of the keyspace involved. Several algorithms can be used and we looked at the relative security of these at the end of Chapter 10. But there is one particular danger which only applies to asymmetrical systems. Look again at Figure 18.5. Imagine what would happen if Maureen were to publish her own public key and persuade Dennis that it was Susie's public key. In good faith, Dennis would encrypt his message with it, but Maureen would be able to decipher it using her corresponding

Figure 18.5 Using a public key system to transmit secure e-mail

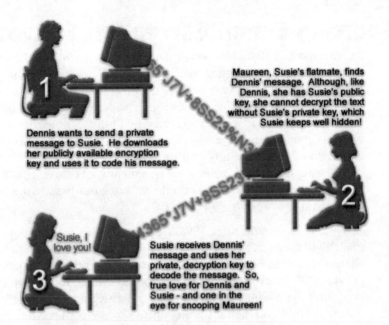

Dennis wants to send a private message to Susie. He downloads her publicly available encryption key and uses it to code his message.

Maureen, Susie's flatmate, finds Dennis' message. Although, like Dennis, she has Susie's public key, she cannot decrypt the text without Susie's private key, which Susie keeps well hidden!

Susie, I love you!

Susie receives Dennis' message and uses her private, decryption key to decode the message. So, true love for Dennis and Susie - and one in the eye for snooping Maureen!

private key. In any public key system, the integrity of the published keys is critical. If you intend using such as system, you must make sure that your correspondents are who they say they are and that you are using the correct public keys.

To sum up, the strength of public key encryption mechanisms is irrelevant without a discussion of the strength of the public key validation protocol. A symmetrical system does not require such a protocol, since the key is secured at a single location. You need to consider both the strength of the encryption algorithm and the security of your published key.

Techno Talk blah blah blah blah

Technical types might be interested in the opinion of cryptologist Terry Ritter who, in 1993, commented: 'When we have a public-key cipher and use an unvalidated key, our messages could be exposed to a spoofer who has not had to break the cipher. Thus, discussion of the technical strength of [an encryption system] is insufficient to characterize the overall strength of such a cipher. In contrast, discussion of the technical strength of a secret-key cipher is sufficient to characterize the strength of that cipher.'

As well as providing security for data transmissions, asymmetrical public key systems are also used to protect digital signatures and other systems used for transferring funds across the internet. We will look at this technology in more detail in Chapter 19.

Sourcing E-mail Encryption Software

As with most of the subjects we have discussed, there is a choice of e-mail encryption software. You can even make use of the encryption systems built into some e-mail clients, but their security is very weak and should not be relied on for highly sensitive messages. One encryption system that is widely used and widely respected is Pretty Good Privacy (PGP), originally created by Philip Zimmermann and now distributed by Network Associates. PGP makes use of fairly strong encryption technology[1] and also allows you to digitally sign your messages in a way that allows others to verify that the message actually comes from you. This means, of course, that it goes some way towards fulfilling both of the criteria we agreed earlier as vital for effective asymmetric encryption. It is also free for personal use.

PGP has been around since 1991. Current releases contain plug-ins for all the major e-mail clients such as Microsoft's Outlook, Outlook Express, Qualcomm's Eudora®, and Claris E-mailer®. Plug-ins install themselves into their respective e-mail programs and provide PGP encryption and decryption functions from a series of buttons in the program's main window. In addition, PGP integrates with the Windows shell to add file encryption and digital signing entries to the context menu which appears when a file is right-clicked (see Figure 18.6). One important fact with PGP is that it offers a level of encryption not always available in countries outside the US. (You will remember that American authorities are strongly opposed to exporting powerful encryption software!) This means that non-US users are not disadvantaged as they are with some other encryption programs.

Figure 18.6 PGP functions available from a file's content menu

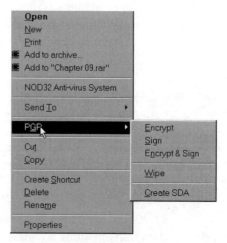

[1] PGP uses the RSA encryption algorithm we looked at in Chapter 10. This is not the securest cryptosystem available and some fears have been expressed that it is not strong enough to withstand the tools available to the security services. If your e-mails are likely to interest the NSA or GCHQ, I suggest you look to a more secure system which uses BlowFish or TwoFish encryption.

```
This email is highly confidential.
It is nothing less than a complete
record of our plans to dominate
the entire world.  Below you will
find details of how all national
governments are to be brought
down. We are including a timetable
of events and a list of all our
co-conspirators.  We are also
appending information on the
various international corporations
which are funding our project and
a record of the money they have
```

```
qANQR1DBwU4DBnEf2mddcH0QB/9VEc7CRt
YqDAGYo8bBuy7f8JtOtq3DJa8VskJn
rrQfNorJ3MG8aqjklQMRLN/z8d6lq9Hj/G
VtKMMO4ocjSbyoX6VED4fdHGpPBAsW
QeN+pYlgyYzLfSN5ujN9ZMFEGGEd3vpzOm
D5VqEb/c77CiF6cftJrWkQqLWbmJEs
qfffFK6Ln41PjTjcB5J2K9LazAsZ21KciKZ
sJ5E8adnqk2tIHxGkg80uxckv/zZvQ
xk1+p1kNUT9j7qbDq8TUO72r/C5qM4gdKI
dFfruTrpnpJDnW1eNZJfyb3r6nfc9J
BCYW15Omul7GCdJDIhK8ptEm6XoWbOAX3y
O4da2/N/Jg99stCADrXemakqI61Oz7
2im2uI/comnPtVGzzc8mMMW8rGneDrdxoV
```

Figure 18.7 An e-mail message as plain text and after it has been PGP-encrypted

Despite being free, PGP is a highly professional and well-written program. During installation, you are asked for a pass-phrase which is then used to generate your public and private keys. These are validated by your name and e-mail address. You then publish your public key by sending it to a PGP key server on the internet from where people who wish to send you private e-mail can download and use it to encrypt their messages. Of course you retain your private key, so that only you can open and read the e-mails that you receive. When you wish to encrypt an e-mail, you must first download the intended recipient's public key. With this installed, you write your message as normal, then click the encryption button in your e-mail client. Decrypting a message is equally simple. Figure 18.7 shows an e-mail before and after encryption with PGP.

PGP has proved so reliable that it has become the *de facto* standard for e-mail encryption. There are other programs available, but none with the user base of PGP. This is important for two reasons. First, you need to be sure that whoever you are sending messages to is using the same encryption technology that you are and, second, asymmetric encoding is made much easier if public keys are available on the web. PGP offers this by storing them on its own server.

If you need something stronger and are concerned about lodging even a public key with a third party, you might consider ShyFile. ShyFile incorporates a unique algorithm which makes use of a variable key space to determine how your text is encoded. In simple terms, your message is mixed with characters generated at random, then scrambled even further. No ShyFile encryption has ever been broken (at least, to my knowledge), and the fact that it has been designed and published in Germany gets rid of any nagging worries about collusion with the US security agencies.

One final warning: do not confuse security with integrity. Just because your e-mails are securely encrypted does not mean that someone who intercepts them cannot mutilate them. If encrypted text is jumbled, not only does this destroy the data it carries, but it also means that it cannot be decrypted at the far end.

If you have followed the advice in this and the previous few chapters, you are now well on your way to becoming a secure internet user. In Chapter 19, we will be looking at some of the more disturbing aspects of the web, including how commercial interests are targeting you and what you can do about it. We will also be considering online shopping and how you can transfer money safely. Join us after the break …

Pretty Good Privacy is available as a free download for non-commercial users from www.pgp.com A trial version of ShyFile can be obtained from www.shyfile.net Other encryption programs can be investigated at one of the web's many download sites.

Chapter 18 – Security Checklist

1 Electronic mail (e-mail) is a highly insecure method of communicating. If it is transmitted in plain text, it can be intercepted and read by anyone who gains access to the data lines carrying it. This applies to both locally managed e-mail and web-based services. In fact, web-based e-mail is even less secure because it is stored on a remote server for an extended period.

2 Of particular concern is a growing trend for national governments and security agencies to develop systems which can intercept and read private e-mail. Several authorities now have software which can do this and there are plans for even more draconian measures such as storing all private messages in a data warehouse for up to seven years.

3 Another major problem with e-mail is that once you start using it, you inevitably attract the attention of spammers. Spam is defined as unsolicited e-mail – although some companies claim it is a legitimate marketing tool. Spam is not only a nuisance, it also costs you money to download, wastes valuable space on your computer and can carry dangerous attachments. To deal with the problem you should configure suitable filters within your e-mail client or install anti-spam software to intercept and manage incoming messages.

4 As we noted previously, e-mail is now the principal vector for the transmission of viruses and other malevolent code. Suggestions for blocking this danger were listed in Chapter 5.

5 If you need to send confidential information by e-mail, you will need to install reliable encryption software. Data transmission encryption usually makes use of asymmetrical systems which require both a private (decryption) key and a public (encryption) key. You must ensure both that the strength of the encryption is adequate to your security needs and that the public key is safely stored and validated in case someone tries to 'spoof' your security by substituting his own public key for yours.

6   Remember that encrypting an e-mail does not protect the integrity of the data it contains. If your message is intercepted and modified, the data is lost and decryption software will no longer be able to decipher the text.

Web Crime And Commerce

In This Chapter

➤ Who watches the watchmen?

➤ Internet crime

➤ Commercial profiling

➤ Website privacy policies

➤ Spyware – the commercial snooper at work

➤ Your Internet Service Provider (ISP)

➤ Purchasing online

➤ Digital signatures

➤ Secure storage for personal details

In God we trust. All others we monitor.   *The motto of the National Security Agency*

Who Watches The Watchmen?

Right about now you might be suffering from an acute attack of paranoia. After reading the last few chapters, you could be left feeling like a microbe under a microscope with huge official eyes peering down at you and faceless snoopers recording your every action. You might even be wondering how the cheerful anarchy of the internet got twisted into Big Brother's ultimate weapon. I have already listed dozens of threats to your privacy – and this chapter looks at even more. So is internet anonymity merely a dream? Are you inevitably going to end up stamped and filed in some bureaucrat's database or as a mere marketing statistic? Are you doomed to a life of unsolicited e-mails and personalized advertising? Don't you just love these rhetorical questions?

I would love to be able to offer some reassurance at this point, but I am afraid that I can't. The web really is a dangerous place, and when you plunge into it, you expose yourself to all kinds of hazards. In previous chapters we have looked at the most common problems and suggested ways in which you can try to protect yourself. It must be admitted, however, that all you can hope to do is to minimize those dangers – they will never disappear completely. One of the problems it that this book is out-of-date. If I wrote it again tomorrow, it would still be out-of-date. If I e-mailed you a personal update every time circumstances changed, it would still be out-of-date. The reason is obvious. Internet technology develops at an unbelievable rate and those of us on the side of the angels are always one step behind the developers. Sometimes this means that we are tracking down new browsers, new anti-virus software, improved firewalls and all the other good things that help to protect us. More often than not, we are trying to follow the ungodly as they pervert technology to suit their own ends.

This chapter is a kind of pot-pourri of bits and pieces which do not justify a chapter to themselves. In particular we look at web crime and web commerce – subjects which sometimes are not too far apart. Because of limited space, I have been obliged to cram some quite complicated subjects into only a few lines. If you need further information on anything in this chapter, I suggest you look on the web. Try entering the subject into a search engine and see what comes up.

Internet Crime

Most of the problems we have discussed so far have involved legal practices. Some of them might have been unethical, but none of them actually broke the law. Now we need to look at the other side of the coin and examine internet crime and how it can affect you as an individual. Crime on the web can be quite hard to identify and even harder to prosecute. Because of the international nature of the internet, it is often difficult to establish in which jurisdiction a crime was committed. This then raises questions like who should investigate, who should prosecute and who should punish the wrong-doers? Figure 19.1 illustrates the problem.

There is a famous old joke which goes 'on the internet, no one knows you're a dog!' This might have been true in the beginning, but as we have seen, these days anyone who makes an effort can not only discover that you're a dog, but also what breed of dog you are, if you know how to roll over and which brand of pet food you

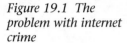

Figure 19.1 The problem with internet crime

A criminal in South Africa steals credit card details from a computer in France and uses them to buy a DVD player in the US. Where are the crimes committed?

prefer. As we have seen, such information is usually used to target you with goods and services, but it can also be used in a much more devious way. It can be used to impersonate you!

The crime in question is known as identity theft, and is becoming more and more common. It is estimated that each week up to 20,000 web users have their identities stolen. In many cases the victims are completely unaware that they are being impersonated. Using the techniques we have already looked at, hackers extract details from your online purchasing, your browsing and your e-mail and put them together until they have enough information to assume your identity. They can then make purchases in your name – often using your own credit card – or sign up for online services. This type of crime can take weeks to discover and even longer to sort out. It can mean you losing your credit card and your credit rating. In some cases, you will be liable for all or part of the debts incurred in your name. Hackers can also use this information to impersonate you in online chat rooms or other virtual gatherings. While this might not harm you financially, your reputation can suffer and you might end up being investigated for criminal activities.

Equally nasty is online stalking. If you expose enough information about yourself, you might find that you attract the attentions of a stalker. Often such maladjusted individuals will shower you with unwanted e-mails, follow you into chat rooms or even turn up on your real-life doorstep. This can be particularly dangerous for children who can be 'befriended' online by twisted types who are 'grooming' them for criminal or sexual activities. I shall be looking at this horror in more detail in the following

311

chapter. Stalkers often turn from artificial friendship to serious harassment. You might find your in-box filled with hate e-mail. Another trick is to sign you up for dozens of newsletters or register your address with porn sites.

Maureen The Leisure Surfer

As a regular visitor to chat rooms and internet discussion forums, Maureen has made many good friends. Unfortunately, one friend she is particularly fond of has dishonourable intentions. 'Sandra' is not a nineteen-year-old college student. He is a forty-five-year-old criminal who uses web chat rooms to track down potential victims. Maureen is upset because 'Sandra' has run out of money and can no longer afford to stay at university. Kind and generous, Maureen has already tried to help by sending money through the PayPal system (see below), but 'Sandra' wants more than that. He is currently working on getting hold of Maureen's credit card details – he has asked her to help him buy college books. When Maureen succumbs, 'Sandra' will simply disappear from the internet and 'Judith' will take her place.

In many ways, the web is a make-believe world. In real life, commercial institutions have solid bricks-and-mortar presences which enable us to judge their probity and integrity. On the internet however, a professionally designed website can easily fool us into believing in a company that has no real substance beyond a few lines of HTML code. The web is awash with investment opportunities of all kinds and it is hard to know which are trustworthy and which are distinctly dubious. Even financial institutions that are household names have been spoofed. They can turn out to be nothing more than a faked site hosted on a domain with a similar name. (This is simple to do. A fraudster might register a name like www.americanexpres.com – note the single 's' – and rely on occasional rushed typing to bring in victims.) Invest in a web scam, and you are unlikely to retrieve any of your money. By the time you discover the truth, the nameless and faceless fraudsters will already have disappeared.

Online purchasing is also a risky business. Again it is impossible to distinguish between honest merchants and those who are only there to cheat the consumer. Purchase something online and any number of things can go wrong. Inferior goods can be delivered – if anything is delivered at all! Promised refunds can fail to materialize. You might find your credit card is overcharged or even double charged. Sorting such problems out can be a nightmare, particularly if the merchant is being deliberately obstructive. To quote one online commerce specialist: 'Bad merchants rely on the profound user isolation on the web to get away with the abuse.'

It would be comforting if the above represented the full extent of internet crime, but the examples I have mentioned are just drops in the ocean. A comprehensive list of all the scams, thefts and other criminal activities on the web would fill several encyclopaedias. If you wish to know more, try entering 'internet crime' into a search engine and standing well back. I shall be looking at web shopping later in this chapter, so I will close this section with some general advice on protecting yourself from the criminals who haunt the internet.

➤ Never reveal any details about yourself or your family and friends in web forms unless you are completely convinced of the integrity of the site owners.

➤ Unless it is vital, never give out personal details in e-mails, online chat rooms or postings to newsgroups. Even your e-mail address should be considered as confidential information.

➤ Never respond to online appeals for money unless they come from a recognized charity. This sounds harsh, but the simple fact is that most beggars on the web are not what they seem. How can you hope to sort the real from the fraudulent?

➤ If you are considering investing money in any enterprise or scheme that is promoted on the internet, make sure that there is reality behind the website. Phone books or directory enquiries can confirm that a company exists. If possible, visit their premises or ask for sales literature. Check with friends living near their physical location. In short, do whatever is necessary to ensure their offer is viable.

➤ Use Chapter 16's recommendations on browsing anonymously to keep your online activity as private as possible. By making yourself a very small target, you make it more difficult for fraudsters to identify you.

➤ Whenever you reveal personal details or part with money, make absolutely certain that the page is secure. This is normally indicated by an *https:* URL, and some browsers display a small padlock or key somewhere on the screen. (I will look at this in more detail in the section on online shopping.)

Commercial Profiling

On several occasions I have mentioned commercial interests scraping together personal details in order to target you as a customer. I promised to explain this in greater detail, and I do try to keep my promises. This process is known as 'profiling'. Some degree of profiling is done by many websites, often for perfectly honourable reasons, but there are also various dedicated profiling operators who use web data to create detailed pictures of potential customers which they then sell to merchants or online marketing companies. If you find spam connected to your own interests suddenly appearing in your e-mail, you can be certain that somewhere along the way you have been profiled. Profilers use a number of devices to collect information. I have mentioned most of these in passing, but let me bring the common ones together in Table 19.1.

Table 19.1 Have You Been Profiled?

Technique	Explanation
Cookies	As you know, cookies are small text files containing data that you have willingly, or unknowingly, revealed to a website. Cookies are supposed to be site-specific, but some sites share or sell such information to commercial profilers.
Third-party cookies	Similar to the above, but with one important distinction. Some site owners agree to create cookies on behalf of third parties such as profilers. These have nothing whatsoever to do with your browsing, they are there solely to extract personal details.
Banner advertisements	When you click on a banner ad, you are not only transported to the related content, but your interest in the product or service on offer is also recorded and added to your profile.
Web bugs	We looked at these earlier. Web bugs are small invisible images coded to place cookies or run scripts on your computer without your knowledge. They often attempt to bypass your browser settings.
Online registrations	When you register with a website or sign up for a service, your details are supposed to be kept confidential. Some sites do not respect this and sell their subscription lists to commercial profilers.
Web forms	Many sites on the web contain forms which you complete to order software, to make enquiries or to use a particular feature. Once again, you might assume that the information you provide will be kept private, but unethical site owners often sell this information to third parties.
Data mining	Date mining is a decidedly underhand practice. Some sites attempt to extract personal details under false pretences. You might be asked for a credit card to establish your financial status or your postal address to establish whether additional tax should be charged. The information you provide in response to such questions might be used for the stated purposes, but it might also be passed on to profilers to add to the information they already hold.

Despite the claims of the profilers, most of the information they assemble is wildly inaccurate, but, of course, you have no possibility of checking or correcting it. If you are looking into retirement homes for an elderly friend, a profiler might well assume that you yourself are a pensioner. You might find yourself bombarded with spam offering you senior citizen discounts. (This happened to a friend of mine who is 26 years old.) Probably the most offensive form of inaccurate profiling is that which links you to the amusingly named 'adult content'. Most web users at some stage or other finds themselves on a porn site. This might be out of interest or because the pornographers are particularly clever at suckering you in with misleading advertising or so-called 'look-alike' domains. If such a visit is added to your profile, you might find yourself swamped with smutty offers. This is even more disturbing when it happens to youngsters. Of course, an ethical profiler would offer you the right to look at, edit, or even delete, the information they hold, but this option is seldom available.

Website Privacy Policies

In response to growing concerns about privacy on the internet, many websites now publish an online privacy policy document. Far too many people assume that because a site has such a policy, it is guaranteeing your privacy. If anyone bothered to read these things, they would soon discover that the exact opposite is often the case. A policy which assures you absolutely no privacy is still a privacy policy – if you see what I mean. I know that reading small print is a tedious business, but I urge you to read such policies before passing over any information that could be used to profile you.

Much of the difficulty in assuring privacy is that the model adopted across the web is 'opt out' rather than 'opt in'. This means that unless you specifically advise a site that your personal data is confidential, it is assumed that you don't mind sharing it with every advertiser and marketing operation on the web. Bear in mind also that some sites cancel your opt outs after a set period (and often without advising you) and that if you fail to renew them, they assume that they are now free to distribute your personal details as they wish. Obviously it would be fairer to work from the opposite direction and assume that data was confidential unless you specified otherwise. Such fairness is the exception in the commercial heart of the internet.

Spyware – The Commercial Snooper At Work

Of all the techniques used to profile you, undoubtedly the most invasive is spyware. Spyware is pure deception, though still legal in most regions. A spyware program is a small piece of software hidden within another application. When installed, it takes up residence on your hard drive and begins recording information about you. Some varieties merely note the files you download and the websites you visit while others log much more personal details. What they all have in common is that in some point in the cycle, they 'phone home'. This connection is usually masked by your own internet access so you might have no idea that a spyware program is uploading all the information it has gleaned to a server somewhere on the web. Some people still have difficulty in believing that something as insidious as this could have taken up residence on their personal computers, so here are one or two examples.

RealNetworks Incorporated have formally admitted that their RealDownload software can be used to track users' download habits. Following the uproar when users

*Figure 19.2 The
Sniffem packet sniffer
in action*

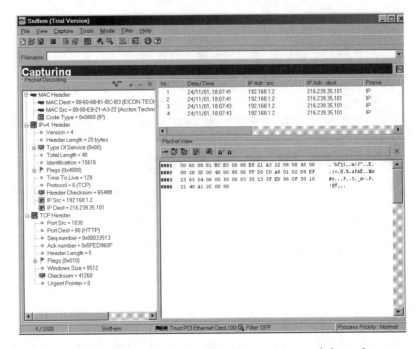

discovered this feature, the corporation now claims that later versions of the software no longer transmit the infamous **downloadid** – a digital code which identifies individual users, but merely reports the names of the files downloaded and where they have come from. RealNetworks admits that this information is used to customize advertisements which are then aimed at specific users. RealNetworks distribute several software products including the popular RealPlayer. Many people feel that all their software is now tarnished and refuse to use any of it.

The same technology is employed in NetZip and the downloader provided by Netscape/AOL, among others. To prove if such products are operating concealed spyware, it is necessary to check the data sent by your computer to see where it is going and if it contains personal details. Fortunately, it is simple enough to check for this kind of activity using a readily available network tool known as a packet sniffer. A packet sniffer is a program which monitors the packets of data being sent to and from a computer. It is often used by a network administrator to monitor traffic across the network and to identify abuses of the system. Figure 19.2 shows the Sniffem packet sniffer in action. Analysing the information displayed in the *Packet View* pane reveals the data being transmitted and received – in this case a request to the Google search engine. Turning a sniffer onto the download utilities listed above reveals that they are, indeed, sending detailed reports back to base every time they are used to download a file. These reports not only contain the URLs of the files being downloaded, they also include unique IDs which can be used to identify the computers calling for the downloads.

Similar technology is used by the commercial profilers known as Radiate. Founded in 1996, Radiate has designed programs which can be easily embedded into software products and used not only to profile their users but also to display targeted advertising while the software is in use. An embedded Radiate module has the ability to roll out these adverts even while the user is not connected to the internet. Conducent is another company whose software offers this feature. Their system uses the internet to quietly deliver targeted advertising to the program in which their software is embedded. Ads can then be displayed off-line by the offending application.

We can define spyware as any software which employs someone's internet connection in the background to upload personal data without that person's permission. This is often referred to as using the internet 'backchannel'. But unlike internet profiling by indirect means which you can do very little about, spyware can be fought and defeated. There are two steps you should take. The first is a firewall which, when properly configured, will prevent any program connecting to the internet without your explicit permission (see Chapter 24 for details). The second is to make use of anti-spyware software, which is not only a tongue-twister but is also the gorilla's pyjamas when it comes to eradicating the nasty little beasts.

The prince of anti-spyware programs is Lavasoft's Ad-aware, illustrated in Figure 19.3. It relies on the fact that Windows keeps records of all the software installed and all the processes running on your computer. Fire up Ad-aware and it checks your hard disk for any known spyware programs, then checks your system for spyware processes. Better yet, when it finds them, it kills them and deletes the spyware modules. This program is essential to good web security. Get it, install it and use it regularly.

Check This Out...

A feature-limited version of Sniffem can be found at www.sniffem.net There are many other packet sniffers available on the web, but be cautious! A packet sniffer is a hacker's tool and you might download more than you bargained for (see Chapter 23 on Trojans!) You can download Ad-aware for free from www.lavasoft.de If you are interested in the programs and policies of Radiate or Conducent, you can learn a lot from their websites at www.radiate.net and www.conducent.net, but don't leave any information about yourself or you might get a visit from a whole heap of advertising!

317

Figure 19.3 Lavasoft's anti-spyware program

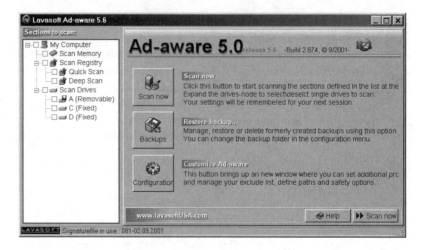

Your Internet Service Provider (ISP)

You might think that your friend and ally on the web would be your ISP. After all, you pay them to connect you and they seem very keen to attract your business. (There is a site on the web which hopes to collect one million free AOL CD-ROMs!) In fact ISPs are often the worst offenders. Unless you are using a secure socket connection – don't bother looking, you almost certainly are not – your ISP can monitor all your online activity including the sites you visit, any information you supply and anything you download. Most ISPs insist that they respect their clients' privacy and that they would only snoop if you were found to be doing something illegal or were under investigation.

In most countries, people have a wide choice of ISPs. If you have the choice, consider reselecting your ISP from a personal privacy perspective. You might like to consider the following points.

➤ Cheapest is not always best! An ISP that can obtain a decent revenue from its subscribers is less likely to need to raise extra cash by selling their details to a third party. Even if some ISPs offer cheaper connection rates, part of that advantage might be swallowed up by the endless spam you will pay to download when the profilers get their hooks into you!

➤ Smaller can be better. Small ISPs often offer a more personal service that the large corporations. I might even suggest that they are likely to be managed by less commercially minded people, but perhaps that is stretching it.

➤ Read the privacy policy – then read it again. If an ISP admits that it is gathering information, even if it claims that information is for internal use only, I would go elsewhere. Logging information is a bureaucratic disease and once it starts, it often infects a whole organization. Even if today's management is sincere, there is no guarantee that an ISP will not be bought out by a less scrupulous enterprise which will find all that valuable personal data stored on its newly acquired computers.

➤ Check the web. The best guide to an ISPs integrity is to read the opinions of its members, and you will find plenty of these on the internet. A good search engine will guide you to relevant information.

➤ Finally, if all else fails, follow your instincts. Smarmy advertising, endless assurances of special qualities, a long, careful look at the ISP's own portal – all of these things will help to give you a feeling about whether or not you can trust their claims. Be suspicious!

Purchasing Online

Sooner or later you will certainly wish to purchase something from a website. In the last few years the internet has become a shopper's paradise. You can now buy almost everything online and the choice and variety continue to grow. Of course this development has created problems. The popular press enjoys running stories about dishonest merchants who take the money and run. There has also been concern expressed about the security of online transactions. To buy, you need to expose your credit or debit card details, and this by itself is enough to scare many people away from online shopping. Of course, these same people will happily hand their credit cards over to waiters or shop assistants and sit quite relaxed while they take them behind counters or into back rooms. Research has proved that you are far safer using your credit card on the web than using it on the high street.

Most websites that offer transaction handling, provide a secure area which uses encryption technology to protect the confidential information that is required. As you click to enter this area, you should be presented with a warning box like the one in Figure 19.4. I suggest that you do not click the **In the future, do not show this warning** check-box. You need to know when your connection is secure. Click **OK**, and you can enter the secure area. Your browser should now display a padlock or a key icon somewhere in the window and you can click this icon to read a certificate which verifies the security of the site. If your browser does not show a padlock, look at the address bar and make sure the page address now reads **https://whatever** rather than **http://whatever**. This indicates that you are connected to a secure server. As a final proof, you can right-click your mouse anywhere on the web page (not on the graphics) and one of the options on the drop down menu will tell you if the site employs secure encryption.

Figure 19.4 The security alert shown by a browser when you enter a secure area

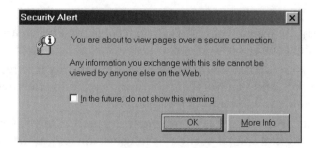

HTTPS – the secure hypertext transfer protocol – has had its critics. By now you are aware that encryption strength varies enormously and you are possibly wondering just how secure HTTPS encryption is. Wonder no more! The straight answer is that it is secure enough for most transactions, but not up to withstanding a concerted attack.

HTTPS relies on technology called SSL (Secure Sockets Layer). I mentioned this briefly in the previous chapter. Originally designed by Netscape®, SSL is intended to prevent eavesdropping, tampering, and the forging of spoof messages. It is essentially a public key system which allows server and client to negotiate an encryption algorithm and suitable keys before any actual data is transmitted or received. After these negotiations, encryption such as DES is used to encode data and to authenticate the identity of the users. It also provides a message integrity check to prevent spoofing.

HTTPS (Hypertext Transport Protocol Secure) uses SSL to establish a secure connection. An *https://*address directs the message to a secure port number rather than the default web port number of 80. The session is then managed by the SSL security protocol.

Hackers sneer at the security provided by HTTPS servers, but at present it seems to provide adequate protection. The reality is that you as a consumer are far less at risk than merchants on the web who have to cope with regular waves of stolen credit cards and spoof transactions. If you're a customer, the chance of your credit card number being intercepted on the web is extremely small. But as a merchant, the possibility of receiving orders using a stolen credit card is significant. The list that follows suggests ways of maximizing your security when shopping online.

➤ Make sure that you only reveal credit card information in the secure area of a merchant's site. Use all of the checks described above, and if you are not totally satisfied, do not buy. (*Note*: older browsers might not support the use of secure server (SSL) technology. If yours does not, consider upgrading to the latest version.)

➤ Never send your credit card number by e-mail. If the merchant does not offer secure transactions, send him a cheque through the post or look for another supplier. Remember – unencrypted e-mails are never secure.

➤ Always check out a site's return policy before buying. If there is no return policy or it does not offer adequate customer protection, go elsewhere. Make sure the site accepts returned goods without too much grief and that you are not going to incur a charge for the merchant's own administrative errors.

➤ Be extremely cautious when filling out online order forms. Never give more information than is necessary – most forms indicate the essential information in some way. Ask yourself why a site is asking a particular question. If the information requested has no relevance to your purchase, do not provide it and if that prevents the transaction from going ahead, look somewhere else. Be particularly cautious of handing over your e-mail address. While many merchants require this to establish your identity, try to make sure that the information will not be passed on to third parties.

➤ Check if the site has a privacy policy. If it has, read it and make sure you are happy with the contents. If there is no policy, it is safest to assume the worst and expect that any personal information you provide will be shared with unknown parties.

➤ Finally, make sure that you establish working lines of communication with the merchant. Note down any confirmation or order numbers you are supplied with. Check that the site provides a customer service telephone number or at least an e-mail link.

Digital Signatures

When we looked at public key encryption, I mentioned that it had other applications in providing online security. One of the most important of these is in making possible digital signatures. Digital signatures are important in several ways. They can be used to authenticate documents, they allow users to sign contracts without being physically present, and they make possible the exchange of digital cash.

PGP, the industry standard asymmetrical encryption system we discussed earlier, allows you to securely sign a message or a file, with or without encrypting it. A digital signature is uniquely generated by PGP, based partly on the contents of the message and partly on your private key. The authenticity of your signature can be checked subsequently by anyone using your public key. Because your digital signature is generated (in part) by the contents of the message, if even one character of the message has been changed, PGP will report that your signature is invalid. Digital signatures have an important part to play in online business activity. You can send a signed message to someone, knowing that he can confirm that it comes from you and that is has not been tampered with.

It is worth noting that digital signatures are, in many ways, more secure than traditional hand-written signatures. Written signatures can be forged or copied from document to document A digital signature, on the other hand, only applies to a single document. Any attempt to transfer a digital signature to a second document ensures that it fails a validation test.

Encryption also allows the transfer of money across the web. Digital cash can be defined as a system which allows a person to pay for goods or services by transmitting a digital representation of payment from one computer to another. It comes in two varieties, usually defined as anonymous and identified. Anonymous digital cash is the web equivalent of the banknote, with each certificate carrying a digital identifier and representing a specified sum of real money. Like the serial numbers on banknotes, these identifiers are unique. This type of cash is reusable on the internet and carries no information which refers to the user. Anonymous digital cash, like paper money, can be withdrawn from an account and spent without leaving a transaction trail. Additional security comes from using numbered bank accounts and 'blind' signatures rather than identified accounts and personal signatures. Identified digital cash is the online equivalent of writing a cheque or using a credit card. These transactions carry information which reveals the identity of the purchaser. They therefore allow banks and merchants to track a payment as it moves through the system.

Figure 19.5 Security on the PayPal website

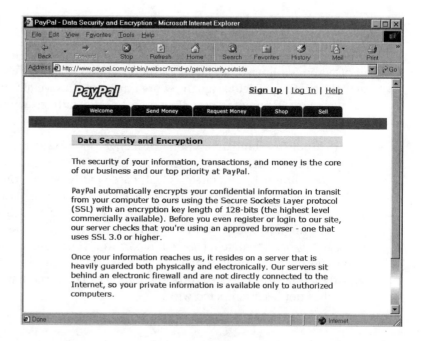

The PayPal service is online at www.paypal.com There is a small registration fee which is credited back to your account when you start using it. For information on digital cash services, check the website of your own bank – or some other bank if yours is too old-fashioned to offer them!

Many pundits predicted that digital cash transactions would have become commonplace on the web by now, but the technology has been slow to catch on with some spectacular failures along the way. A number of different banks and finance houses launched their own digital cash systems and it is possible that the choice available worried the consumer. It is still unclear which ones will come to dominate the market. On the other hand, digital payment services such as PayPal, which allow anyone with a credit card to pass funds to anyone with an e-mail address, have proved a great success. Figure 19.5 shows the Data Security and Encryption page from PayPal's website.

Secure Storage For Personal Details

I want to end this chapter with a brief look at the security aspects of storing your confidential personal data on a computer. I touched on this way back in Chapter 10, when I suggested a method of storing all your passwords in a single encrypted file – but we have all become a lot wiser since then! A number of different third-party applications claim to provide the facility to store personal details for you so that they can be entered into forms quickly and efficiently. (One of these, you will recall, was Gator – the little spyware utility which offers to take care of your details, then secretly uploads them to its masters.) I would be highly suspicious of any third-party program intended for this purpose – particularly if it was available for free – but what of the similar feature built into your browser?

Internet Explorer, for example, provides a feature called AutoComplete. To access this, click **Tools > Internet Options > Content > AutoComplete**, and you will be presented with a box like Figure 19.6. If you check the **Forms** or the **User names and passwords on forms** options, the browser will prompt you to save the details you enter into web forms and will subsequently offer to fill in this information for you the next time you encounter an online form. You can clear this information if you wish by clicking the **Clear Forms** or **Clear Passwords** buttons. If you make use of AutoComplete, the information is stored to your hard disk without any serious security, but is probably adequate for less sensitive data. For such details as site access passwords, the AutoComplete function can prove very useful and a significant time saver. Similar features are offered by Netscape, Opera® and other browsers.

The big question comes with storing highly sensitive information such as your credit card number. If you wish to securely store confidential details, I would look to your encryption software rather than a dedicated program. Steganos, for example, the

Figure 19.6 Internet Explorer's AutoComplete Settings

complete security suite published by CenturionSoft, includes a utility called the Password Manager which uses AES encryption to encode passwords, PIN numbers and credit card details. But any encryption software can be used. The simplest solution is to create a text file which contains the information required. Something like this:

Credit card: VISA

Credit card number: 1234 5678 9124

Expiry date: 30.11.2003

PIN number: 5432 etc...

Now give it an innocuous name such as **install_log.txt** and encrypt it to an obscure folder on your hard disk. When you need to access the data, open it up and cut and paste the text into the relevant boxes in the online form. After you have finished your session, restart Windows to clear the contents of your clipboard. Why spend money on specialized software when there is a simple solution such as this?

This chapter has been a bit of a mess, covering all sorts of odd bits and pieces. Now we need to firmly focus on one of the most controversial and complex aspects of internet security – watching over the online activities of our children. For the first time, we are moving to the other side of the fence – becoming Big Brother. And this calls for a new chapter.

Chapter 19 – Security Checklist

1   Some activities on the web are not so much unethical as downright illegal, though internet crime is notoriously difficult to investigate and prosecute. Crimes include identity theft where a hacker assembles enough information to be able to assume your identity and buy goods and services in your name.

2   Online stalking is a particularly nasty activity. Someone will find out enough about you to pursue you across the internet, sending you e-mails, turning up in the chat rooms you frequent or even appearing in person on your doorstep. Some stalkers have even worse intentions, befriending children with a view to persuading them into sexual or criminal activities. Keeping a low profile minimizes the chances of attracting this kind of attention. Online stalking amounts to harassment and in many countries is illegal, but is difficult to prosecute since the stalker can disappear leaving no traces for the police to follow.

3   The nature of the web makes it possible for a confidence trickster to erect a very convincing facade behind which is no real substance. Before parting with money online, you need to make sure that the merchant or business that you are dealing with is sound and not merely the product of a conman's imagination. Investigate offers thoroughly – off the web if possible – and don't be in too much of a hurry to hand over your cash. Remember the old adage: if an offer sounds too good to be true, it almost certainly is!

4   Commercial profiling refers to the unpleasant business of gathering information about potential customers and selling that information to merchants or web marketing companies. Personal details can be obtained in a number of ways including cookies, web bugs, advertising responses and online forms. Once again, the safest way to deflect such interest is to browse anonymously and restrict the amount of personal information you release.

5   Spyware are programs concealed within other applications which record personal details from your computer then use the back-channel of your internet connection to pass these details on to interested parties. They are dishonest and invasive and should be declared illegal. Unfortunately a lot of software these days contains spyware. Use Lavasoft's Ad-aware to detect and remove spyware programs currently installed on your own computer.

6   You might expect your ISP to take on some responsibility for sheltering you from some of this web nastiness – after all you pay him to provide your connection. In fact, some ISPs are part of the problem. It might be worth reassessing your ISP from a security perspective. In particular, you might check your ISP's privacy policy to make sure that they are respecting the confidentiality of your personal details.

7   When you are shopping online, you need to make sure that transactions take place through a secure server. This is indicated in several ways – a padlock or key icon in the browser bar, an *https://* page address, and a warning box when you enter are the easiest to recognize. Never make any transactions over an insecure server since all the information you reveal can be seen by outsiders.

8   It is often useful to store confidential data such as credit card or PIN numbers on your computer. There are various third-party programs which offer this, but my advice is to ignore them and stick to your preferred encryption software. If this facility is not offered as a feature, consider writing your information to an ordinary text file, then encrypting it.

Where Do The Children Play?

In This Chapter

- ➤ The moral dimension
- ➤ Do you know where your children go?
- ➤ Pornography, violence, racism … keeping the horrors at bay
- ➤ Your children as marketing targets
- ➤ The dangers from internet chat rooms
- ➤ Safe sites for children

The Moral Dimension

There can be few subjects more controversial than the dangers children are exposed to on the internet. Most parents, quite rightly, are concerned about potentially harmful content or that their offspring might be exploited by other web users. There is also a moral dilemma. The web is a bastion of free speech and free expression which, so far, has managed to resist any form of censorship. Most people would consider this to be a good thing. On the other hand, there is the ever-present fear that children might be psychologically harmed by some of the more violent or sexually explicit content that is so freely available. I'm not sure there is any real evidence for this, but the worry remains.

Even the most liberal of parents feel the need to place some restrictions on children's browsing – if only because young children have not yet developed the ability to view disturbing content objectively. I myself would try to resist any attempts to censor the internet. In my opinion, the right to free expression is more important than unspecified dangers to anybody's mental health. But I have a young daughter, and I do feel it my duty to protect her from assaults on her senses, in the same way that I try to protect her from sharp knives and vicious dogs.

All this means, of course, that at this point in the book we are changing sides. So far, we have been concerned mainly with resisting the intrusions and restrictions of others. Now we must consider if we ourselves should be intruding and restricting. If we have been offended by the attempts of government and commerce to spy on our online activities, we are now placed in the position of spying on our own children. That we intend doing so for their own good is not much of an argument – an official busybody monitoring our e-mail might say the same thing! At the end of the day, you will have to make up your own mind how far you will go to protect your children. This chapter will tell you how to do it. The moral dimension I leave to you.

Do You Know Where Your Children Go?

Most parents are naturally anxious about allowing their children unrestricted access to the internet. Children are always excited by the electronic media and are often faster and more efficient than their parents in learning and using new technology. Because of both real and imagined dangers, most parents feel obliged to take an active role in guiding their children's online activities. While the web contains many dark and unpleasant places, as well as real threats, there is also a vast amount of exciting and interesting content designed to appeal to children of every age. Both national governments and industry are trying to make the internet a safer place for children. Later in this chapter we will be looking at such innovations as site rating systems and content blocking software. But parental guidance is still the most effective means of control.

The major problem here is the sheer speed of the internet. You can sit with your children for several hours, guiding them through nice, comfortable web pages, but get up for a cup of coffee and before you have left the room they have jumped to a porn site or found a page which tells them how to make Molotov cocktails from household products. Return with your drink, and they are back at www.lego.com, looking as innocent as new-born lambs. Are you prepared to check the internet logs every day to see where they went when your back was turned? And bear in mind that 'checking up on me' is one of the greatest crimes a parent can commit.

Like most of us, children are excited by the forbidden. Many authorities recommend that you sit down with your youngsters and agree a 'family code of conduct' with negotiated limitations on access times and the type of sites visited. Only you can decide if your own children are likely to abide by such an agreement. In my experience, for what it is worth, cheating parental restrictions is an essential skill for teenagers. Older children are also likely to come under pressure from less inhibited friends to look at forbidden content. Peer pressure is a frighteningly powerful force when you are growing up and to be the only boy in a class not to have looked at pictures of explicit sex would be almost unbearable.

If we adopt a typically suspicious parental attitude, we will assume that web-wise children are going to track down and view what we consider to be inappropriate content. We can either ignore this on the grounds that it is too late to undo the damage or we can employ tracking tactics and chance the stamped feet, slammed doors and extended sulking. So now we are going to do all those things that we spent the last few chapters learning to evade. The table overleaf brings together a range of snooping tactics we have already looked at.

Already this is looking like a war between children and adults! Perhaps I am over-rating the subtlety and technical competence of the next generation, but I doubt it! I hope that you won't need to employ such heavy-handed tactics. Let's just say that I am preparing for the worst and hope it won't be necessary. In case it is, here is how to handle the suggestions made in the table.

If you need to disable access to some of the controls in Internet Explorer, there are several programs that can help you. X-Setup, the Windows configuration manager we have looked at before, provides these options, as does Windows Security Manager, the utility we discussed in Chapter 11. Figure 20.1 shows the relevant section of the program. From here you can **Disable the 'Internet Options' item in IE browser** and protect that setting with a password. There are also other control options available to

Figure 20.1 Using Windows Security Officer to control use of Internet Explorer

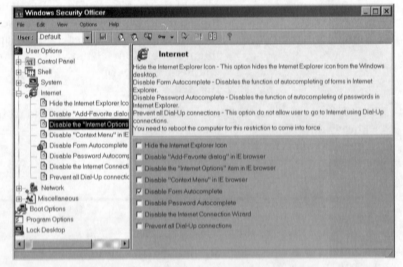

Table 20.1 Snooping Tactics

What you can do to see where your children have been	What your children can do to try and stop you	How you can counter their actions
Check your computer's browser logs. For Internet Explorer, these are stored in **C:\Windows\History**.	They can delete the records or, depending on the browser used, configure it not to store records. They can use clean-up software to erase their web tracks.	You can make regular back-ups of the browser records. You can configure your system so that the browser settings can't be changed. You can prevent new software being installed.
Check your computer's browser cache. For Internet Explorer, visited page content is cached in **C:\Windows\ Temporary Internet Files**.	Again, they can delete these records, but with Internet Explorer, they cannot remove the cache altogether. They can use clean-up software to erase their web tracks.	You can make regular back-ups of the cache, but a better option would be to configure your browser to store the data in a different (and less obvious) folder – preferably an unshared folder on a network drive.
Install a 'snooper' program to record keystrokes and take regular snapshots of the desktop while your children are online.	They can download and install an anti-snooper (see Chapter 17) to check if and when a snooper is operating.	Snoopers are hard to defeat. Even knowing that one is installed might be enough to keep their browsing honest. You can prevent new software being installed.
Install more sophisticated web-monitoring software.	Most of these are designed to be childproof, though the really inventive youngster might be able to track down counter-measures on the web.	I shall be looking at some of these programs later in the chapter.
Beg, borrow or steal heavy duty data recovery tools from the police or the security services.	Now you are being ridiculous. No wonder your children aren't honest with you!	

*Figure 20.2 Changing
IE's cache folder*

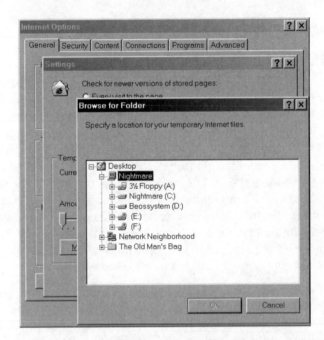

limit browser usage. I am not saying that this type of control is fool-proof. A resourceful youngster might well find a way around these settings – installing a different browser would do it, but at least you are making life difficult.

If you need to change the default folder for the browser cache, you can do this from within Internet Explorer. (If you've disabled **Internet Options** already, you will have to temporarily re-enable them to do this.) With IE open, click **Tools > Internet Options** and select the **General** tab. Within the **Temporary Internet files** section, click **Settings** and in the window which opens, click **Move Folder**. You will see a box looking like Figure 20.2. From here you can browse to a folder which suits your purposes. If the computer is part of a network, I suggest using a folder on another machine to which your children do not have read/write access. If not, select a folder which is not obvious and hope for the best.

With all this configured, you now have a sporting chance of finding out where your youngsters are browsing. If you feel that you need this degree of monitoring – and you know your own children best – my advice would be to invest in some proper monitoring software (see later in the chapter) and let your children know that it is installed. This saves you from any accusations of deviousness, and often the mere presence of such software keeps young web users honest. My final suggestion at this point is that you locate the computer used for web browsing in a busy room in the house rather than a bedroom or attic. In this way you will be able to keep a discrete eye on your children's online activities without them feeling that they are being supervised.

Pornography, Violence, Racism ... Keeping The Horrors At Bay

As I stated at the top of this chapter, parental involvement is the key to safe browsing, but even the most dedicated parent cannot watch over his or her children all the time. With what most parents would term inappropriate content so prevalent on the web, it is merely a matter of time before your children encounter it. Hard core pornography is probably the content that worries parents the most, although personally I would rate violence, cruelty and racial intolerance much more dangerous to a developing mind. Unlike television – the other often cited curse of youth – the web is not a purely passive medium. Pornographers, in particular, are adept at luring people into their sites with misleading links, banner advertising on unrelated sites and cunning entries in search engines. Figure 20.3 shows the results from the WebCrawler search engine against the term 'teenager' in the top window. The fifth most prominent link connects to the hard core porn site shown in the window below it.

Even if your children are completely happy about you organizing their browsing, they are almost certain to stumble on unsuitable material by accident. As a parent, you are left with only three choices. First, you can forbid any web browsing unless a responsible adult is present, second, you can just let them go wherever they wish and trust that you can explain or justify the hateful or obscene material that they are bound to find or third, you can invest in some variety of content filtering software.

Because of the way in which the web works, content filtering is a relatively simple proposition. When a browser requests a page, a lot of information is revealed before and during the download process – information which a filter can use to prevent the page being displayed. Some possible filters are examined in Table 20.2 overleaf. This is by no means a comprehensive list of filter types but it does indicate how effective filtering software can be if it is properly set up.

There are three basic technologies available to help parents who wish to restrict their children's access to unpleasant web content. The first, and probably the least effective, is the online content blocking service offered by some ISPs. Although these features are easy to use, they are frequently inefficient and can be bypassed by any technologically aware teenager. Online filters, like the filtering software we will look at shortly, can be difficult to fine tune. Set the filters too low and unsuitable content can slip past them. Set them too high and you might block out perfectly sound and educational content. You might not want to let your son look at Fanny with her bits out, but do you also want to cut off his access to classical nude paintings?

Another line of defence is offered by website rating systems. There are several of these in operation, and one of the most respected is the ICRA system which is integrated into both Internet Explorer and Netscape. The Internet Content Rating Association is an independent organization that aims to protect children from potentially harmful

Figure 20.3 A top search engine listing for 'teenager' links to this hard core site

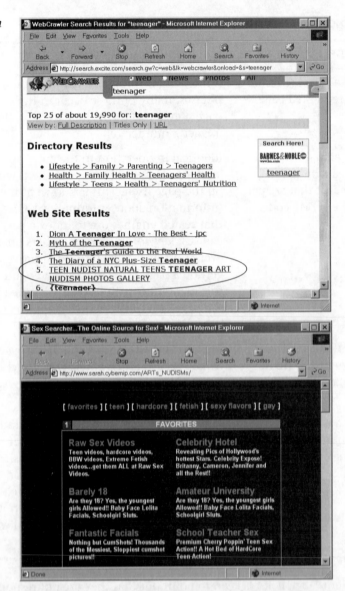

material while still supporting the right to free expression. It attempts to provide parents with the information they need to permit or deny access to web resources by clearly labelling their contents. This is a two-stage process.

Web authors are requested to fill in an online questionnaire which describes the content of their pages in terms of what they do or don't contain. From their answers, ICRA creates a content label (a short piece of computer code) which the author adds to his site. Parents who wish to use the system can then configure their browsers to permit or deny access to rated sites according to the information provided by the

Table 20.2 Content Filtering

A filter can look at	How the filter operates
The address (URL) of the requested page.	A filter can be programmed with a series of key words or phrases. If any of these occur in the URL, the filter refuses the page. Key terms might include 'sex', 'hot action', 'rape', 'nigger', 'murder', etc.
The actual text that appears on the page or words that are part of the HTML code.	Identical in operation to the entry above. Most web pages contain a variety of textual content which does not appear on the page itself. This is known as meta-information (information about information). One example is the data that search engines use to index a page, defined in HTML code as 'keywords'. Pornographers often use these to include every possible sexual term to improve their chances of getting a page listed in a search engine. A good filter will scan this meta-information for any banned keywords and refuse the page even if the text that appears in the browser window is harmless.
The names of the images that will be displayed.	Again this is a text filter so any image entitled **hot sex.jpg** will be turned away. Filters can also check the address of the image and refuse pictures such as **www.oolala.com/hot sex pics/harmless.jpg**.
The actual composition of an image in terms of the colour palette it uses.	This is a relatively new technology and not yet totally reliable. The concept behind it is that most pornographic pictures use a high percentage of flesh tones in their palettes. The filter can compare the proportion of flesh tones to other tones and if they exceed a preset level, refuse the image. Unfortunately, this technology will not prevent your son from downloading images of ladies in tight-fitting, black Latex!

content label. ICRA is keen to point out that they are not responsible for rating web content – this is left to the site authors themselves.

To use this rating system in Internet Explorer, click **Tools > Internet Options > Content**. Then click the **Enable** button in the **Content Advisor** section. You will see a window looking like Figure 20.4. (Most browsers will still refer to the RSACi rating system which is currently being phased out, but the ICRA ratings are similar.) Using the slider in this window, you can set your preferred levels for content such as language, nudity, sex and violence. The slider's caption will explain what this lets

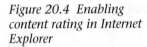

Figure 20.4 Enabling content rating in Internet Explorer

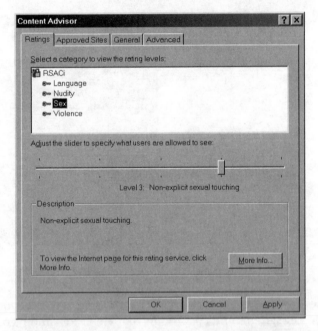

through for the five levels available in each category. In this way you can customize the filtering to suit your personal prejudices. Other tabs in this window allow you to create a list of sites which can always be visited or can never be visited – this bypasses the rating system, to set a supervisor password to lock your settings against intruders, or to change the ratings system you are using.

Website rating systems are useful in many cases, but they still do not solve all the problems with filtering content. Only a small minority of site owners apply for a rating. If you as a parent block all sites without a content label, you will cut your offspring off from most of the web.

Finer control is provided by third-party filtering software which can not only block objectionable page content but also control access to other internet resources such as newsgroups, chat rooms and e-mail which contains adult material. There are many of these 'nanny programs' available and, as always, some do a much better job than others. One of the best is Net Nanny – a comprehensive suite of utilities which provides parents with all the controls they need and locks those controls away so the children can't get at them.

Unlike some filtering software, Net Nanny relies on a team of human researchers to review sites on the web. New sites are constantly being added to the company's list, and the entire list is made available to subscribers. They can then block or permit access as they see fit. Net Nanny also provides traditional filtering tools as shown in Figure 20.5. The program can also be configured to prevent children from giving out personal information such as family names, addresses, phone numbers, e-mail

Figure 20.5 Net Nanny's words and phrases filter

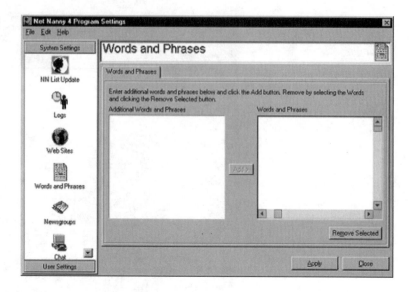

addresses and credit card numbers. It provides an effective monitor which tracks the websites, newsgroups and chat rooms that are visited and records the information your offspring send and receive. Finally, Net Nanny blocks access to known paedophilia sites using information provided by SOC-UM, a non-profit organization dedicated to the prevention of child abuse.

All in all, Net Nanny, Cyber Snoop and similar programs provide a thorough and well-organized solution to controlling web activities, but I must emphasize once more that the finest filtering software on the planet is no substitute for sound parental guidance. I shall close this section with three suggestions for parents who are not confident of their internet skills.

➤ Work hard to become fully web-literate. Even if you have never browsed before, it doesn't take long to become competent. You cannot hope to guide your web-skilled children if you have no idea what they are talking about.

➤ Try to keep up with developing technologies. If your children tell you they are downloading MP3s, should you be pleased or worried? Should you encourage or ban streaming media? If you don't know the terminology, you have lost the battle.

➤ Encourage your children towards the best side of the web. All right, there is a lot of evil out there, but there is also a wonderful and almost limitless resource, which can educate, entertain and expand a child's imagination.

To find out more about the ICRA ratings system, visit www.rsac.org A wealth of useful information is also available from www.safekids.com and www.safeteens.com Both these sites contain up-to-date information on blocking software and internet content rating systems. Net Nanny can be bought online from www.netnanny.com You will find Cyber Snoop at www.pearlsw.com

Your Children As Marketing Targets

Advertisers were very quick to discover that the internet is an ideal tool to sell products and services to children. All the abuses such as activity monitoring and profiling, which we have previously looked at as dangers to your privacy, are also being aimed at your young ones. Because children are usually less discerning, web advertising is often hidden in children's entertainment sites. Not only are such sites proliferating on the web, but they are also being used to gather information on you and your family.

In 1996, the US-based research organization Center for Media Education (CME), produced a report which exposed a wide range of techniques regularly used by internet marketers to collect detailed data and to compile individual profiles on children. To quote from the report, these included:

➤ 'eliciting personal information from children through surveys, games and clubs;

➤ using product "spokescharacters" to develop interactive relationships with children;

➤ monitoring children's online activities and compiling detailed personal profiles on them for future sales pitches;

➤ aiming personalized advertising at individual children;

➤ blurring the line between education or entertainment content;

➤ encouraging children to click on icons which transport them to advertising sites.'

(Copyright © 1996 The Center for Media Education)

Such practices are despicable for two reasons. They not only invade children's privacy – nothing new there, of course – but they also attempt to exploit children's inexperience and vulnerability. Here are some examples. Children are offered the chance to win prizes if they fill out online questionnaires about themselves and their families. Such information goes straight into a profiler's database and will subsequently be used to target the child and his relatives with customized advertising. Online games have been designed around well-known 'spokescharacters' (love that word!) such as Tony the Tiger, Winnie the Pooh and the Snap! Crackle! & Pop! trio. This type of interactive product placement encourages children to click on icons within their favourite games, which immediately transport them to advertising sites. It seems that there is nothing online marketers won't stoop to.

The Center for Media Education went on to produce a series of recommendations including the following.

➤ Personal information should not be collected from children, nor should personal profiles of children be sold to third parties.

➤ Advertising and promotions targeted at children should be clearly labelled and separated from content.

➤ Children's content areas should not be directly linked to advertising sites.

➤ There should be no direct interaction between children and product spokescharacters.

➤ There should be no online microtargeting of children, and no direct-response marketing.

Of course, these were only recommendations but some of their suggestions found a home in the Children's Online Privacy Protection Act (COPPA) which came into effect in the US in April 2000. Among other provisions, COPPA requires commercial websites to get permission from parents before collecting, using or disclosing personal information obtained from children under 13. It also compels websites to post a privacy policy describing what personal information is collected from children, how it is to be used and if it is made available to third parties.

While legislators in the rest of the world have yet to catch up, we parents are expected to make up for their indecision. You might consider the suggestions made in the following list.

➤ Make sure that your children are fully aware of the profiling and targeting techniques we have looked at in this book. Explain to them the importance of anonymity on the web and how they might be used to get to their parents. In my experience, most children love secrecy for its own sake and will be delighted to conspire with you to beat the system.

➤ Convince your children that they must never fill in online forms, subscribe to services, enter competitions or do anything else which involves them giving out personal details without your permission. If your children are old enough, you might organize a web-based e-mail account for them so they can communicate with their friends, but stress that even then they must not include personal information in their messages.

➤ Try to establish a mutual support relationship, so that your children automatically come to you for an explanation of anything they don't understand on the web. While it is vital that you don't frighten your children, or discourage them from using the internet, it is important that they are aware of at least some of the dangers.

The Dangers From Internet Chat Rooms

One of the internet's greatest attractions for children, especially teenagers, is its interactivity. Making friends online appeals to many youngsters, and such global friendships can really benefit a child's social skills. It is important to remember, however, that such friends are not always who they claim to be. Online communication allows people to adopt bogus identities. This does not always mean that they have any unpleasantness in mind. It might be no more than their own way of protecting their privacy.

Michael The Concerned Parent

Michael's teenagers, like many others, are regular users of instant messaging and internet chat rooms. Michael is very conscious of the dangers these can represent, but does not want to cramp their style too much. His children have agreed to abide by some basic rules Michael has laid down. They don't give out personal details and they never agree to actually meet any of their online correspondents. Michael makes a point of never reading any of his children's communications. He feels that this would be an unpardonable intrusion into their own rights to privacy. While this attitude is understandable, it is not necessarily in his youngster's best interests. His son has now hooked up with a hacking crew who are only too delighted to teach him how to break into computers and rifle their contents. Michael's boy is now hovering on the edge of breaking the law.

Of course there are predators who prowl internet chat areas with despicable motives. I have already mentioned the practice known as 'grooming'. A 'chatmate' – nearly always a man – will befriend a youngster by pretending to be a friend of a similar age and gender. He will build up the child's trust by flattering her and confiding in her. He might try to move to a more private form of communication by exchanging e-mail addresses with her. After a while, depending on his motive, he might gently divert conversation towards sexual matters. He might describe invented sexual experiences and ask the girl if she has any to share. He might even persuade her to e-mail him photographs. All the time he will stress the importance of keeping their relationship a secret. This comes naturally to most youngsters who share things with their best friends that they would never think of telling their parents. Eventually, he might even try to arrange a meeting with the girl … I won't continue.

Not all such chat room encounters are designed for sexual reasons. There are various recorded cases where predators have persuaded young friends to join them in criminal activities. There are also many instances of crooks using online chat to extract details of parents' credit cards and bank accounts. The attraction for the predator, of course, is almost complete anonymity. Using an assumed identity and internet privacy

Figure 20.6 A typical teen chat room at www.chattownusa.com

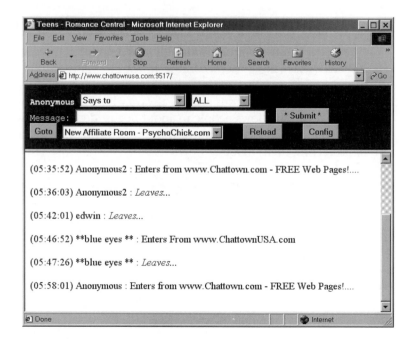

software, the criminal's real personality is never exposed. Even if his false identity is revealed, he can reappear in the same chat room ten minutes later as someone else entirely.

Figure 20.6 shows a typical chat room – Teens-Romance Central at www.chattownusa.com (I must stress that Chattown is a perfectly respectable service and was not singled out for any particular reason.) Like many chat rooms, Chattown does not require you to log-in or identify yourself in any way. You will see from the window that I have just entered as Anonymous. I could be anybody and can now send messages as a wide-eyed sixteen-year-old rather than an overweight parent with a mortgage and a hangover!

If your children are keen to use internet chat services, try to steer them towards the moderated ones where someone keeps an eye on the conversation and can interfere if there is any suspicion of misconduct. You will find the addresses of such sites from a good search engine or from the links at the end of this chapter. I would also suggest you consider impressing the following rules on your offspring.

➤ Your children always use a nickname in a chat room and never reveal their real names. Even a Christian name might give ammunition to online predators.

➤ As always, they should not reveal any personal details without your permission. Since this will certainly prove restrictive, you, yourself, should vet and approve online friends before relaxing this rule.

340

➤ If your children use passwords to log into their chat rooms, they should never reveal them to anyone. This will prevent predators from assuming their identities.

➤ Should your children receive offensive e-mails or other junk, send copies of them to your Internet Service Provider. ISPs will not always respond, but the more conscientious will try to protect youngsters using their services.

➤ Finally, consider using the filtering software we looked at earlier to restrict access to chat rooms (and internet) newsgroups which contain offensive material.

Safe Sites For Children

I will close this chapter with a short list of web addresses that you might find useful in organizing safe browsing for your children. Of course I cannot guarantee the content provided and it is a sad fact that some of the most popular children's sites attempt to advertise goods and services to their visitors. I suggest you visit some of those listed below and make up your own mind.

The following sites are recognized as safe and 'child-friendly':

➤ Disney's Family (www.family.com);

➤ Early Childhood (www.earlychildhood.com);

➤ Family Entertainment (www.familyentertainment.net);

➤ Family Internet (www.familyinternet.com);

➤ Love@Home (www.loveathome.com);

➤ Mr. Rogers' Neighbourhood (www.pbs.org/rogers);

➤ TeamDiscovery.com- Sports Resource Centre (teamdiscovery.com);

➤ The Whole Family (www.wholefamily.com).

You might also find the following child-safe search engines useful. You can be sure that none of these will return inappropriate links:

➤ Yahooligans (www.yahooligans.com);

➤ Fact Monster (www.factmonster.com);

➤ Wonderful Kids Club (www.mikesart.com/links/dlmtools/familysafesearch.htm).

And that's it as far as our look at the wondrous world of the internet is concerned. In Chapter 21 we will be taking on an entirely new subject and examining the activities of hackers and how they threaten our security.

Chapter 20 - Security Checklist

1   After you have settled your conscience concerning the ethics of snooping on your children, you will have to make a choice as to the best method of monitoring their browsing. You can check a computer's browsing records or install monitor software such as a key logging program. If your children are computer-savvy, you might also need to reconfigure software to prevent them from deleting their tracks.

2   If you decide that you are going to control your children's browsing, you will need to consider some kind of filtering software. There is a wide choice available, including address filtering and word filtering types. Some ISPs offer filtration at portal-level, there are website rating systems available which rely on site authors submitting details of their pages or you might choose to purchase filtering software such as Net Nanny.

3   Perhaps the most important tool you can employ to safeguard children's browsing is simple parental guidance. It is important that you make yourself familiar with web technologies and that you steer your offspring towards the more positive and pleasant side of the web.

4   Like yourself, your children can quickly become targets for unscrupulous business interests. It is important that children are made aware of this danger and advised never to pass on any information which might subsequently be used for online marketing.

5   There are particular dangers attached to online chatting. Web chat rooms are often used by criminals or sexual perverts to 'groom' children for subsequent attentions. Children must never reveal personal details to anyone in a chat room. Some filtering software also includes features which can restrict access to undesirable sites.

Part 5
Trespassers Will Not Be Forgiven

Part 5 is concerned with heavy-duty attacks on your system and how to protect yourself from hackers and the tools they employ. I start by telling the history of hacking and show how it has developed from creating ingenious hardware and software to breaking into systems to steal data or render them useless. I show you ways of avoiding the attentions of the hackers and how to recognize a hacker attack. I then describe the most invasive hacker tool – the Trojan horse program. I show you how Trojans are used to gain access to and take control of your system for nefarious purposes. I'll help you to recognize Trojans at work and look at the software needed to exile them from our computers.

Finally, I focus your attention on that most critical defensive program, the software firewall. I help you to compare different firewalls and look at how they prevent outsiders from entering your systems. I show you how to set up a suitable firewall on your own computer and how to configure it for maximum security. Part 5 closes with a comprehensive checklist for establishing a total security strategy for your computer.

By the end of Part 5, you will understand the activities of hackers and what they are trying to achieve. You will have installed protection against Trojan programs and built yourself a firewall to control data coming in to and going out of your system. By implementing all the procedures recommended in this book, you will have a totally secure computer system, strong enough to withstand all attacks whether accidental or deliberate.

Hello Hackers, Everywhere!

Hacking And Cracking

Ask any computer security specialist what he considers to be the greatest danger to a major network installation, and he will probably reply with one word – hackers! The term has grown from its very specific origins, and is now used to cover almost all varieties of computer crime from breaking into systems to modifying shareware programs so they no longer ask you to pay for them. Some computer hobbyists quite like to be called hackers. The term suggests an untamed, free-spirited outlook on technology. There is even a certain romanticism. Like the buccaneers, highwayman and Robin Hood before him, a hacker is not so much breaking the law, as righting the wrongs imposed on free men and women by big business and repressive governments.

Of course this is all nonsense. Hackers destroy data, wreck computers and cost us all a lot of money. Where is the romance in breaking into an ordinary person's computer and stealing his credit card number? I have lost count of the number of shareware authors who have given up producing programs because cracked versions of their code have reduced their income to peanuts. Hackers sometimes claim to be supporters of free information, but their combined efforts to vandalize the internet is largely responsible for the current interest in controlling and regulating it.

And if you think that your own insignificant little network is beneath a hacker's notice, think again. Most attacks are aimed at private individuals or small company networks, simply because they are the easiest targets. You cannot afford the costly layers of protection which safeguard a bank or a major corporation. Like the muggers who avoid the well-lit and policed main streets, hackers dwell in the darker corners of the internet where they can prey on the weak and defenceless.

This is a short chapter but an important one. The remainder of this book is concerned with protecting your computer against invasion from outside, so it is important from the outset that you understand the nature of your enemy. In this chapter we will look at the origin and development of hacking, the tools hackers use against you and the damage they can do. Some aspects of their craft we have covered in previous chapters, others will be new to you. Read this chapter and you will discover how a lofty ideal has fallen into ruins.

What Is A Hacker?

Here is the definition of a hacker from the 1994 *Que's Computer User's Dictionary*:

> *a computer enthusiast who enjoys learning everything about a computer system and, through clever programming, pushing the system to its highest possible level of performance*
>
> (*Copyright © 1994 by Que Corporation*)

Here is the definition of a hack from the same book:

> *an inordinately clever rearrangement of existing system resources that results, as if by magic, in a stunning improvement in system performance – or an equally stunning prank*
>
> (*Copyright © 1994 by Que Corporation*)

Can you recognize the current generation of thieves and vandals from these descriptions? Hackers were not always the bad guys. Not so many years ago, hackers were the driving force behind hardware and software development. They took the immature art of computing and turned it on its head, wrestling control away from big business and opening the door to true personal computing. Without the original hackers, it is doubtful that you would be sitting at your computer today. The hardware hackers designed and built the first practical personal computers by assembling off-the-shelf components in a brilliantly creative way. Before the hackers, computers were huge, lumbering monoliths affordable only by governments and massive corporations. The hardware hackers put the PC on your desktop. And the software hackers gave you the software that makes it work. Even the mighty Microsoft started life as a tiny hacking company. Hackers put together the code which allows your computer to work and you to be productive. All hail the original hackers!

In the 1980s the press redefined the term hacker. Despite loud protests from the real hacking community, which still exists today, the word was hijacked and used to describe those sorry individuals who specialize in breaking into computer systems. Hacker hysteria was born and the original concept of hacking as a creative art died at the same time. The hacker's dream of getting an idea, then hacking programs or machinery together to make that dream a reality has given way to the idea of hacking into someone else's computer and doing bad things to it. The hackers of yesterday don't even acknowledge today's crop of cyber-vandals. They refer to them as crackers or script kiddies. It pains me to even use the term hacker for such people, but the press has latched onto the word and we can but follow!

The 'Hacker Ethic'

Way back in 1984, Steven Levy wrote a book about the original hackers called (honestly enough) *Hackers*. In it, he outlined the code of these 'heroes of the computer revolution' which he called the 'Hacker Ethic'. This is it.

1 *Access to computers – and anything which might teach you something about the way the world works – should be unlimited and total. Always yield to the Hands-On Imperative!*
2 *All information should be free.*
3 *Mistrust authority – promote decentralization.*
4 *Hackers should be judged by their hacking, not bogus criteria such as degrees, age, race or position.*
5 *You can create art and beauty on a computer.*
6 *Computers can change your life for the better.*

(Copyright © Steven Levy 1984)

While this ethic was never formalized or promoted, it was – and still is – widely accepted by those we might refer to as the real hackers. It is also easy to see how this ethic can be twisted to justify the computer attackers of today. 'Access to computers...should be unlimited' might be used to excuse breaking into private systems. 'All information should be free' provides a tenuous justification for stealing your private details. Of course, the real hackers were not interested in breaking and entering or data theft. Their ethic was to improve machine processing as an art form, to create new and beautiful software and to bring the benefits of the computer revolution to everyone.

The current generation of hackers have simply lost the plot. While they might see themselves as the natural successors to our original hackers, somewhere along the line they have distorted the honesty of the Hacker Ethic to excuse a miserable brand of crime and cyber-vandalism. They have also chosen to ignore the vital sixth element of the ethic – 'computers can change your life for the better'.

Hackers On The Internet

Having said this, it is a mistake to write off all of today's hackers as mindless vandals. Certainly there are some for whom wanton destruction is an end in itself, but most have managed to concoct some justification for their activities. They might claim, for example, to attack major websites in order to highlight weaknesses in their security or to crack shareware programs because it is wrong to profit from computing. By understanding the twisted logic behind these excuses (and not forgetting urban deprivation and personality disorders) we can begin to make sense of the anti-social activities they indulge in.

RatZnuTZ The Cracker (Artist's Impression)

Remember RatZnuTZ (real name Justin Longbottom)? Our own personal hacker, like many of his peers, is convinced that he is a potent force for change. As a disaffected teenager, he has found a place in the hacker community which gives him a sense of purpose and a sense of belonging. In many ways, hacker groups are the online equivalents of street gangs. RatZnuTZ is not a bad person – away from his computer, he is a normal teenager – but hacking has become his cause, at least until he discovers girls!

Hackers often form groups with names which are intended to make them sound potent – DooMSlayerZ, HellZcoDerZ, things like that. These groups often specialize in particular forms of attack. One form which is becoming more popular is the Denial of Service (DoS) attack I have mentioned earlier. DoS attacks are intended to lock out legitimate users by plaguing websites with repeated requests until the site can no

It is worth pointing out that worms are not necessarily harmful. The first worm on the internet, the so-called Morris Worm, was designed by a university student as an experiment and did not carry a viral payload. Unfortunately, it propagated so enthusiastically that it sucked up vast amounts of internet resources and almost brought the whole thing to a grinding halt.

longer cope with the traffic. Such attacks are usually managed by automated scripts, but a more cunning variety, the Distributed Denial of Service attack (DDoS) is run from multiple computers, often without the knowledge of their owners. Hackers can plant Trojan horse programs (see Chapter 22) in hundreds or even thousands of computers, then launch a co-ordinated attack in which all those commandeered computers launch requests at the same time. Site owners who are subjected to DoS attacks find that they can no longer do business on the web.

There are also hacking groups that specialize in propagating computer worms and viruses. As we noted in Chapter 5, worms are essentially self-replicating programs which can spread exponentially over a network.

To most web users, hacking involves breaking into other people's computers. In Chapter 22 we will look at Trojans – the tools most commonly used for such attacks – but there are other, equally worrying ways in which hackers can get at your data. In Chapter 19 we looked at online financial transactions and described the SSL (Secure Sockets Layer) protocol which provides the security. As we noted, SSL is a fairly secure protocol and cracking it is beyond the skills of most hackers. Instead of battering at a locked door, a hacker can try so-called 'session hijacking'. When you contact a secure server, the server establishes a session ID to identify your connection. This is only done once. An enterprising hacker can hop in at this point and extract the session ID. He can use this to redirect the rest of the transaction to his own computer. The SSL protocol doesn't notice that the user's IP address has changed. The hacker has effectively assumed your identity.

As you know, when you attempt to connect to a web server, the address you type into your browser has to be translated into that server's numeric IP address by a DNS (Domain Name Service) server. DNS servers maintain a constantly updated database of these entries to ensure that a site's domain name (www.cocacola.com) is mapped to the correct IP address (204.146.144.253). A 'DNS spoof' involves a hacker breaking into a DNS database and modifying an entry to redirect your browser to a different site. Let's say you wanted to pay a bill using your online bank account. You type www.mybank.com into your browser, but instead of sending you there, a knobbled DNS server redirects you to www.thievingscum.net – a fake site which looks like your bank's genuine site. You might well be persuaded to hand over personal details such as your account and PIN numbers which a hacker can then use to access your account at the bank's actual site. Such sophisticated hacks are becoming more common.

Figure 21.1 Two hacked web pages.

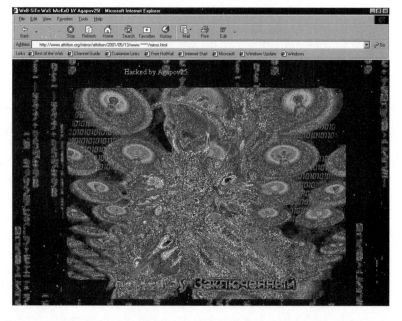

Of course, some hackers cannot aspire to such lofty hacks. They are limited to breaking into sites and messing them up – a rather feeble activity known as web defacement. As we have seen, web pages are simply computer files stored on a web server. If a hacker can gain access to these files, he (or she in the first example shown!) can simply modify the HTML code. Figure 21.1 shows examples of two hacked web pages.

Finally in this section I should mention the hacker technique known as 'social engineering'. This is a polite way of describing a range of techniques used to dupe people into giving out confidential information a hacker might need. Hackers have been known to pose as representatives for a software vendor and ask employees for information on their company network. Sometimes they pretend to be working for a company and seek help from other employees because they have forgotten passwords and network IDs. There are records of many similar tricks, used by hackers to bypass security precautions.

The Hackers' Tools

If the original hackers were limited only by their skills, today's breed have a much easier life. Instead of solving problems with imagination and creativity, the new-style hacker has a ready-made toolbox of utilities he can use to crack into other people's systems. Some of these tools are complex and require considerable knowledge of the underlying technologies if they are to be used efficiently. Others are virtually click-n'-hack, and it is these simple but damaging tools which have empowered vast numbers of otherwise ineffectual hacker wannabees. It is also worrying to note that the sheer number of hacking tools is on the increase, while the growth of the internet has made them accessible to more people.

Take, for example, the Denial of Service attacks we looked at in the previous section.There are various DoS tools including Tribal Flood Network, Stacheldraht and WinTrin. They tend to work in a similar way, recruiting unsuspecting computers – known as zombies – and implanting them with the attack program. Packetstorm (www.securify.com) carries a great deal of information on the subject of DoS attacks along with advice from companies such as Sun and Microsoft on avoiding them. They also provide a range of DoS detection utilities such as ddosping produced by Foundstone Inc., a US-based security consultancy.

Another essential tool for the keen hacker is the packet sniffer. Like many other tools, this was originally developed to help network administrators resolve system problems. (We looked at packet sniffers in Chapter 19.) Such tools, like guns and knives, are not inherently bad. It is only when they are used for illegal activities that they become dangerous.

Port scanning programs search for open and listening ports on remote computers. A port is an abstraction that enables a process on one machine to communicate with a process on another machine over a network. Popular net services like the WWW, FTP, and Telnet each use different incoming ports (numbers 80, 21 and 23, respectively). Open ports are potential vulnerabilities since by definition they 'listen for' or accept connections from random machines on the net.

There are two types of port scanner. The first type, illustrated in Figure 21.2, searches a range of IP addresses for a particular open port. In our example, this is port 12345. The

Figure 21.2 Port Scan, as its name suggests, is a high-speed port scanner

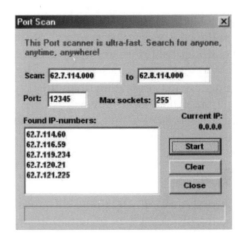

second type – and one that is almost exclusively used by hackers – searches IP addresses for the presence of a Trojan server. One comparison that is often used is that a scanner is the online equivalent of a burglar going from house to house and trying doorknobs. Dozens of port scanners are available on the internet, each with their own special features.

Another hacker tool which has become very prevalent in network attacks is the so-called 'war dialler'. This is a software utility which dials telephone numbers one after another looking for a network connection. A war dialler can spot the different tones used by faxes and modems. Left unattended, it can check thousands of numbers, compiling a list of those which respond with a suitable network signal. A hacker can then try these numbers in an attempt to establish a direct network connection. In theory, network access is protected, but far too many employees bypass system security by connecting their modems to outside lines, thus providing hackers with a way in to the network.

One thing a hacker always needs is anonymity. Since most of his activities are illegal, he naturally wishes to hide from retribution, and calling himself PoiSonBoT is only part of the answer. Security specialists grow ever more vigilant and now employ a tactic called traceback to follow a hacker's trail back to his home computer. (Most hackers really do work from their own bedrooms!) An experienced hacker tries to leave no evidence of his activities – a technique know as traceback avoidance. Properly managed, this can provide almost complete secrecy. As we have seen, internet communication is carried out between computers rather than between people. Wise hackers use all the privacy techniques we looked at in Chapter 16, including proxies and anonymizing sites.

Since most hacking tools are designed to crack open secure systems such as UNIX and Windows NT, the Windows 98 user is left with only limited resources. Luckily, Microsoft provides a few useful tools as part of the Windows distribution. Netstat, a

Figure 21.3 Using the DOS Ping command

```
C:\Windows>ping google.com

Pinging google.com [216.239.35.100] with 32 bytes of data:

Reply from 216.239.35.100: bytes=32 time=281ms TTL=48
Reply from 216.239.35.100: bytes=32 time=284ms TTL=48
Reply from 216.239.35.100: bytes=32 time=285ms TTL=48
Reply from 216.239.35.100: bytes=32 time=293ms TTL=48

Ping statistics for 216.239.35.100:
    Packets: Sent = 4, Received = 4, Lost = 0 (0% loss),
Approximate round trip times in milli-seconds:
    Minimum = 281ms, Maximum = 293ms, Average = 285ms

C:\Windows>_
```

utility we shall be using in Chapter 22, can provide a lot of information if your goal is hacking a local network. Another useful tool is the Tracert utility which traces the route between your computer and a remote server. Like netstat, you need to use Tracert from the MS-DOS prompt. Typing **tracert www.microsoft.com** on the DOS command line will show you all the computers that are routing your call to Microsoft and how long each 'hop' takes. Windows also provides a useful terminal emulation program called Telnet. Finally, never forget the humble Ping utility. Again, you will need to work in a DOS session, but typing **ping google.com** produces the response shown in Figure 21.3. Ping sends small packets of data to the remote server and checks how long it takes that server to respond. In this example, the round trip took just 285 milliseconds. Hackers often use the Ping command in a Denial of Service attack – the so-called 'Ping of Death'. Send enough pings, and you will keep the server so busy that it cannot do anything else.

The top echelons of hackerdom design and program new tools to suit their needs. This is one part of the Hacker Ethic which has survived the fall. Like other programmers, hackers can be quite passionate about writing efficient, bug-free code, and it must be admitted that some hacker programs are masterpieces of compact functionality. Such tools are often made available to other hackers via dedicated sites on the web. This means that new tools are constantly appearing, leaving security professionals to track them down and design suitable counter-measures. But for the talentless hacker who cannot create or even download tools, there is always the option of buying a DIY hacking outfit as you will see from Figure 21.4!

A Hacker Speaks ...

So far, this chapter might leave you thinking that hackers are an unstoppable force and destined to rule the web – but this way lies paranoia! Aside from their anti-social interests, hackers are pretty much the same as the rest of us. Their antics can be

Figure 21.4 Hacker shopping on the internet

contained and they can be caught and prosecuted for their crimes – and often are. At the same time, there are hackers who actually benefit the system. They sometimes develop and improve excellent tools, and if ordinary network tools can be perverted by a hacker, there is no reason why a hacker's tool cannot be turned to good use.

If you would like an insight into the mind of a hacker, the following snippets come from an FAQ posted on a hacker site on the web. Its purpose is to advise would-be hackers on how to get started. I have not touched the spelling or grammar.

> *… there you are sitting in front of your computer twiddling your thumbs, scratching your head wondering how to hack your friends your computer. How do I get access to it and do what you have to do.*

> *GETTING ACCESS TO ANOTHER PERSONS COMPUTER*

> *To get access to your victims computer, you need 2 things:-*

> *(1).... Their IP address or Host name,*

> *(2).... Their computer must be infected with the trojan Server or Patch.*

> *There are many ways of getting into someones computer, I will briefly run through the more common methods…*

> *…After about 30 seconds or so of scanning, I had 5 unknown IP addresses…*

> *…software has been designed to mask the trojan server, by adding the server to a geniune file. For example this software can add the server to a game like Flight Simulator, or to a*

MP 3 music file. Send your masked server to your victim, and when they open the attachment it automatically installs the server into their Windows Registry. All you have to do now, is wait until their connected to internet and then use your client to gain access. Once you have access and you are on their computer, an option you have is to password protect your server, thus only giving you access too their computer and making less ulnlikely that you will be detected.

Once connected too a victim, just start experimenting, be careful thou as this is illegal. Please don't destroy, delete or infect anyones computer with viruses etc etc as this is very lame and you give other people who care a bad name...

...if you have a person in mind that you want to hack, and after scanning their IP address for all trojans you find that they are not infected...then what next ??? It's time for you to infect their computer using the server part of the download. The hardest part of all this is getting the server part to your victim and then getting them to open it up and run it.

There are many ways of getting servers on other peoples computers-

(1) Direct access – Infection caused by floppy discs or CD – Roms

(2) ICQ – Send server through ICQ

(3) Email – Send the server to them by email.

(4) Downloads – If you own a web site, design a good program, and provide them with the URL download.

Understanding Software Ports

To understand the finer points of hacking – and particularly the use of Trojan horses, which is coming up next – you need to be familiar with the concept of ports. Most computer users are aware of the hardware ports which are usually located round the back of a machine and allow you to plug in peripherals such as printers, modems and keyboards. Here we are concerned with software ports, the channels by which different processes and network services connect to your operating system and application software. Forget one parallel and two USB ports, your computer can make use of up to 65,536 software ports (port numbers from 0 to 65535).

Ports provide a range of different functions such as transmitting and receiving data. They can be open or closed. What a port is doing at any one moment is known as its state and from our security perspective we are most concerned with a port in a listening state. A port in a listening state – usually referred to as a listening port – is doing exactly what it sounds like. It is waiting for something to send it a signal. When it hears the right signal, it responds to let the signaller know that it is ready and waiting. Web servers, for example, are usually configured to listen on port 80. If you wish your browser to connect to, say, Yahoo!, you might type www.yahoo.com into the address bar. Yahoo!'s full address is www.yahoo.com:80 – the IP address followed by the port number, but in most cases the port number is assumed. Figure 21.5 shows a very small part of a massive web-based port table listing the services which connect to all 65,536 software ports.

In most cases you will not need to figure out port numbers for the services you use because they conform to an agreed standard which ensures that the same port is always used by the same service. Here are a few of the most common service/port combinations.

➤ Web servers listen on port 80.

➤ FTP (File Transfer Protocol) servers listen on port 21.

➤ Servers that provide Telnet connections listen on port 23.

➤ POP3 e-mail servers listen on port 110.

You will notice that so far I have only listed server ports. Client software also requires ports for information transfer and can use any port number from 1024 upwards. Take a typical client application like your web browser. When your web browser connects to a server – on port 80, you will recall – your browser suggests a port for the server to reply to and the first page you request will normally be downloaded to the suggested port. Click a link, however, and your browser will ask for the new page to be sent to a different port. Access a page which uses HTML frames or includes Java applets, and each of these elements will require its own port. Before you know it, you can have dozens of open ports on your computer.

Figure 21.5 A web-based port table showing the services which use the first nine ports

number	tcp/udp	service	Explanation
0	tcp/udp	#	Reserved
1	tcp/udp	tcpmux	TCP Port Service Multiplexer
1	ddp	rtmp	Routing Table Maintenance Protocol
2	tcp/udp	compressnet	Management Utility
2	ddp	nbp	Name Binding Protocol
3	tcp/udp	compressnet	Compression Process
4	tcp/udp	#	Unassigned
4	ddp	echo	AppleTalk Echo Protocol
5	tcp/udp	rje	Remote Job Entry
6	tcp/udp	#	Unassigned
6	ddp	zip	Zone Information Protocol
7	tcp/udp	echo	Echo
7	udp	fw-1_7	echo-udp
8	tcp/udp	#	Unassigned
9	tcp/udp	discard	Discard

Here are a few examples of client software and the ports they normally open.

➤ ICQ: IN on port 20000 – 20019, OUT on port 4000.

➤ Internet Phone: port 22555.

➤ MSN Messenger: IN on port 1863, 5190 or 6901, OUT on port 6891–6900.

➤ Napster: port 6699.

➤ Net2Phone: port 6801.

➤ Quake2: port 27910 (client and server).

➤ Yahoo Messenger: Chat on port 5000–5001, Phone on port 5055.

It is important to remember that any open port represents a security risk to your system. An open port means that data can flow in one or both directions. Hackers use ports as doorways into your system. The obvious solution is a gatekeeper, and the most effective gatekeeper is a firewall. We shall examine firewalls in Chapter 23. Until then, we will take a few pages to look at the hacker's favourite utility and one which exploits software ports in a frightening fashion – the aptly named Trojan horse.

Sorry, but I am not going to include links to any of the hacker software discussed in this chapter! If you want to get involved in that sort of business, you will have to find them yourself. Instead, you might like to amuse yourself at www.attrition.org which takes an anarchic and very funny view of hacking or look at the archives on defaced.alldas.de which stores copies of most website defacements.

The Trojan Horse

In This Chapter

➤ The Trojan wars

➤ Additional dangers from new technologies

➤ Spotting a Trojan at work

➤ Protecting yourself against a Trojan horse

➤ Anti-Trojan software

The Trojan Wars

I have mentioned Trojan horses several times in this book. Now it is time to get serious about them. Despite the classical name, Trojan horses (or Trojans) represent a very modern danger to computer security. First, some definitions. Strictly speaking, a Trojan is the apparently harmless program which is used to conceal malicious or harmful code, but this was soon turned around and became the accepted name for the harmful code itself. (From this definition, you will realize that the spyware modules we looked at in Chapter 19 can be defined as Trojans.) Additionally, the term Trojan is often used to describe a malevolent client/server system, where the server is secretly infiltrated into a computer and the client is used by a hidden operator for the unauthorized collection, falsification or destruction of data. This is the threat we are going to focus on in this short, but vitally important chapter.

Figure 22.1 How a client/server Trojan operates

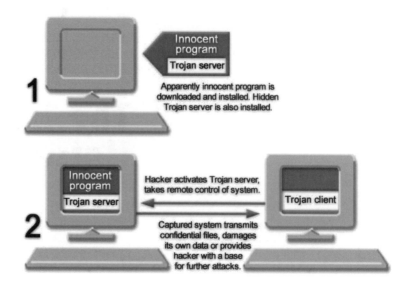

The term 'Trojan horse' comes from classical Greek literature. After unsuccessfully besieging the city of Troy for many years, the Greeks tried a last trick. They constructed an enormous wooden horse which they left outside Troy as an offering to the gods. Then they pretended to sail away defeated. The Trojans, with quite staggering stupidity, pulled the horse inside the city and, during the night, the Greek warriors hiding inside jumped out and slaughtered everybody. As you can see from this potted myth, we should really be talking about a Greek horse.

Figure 22.1 illustrates how a client/server Trojan operates. You innocently install a program within which is concealed the server module of the Trojan. The server hides itself away on your hard disk. The hacker meanwhile activates his client module which makes contact with your server. Now he has control of your system and can instruct the server to transmit confidential information or to damage or destroy your files. He can even use your computer as a base from which to mount further attacks on other systems. You can become an unknowing pawn in a major Denial of Service (DoS) war, while the hacker himself keeps well away from the conflict.

Let us look at one such Trojan in detail to understand how dangerous they can be. Back Orifice 2000 – a pun on Microsoft's Back Office® software – first hit the web in July 1999. It was a successor to the original Back Orifice Trojan, but considerably more devastating. It was designed by a group of hackers calling themselves 'The Cult of the Dead Cow' (a name borrowed from the novel *Illuminatus*). Unlike Back Orifice, Back Orifice 2000 – more commonly known as BO2K – runs on Windows NT systems as well as on Windows 98. This makes it much more dangerous to corporate systems which usually rely on the added security of an NT network. As well as BO2K itself, the hackers also released the source code on the internet, inviting others to modify it and create new varieties of Trojan.

360

BO2K is a good example of the so-called Remote Administration Tool (RAT). RAT Trojans are often promoted as genuine utilities which enable users to manage their computers over a network, and they do indeed provide this facility. Unfortunately, they also allow outsiders with the RAT client to access the installed server. BO2K comes in many different disguises. One of the most common is an attachment called **joke.exe.** Once the BO2K server had been installed, the remote client allows its users to access and manipulate the victim's computer whenever he is connected to the internet. Here is a list of some of the 70 different commands that are available at the client end and their effects on the server.

➤ Reboot Machine: shuts down and reboots the machine.

➤ Lock-up Machine: freezes remote machine, which then requires a reboot.

➤ List Passwords: retrieves a list of users and their passwords.

➤ Get System Info: retrieves a variety of information on the remote machine, including its name, the processor it uses, the operating system, the memory and a list of fixed and remote drives.

➤ Log Keystrokes: logs the remote user's keystrokes to a file.

➤ TCP File Send: connects to a specified port and sends a file to the remote machine.

➤ Capture Screen: creates an image of the screen currently displayed on the remote machine and saves it to a file.

➤ Delete File: deletes a file from the remote machine.

As you can see even from this shortened list, BO2K is a horrifying bit of technology which effectively hands over control of your computer to an outsider.

Marketing specialists used to divide promotional campaigns into 'rifle shot' and 'scatter gun'. The first indicated a campaign which was tightly targeted at particular individuals, while the second type was simply blasted at the public in the hope that someone would get hit. Carrying the concept over to hacking, the RAT Trojans represent scatter gun attacks. It is almost impossible to target a Trojan victim. As a hacker, you can never be certain that an individual will download and run the program which installs the Trojan server. Instead you resort to broadcast techniques. You conceal the Trojan in newsgroup postings, e-mail attachments and even downloadable software and you wait for web users to pick it up.

Now, still as a hacker, you need to track down infected machines. Some Trojan servers are configured to contact their masters once they have been installed. They can use e-mail, ICQ or even Yahoo or AOL instant messaging. Another technique requires the hacker to identify infected computers using a scanner. As we saw in Chapter 21, a scanner is a program which attempts to connect to a wide range of IP addresses on the internet. If any computers respond, the hacker can then establish a connection to the Trojan's listening port and go into action.

Additional Dangers From New Technologies

A Trojan server can only be activated over a network – usually the internet although there have been high-profile reports of Trojans used on large corporate networks. For most people this means that they are only at risk of remote control when they are browsing the web. To access your system, the hacker with the Trojan client must be online if he is to control operations in real time. You'll remember that a standard modem connection results in you getting a different IP address each time you dial in. This can make it very difficult for the hacker to track down the right address to connect to. The situation changes dramatically with new broadband connections where you will have a static IP address. Once the hacker has identified this, he can lurk in the dark until you connect and then go straight into action.

There are also various programs which operate exactly like RAT Trojans but which are promoted as network analysis tools. One of the earliest Trojans, NetBus, is now claimed by its author to be a sophisticated remote management program. It can certainly fulfil this task, but it is also a very effective Trojan. (Honourable software products like LapLink and PCAnywhere make use of similar technology.)

Spotting A Trojan At Work

By definition, a Trojan is designed to operate in secrecy. The first indication you might see is your computer operating in a strange manner. If you look back at the list of Back Orifice commands above, you can identify some of the events that might make you suspicious. If your computer suddenly reboots or stops working, if files start disappearing or appearing, if your computer is buzzing and whirring when you are not consciously processing data, all of these suggest outside interference. Of course they can also indicate a virus or badly behaved software, so it isn't safe to assume a Trojan is at work. The following list suggests symptoms of a Trojan infection. It is based on the commands built into the most popular Trojan clients.

➤ If your computer performs an unexpected reboot ...

➤ If your computer suddenly locks up ...

➤ If you find someone else has access to your passwords ... (Some Trojans have the ability to retrieve a list of passwords from your computer's memory.)

➤ If you find that files or folders are unexpectedly moved, created, copied or deleted from your hard disk(s) ...

➤ If inexplicable message boxes appear on your screen ...

➤ If network shares are added to or removed from your system ...

➤ If software processes start or end without your intervention ...

➤ If you find that your Windows Registry has been modified ...

➤ If your computer suddenly starts playing sound files (looped playback is possible) or images and movie stills are displayed …

➤ If you find that files or folders are being compressed or decompressed without your intervention …

➤ If you find that your browser's plug-ins no longer operate or new plug-ins appear … (For example one common plug-in can initiate a video stream and 'highjack' a remote system.)

➤ If the door to your CD-ROM drive opens and closes for no apparent reason …

… you might suspect that a Trojan server is at work

Of course, spotting Trojans from their activities is a very reactive solution in any case. What we need is a proactive technique that can spot the Trojan before it does any damage. One useful tool here is the little DOS utility called netstat. Netstat is a network monitor built into Windows. You will have to run it from the DOS prompt. Click **Start > Programs > MS-DOS Prompt** to open a DOS session.

On the command line, type **netstat –n**, the response will be a list of all your computer's current network connections. We are interested in the ports which are open and currently listening for a connection, so type **netstat –a**, you will see a list something like Figure 22.2. Now you can check and make sure a Trojan server is not listening on a port. The first two columns are the relevant ones. The first column shows the protocol in use. The second shows the port number (after the colon). Armed with this information, you can check the list of common Trojans given in Appendix 1. The following table shows the most common Trojans and the protocols and ports they normally use.

Figure 22.2 Using netstat to find listening ports

```
Microsoft(R) Windows 98
  (C)Copyright Microsoft Corp 1981-1998.

C:\Windows>netstat -a

Active Connections

  Proto  Local Address          Foreign Address      State
  TCP    Palimpsest:10500       UAIO:0               LISTENING
  TCP    Palimpsest:44334       UAIO:0               LISTENING
  TCP    Palimpsest:44334       UAIO:0               LISTENING
  TCP    Palimpsest:137         UAIO:0               LISTENING
  TCP    Palimpsest:138         UAIO:0               LISTENING
  TCP    Palimpsest:nbsession   UAIO:0               LISTENING
  UDP    Palimpsest:1030        *:*
  UDP    Palimpsest:44334       *:*
  UDP    Palimpsest:nbname      *:*
  UDP    Palimpsest:nbdatagram  *:*

C:\Windows>
```

Table 22.1 Common Trojan Protocols And Ports

Trojan horse	Protocol	Port numbers
Back Orifice	UDP	31337 and 31338
Deep Throat	UDP	2140 and 3150
GirlFriend	TCP	21544
Masters Paradise	TCP	3129, 40421, 40422, 40423 and 40426
NetBus	TCP	12345 and 12346
NetBus 2 Pro	TCP	20034
Sockets de Troie	TCP	5000, 5001 and 50505
Whack-a-mole	TCP	12361 and 12362

Another solution, of course, is to use the anti-Trojan software discussed later in this chapter.

Protecting Yourself Against A Trojan Horse

The best solution – and one that the ancient Trojans should certainly have tried – is not letting the Trojan into your system in the first place. To get inside, a Trojan program has to be downloaded and installed, so all my usual warnings against running e-mail attachments and loading uncertain software apply. It has often been said that the most effective tool in implementing a secure system is an aware user. Knowing what a Trojan is and what it does, makes you better equipped to resist an infection.

One of the most effective weapons against the Trojan invasion is the firewall discussed in the following chapter. If a Trojan does gain access to your system, a good firewall has the ability to alert and block any attempts to access TCP or UDP ports internally or externally. Even with a firewall in place, it is worth undertaking some preventative maintenance. A Trojan is nothing more than a software program. However cleverly it has been coded, it still obeys the same rules as the other software installed on your computer. It requires executable and support files, it takes up space on your disk and it needs entries in the Windows Registry.

Prepare for trouble by making a secure copy of all those files which a Trojan might attempt to modify. This means copying your Windows Registry and the system files **win.ini**, **system.ini**, **config.sys** and **autoexec.bat** (if they exist). It is also a good idea to run netstat to build a profile of the TCP and UPD ports which are legitimate for your system. If you go to the DOS prompt and type **netstat -an >> netstat.txt**, this will write netstat's output to a text file called **netstat.txt** which can be viewed in your text editor. If you subsequently suspect a Trojan attack, you can compare these files with the current versions, using Table 22.2.

Table 22.2 If You Suspect A Trojan Attack ...

File to check	Look for	Notes
The Windows Registry	Changes to **RunServices** and **Run** keys for example: *HKEY_LOCAL_MACHINE\ SOFTWARE\ Microsoft\Windows\ CurrentVersion\RunServices* or *HKEY_LOCAL_MACHINE\ SOFTWARE\Microsoft\Windows\ CurrentVersion\Run*	As implied by the names, these keys are used to run software or software services on your computer. New keys which do not relate to software you have installed suggest programs which are operating without your permission.
win.ini and **system.ini**	New entries introduced by **run** or **load**.	These system files can be used to load programs during the start-up process.
autoexec.bat	New entries which start an executable file such as **[something].exe**, **[something].com** or **[something].bat**. Pay particular attention to lines that indicate programs located within your Windows folder.	As we noted earlier, autoexec.bat is a text batch file which can fire up programs during start-up.
netstat.txt	New ports which have appeared since your original listing.	Many applications open ports, so this does not necessarily indicate Trojan activity. Check the ports opened against those listed in Appendix 1.

Other problems come from the sheer sophistication of some Trojan servers. Earlier in the book, I recommended the use of encryption software to hide critical data. A Trojan can bypass this security. Once installed, the server can send all keyboard entries to the attacker. It doesn't matter how well you encrypt a stored password, once you type it in the open, your keystrokes are transmitted and your password is lost. Let us say you use an online banking service. You start a transaction with a hacker monitoring your key strokes. Just before you close the transaction, the hacker locks your computer and blanks your screen. He then takes over the transaction, changes the data as necessary and transfers the funds to his own account. The worst of this is that you might well attribute the problem to a technical breakdown and only later realize that your money has been stolen.

Identifying specific Trojans can be a difficult operation. Most of them rely on stealth technology to hide from standard security software. For example, Back Orifice 2000, the Trojan we analyzed, modifies the following Registry key: HKEY_LOCAL_MACHINE\SOFTWARE\Microsoft\Windows\CurrentVersion\RunService by adding the following value: "Umgr32.exe"="C:\\Windows\\System\\Umgr32.exe e". *Umgr32.exe* is the default file name for Back Orifice 2000, but this can be modified by whoever is trying to distribute the program. If the file name is modified, the Registry value still contains the path to the designated file name, but many people will hesitate to remove the entry in case it is a legitimate part of the operating system.

The simple fact is that you cannot rely only on firewalls and virus scanners as protection against Trojan software. A firewall configuration is often static, while a Trojan can choose its configuration dynamically. The virus scanner may not detect a well-hidden Trojan or a new variety of the Trojan, particularly if your virus signature file has not been recently updated. To ensure that Trojans are detected and removed, you need to install dedicated software.

The clever use of Java programming can increase the possibility of Trojan horses getting into your system. Java applets are usually loaded without requiring separate permission for each one. It is possible to design a Java applet to mimic a legitimate request for online information. In this way it can operate as a Trojan horse in confidential transactions and quietly report on the keystrokes used to input critical data such as passwords or credit card numbers.

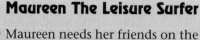

Maureen The Leisure Surfer

Maureen needs her friends on the internet and when they send her e-mails, she is quick to open them. Recently she received an e-mail from a friend which invited her to check the jokes contained in an attachment. Of course Maureen's friend had not intended to send the e-mail, the Trojan server on his computer had taken care of that. Maureen's computer is now a slave to the Trojan's master as well. Although her computer is now a little unpredictable, Maureen has put that down to the odd technical glitch. She continues to live her online life, totally unaware that her machine is just one of a regiment of computers in the front line of an attack on an anti-hacker website.

Anti-Trojan Software

There is a large number of Trojan horses currently on the loose, but only a handful of them cause regular problems. Many anti-virus programs claim to detect and remove Trojans, but some of them are singularly inept in this department. Remember that a Trojan is not a virus as such. Certainly a Trojan can carry a virus or can be used to imitate the effects of a virus, but a Trojan, as we are defining the term, is a client/server program which provides remote management facilities using the internet as a vector. Some Trojans are particularly crafty in fooling virus scanners. They change their configuration and file lengths to constantly stay ahead of the latest virus definitions. In addition to this, Trojans are adept at hiding from AV software. Virus scanners are often only set up to check obvious executable files such as those with the classic **.exe** extension. A Trojan server can start from the Registry using a name such as **ftplog.txt** which might easily be missed by a scanner.

This leaves us needing a dedicated anti-Trojan program, and there are quite a few of these about. The best programs use a number of different techniques to detect and destroy active and passive Trojan servers. Jammer, for example, offers three lines of defence. First, it monitors your Registry. As we have noted, in order to run, any software program has to modify the Windows Registry and a Trojan is no different. Jammer detects any changes to the Registry keys that handle system start-up and alerts you by displaying a dialog box which enables you to stop a particular key from operating. Jammer also monitors your computer ports for any sign of scanning. If such an attempt is detected, the scan is blocked and the attacker's IP address and, where accessible, the name of his ISP is recorded. Finally Jammer constantly monitors your system for any sign of Trojan activity.

Figure 22.3 TrojanShield scanning for Trojans

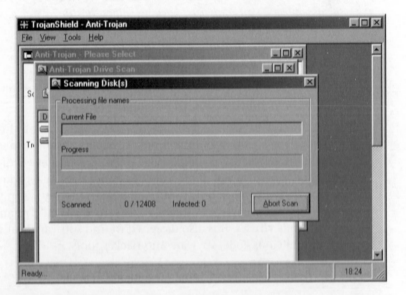

Figure 22.3 shows one of the most efficient anti-Trojan programs in operation. Like similar utilities, TrojanShield packages a series of applications into one suite. The console module constantly checks for intrusion attempts, while the tracer module tries to track down the intruder. The anti-Trojan module scans for Trojan servers. What lifts TrojanShield above some of the other anti-Trojan products are the process and start-up managers.

The process managers we looked at before – utilities such as WinPatrol and the trusty **Ctrl-Alt-Delete** three-finger salute – are intended to display all the processes running on your computer. This does not always reveal Trojans. The TrojanShield version does and allows you to terminate any processes you are not happy with. We have also looked at start-up managers earlier in the book. Trojan servers are designed to configure themselves so they start with the system either by loading from an entry in the Windows Registry or from one of the system start-up files. Many Trojans make themselves invisible to traditional start-up managers, but TrojanShield's start-up manager usually finds them and allows you to block them before they take over your system.

A very different approach has been taken by a new generation of anti-Trojan software. As we noted at the very start of this chapter, the term Trojan horse has been redefined over the last few years. Originally referring to the software in which a program was concealed, then turned around to mean the concealed program, many people now use the term to refer to the client/server programs we have been looking at. Strictly speaking, these should be called 'backdoors' and are one of a number of new menaces which are not strictly viruses. Our example of this type of software is PestPatrol which claims to handle:

> *ANSI bombs, answering machine hacks, carding, denial of service attack tools, disassemblers, virus droppers, hacking guides, hostile Java, icq, mail bombers, password crackers, phreaking, surreptitious remote control, remote monitoring, network scanning, sniffers, spoofers, spyware, surveillance, Trojans, Trojan creation tools, virus creation tools, virus writing tools, and word lists used by password crackers.*

It is in this grey area that traditional anti-virus programs often go astray. PestPatrol lumps all these together and calls them pests.

Figure 22.4 shows PestPatrol's configuration window. From here you can decide the file types to be checked and the drives or folders to be scanned for infection. You can also instruct PestPatrol to look for the spyware modules we discussed earlier. PestPatrol can be configured to watch for someone using the hacker tools we mentioned in Chapter 21. It also provides an online update system to keep your pest definitions up-to-date. To sum up, while PestPatrol is designed to find Trojans the way an anti-virus product finds viruses, it is also designed to find software that might fall into the grey areas of malicious code, spyware and hacker tools.

Figure 22.4 PestPatrol's configuration screen

Whether you call them Trojan horses, RAT Trojans, backdoors or pests, the type of client/server programs we have analysed in this chapter represent a real danger to computer security. In Chapter 23 we will look at the last great security tool, the mighty firewall.

Jammer can be downloaded from www.agnitum.com. TrojanShield is available as 15-day-valid shareware from www.trojanshield.com An evaluation version of PestPatrol can be obtained from www.pestpatrol.com The Cleaner is also available as a free trial version from www.moosoft.com

Chapter 22 – Security Checklist

1 A Trojan client/server program is a common form of attack. The server is secretly installed on your computer, while the hacker makes use of the client module to take control of your machine. Such attacks are normally tried over the internet, but they can also be applied to corporate networks.

2 Most Trojan servers are distributed via the internet and end up attacking computers pretty much at random. Finding the IP addresses of infected machines usually requires the use of a port scanner, but the increasing use of broadband connections which give each computer a static IP address makes the hacker's task much easier.

3   You might be able to detect a Trojan at work by spotting symptoms such as unusual computer behaviour. You can also use the netstat utility built into Windows to check for open network ports used by Trojans. Appendix 1 carries a useful checklist of Trojans and the protocols and ports they make use of.

4   Most Trojan servers are carried as e-mail attachments or embedded within apparently harmless software downloads. Our usual precautions are required to prevent this type of infection. A good firewall will prevent a Trojan server from contacting the remote client.

5   Sensible anti-Trojan security precautions involve making a secure copy of all system files including the Windows Registry. These can subsequently be checked against the current versions to verify that Trojans have not modified them.

6   Trojan servers can be sophisticated enough to bypass many of the more obvious security precautions such as encryption. For example, some Trojans can log keystrokes. If you type a password into a web form, the Trojan will record the keys used and pass the information back to the controlling hacker. Anti-virus software cannot be relied on to detect and delete Trojan programs.

7   To be certain of dealing with Trojans, you might need to install a dedicated anti-Trojan program such as Jammer or TrojanShield. Such software uses a range of techniques to detect and remove Trojans, including Registry monitoring, process management and port scanning.

Building A Wall Around Your Computer

The Mighty Firewall

Several times in this book I have referred to a firewall and each time I have postponed discussing it in any detail. You have waited long enough. If ever a piece of software deserved a chapter to itself, it is the mighty firewall. Properly configured, a firewall will protect your computer from attackers trying to get in and prevent anything from getting out without your permission. In many ways it is the ultimate defence. Some people will tell you that the term derives from architecture, but I prefer to think it comes from American stock car racing. Stock cars are constructed with a flame-proof barrier which shields the driver from engine fires. This is the firewall.

A firewall is such a good idea that it is amazing that one is not built into all operating systems as standard. It's been a long time coming, but now it is! Windows XP, the latest version of Microsoft's operating system, contains its own integrated firewall. How effective it will prove to be has yet to be established. Certainly Microsoft's attempt at a firewall has a lot to live up to. There are some formidably efficient products currently available, and old hands might be unwilling to gamble with proven security. We shall see.

This is not to say that there aren't impostors about. Many products which provide some degree of network security are claimed by their manufacturers to be firewalls. Some of these provide such a weak layer of defence that they are less than useless. Since the correct operation of a firewall can be precisely defined, there should be no difficulty in identifying a product worthy of the name. As is so often the case, unscrupulous manufacturers try to trade on consumer ignorance. In the next section I am going to explain exactly what a firewall is and how it works. After reading this, you will be an expert and impossible to deceive.

How A Firewall Works

A firewall is basically a very simple device, which is why it is so effective. It is not, of course, a physical barrier to data transmission, like a switch. Instead it is a wall of computer code which will not allow packets of data to pass through in either direction unless they conform to a set of rules which you, as the operator, define. As data arrives at the wall it is inspected by the firewall software. If it doesn't pass the tests, it is refused entry – if it does, it is allowed through. A good firewall is a stern judge. There is no appeal against its decisions and no way of getting round it. There might be no such thing as complete protection, but a properly configured firewall comes damn close!

Way back in Chapter 14, I referred to data packets. All communication over a network – whether that network is simply two computers wired together or the mighty internet itself – consists of machines exchanging individual packets of data. Packets travel back and forth between connected computers as simply illustrated in Figure 23.1. A typical packet sequence might consist of one machine sending a request, the two machines agreeing a protocol, the receiving machine transmitting the requested data and the first machine acknowledging receipt. Of course some communications are enormously more complicated than this, but the basic sequence of packet exchange remains the same.

Now think for a moment about the packets themselves. Whatever other information it contains, each packet must carry a destination address – so it is sent to the correct computer – and a return address – so that the receiving computer knows where to reply to. Network addresses consist of two components: an IP address which uniquely identifies the computer on the network and a port number which specifies where to connect a particular type of service. In short, any computer communication is a two-way conversation consisting of individual packets of data travelling between two connected machines.

372

Figure 23.1 Computer communication consists of a stream of individual data packets

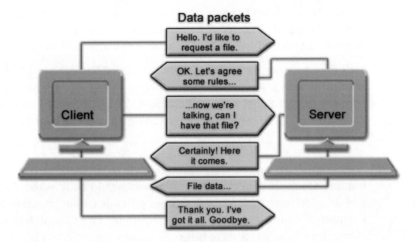

Data packets

Now a firewall sits at the interface between a computer and a network, and from there it can inspect each data packet before it is allowed in to or out of your system. This means that it can vet packets before they are seen by your computer's software. If a packet arrives carrying the correct IP address, the firewall will then look at the port it is requesting. (You will remember from the previous chapter that software ports are associated with different services or types of communication.) If your firewall has been told to accept data on that port, it will then pass the packet on to your system software. But there are no compromises in a firewall's rules. If a packet does not conform to the rules, it is firmly rejected and that port is slammed shut.

A good firewall can be fine tuned by configuring rules based on the four pieces of information each packet must carry. Table 23.1 looks at a sample of firewall rules.

Table 23.1 Sample Firewall Rules

	Client's IP address	**Client's port number**
Server's IP address	Permit all packets to the client which originate from a particular server.	Refuse all packets from a particular server which are intended for a specified port.
Server's port number	Refuse only those packets from a particular server whose return address specifies a particular port on that server.	Permits only those packets from a server which are intended for a specified port but whose return address does not specify a particular port on the server.

As you can see from the table, it is possible to create quite complex rules by manipulating the four information elements that a packet carries. This means that a firewall can be highly selective in which packets it allows in.

Let's take an example and see how this works. You are already familiar with the concept of a web server. Connections to a web server are normally configured to connect to port 80 which handles the HTTP protocol. If you wished to set up your computer as a web server, you could define a rule for your firewall which stated:

Allow any incoming connections to port 80, but close all other ports.

Now any clients on the web would be able to connect to your web server via port 80, but any attempts to access any other port would be rejected. Even if your system was running software which opened other ports (a Trojan program for example – see Chapter 22), nothing could connect to them. The firewall would ensure that to other computers those ports were not only closed, but effectively invisible.

A firewall can not only block incoming data packets, it can also control your outgoing connections. When you wish to connect to a web server, your outgoing packet contains the IP address and port number of that server. Most firewalls are preconfigured to accept this type of packet using a rule such as:

Permit connections from my IP address to any server address on port 80 (HTTP).

As we have seen, network communication requires the exchange of packets, so what happens to the return packets from the web server you are trying to contact? Again, this is no problem for a firewall. As each packet of data is received, a packet is returned acknowledging its receipt. Such packets carry a special piece of information known as the ACK (acknowledge) bit. When you think about it, only the very first packet – the one which is sent to initiate the connection, does not carry the ACK bit. All the others, whether they are carrying requested data or asking for new data, will also be acknowledging the preceding packet. By checking for the presence of the ACK bit, a firewall can determine whether a packet is part of an existing communication, which would be allowed automatically, or initiating a new communication, which would be checked against the rules.

Some firewalls are clever enough to provide filtering at the application level. This is one step up from simple packet inspection and requires the firewall to work out which application is sending or receiving packets, and then apply rules to these. A rule at this level might be:

Always allow Internet Explorer to connect to any server address on port 80 (HTTP).

Figure 23.2 shows this type of configuration. ZoneAlarm Pro is a personal firewall we will be looking at later in this chapter. From the illustration you can see a list of programs which are allowed network connections of some kind. Rules for each program are divided between local network and internet groups. They can involve

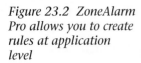

Figure 23.2 ZoneAlarm Pro allows you to create rules at application level

automatic approval (as shown by the tick to the right of the application name) or ask before passing (the question mark). The **Options** button allows you to fine tune these generalized rules down to the IP address and port level.

Most firewalls also provide a warning box when an unexpected attempt at a connection is encountered. The warning will usually tell you where the intercepted packet has come from and where it is trying to get to. This is a useful feature since, first, it lets you know if someone is trying to break into your system and, second, it points you to the address of the culprit. The information provided can be difficult to analyse, but could enable you to alert your ISP, or network administrator where appropriate, that hackers are on the rampage. Since connections involve packets travelling in both directions, you will also be alerted when a program on your own computer attempts to contact a network server. This is particularly useful in helping you to track down and eliminate spyware modules or Trojan horses which have infiltrated your system.

Not all firewalls offer the full range of features I have described. Let me close this section with a short list of features which a class one firewall should provide. Your own security might not require all of these, so you should pick your firewall according to its ability to meet your needs.

➤ A firewall should provide packet-level monitoring to shield your computer from unwanted network intrusions by verifying each packet of inbound or outbound data received.

➤ A firewall should provide application-level filtering which allows you to control network connections based on the programs you are running on your computer.

➤ A firewall should allow you to define simple or complex rules which can be designed to fit your networks needs.

➤ A firewall should provide effective visual warnings of any attempts to establish a network connection from inside or outside your computer.

➤ It goes without saying that a firewall should be easy enough to set up and totally reliable in operation.

 Technically inclined readers might be interested in some of the methods used by a firewall to monitor connections. As we have seen above, packet filtering simply checks packets and passes or refuses them based on the rules you define. More complex is status inspection which requires the firewall to remember the status of each connection and use this information to make a more informed decision on whether or not a packet should be allowed to pass. Finally, some firewalls make use of a proxy service. You will remember from Chapter 16 that a proxy server stands between your computer and a network, intercepting and handling requests. A firewall-based proxy server adds another level of security to your system since both client and the server only see the proxy and not your computer.

Firewall Strengths And Weaknesses

I hope you are still with me at this point. Firewalls are complex entities and it is often fear of installing one which prevents users from taking advantage of the security they provide. Of course, if your computer never connects to a network or if your network is a tightly controlled local affair with no external access, you do not need a firewall. But you should seriously consider installing one if any of the following are true.

➤ You use your computer to access any network – and especially the internet – and wish to protect your system against outside invaders.

➤ You wish to prevent malicious software, installed without your permission, from passing out your private data. This includes spyware and Trojan programs.

➤ You need to access your own computer remotely. (This includes the use of any remote control programs such as PC Anywhere or Laplink.)

➤ You are operating any sort of internet server such as Microsoft's Personal Web Server – even if that server is only intended for your local network.

Despite their strengths, firewalls cannot solve all your security problems. For a start, they provide no protection against internal attackers. Disgruntled employees or even members of your own family are quite capable of creating breaches for their own use and these breaches can subsequently be exploited by outsiders. Some firewalls are configured to give network users private IDs that can't be accessed from the internet. These IDs can be spoofed to allow illegal access to the network. Some security experts estimate that over 80 per cent of all security attacks come from inside the firewall. However diligent companies are about external security, their systems are still at risk if they forget to address internal security issues.

Eugene The Businessman

Eugene is confident – perhaps too confident – about the security provided by his network's firewall. He has not reckoned on the attentions of Harry, his customer service representative. Harry feels hard done by. He was bypassed for an internal promotion a few months back and is now determined to exact his revenge. When he is not fielding calls from unhappy customers, Harry beavers away trying to wreck his employer's computer system. He configures special firewall rules which allow outsiders access to undefended ports, then he posts information on these weaknesses to hacker newsgroups. So far no one has responded to these messages – Eugene's company is hardly a high-profile target, but sooner or later some bored hacker will come calling. Harry will get his revenge and Eugene will be looking for a new customer service representative.

Hackers attempt to breach firewalls by implanting viruses in e-mail attachments or other material downloaded from the internet. These viruses can be designed to burrow into a network and discover private IDs and other data which can be used to bypass the firewall. They can also make use of the denial of service attacks (DoS) we looked at in Chapter 21 by sending so many data packets from commandeered computers that the firewall is overwhelmed, and the network administrator is forced to shut down the system as a protective measure.

Third-party Firewall Software

As always when we come to consider third-party software, there is a wide choice of firewalls available. In this case, however, because our requirements are so precise, we are in a better position than most to rate the various programs on offer. One of the best ways to test a firewall is to use Steve Gibson's excellent (and free) Firewall Leakage Tester utility, shown in Figure 23.3. With a firewall installed and running, you start the program and click the **Test for Leaks** button. Firewalls that operate at the application level will then ask whether the Firewall Leakage Tester should be permitted to access the internet. You say no, and the tester then strains to get through the firewall. If it can't find a path out, the message shown in Figure 23.3 appears and you can consider

Figure 23.3 Gibson Research's LeakTest firewall tester

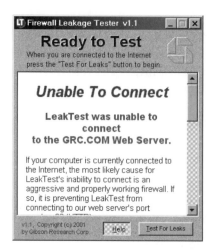

your firewall safe. The Firewall Leakage Tester has been widely used to test different programs. Those that have passed the test include the McAfee Firewall, the Tiny Personal Firewall, the Symantec/Norton firewall and, my own personal favourite, ZoneAlarm Pro. Those that failed the test include AtGuard, BlackICE Defender and the eSafe Desktop firewall.

Not surprisingly, we won't be looking at any of the failures. Of the successes, two products stand out in my opinion. The Tiny Personal Firewall is an excellent free program, but not, perhaps, one for the beginner. Configuring the Tiny firewall can be quite a complex operation and requires a user to spend some time learning about rules, ports and protocols. Figure 23.4 shows one section of the firewall configuration

Figure 23.4 Configuring rules for the Tiny Personal Firewall program

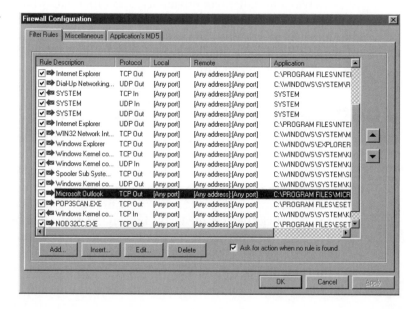

Figure 23.5 Editing firewall rules

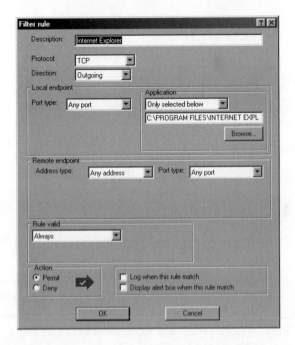

window, which lists the filtering rules currently in operation. To an extent, rule creation can be left to the firewall. When it encounters a packet or an application trying to connect in either direction, it throws up a warning window which offers to create a rule based on the decision you make. Such a rule can then be applied to any similar encounters.

Once created, a rule can subsequently be modified. Figure 23.5 shows a rule which permits Internet Explorer to access the internet using TCP (the Transmission Control Protocol). You will notice that the rule only applies to outgoing connections and only to the specific application. The **Remote endpoint** section refers to servers to which the application is permitted to connect. This is set to **Any address** and **Any port** – sensible settings for an internet connection, but these could be changed to only allow access to a specified IP address such as a proxy server or addresses within a predefined range such as **123.123.123.0 to 123.123.123.255**. As set up the rule is valid at all times, but once more this could be changed to only permit the connection at certain times on certain days. Finally, note that the rule can be easily inverted to **Deny** rather than **Permit** the connection, by using the radio buttons at the bottom of the window.

I have gone through this rule in some detail because it illustrates the way in which most firewalls can be configured. If you prefer a simpler, less flexible but equally powerful firewall, you cannot do better then ZoneAlarm – a free download – or ZoneAlarm Pro – it's big brother.

379

Check This Out...

The Tiny Personal Firewall can be downloaded free of charge from a number of the web's larger software archives, including Tiny Software's preferred source at <u>download.cnet</u>.com The free version of ZoneAlarm, and the paid-for, but better equipped ZoneAlarm Pro can be found at <u>www.zonelabs.com</u>

I have never been able to fault ZoneAlarm which, as far as I can see, is flawless in operation and extremely simple to set up. ZoneAlarm gets away from the concept of defining filter rules in favour of application-level controls. Look back to Figure 23.2 to remind yourself of this method. During installation, ZoneAlarm asks you if you wish to create a standing rule for your browser. After this, any application which attempts a network connection is frozen while ZoneAlarm asks whether you wish to allow it. You can agree or refuse each time an application tries to connect or you can instruct ZoneAlarm to generate a fixed rule which is applied as required.

An additional feature of ZoneAlarm Pro is its ability to quarantine e-mail attachments. We know how hazardous these can be. Clicking **Security** > **Advanced** brings up the window shown in Figure 23.6. The different tabs allow you to adjust ZoneAlarm's security settings for both your local network and the internet, to identify computers which you wish to be placed in your local zone and to access the MailSafe feature. While we have discussed some of the e-mail attachments which can be dangerous, MailSafe can handle a much wider range. If it encounters a listed attachment, MailSafe

Figure 23.6 Using ZoneAlarm's Mailsafe feature

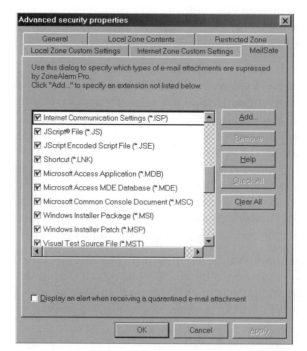

renames it to **[original name].zl*** (where ***** represents a number or a letter). With the attachment thus prevented from running, you have the option of changing its extension back to what it was. If you are uncertain of the file's validity, you can double-click on it to launch a wizard which provides options for opening, deleting, renaming or making further checks on its origins and content.

While as always, the final decision is yours, I believe that there is no better way to protect your system than by installing a good firewall. With both of our 'featured products' available in free versions, you cannot even plead poverty as an excuse. Take my advice and get one today.

Physical Barriers To Intruders

'There's no better computer security than a padlock.' I can't remember who said that, but he (or she) was absolutely correct. We have spent a lot of time looking at different types of software security products, but at the end of the day, a computer which is switched off and safely locked up is probably the only computer which is 100 per cent secure. Among all the high-tech solutions, it is easy to overlook the simple mechanical precautions which cannot be bypassed by clever hackers.

Prevents Outside Access

For instance, you can unplug your modem or network cable. This low-tech operation removes, at a stroke, any possibility of an external software attack on your system. Switching off your computer, although increasing the chances of mechanical failure (see Chapter 2), is a one-step answer to computer security. Depending on your circumstances, locking the door to your computer room might be an effective solution to safeguarding your data, as might storing data on removable disks which can be locked up in a safe.

Hardware Locks

With all the online dangers to computer security, it is easy to overlook plain old-fashioned theft. Many companies suffer from continuous pilfering which doesn't stop at floppy disks and the occasional pack of paper. Keyboards, mice and even whole computers can disappear. Home users are also at risk. Burglars are always interested in an expensive computer, with Personal Digital Assistants (PDAs) and laptops particularly favoured. The obvious solution is to lock such items to your desktop. Today's mechanical security products are neat, efficient and non-intrusive. Look, for example at the range of desktop locks shown in Figure 23.7. The items illustrated are from the GoLocks range marketed by Noble Security Systems. They include a security cable which protects the CPU, monitor, keyboard and mouse with a single rail mounted system. There is even an option which can secure computer memory against theft.

Figure 23.7 A range of PC and peripheral locks from Noble

For companies facing expensive equipment theft, security measures might include security locks, round-the-clock guards or even biometric systems which use personal characteristics such as fingerprints to authenticate users. In more secure environments, biometrics is replacing password security. Computer workstations might be equipped with a fingerprint reader. A user needs to place his finger on a scanning device which confirms his print against those of authorized staff before he is permitted to access his machine. Companies also face the risk of internal sabotage. We have already seen how disgruntled employees can damage a computer system in return for some real or imagined slight. An employee who feels he is underpaid might decide to increase his earnings by stealing and re-selling company property. Once again, mechanical locks are a sensible precaution.

A computer network is always physically vulnerable. Thieves – both casual and professional – regularly break into office buildings to steal or simply to vandalize. Sensible precautions include locking critical data servers into secure rooms, bolting expensive equipment to floors or desks and marking all hardware with indelible and concealed labels to aid recovery. Security companies have come up with some cunning ideas to deter theft. Laptops can be equipped with audible alarms which scream when they are snatched. There are also add-on components designed to emit radio signals which can be tracked with specialized positioning systems. How much of this is appropriate to your needs will depend on the value of your equipment and the data it stores. But with a good computer costing roughly 100 times the price of a simple desktop lock, the mathematics are hard to dispute!

And that's it! It has been an exhausting ride to get this far – thank you for your patience. In this book I have tried to cover most aspects of computer security. I have done my bit – now it is over to you. The final chapter brings together most of the suggestions from previous chapters in a comprehensive security plan. Your mission, should you choose to accept it, is to put the plan into practice. Good luck!

Chapter 23 – Security Checklist

1   A firewall is a software barrier installed on a network. It examines each packet of data as it tries to arrive or depart, and passes only those which conform to a set of predefined rules. By default, a package is blocked.

2   Some firewalls also allow filtering at application level. Here you can specify which applications can connect to which services.

3   There are various third-party firewalls available, some of which are not considered to be secure. Among the better ones are ZoneLabs' ZoneAlarm and the Tiny Personal Firewall, both of which have been proved effective by firewall leak testers. If you intend taking your computer security seriously, get one and install it now.

4   One security precaution which is often overlooked is providing simple, physical barriers to computer access. Computers can be switched off, hardware can be secured with locks and rails and the doors to computer facilities can be locked shut.

Now DO Something ...

Developing A Security Strategy

This is the final chapter – we can both breathe a sigh of relief. To help you to work out your own security strategy, the table below brings together suggestions from the rest of the book and groups them into categories. Each suggested action is given a priority (low, medium or high) to help you develop a logical plan of action. Note that within each priority actions are in alphabetical order.

Category 1 Hardware Security

Priority	Action
High	Always unplug your modem from the telephone socket when you are not online. This will prevent lightening strikes from using the cable to zap your computer.
High	To safeguard against electrical surges and spikes, invest in an electrical extension cable with surge protection and plug your computer into that rather than the mains.

High	Save your work regularly to minimize lost data if there is a power cut.
Medium	Before you attempt any DIY computer building, read the manuals that relate to the hardware you have chosen and write down any information printed on the components themselves. Make diagrams of connections and jumper settings.
Medium	If your data is critical, consider leaving your computer switched on all the time to avoid the stress that power-ups impose on your hardware.
Medium	One security precaution which is often overlooked is providing simple, physical barriers to computer access. Computers can be switched off, hardware can be secured with locks and bolts and the doors to computer facilities can be locked shut.
Medium	Try to plan your hard disk(s) configuration to provide the maximum protection for stored data. There are several options here, with the securest being a pair of drives, each of which store all your essential data. If this is not viable, at least try to physically separate your programs from your data using logical drives.
Medium	Try to work in a cool environment and keep smoke away from your computer.
Low	Approach buying a new computer with caution – an upgrade might be more cost-effective. Start with a written list of requirements and check what is offered against that list. Beware of bundles – the peripherals offered are seldom the ones you really need.

Category 2 Software Security

Priority	Action
High	Before you make any changes to your system's start-up files, take the precaution of saving back-ups of the originals to a secure location. In addition to saving a copy of the Windows Registry, you should also save **Autoexec.bat**, **Config.sys**, **System.ini** and **Win.ini** by copying and renaming them.
High	Watch out for programs which load at start-up without your permission. They can use up vital system resources and you cannot be certain they are operating in your best interests. You need to monitor every process which auto-loads and remove those which are not contributing to your needs.

Medium	Be cautious when it comes to installing your operating system. Windows' 'typical' installation can load your computer with utilities you don't need, some of which can be security hazards. Choose the 'custom' option and make your own decisions.
Medium	If you are installing new software from any source, do not assume that it is free from bugs. While the major manufacturers can afford extensive prerelease testing, smaller companies and individual programmers cannot. Remember that badly written programs will not only crash and burn, they can also damage your operating system.
Medium	If you decide to install trial applications, make sure you only add one at a time. The best option is to install a program, then thoroughly test it for several days before deciding whether to keep it or not.
Medium	Microsoft provides a Windows Update system which allows you to download and install updates to the operating system from the internet. Make use of it to keep your computer's OS in good shape. It is also worth checking for any new security patches available from the Microsoft website.
Medium	When obvious steps fail to work, rogue programs can often be halted from the Close Program box, generated by pressing down the **Control (Ctrl)**, **Alt** and **Delete** keys simultaneously. The resulting window will show you all the processes running on your computer and give you the opportunity to shut each one down individually.
Low	Avoid installing a brand new Windows distribution as soon as it is launched. Wait for the second, or even third, release, by which time most of the bugs and security holes will have been sorted out.
Low	Be prepared for software breakdowns. Know the signs and watch out for them. If your applications crash, you can try restarting them or even restarting your system, but be prepared to get rid of applications that constantly misbehave.
Low	Carefully consider the application software you need. Pick software logically to suit your needs and budget. Do not be tempted to load up applications just because they're available or cheap.
Low	It is worth keeping your workspace tidy, cleaning out your hard drive(s) and running an error checker on a weekly basis. Housekeeping not only makes it easier to find the files you need, it also frees up space on your hard disk and keeps your computer running sweetly.

Low	Take a note of any error messages that are thrown up by the operating system. While these are often mysterious, they can suggest how to resolve the problem indicated.
Low	Uninstall routines often fail to clean up properly. They can leave a lot of debris behind to clutter up your hard disk. Using good-quality uninstaller software can solve this problem, but otherwise you will need to resort to manually removing files, folders and shortcuts. There will often be orphaned entries left in the Windows Registry, but you should not attempt to clean these up unless you really know what you are doing.

Category 3 Protecting Your Computer Data

Priority	Action
High	Decide on suitable passwords or pass-phrases. Long and unpredictable are the golden rules. Always avoid single words or phrases that might be guessed by someone who knows you. Select multiple words or a mixture of random letters and digits. And remember never to write your passwords down anywhere.
High	Don't delay working out and implementing a back-up strategy. Although setting one up initially can take a lot of time, once the folders and files you wish to secure (your back-up set) is decided, back-ups can be handled quickly and smoothly. They can even be automated to take place in the background with no user intervention at all.
High	Look closely at the data stored on your own computer and decide how much, if any, needs to be encrypted. Remember that you cannot assume that your computer is secure. Friends, relatives and colleagues at work can sit down at it, and if you have a network or internet connection, hackers can access it remotely. If you store any kind of critical data on your machine, encryption is vital.
High	Secure file deletion requires the use of specialist wiping software. Any number of suitable tools are available from the internet. Check out the features and costs of several before installing your preferred program.
High	When deleting a file, the number of times you overwrite file data should be determined by the file's sensitivity. One pass would be sufficient for a mildly confidential file which is unlikely to be of interest to anyone else. At the other end of the scale, the so-called

Guttman Method which proposes 35 passes would render even the most hazardous files unrecoverable.

High   Total security might involve storing your encrypted files in special containers, which can be unlocked and mounted as virtual drives. A further refinement would be to create your encrypted containers on removable media which could be securely stored away from your computer. Using rewritable CD-ROMs is a good way of doing this.

High   When you create or edit a file, all sorts of traces of that file are also created. Some of these are shortcuts to that file, intended to help you find it quickly. Others are references to that file within the relevant application. There are also temporary versions of the file created by the application. Secure file deletion requires that all these traces are also erased from your computer.

Medium   A simple way of hiding individual files is to store them in a folder which is not normally used for data, and/or to change their extensions so that they appear to be different types of files. A more complex, but much more effective technique is to create a false file type which appears to the OS to be legitimate and to change each file's extension to match the new type.

Medium   Locking your screen-saver so that the desktop cannot be accessed without a password is a simple precaution to prevent snoopers from looking at your work while you are absent from your computer.

Medium   To establish your back-up set, you need to consider not only your data files, but also operating system and application files.

Medium   You will also benefit from securely locking your desktop. Before installing a locking program, it is sensible to reconfigure your system's BIOS to prevent an intruder from getting past your lock.

Low   You will need to decide on the back-up media to use. There are several options listed in the table earlier in the chapter. Consider such criteria as price, read and write speed and storage capacity. A good choice for many people is a CD writer, although regular back-ups might get through a lot of CD-ROMs.

Category 4 Enemy Action

Priority	Action
High	Be vigilant! Watch for symptoms of virus activity on your computer. In general, be suspicious of any unexpected computer activity. If your hard drive is whirring or your computer does strange things, don't assume everything is all right. Investigate at once.
High	Invest in a good anti-virus program, install it, use it and keep it up-to-date by downloading new anti-virus definitions as soon as they are published.
High	Kill the Windows Scripting Host unless you have a specific need for it and, while you are at it, disable scripting by moving your e-mail client to the Restricted Zone.
High	Never install new software without checking it for viruses – and make sure you check it using the most up-to-date set of virus definitions available for your scanner.
High	Never open an e-mail attachment unless you are absolutely certain that it is genuine. Remember that your friends and colleagues can inadvertently spread viruses, so a recognized name on the message does not guarantee its safety. If in doubt, delete it immediately.
High	Sensible anti-Trojan security precautions involve making a secure copy of all system files including the Windows Registry. These can subsequently be checked against the current versions to verify that Trojans have not modified them.
High	There are several third-party firewalls available, some of which are not considered to be secure. Among the better ones are ZoneLabs' ZoneAlarm and the Tiny Personal Firewall, both of which have been proved effective by firewall leak testers. If you intend taking your computer security seriously, get one and install it now.
High	To be certain of dealing with Trojans, you might need to install a dedicated anti-Trojan program such as Jammer or TrojanShield. Such software uses a range of techniques to detect and remove Trojans, including Registry monitoring, process management and port scanning.
High	Watch out for Office macro viruses which can creep in inside documents. Make sure you set your macro security to the highest possible setting.

Medium	Change your computer's boot-up sequence so that it starts from your hard disk and not from a floppy.
Medium	You might be able to detect a Trojan at work by spotting symptoms such as unusual computer behaviour. You can also use the netstat utility built into Windows to check for open network ports used by Trojans.

Category 5 Online Security

Priority	Action
High	Always remember that as soon as you connect your computer to a network, you expose it to a new level of risks. A network connection implies providing access in to and out of your computer, and there are plenty of people who will abuse that access.
High	If you need to send confidential information by e-mail, you will need to install reliable encryption software. You must ensure both that the strength of the encryption is adequate to your security needs and that the public key is safely stored and validated in case someone tries to 'spoof' your security by substituting his own public key for yours.
High	It is often useful to store confidential data such as credit card or PIN numbers on your computer. Consider writing such information to an ordinary text file, then securely encrypting it.
High	Like yourself, your children can quickly become targets for unscrupulous business interests. It is important that children are made aware of this danger and advised never to pass on any information which might subsequently be used for online marketing.
High	Spyware are programs concealed within other applications which record personal details from your computer then use the back-channel of your internet connection to pass these details on to interested parties. Use Lavasoft's Ad-aware to detect and remove spyware programs currently installed on your own computer.
High	There are particular dangers attached to online chatting. Persuade your children that they must never reveal personal details to anyone in a chat room. Some filtering software also includes features which can restrict access to undesirable sites.

High	To permanently delete any traces of your browsing, you will have to rely on third-party clean-up software such as WindowWasher or CyberScrub. These will flush out all the records stored on your system and overwrite them so that they cannot be retrieved.
High	You need to enforce three security rules. First, a network must be protected against unauthorized intruders. Second, an authorized user must only be able to access those shares he has permissions for. Third, data on the network must be protected against deliberate or accidental damage.
High	When shopping online, you need to make sure that transactions take place through a secure server. This is indicated in several ways – a padlock or key icon in the browser bar, an *https://* page address, and a warning box when you enter are the easiest to recognize. Never make any transactions over an insecure server since all the information you reveal can be seen by outsiders.
Medium	Browsing records are stored in several different ways. Cookies are small text files loaded on to your computer by a website, your **Temporary Internet Files** folder is the cache in which Windows stores all the page content from the sites you visit and your **History** folder stores web addresses you have visited in the previous three. Anonymity requires that all of these records are deleted.
Medium	Configure your internet connection so that it cannot dial into the internet without your permission. A lot of programs these days try to exploit the default setting to contact websites whenever they want to.
Medium	If you decide that you are going to control your children's browsing, you will need to consider some kind of filtering software. There is a wide choice available, including address filtering and word filtering types. Some ISPs offer filtration at portal level, there are website rating systems or you might choose to purchase filtering software such as Net Nanny.
Medium	If you decide to monitor your children's web use, you can check your computer's browsing records or install monitor software such as a key logging program. If your children are computer-savvy, you might also need to reconfigure software to prevent them from deleting their tracks.
Medium	Internet connections can be created in several ways. It is worth taking the extra time to set your connection up manually. In this way you maintain the maximum control over your internet activity.

Medium	It is important to maximize the security offered by your browser. Security settings can be configured from within Internet Explorer. You should change any potentially hazardous setting to either disable or prompt. The prompt setting gives you the option of allowing an activity but can prove irritating as confirmation boxes keep popping up when you are browsing.
Medium	Remember that encrypting an e-mail does not protect the integrity of the data it contains. If your message is intercepted and modified, the data is lost and decryption software will no longer be able to decipher the text.
Medium	Spam is defined as unsolicited e-mail – although some companies claim it is a legitimate marketing tool. To deal with spam you should configure suitable filters within your e-mail client or install anti-spam software to intercept and manage incoming messages.
Medium	To control access to network resources, work out a detailed resource management strategy. Decide which folders you wish to share, who will have access to them and what form that access will take. Where practical, restrict access to read only. This prevents users from modifying files.
Medium	To privatize your browsing, you can use a proxy server. In addition to adding anonymity, using a proxy server can speed up your access speed by sending you commonly requested resources stored in its own data cache.
Low	It might be worth reassessing your ISP from a security perspective. In particular, you might check your ISP's privacy policy to make sure that they are respecting the confidentiality of your personal details.
Low	To speed up your browsing, consider employing software to filter unwanted content out of the pages you download. Such programs can be configured to recognize advertisement blocks from their dimensions and can often control other annoying web elements such as animations.
Low	You should also consider the possibility that your browsing is being monitored locally. There are programs which can check for these so-called 'snoopers' and advise you if you are being watched.

Part 6
Resources

I've provided two appendices intended to help you in your search for security.

Appendix 1 lists all the common Trojan horse programs along with details intended to help you with identifying any at work in your own system. Appendix 2 is a useful checklist of all those Three-letter Acronyms (TLAs) which computer specialists use to confuse the rest of us.

List Of Common Trojan Horses

This appendix provides two lists to aid in the identification of Trojan servers. The first lists these by port number and the protocol they make use of.

Port number	Protocol	Name of Trojan(s)
2	TCP	Death 1.0
21	TCP	Blade 0.80 Alpha
21	FTP	Dark FTP, Cattivik FTP, CC Invader 1.0, Invisible FTP
23	TCP	My Very Own Trojan, tRuVa Atl 1.2
25	TCP	Ajan 1.1, Antigen, Email Password Sender 1.03-1.6, Gip1.10, Kuang2 0.17A-0.30, Mail Bomb Trojan, Magic Horse Trojan, Moscow Mail, Taprias, WinPC
31	TCP	Agent 31
58	TCP	DMSetup
59	TCP	DMSetup
79	TCP	Firehotcker
80	TCP	711 Beta, Exector, Web Serve 2

Port number	Protocol	Name of Trojan(s)
80	ACK	AckCmd
12	UDP	Jammer Killah 1.2
146	TCP	The Infector 1.3
170	TCP	A-Trojan
334	TCP	3.1–3.1.1
411	TCP	Backage 3.2 SE
420	TCP	Incognito 1.2
455	TCP	Fatal Connections 2.0
456	TCP	Hackers Paradise 2 beta 3, Masters paradise 98 beta 2–99 beta 9.9d
555	TCP	iNi Killer 4.0 pro, phAse zero 1.0–1.1, Stealth Spy
666	TCP	th3r1pp3r'z trojan 1.0–1.1
667	TCP	SniperNet 2.1
669	TCP	DP Trojan 2.5
692	TCP	GayOL 1.6
1001	TCP	SK Silencer, Web Ex 1.2–1.4
1010	TCP	Doly Trojan 1.35
1011	TCP	Doly Trojan 1.11
1015	TCP	Doly Trojan 1.5
1016	TCP	Doly Trojan 1.6–1.70 SE
1024	TCP	Latinus 1.0–1.1 beta, NetSpy 0.6.98 Build A
1025	TCP	NetSpy 0.6.98 Build A
1053	TCP	Thief 2
1054	ACK	AckCmd
1066	TCP	B.F. Evolution 5.3.12
1212	TCP	Kaos 1.1–1.3
1234	Telnet	Ultor's Telnet Trojan
1243	TCP	SubSeven 1.0–1.8
1245	TCP	VooDoo 6
1256	TCP	Project nEXT 0.5.3 beta

Port number	Protocol	Name of Trojan(s)
1269	TCP	Maverik's Matrix 1.7–2.1
1272	TCP	The Matrix 1.03
1349	UDP	Back Ofrice DLL
1441	TCP	Remote Storm 1.2
1492	FTP	FTP99cmp
1777	TCP	Scarab 1.2c
1967	FTP	WM FTP Server
1981	Telnet	Bowl 1.0, Shockrave
1999	TCP	BackDoor 1.00–1.03, Transmission Scout 1.1–1.2
2000	TCP	Last 2000, Transmission Scout 1.1–1.2
2001	TCP	Trojan Cow 1.0
2023	TCP	Ripper Pro
2130	UDP	MiniBackLash 1.0a
2115	TCP	BUGS
2140	UDP	The Invasor
2311	TCP	Studio 54 1.0
2565	TCP	Striker 1.0
3000	TCP	InetSpy beta 1, Remote Shut 1.2–1.4
3031	TCP	Microspy 1.0
3150	TCP	MiniBackLash 1.0a
3250	UDP	The Invasor
3456	TCP	Doly Trojan 2.0, The Terror Trojan
3459	TCP	Sanctuary
3700	TCP	Portal of Doom V.3 Beta
3777	TCP	Psychward The First
4000	TCP	Skydance 2.16 Beta
4242	TCP	Virtual Hacking Machine
4321	TCP	Bo-Bo 1.0 Final Beta
4444	TCP	Swift Remote 1.06

Port number	Protocol	Name of Trojan(s)
4567	TCP	File Nail 1
4653	TCP	Cero 1
5000	TCP	Bubbel
5011	TCP	One of the last trojans
5025	TCP	WM Remote Keylogger
5031	TCP	Net Metropolian 1.00–1.04
5400	TCP	Blade Runner 0.80 Alpha
5401	TCP	Blade Runner 0.80 Alpha
5402	TCP	Blade Runner 0.80 Alpha
5534	TCP	The Flu
5569	TCP	Robo Hack 1.2
5880	TCP	Y3K RAT 1.4–1.5
5882	UDP	Y3K RAT 1.0
5888	UDP	Y3K RAT 1.0
6000	TCP	The thing 1.6
6400	TCP	The thing 1.1–1.5
6661	TCP	Weia-Meia 0.1
6666	TCP	Dark Connection Inside 1.2 beta
6667	TCP	SubSeven ICQ Fix
6669	TCP	Host Control 1.0
6712	TCP	Funny Trojan
6912	TCP	ShitHeep
6969	TCP	Gatecrasher 1.1–1.2
7000	TCP	Remote Grab 1.0
7001	TCP	Freak 88's DAS
7300	TCP	Net Monitor 1.0
7301	TCP	Net Monitor 1.0
7306	TCP	Net Monitor 1.0–2.01
7307	TCP	Net Monitor 1.0

Port number	Protocol	Name of Trojan(s)
7308	TCP	Net Monitor 1.0
7579	TCP	QAZ Trojan
7626	TCP	Glacier 3.0
7777	TCP	Tini
9000	TCP	Netministrator
9400	TCP	InCommand 1.0–1.6 beta 6
9876	TCP	RUX
9989	TCP	iNi Killer 1.2–3.2 pro
10085	TCP	Syphillis 1.18 Alpha
10100	TCP	Control total beta 4, Gift 1.07.0
10101	TCP	BrainSpy Beta
10607	TCP	Coma 1.0.9
10666	UDP	Ambush 1.0
11223	TCP	Progenic trojan beta 1.0–1.0, Secret Agent 1.0
12345	TCP	NetBus 1.20–1.70
12349	TCP	BioNet 0.84–3.09
12624	TCP	ButtMan 0.9N
13013	TCP	Psychward 01
13014	TCP	Psychward 02–03
13473	TCP	Chupacabra 1.0
15382	TCP	SubZero Alpha
16484	TCP	MoSucker 1.0–MoSucker 1.1
16969	TCP	Priority
17166	TCP	Mosaic 2.00
17569	TCP	The Infector
17593	TCP	AudioDoor 1.2
20001	TCP	Millenium 1.0–2.0
20002	TCP	AcidkoR
20005	TCP	MoSucker 2.0–2.1b

Port number	Protocol	Name of Trojan(s)
20034	TCP	NetBus 2.0 Beta–NetBus 2.10
21544	TCP	GirlFriend 1.0 Beta–1.35, Kid Terror 1.0, Maverik's Matrix 1.0–1.6
22222	TCP	Ruler 1.3 Test version
23005	TCP	NetTrash 1.01
23006	TCP	NetTrash 1.01
23023	TCP	Logged 1.0
23032	TCP	Amanda 2.0
23432	TCP	Asylum 0.2
23456	FTP	Evil FTP
23777	TCP	InetSpy beta 1
24000	TCP	The Infector 1.7
25685	TCP	MoonPie 1.0–1.2
25686	TCP	MoonPie 1.0–1.2
25982	TCP	MoonPie 1.1
29104	TCP	NetTrojan 1.0
29891	UDP	The Unexplained
30001	TCP	The Infector 1.7 version 2
30001	TCP	Err0r32 beta
30029	TCP	Aol Trojan 1.1
30100	TCP	NetSphere 1.27a
30101	TCP	NetSphere 1.27a
30102	TCP	NetSphere 1.27a
30947	TCP	Intruse 1.27b
31337	UDP	BackOrifice 1.20, Freak trojan 2k
31338	UDP	DeepBO
32100	TCP	Peanut Britter 0.2 beta
33333	TCP	Blackharaz, Prosiak
33577	TCP	Psychward small 01–02
34324	TCP	Bigluck

Port number	Protocol	Name of Trojan(s)
37237	TCP	Mantis 0.1b
40412	TCP	The Spy Beta 1
41337	TCP	Storm 1.2
41666	TCP	Remote Boot Tool 1.0
41666	UDP	Remote Boot Tool 1.0
47262	TCP	Delta source 0.5–0.7
47262	UDP	Delta source 0.5–0.7
50130	TCP	Enterprise
50766	TCP	Fore 1.0 Beta
51966	TCP	CAFEiNi 0.8–1.1
53001	TCP	Remote Windows Shutdown 0.02b
54321	TCP	SchoolBus .6–1.60
55165	TCP	File Manager Trojan
55166	TCP	File Manager Trojan
61466	TCP	TeLeCoMMaNDo 1.5.40
65000	TCP	Devil 1.3
65535	TCP	RC

The second table lists most of the common Trojan servers against the Windows Registry location from which they start up and the default file name of the server program.

Trojan name	Location in the Windows Registry from which the server is configured to start up (See note below.)	Default file name of the Trojan server
AntiGen	...\CurrentVersion\Run	antigen.exe
Back Orifice	...\CurrentVersion\RunServices	boserve.exe
BackDoor	...\CurrentVersion\Run	icqnuke.exe or readme.exe

Trojan name	Location in the Windows Registry from which the server is configured to start up (See note below.)	Default file name of the Trojan server
Big Gluck	...\CurrentVersion\RunServices	bg10.exe
Blade Runner	...\CurrentVersion\Run	server.exe
Bugs	...\CurrentVersion\Run	Bugs.exe
Back Orifice	...\CurrentVersion\RunServices	boserve.exe
Deep Throat	...\CurrentVersion\Run	server.exe
Deep Throat v2	...\CurrentVersion\Run	SystemPatch.exe
Delta Source		Server.exe
Devil		ICQFlood.exe
Doly Trojan	...\CurrentVersion\Run	tesk.exe
Email Password Sender	...\CurrentVersion\Run	eps.exe
Executer		Exec.exe
Firehotcker BackDoorz		server.exe
Fore		foresvr.exe
FTP99cmp	...\CurrentVersion\Run	FTP99cmp.exe
Gaban Bus		Patch.exe
Gate Crasher	...\CurrentVersion\Run	Server.exe
GirlFriend	...\CurrentVersion\Run	windll.exe
Hack '99 KeyLogger	...\CurrentVersion\RunServices	Server.exe
Hack 'a' Tack	...\CurrentVersion\Run	expl32.exe
HackCity Ripper Pro		RipServer.exe
Hackers Paradise		server.exe or explorer.exe
icKiller	...\CurrentVersion\Run	ICKiLLeR.exe
ICQ Trojan		icqtrogen.exe or Command.exe and FindFast.exe
iNi-Killer	...\CurrentVersion\RunServices	server.exe
Kuang2	...\CurrentVersion\Run	K2pS_FULL.exe or K2pS.exe

Trojan name	Location in the Windows Registry from which the server is configured to start up (See note below.)	Default file name of the Trojan server
Masters' Paradise		icqcrk.exe) or uagent.exe or Agent.exe) or Angel.exe) or progman.exe
Millenium	...\CurrentVersion\Run	spy.exe or modem.exe
NetBus	...\CurrentVersion\Run	Patch.exe
NetBus Pro	...\CurrentVersion\RunServices	NBSvr.exe
NetMonitor	...\CurrentVersion\Run	spyserver.exe and netspy.exe
NetSpy	...\CurrentVersion\Run	server.exe or server.exe
Phase Zero		phase.exe
Phineas Phucker	...\CurrentVersion\RunServices	Phineas.com
Portal of Doom	...\CurrentVersion\RunServices	Server.exe
Priority	...\CurrentVersion\RunServices	PServer.exe
Progenic	...\CurrentVersion\Run	AntiNuke.exe
Prosiak	...\CurrentVersion\RunServices	prosiak.exe
Psyber Stream Server		Wave.exe and wave.dll
Remote Grab		gserver.exe
Remote Windows Shutdown		RmtEwxS.exe
Robo-Hack		robo-serv.exe
Satanz backDoor		WinVMM32.exe
ShockRave	...\CurrentVersion\RunServices	shockrave.exe
Shtirlitz	...\CurrentVersion\Run	faxmgr.exe
Sivka-Burka		hs.exe
SK Silencer		Server.exe
Sockets de Troie		lame.exe
SpySender	...\CurrentVersion\Run	client.exe

405

Trojan name	Location in the Windows Registry from which the server is configured to start up (See note below.)	Default file name of the Trojan server
Stealth Spy		telserv.exe and tserv.dll
Stealth	...\CurrentVersion\Run	Zip.exe
Striker		ServerS.exe
SubSeven	...\CurrentVersion\Run or ...\CurrentVersion\RunServices (Can also be triggered from an entry in *win.ini* file (*run=* or *load=*) or an entry in *system.ini* (*shell=*).	Server.exe
Tapiras	...\CurrentVersion\Run	tapiras.exe
TeleCommando	...\CurrentVersion\Run	TeLeCoMMaNDo Server.exe
Terminator		param1.exe and param2.exe and param3.exe and sat.exe and uninst.exe
The Invasor	...\CurrentVersion\Run	runme.exe
The Spy	...\CurrentVersion\RunServices	SpyServ1.exe
The Trojan Cow	...\CurrentVersion\Run	CowServer.exe
TN	...\CurrentVersion\Run	tnsrv.exe
Ugly FTP		UglyFTP.exe
Ultor's Trojan		t5port.exe
Voice		Wave.exe and wave.dll
Voodoo Doll		adm.exe
Web Ex	...\CurrentVersion\Run	Task_Bar.exe
WinCrash	...\CurrentVersion\Run	server.exe or cfg95.exe and ICQFuckerExtentions.exe and win32cfg.exe

Note: In the table above, replace the three dots before the key name with *HKEY_LOCAL_MACHINE\SOFTWARE\Microsoft\Windows*

A Useful List Of TLAs (Three-letter Acronyms) And Some Two- And Four-letter Ones As Well

TLA	What it means
API	Application Program Interface. The software provided by Microsoft so that third-party programs can make use of the graphical and resource handling features of the Windows operating system.
ASP	Active Server Pages. Microsoft's proprietary interactive web page system.
AV	Anti-virus.
BIOS	Basic Input Output System. A set of simple programs which handle computer start-up functions and provide low-level control for keyboards, disk drives, etc.
BSOD	Blue Screen Of Death. An amusing joke built into Windows. The BSOD warns you that your system is near death and then suggests some ways in which you might be able to make it recover. You will have to reboot your computer.
CLI	Command Line Interface. The original method by which man communicated with computers. A CLI requires you to type instructions on a command line such as the one you see in a DOS session.
CMOS	Complementary Metal-Oxide Semiconductor. The special chip on a computer's motherboard which stores the basic system configuration.
CPU	Central Processing Unit. A computer's inbuilt memory, data processing and control circuits. Nowadays, the term is often applied to the processor itself.

TLA	What it means
DLL	Dynamic Link Library. A special type of file which Windows uses to share resources between the operating system and application programs.
DNS	Domain Name Service. A server on the internet which stores a database of numeric IP addresses against their textual equivalents. When you type a web address into your browser, it is a DNS server which translates that address into the numeric IP address of the site.
DoS	Denial of Service. A form of network attack where a server is swamped with thousands of small data packets which prevent it from operating normally. Where this attack comes from a series of co-ordinated computers, it becomes a Distributed Denial of Service (DDoS) attack.
DSL	Digital Subscriber Line. A recent type of connection to the telephone network which allows for always-on, high-speed internet connection.
DTP	Desktop Publishing – as if you didn't know. A process which allows you to create and publish documents on a personal computer.
FAT	File Allocation Table. A special file which stores details of how files are arranged on your hard disk.
FTP	File Transfer Protocol. An older internet protocol which allows files to be moved across a network. FTP is still used on many servers to ensure error-free up- and downloads.
GCHQ	Government Communications Headquarters. The UK's equivalent of the US NSA. A government organization concerned with intercepting and monitoring communications.
GUI	Graphical User Interface. A component of modern operating systems which represents programs and data as on-screen icons which can be manipulated with a mouse.
HTML	Hypertext Mark-up Language. The code used to mark up pages on the web so a browser knows how to display them. HTML is now being supplanted by DHTML (Dynamic HTM) and XML (eXtensible Mark-up Language) which provide more opportunities for web authors to provide interactive content.
HTTP	Hypertext Transfer Protocol. The protocol which allows resources on the web to be accessed by means of hyperlinks.
HTTPS	Hypertext Transfer Protocol Secure. A web protocol which uses SSL (see below) technology to allow encrypted access to secure web resources.
IDE	Integrated Drive Electronics. A type of hard disk interface standard on modern personal computers.
ISDN	Integrated Services Digital Network. A recent type of connection to the telephone network which allows high-speed access over a digital phone line.

TLA	What it means
ISP	Internet Service Provider. A company which provides a connection from your local computer to the internet backbone.
MIME	Multipurpose Internet Mail Extensions. The technology used to bundle different types of content into a single file which can be sent over a network. Originally designed for e-mail bundles, MIME is now used for most multimedia web content.
NAT	Network Address Translation. A feature provided by many network routers which translates all the addresses on a network into a single address which is presented to the internet.
NSA	National Security Agency. The US government department responsible for maintaining national security.
OEM	Original Equipment Manufacturer. A company which builds hardware.
OS	Operating System. The software application which manages a computer's hardware and processes. Some OSs, like Windows, also provide a graphical user interface (see above).
PDA	Personal Digital Assistant. A computer small enough to fit in a pocket – sometimes a pretty large pocket, it must be admitted. Most PDAs are designed to interface with their desktop equivalents.
PGP	Pretty Good Privacy. A freely available asymmetrical data encryption system which is widely used to code e-mails and other files for network transportation.
POST	Power On Self Test. The routine which operates when you first switch on your computer and checks for the correct operation of essential hardware.
PPP	Point to Point Protocol. The web protocol designed to handle internet communications over dial-up connections.
PSTN	Public Switched Telephone Network. The correct name for the telephone system.
RAID	Redundant Array of Independent Disks. A means of setting up hard disk storage so that different platters store copies of the same information. This speeds up access and improves data security.
RAM	Random Access Memory. A computer's working memory in which active programs and data are temporarily stored. Best thought of as a computer's workbench.
RTFM	Read The F****** Manual. The best advice anyone can ever receive!
SCSI	Small Computer System Interface. An interface which provides a high-speed data bus into which peripheral and integrated components can be plugged.

TLA	What it means
SSL	Secure Sockets Layer. The protocol which allows encrypted communication with a secure web server. (See HTTPS above.)
TCP/IP	Transmission (or Transfer) Control Protocol/Internet Protocol. A set of protocols used to control the transmission of data across the internet. In simple terms, TCP handles packet assembly and distribution, while IP handles addressing.
USB	Universal Serial Bus. A relatively new serial port which provides high-speed, hot-pluggable connections for peripheral devices.
WHS	Windows Scripting Host. Software which provides an environment on your computer in which scripts can run.
WWWC	World Wide Web Consortium (also known as W3C). The independent body which oversees the development and implementation of software standards for the web.

Index